Air Defence Identification Zones and Maritime Frontier Disputes

Essential Air and Space Law

Series Editor

Marietta Benkö

VOLUME 30

The titles published in this series are listed at *brill.com/easl*

Air Defence Identification Zones and Maritime Frontier Disputes

Legal and Political Issues

By

Stephanie Stipsits

BRILL

LEIDEN | BOSTON

Library of Congress Cataloging-in-Publication Data

Names: Stipsits, Stephanie, author.
Title: Air defence identification zones and maritime frontier disputes : legal and political issues / by Stephanie Stipsits.
Other titles: Air defense identification zones and maritime frontier disputes
Description: Boston, Massachusetts : Brill, [2025] | Includes bibliographical references and index.
Identifiers: LCCN 2024041234 (print) | LCCN 2024041235 (ebook) | ISBN 9789004720992 (hardback) | ISBN 9789004721005 (e-book)
Subjects: LCSH: Air defense identification zones. | National security–Law and legislation. | Military readiness–Law and legislation. | Airspace (International law) | Maritime law. | Economic zones (Law of the sea) | Territorial waters.
Classification: LCC K4720 .S75 2025 (print) | LCC K4720 (ebook) | DDC 343/.018403--dc23/eng/20241118
LC record available at https://lccn.loc.gov/2024041234
LC ebook record available at https://lccn.loc.gov/2024041235

Typeface for the Latin, Greek, and Cyrillic scripts: "Brill". See and download: brill.com/brill-typeface.

ISSN 1872-2180
ISBN 978-90-04-72099-2 (hardback)
ISBN 978-90-04-72100-5 (e-book)
DOI 10.1163/9789004721005

This book is printed on acid-free paper and produced in a sustainable manner.

Contents

Acknowledgment

First and foremost, I would like to thank Prof. Irmgard Marboe, without whose support I would never have found my way into the world of international law. This book was also made possible by Prof. Dai Tamada and Prof. Shotaro Hamamoto of Kyoto University. I was very fortunate to be able to spend six weeks in the very stimulating environment of Kyoto University to conduct my research. At Osaka University, I would like to thank Prof. Akira Mayama for giving me the opportunity to visit the National Institute of Defence Studies in Tokyo.

Abbreviations

ADC	Air Defence Clearance
ADIZ	Air Defence Identification Zone
AIC	Aeronautical Information Circular
ANSP	Air Navigation Service Provider
ANP	Air Navigation Plan
ATC	Air Traffic Control
ATS	Air Traffic Services
ATM	Air Traffic Management
CBM	Confidencc Building Measure
ECJ	European Court of Justice
EEZ	Exclusive Economic Zone
ENR	EN Route
ECS	East China Sea
FIR	Flight Information Region
FUA	Flexible Use of Airspace
GA	General Assembly
IATA	International Air Transport Association
ICJ	International Court of Justice
ICAO	International Civil Aviation Organisation
ILC	International Law Commission
IMO	International Maritime Organisation
ITLOS	International Tribunal for the Law of the Sea
FAA	Federal Aviation Administration
FIR	Flight Information Region
GA	General Assembly
GCI	Ground Control Intercept
JASDF	Japanese Self-Defense Forces
NOTAM	Notice to Airmen
PANS	Procedures for Air Navigation
PCA	Permanent Court of Arbitration
SARPS	Standards and Recommended Practices
SC	Security Council
UN	United Nations

Introduction

Air Defence Identification Zones (ADIZs) have their roots in State practice during the Cold War and describe areas of airspace where States impose identification obligations on civil as well as military aircraft. In addition to the traditional concern about foreign military aircraft intruding national airspace, aerial terrorist attacks by hijacked civilian aircraft represent a new threat. Due to the absence of an international legal framework for ADIZs, they constitute a controversial State practice outside national airspace with potential effects on the freedom of overflight over the high seas and on unresolved border conflicts in maritime areas. The spatial dimensions of ADIZs vary drastically and raise the fundamental problem of State authority exercised over foreign aircraft outside national territory. The unilateral declaration of ADIZs by States leads to competing claims on national jurisdiction. The international community is well aware of the problems, but also of the opportunities created by ADIZs. A clarification of apparent legal uncertainties about the rights of States in areas beyond national jurisdiction is in due need. The impact of expanding State activities in international airspace can be seen in the examples of the East China Sea, where China, Japan, and South Korea all extended their ADIZs' claims in 2013, as well as in the establishment of Bangladesh's ADIZ in 2018. The most recent example of an escalation of tensions due to aerial military activities can be seen in the airspace over the South China Sea.

In 1977, the issue of ADIZs was discussed under the aspect of "creeping jurisdiction" when *Cuadra* identified the establishment of ADIZs in international airspace as an unresolved legal concept.[1] China's declaration in 2013 to establish an ADIZ over an area including disputed islands gave new impetus to the discussion. The literature is divided on the question of the legal status of ADIZs.[2] There are differing views on whether a basis can be found in international treaties, or whether a legal basis can be derived from customary international law. Some argue that ADIZs are in fact contrary to international law as they violate the freedom of overflight.[3] Most of the discussions in the

1 Elisabeth Cuadra, 'Air Defense Identification Zones: Creeping Jurisdiction in the Airspace' (1977) 18 Virginia J Int'l L 485.

2 Christopher Lamont, 'Conflict in the Skies: The Law of Air Defence Identification Zones' (2014) 39 Air & Space Law 178; Stefan Kaiser, 'The Legal Status of Air Defense Identification Zones: Tensions over the East China Sea' (2016) 63 ZLW 527; Zoltan Papp, 'ADIZ in the Light of Public International Law' (2015) Pécs J Int'l & European L 36.

3 Kay Hailbronner, 'Freedom of the Air and the Convention on the Law of the Sea' (1983) 77 AJIL 493.

 | DOI:10.1163/9789004721005_002

current literature on the subject argue that newly established ADIZs should follow the concept of the US ADIZ to be consistent with international law.[4] In contrast, the ADIZ established by China over the East China Sea (ECS) was described as illegitimate and not in line with common State practice, and was rejected because it differed in content from the US ADIZ. New submissions focused more on the legality of the Chinese ADIZs.[5] While these contributions provide a notable but brief theoretical framework, the authors have refrained from engaging in depth with the embedding of ADIZs in the overall international legal system. Publications have tended to focus on the analysis of ADIZs within a particular sub-field of international law.[6] The present book seeks to clarify broader conceptual issues related to ADIZs and their impact on maritime territorial disputes. It reconciles various treaty sources to present a coherent picture of ADIZs that is also consistent with current State practice. In particular, this book particular addresses the relationship between ADIZs and the freedom of overflight, drawing on a comprehensive set of case law from various judicial institutions. This book attempts a comprehensive analysis of the scope and content of national laws on ADIZs as well as State responses to the establishment of ADIZs. It aims to clarify relevant terms, categorizes ADIZs under each legal source and draws an overall conclusion.

---

4 Roncevert Almond, 'Clearing the Air above the East China Sea: The Primary Elements of Aircraft Defense Identification Zones' (2017) 7 Harvard Nat Sec J 138; Peter Dutton, 'Caelum Liberam: Air Defense Identification Zones Outside Sovereign Airspace' (2009) 103 AJIL 2.

5 Jinyuan Su, 'The Practice of States on Air Defence Identification Zones: Geographical Scope, Object of Identification, and Identification Measures' (2019) 18 Chinese J Int' L 817.

6 Edmund J Burke & Astrid Stuth Cevallos, *In Line or out of Order? – Chinas Approach to ADIZ in Theory and Practice* (Rand 2017); Mercedes Trent, 'Overview of ADIZ in East Asia' in Federation of American Scientists (eds), *Over the Line – The Implications of China's ADIZ Intrusions in North East* (2020); Ann Mary George, 'Constructing the China threat: the Indian strategic community's discursive interpretation of the East China Sea ADIZ' (2021) 59 Commonwealth & Comparative Politics 297; Taisuku Ikeshima, 'China's Air Defense Identification Zone (ADIZ) and its Impact on the Territorial and Maritime Disputes in the East and South China Seas' (2016) 3 Transcomm 154.

CHAPTER 1

Political and Legal Background

1 The East China Sea ADIZ – the Unresolved Scope of Content and the Influence on Territorial Disputes

The unilateral declaration of ADIZs dates back to the early years of the Cold War,[1] a practice which until recently, has not given rise to much debate. Over the past 70 years, States have created ADIZs as a security measure to identify aircraft bound for national airspace in a timely manner while the aircraft were still in international airspace.[2] In 2013, China followed a long-standing State practice and declared an ADIZ over the East China Sea (ECS).[3] China's establishment of the ECS ADIZ drew strong protests from neighbouring States, such as Japan and Korea, as well as the United States, which sent military aircraft through China's ADIZ.[4] At first glance, the reactions of the international community seemed surprisingly vehement but is due to five controversial aspects:

1. The scope of application includes aircraft not intending to enter China's national airspace, but also those traversing through the ECS ADIZ. This may contradict the practice of most States, which apply ADIZ's rules only to aircraft bound for national airspace.[5]
2. China justified the establishment of the ECS ADIZ on the basis of the administrative need to control air traffic. China's claim was not based on

---

1 Christopher Lamont, 'Conflict in the Skies: The Law of Air Defence Identification Zones' (2014) 39 Air & Space Law 178; Gil Yun-hyung, The History of Air Defense Identification Zones in Northeast Asia' (27 November 2013) https://english.hani.co.kr/arti/english_edition/e_international/612953.html (accessed 20 October 2022).

2 Stefan Kaiser, 'The Legal Status of Air Defense Identification Zones: Tensions over the East China Sea' (2016) 63 ZLW 527.

3 'China establishes 'air-defence zone' over East China Sea', BBC NEWS (23 November 2013) http://www.bbc.co.uk/news/world-asia-25062525.

4 Prior to China's ADIZ declaration, unilateral establishment of ADIZ remained mainly uncontested by States. For ADIZ practice prior to China's see Ruwantissa Abeyratne, 'In Search of Theoretical Justification for Air Defence Identification Zones' (2012) 5 J Transp Sec 87.

5 Roncevert Almond, 'Clearing the Air above the East China Sea: The Primary Elements of Aircraft Defense Identification Zones' (2017) 7 Harvard Nat Sec J 138–146.

 | DOI:10.1163/9789004721005_003

security justifications and the protection of national security interests in airspace.[6]

3. China's ADIZ covers disputed maritime territories, namely the Senkaku/ Diaoyu islands as well as the Ieodo/Suyan reef. Concerns relate to the potential effect of ADIZs on strengthening territorial claims by exercising control.[7]
4. ADIZs in international airspace may have a negative effect on the freedom of overflight as set forward in Art. 87 UN Convention on the Law of the Sea.[8]
5. The geographical scope of the Chinese ECS ADIZ overlaps with the ADIZs of Japan, Korea and Taiwan, creating the problem of concurrent jurisdiction in international airspace.[9]

Overlapping ADIZs are not necessarily a problem. They can be managed cooperatively as in the case of the North American ADIZ which is jointly administered by the US and Canada.[10] However, the situation becomes more complex when disputed territories are involved. Their inclusion may imply the intention to extend control over these territories. The practice of establishing ADIZs in the airspace above the Exclusive Economic Zone (EEZ) and the high seas, in general, has fuelled the debate about their impact on progressive sovereignty claims of coastal States. Although not referred to as "res communis omnium," international airspace can be included to some extent, as it is not subject to the appropriation or sovereignty of any State.[11] International airspace is a specific area beyond national jurisdiction, just like outer space, or the deep seabed, and therefore not an object over which individual States can claim

---

6 Jinyuan Su, 'The East China Sea Air Defense Identification Zone and International Law' (2015) 14 Chinese J Int'l L 284–285; Jinyuan Su, 'Is the Establishment of Air Defence Identification Zones Outside National Airspace in Accordance with International Law? (2020) 32 EJIL 1309.

7 Christopher Lamont, 'Conflicts in the Sky: The Law of Air Defence Identification Zones' (2014) 39 Air and Space L 187.

8 Elisabeth Cuadra, 'Air Defense Identification Zones: Creeping Jurisdiction in the Airspace' (1977) 18 Virginia J Int'l L 485.

9 Peter Kreuzer, 'Chinas Luftverteidigungszone und der Konflikt um die Diaoyu/Senkaku Inseln' (2013) 9 HSFK Report 3.

10 'Time to Regulate Air Defence Zones to Prevent Conflict', South China Morning Post (29 November 2013) http://www.scmp.com/comment/insight-opinion/article/1368612/time-regulate-airdefence-zones-prevent-conflict.

11 Aaron x Fellmeth & Maurice Horwitz, 'Res communis omnium' in *Guide to Latin in International Law* (2nd edn, OUP 2011) (online version).

sovereignty.[12] Nevertheless, in the past, powerful States have asserted exclusive rights over areas regarded as "res communis omnium" and denied other States of access to them.[13] International airspace could suffer a similar fate.

Commentators suggested that China's extension of the ECS ADIZ was aimed at strengthening its claims to the Senkaku/Diaoyu islands, which were purchased by the Japanese government from Japanese citizens in 2012, and over which Japan has administrative control.[14] China, on the other hand, claims that the islands are part of its territory.[15] The only conceivable legal mode of acquisition of sovereignty would be occupation, if the disputed islands were considered *terra nullius* at the time of occupation.[16] Occupation involves two cumulative elements, namely the objective element of continuous effective control over the territory, and the subjective element of the intention to effectively control the territory.[17] In this sense, ADIZs may serve as a means of satisfying these two requirements, namely the exercise of control in the airspace above the disputed territories with the intention of establishing control over the territory. Another view suggests that ADIZs may indeed cover disputed islands without necessarily impinging on the sovereignty of other States.[18]

---

12 Paola Gaeta, Jorge E Viñuales & Salvatore Zappalá, *Cassese's International Law* (3rd edn, OUP 2020), stating there these "areas are spatially delimited and therefore – preceding international regulation – potential objects for claims of sovereignty by individual States"; but also emphasizing that res communis omnium "is not a community oriented-concept; it is geared to self-interest", at 93.

13 Paola Gaeta, Jorge E Viñuales & Salvatore Zappalá, *Cassese's International Law* (3rd edn, OUP 2020) 92.

14 Edmund J Burke & Astrid Stuth Cevallos, *In Line or out of Order? – Chinas Approach to ADIZ in Theory and Practice* (Rand 2017) at 5 referring to Jane Perez, 'China Accuses Japan of Stealing After Purchase of Group of Disputed Islands', New York Times (11 September 2012).

15 Ministry of Foreign Affairs of the People's Republic of China, 'Statement of the Ministry of Foreign Affairs of the People's Republic of China' (10 September 2012), https://www.fmprc.gov.cn/mfa_eng/topics_665678/diaodao_665718/201209/t20120911_701817.html.

16 Terra nullius in this regard means territory that belonged to no-one, see *Western Sahara* (Advisory Opinion) [1975] ICJ Rep 12 79. See on a discussion on the territorial status of the Senkáku/Diaoyu islands Koichi Sato, 'The Senkaku Island Dispute: Four Reasons of the Chinese Offensive' (2019) 8 J Cont' East Asia Studies 52–55; see for an official statement on the Senkaku/Diaoyu islands as part of the Japanese territory, Japanese Ministry of Foreign Affairs, 'Situation of the Senkaku Islands' https://www.mofa.go.jp/a_o/c_m1/senkaku/page1we_000010.html.

17 Malcom N Shaw, *International Law* (9th edn, Cambridge University Press 2021) 363; *Territorial Sovereignty and Scope of the Dispute* (*Eritrea v Yemen*) XXII RIAA (1998) at 315 on fishing practice as not being part of excising control.

18 Jinyuan Su, 'The East China Sea Air Defence Identification Zone' (2015) 14 Chinese J Int' L 303; see also chapter 6.3 of this book.

Another point of concern is the influence of the Chinese ADIZ on the status quo in the region and on the security relationship between Japan and the US in maintaining peace and stability in the East China Sea.[19]

2 Bangladesh's ADIZ – Potential Risks for Civil Aviation

The ECS ADIZ was not the only zone in international airspace to raise concerns. Bangladesh's uncoordinated, ad hoc establishment of an ADIZ in 2018 demonstrated the additional negative impact on the civil aviation industry.[20] On Bangladesh's ADIZ, the International Air Transport Association (IATA) pointed out the risks for civil aviation:

1. There are no details on proper dimension, so stakeholders could not assess the extent and impact of the Bangladesh ADIZ on civil aircraft;
2. The ADIZ penetrated the airspace of two adjacent Flight Information Regions (FIR) and therefore impacted aircraft under the control of Air Traffic Control units in other States;
3. There was no consultation with the International Civil Aviation Organisation (ICAO) and adjacent States during the planning of the Bangladesh ADIZ;
4. There are unclear procedures for obtaining an Air Defence Code (ADC) and consequently, several flights were re-planned via routes not requiring an ADC leading to an increase in flight times.[21]

From the perspective of civil aviation, the International Air Transport Association commented:

> Although IATA recognizes the right of each State to ensure the integrity of its national security, IATA maintains that the implementation of an ADIZ, should be properly coordinated, and together with accurate charting and

---

19 Taisuku Ikeshima, 'China's Air Defense Identification Zone (ADIZ) and its Impact on the Territorial and Maritime Disputes in the East and South China Seas' (2016) 3 Transcomm 154; also US Dep't of Defense Press Release, 'Hagel Issues Statement on East China Sea Air Defense Identification Zone' (23 November 2013) www.defense.gov/news/newsarticle.aspx?id_121223 (accessed 21 November 2022).

20 ICAO Doc SAIOACG/9 –WP29, 'Civil/Military Update' Ninth Meeting of the South Asia/Indian Ocean ATM Coordination Group (26.03.2019 – 29.03.2019).

21 ICAO Doc SAIOACG/8 and SEACG/25 WP 22, 'Imposition Of Military Requirements And Restrictions On International Civil Aviation'(30.03.2018) para. 1.2; The ADC is a permission which needs to be obtained before entering the Bangladeshi ADIZ, see Bangladesh AIP SUPP 01/18 (1 February 2018).

> very clear instructions, clearly promulgated to ensure airlines and international civil aviation is able to comply.[22]

At the international level, ICAO has been particularly critical of the establishment of ADIZs because of the lack of a clear legal basis in international law.[23] The ICAO Secretariat stressed that the Bangladesh ADIZ imposes conditions on aircraft without a legal basis in international law and that the consequences of establishing an ADIZ are not defined in the Chicago Convention or its Standards and Recommended Practices, making ADIZs a non-ICAO procedure.[24] This statement is interesting since both Annex 4 and Annex 15 of the Chicago Convention contain a definition on ADIZs. Accordingly, an ADIZ is defined as:

> Special designated airspace of defined dimensions within which aircraft are required to comply with special identification and/or reporting procedures additional to those related to the provision of air traffic services (ATS).[25]

However, ICAO emphasized that the references to ADIZs in Annex 4 and Annex 15 of the Chicago Convention "solely ensure that, where established, any necessary information is included in the State AIP and aeronautical chart."[26] The ICAO Secretariat underlined that national law has no legal effect in airspace above the high seas.[27]

The lack of civil-military cooperation continued to be a topic of discussion, and ICAO Member States were unable to overcome their differences on the recognition of ADIZs in international law. In a draft conclusion, Asia-Pacific States agreed to minimise the impact of non-ICAO procedures and requirements for military activities affecting civil aviation, in order to avoid an increased risk of

---

22 ICAO Doc SAIOACG/8 and SEACG/25 WP 22, 'Imposition Of Military Requirements And Restrictions On International Civil Aviation' (30.03.2018) para. 1.2.

23 ICAO Doc ATMSG/6 WP 26, 'Civil/Military Cooperation Update', Sixth Meeting of the APANPIRG ATM Sub-Group (ATM/SG/6) (03.08.2018) paras. 2.4–2.7; ICAO Doc APANPIRG 29, 'Final Report', Twenty Ninth Meeting Of The Asia/Pacific Air Navigation Planning And Implementation Regional Group (30.09.2019) para. 3.2.58; ICAO Doc SAIOACG/9–WP29, 'Civil/Military Update' Ninth Meeting of the South Asia/Indian Ocean ATM Coordination Group (26.03.2019 – 29.03.2019).

24 ICAO Doc ATMSG/6 WP 26, 'Civil/Military Cooperation Update', Sixth Meeting of the APANPIRG ATM Sub-Group (ATM/SG/6) (03.08.2018) para. 2.4.

25 Convention on Civil Aviation ("Chicago Convention") (1944) 15 UNTS 295, Annex 4, 9th edn (2009) 1–1 and Annex 15, 18th ed. (2018).

26 ICAO Doc ATMSG/6 WP 26, para. 2.5.

27 Ibid para. 2.7.

military intervention for civil flights operating in airspace where "non-ICAO military requirements and procedures" are imposed.[28] The civil/military cooperation update of 2019 by the ICAO Secretariat highlighted again that ADIZs impose "conditions of flight which had no legal basis in international law" as there was no connection to the States' sovereignty.[29] It further concretised:

> It should be noted that while matters of sovereignty are addressed in Art. 1, 2 and 3bis of the Convention on International Civil Aviation, it did not make any reference to ADIZ.[30]

Moreover, a similar wording was used in the statement namely that "there are no ICAO SARPS or procedures for the establishment and operation of ADIZ" and that ADIZs are, in general, a "non-ICAO procedure."[31] At the thirtieth meeting of the Asia-Pacific Air Navigation Planning and Implementation Regional Group,[32] the issue of civil-military cooperation in the Asia-Pacific region remained one of the highest regional priorities, with ADIZs specifically mentioned as a matter of concern.

This discussion shows that there is still legal uncertainty regarding the establishment of ADIZs. There is no clear provision either permitting or prohibiting ADIZs in international airspace. The ICAO Secretariat believes that there is

28 The Draft Conclusion was agreed on 5.9.2018 by States of the Asia Pacific Region (APAC States): Afghanistan, Australia, Bangladesh, Bhutan, Brunei, Darussalam, Cambodia, China, Hong Kong, China Macao, Cook Islands, Democratic People's Republic of Korea, Fiji, India, Indonesia, Japan, Kiribati, Lao People's Democratic Republic, Malaysia, Maldives, Marshall Islands, Micronesia, Mongolia, Myanmar, Nauru, Nepal, New Zealand, Pakistan, Palau, Papua New Guinea, Philippines, Republic of Korea, Samoa, Singapore, Solomon Islands, Sri Lanka, Thailand,Timor Leste, Tonga, Tuvalu, Vanuatu, and Viet Nam. ICAO Doc APANPIRG 29, 'Final Report',Twenty Ninth Meeting Of The Asia/Pacific Air Navigation Planning And Implementation Regional Group (30.09.2019) para. 3.2.58 ff.

29 ICAO Doc SAIOACG/9 – WP29 para. 2.15.

30 Ibid para. 2.16.

31 Ibid para. 2.17.

32 The Thirtieth Meeting of the Asia/Pacific Air Navigation Planning and Implementation Regional Group (APANPIRG/30) was held at ICAO APAC Office, Bangkok, Thailand from 4 to 6 November 2019. The meeting was attended by 151 participants from 22 Member States, 2 Special Administrative Regions of China, 8 International Organisations (AAPA, CANSO, EUROCONTROL, IATA, ICAO, ICCAIA, IFAIMA and IFALPA). All ICAO Contracting States, who are service providers in an air navigation region and part of that region's ANP, should be included in the membership of that region's PIRG. Furthermore user States are entitled to participate in any other PIRG Meetings as a non-member. International Organisations recognised by the Council may be invited as necessary to attend PIRG meetings as observers.

no legal basis for ADIZs in international airspace based on the framework of the Chicago Convention. However, it is not clear whether it is the zone itself, the enforcement of its boundaries, the powers exercised by States therein, or solely the legislative means underlying it, that is considered to be inconsistent with the Chicago Convention and other pertinent rules of international law. To date, a complaint of non-compliance with the Chicago Convention has not been submitted to the ICAO dispute settlement system.[33]

3 The Strategic Violation of ADIZs' Rules – Geopolitical Challenges and the China–Taiwan Conflict

In 2022, a year of geopolitical turbulence, ADIZs were more prominent than ever on the international landscape. The South China Sea is an area of multiple political interests due to China's increasing territorial advances in the area, particularly towards Taiwan. China's position on Taiwan, which was originally a Chinese province, is clear, namely that "there is but one China in the world, Taiwan is an inalienable part of China's territory" and "it is the common aspiration and sacred responsibility of all Chinese sons and daughters to realize the complete reunification of the motherland."[34] In contrast, Taiwan points to history to argue that it was never part of the modern Chinese State that emerged after the revolution in 1911, nor of the People's Republic of China established under Mao Zedong in 1949.[35]

Following the visit of the Speaker of the US House of Representatives to Taiwan in the summer of 2022, China conducted military manoeuvres in the air and at sea around Taiwan, including the firing of ballistic missiles.[36] China's military exercises focused on six danger zones around Taiwan, three of which overlap with the island's territorial waters and all of which are covered by Taiwan's ADIZ. During the Chinese military manoeuvres, Taiwan reported

33 Art. 53, Art. 54 & Art. 84 Chicago Convention; see also: Benjamyn I Scott & Andrea Trimarchi, *Fundamental of International Aviation and Policy* (Routledge 2009) 51. Since the establishment of ICAO, only 6 disputes have been addressed, however the Council never issued a decision on the merits of the cases, see: Mathieu Vaugeois, 'Settlement of Disputes at ICAO and Sustainable Development' (2016) IV Occasional Paper Series 5, 6.

34 Statement by the Ministry of Foreign Affairs of the People's Republic of China (2 August 2022) https://www.fmprc.gov.cn/eng/zxxx_662805/202208/t20220802_10732293.html.

35 Minister of Foreign Affairs of the Republic of China (Taiwan), 'Foreign Policy Report', Foreign and National Defense Committee of the Legislative Yuan (17 March 2022).

36 David Brown, 'China and Taiwan – A Really Simple Guide', BBC News (8 August 2022) https://www.bbc.com/news/world-asia-china-59900139.

several incursions into its ADIZ, which are not a new phenomenon as China has already started operations in Taiwan's ADIZ in 2021.[37] Newspapers suggest that the US representative's visit was not the only reason for the current increase in incursions in the Taiwan's ADIZ, but that the US–Taiwan arms sale was also a factor.[38] In this sense, violating the rules of the ADIZ may serve political and strategic interests, namely signalling displeasure with the closer diplomatic ties between Washington and Taipei and extending control to counterbalance the US presence in the area.[39]

In response to the intrusions, Taiwan dispatched military aircraft, issued radio warnings, and deployed air defence missile systems to track the Chinese planes within the ADIZ.[40] Amid massive tensions with China, Taiwan's army has also threatened a "counter-attack" if Chinese warplanes and warships enter its territory: Taiwan's deputy chief of the general staff for operations and planning declared that Taiwan has a "right to self-defence" and will launch a counter-attack if Chinese warplanes and ships were to enter the 12-mile zone off Taiwan's coast.[41] In 2024, the situation remains unchanged with neither side backing down and continued Chinese military patrols in Taiwan's ADIZ.[42] China's action in the airspace are part of a bigger picture of gradual extension of State authority in areas beyond national jurisdiction. Chinese coast guard

---

37 Brian F Campbell, 'Record-Setting Incursions into Taiwan's Air Defense Identification Zone: The People's Republic of China's Psychological Operations Designed to Erode US Support for Taiwan' (2022) J Indo Pacific Affairs https://www.airuniversity.af.edu/JIPA/Display/Article/3111071/record-setting-incursions-into-taiwans-air-defense-identification-zone-the-peop/ (accessed 21 November 2022).

38 Adrian Ang U-jin, 'Are ADIZ Incursions China's New Response to US Arms Sales to Taiwan?', The Diplomat (23 July 2022) https://thediplomat.com/2022/07/are-adiz-incursions-chinas-new-response-to-us-arms-sales-to-taiwan/ (accessed 21 November 2022).

39 Adrian Ang U-jin & Olli Pekka Suorsa, 'Understanding China's Aerial Incursions Into Taiwan's ADIZ', The Diplomat (2 June 2021) https://thediplomat.com/2021/06/understanding-chinas-aerial-incursions-into-taiwans-adiz/ (accessed 21 November 2022).

40 Eric Chang, '21 Chinese Military Aircraft enter Taiwan's ADIZ', Taiwan News (3 August 2022) https://www.taiwannews.com.tw/en/news/4614891 (accessed 21 November 2022).

41 Yimou Lee, 'Taiwan Vows Counter-Attack If Chinese Forces Enter Its Territory' (31 August 2022) https://www.reuters.com/world/asia-pacific/chinese-military-continues-high-intensity-patrols-near-taiwan-taiwanese-defence-2022-08-31/ (accessed 21 November 2022).

42 'China trying to 'normalise' military drills near Taiwan: island's top security official', Reuters (11 March 2024) https://www.reuters.com/world/asia-pacific/china-trying-normalise-military-drills-near-taiwan-islands-top-security-official-2024-03-11/.

vessels are intensively patrolling the Taiwan Strait and in the South China Sea, including the inspection and boarding of foreign vessels in these areas.[43]

Clearly, due to the absence of a legal basis for ADIZs in international law, violations are more likely to occur when there is an imbalance of power between the States concerned. The tactic of ADIZs penetration is used for a steady progression of small, incremental steps to secure the State's aims while remaining below the threshold of armed conflict.[44] The State whose ADIZ has been violated risks escalating the conflict if it attempts to counter the violations without a solid legal basis on which to base its actions. A comprehensive analysis of the ADIZ concept in international law thus contributes to the de-escalation of conflicts.

43 'China says its coast guard patrols around Taiwan islands 'beyond reproach', Reuters (28 February 2024) https://www.reuters.com/world/asia-pacific/china-says-its-coast-guard-patrols-around-taiwan-islands-beyond-reproach-2024-02-28/.

44 The strategic violation of ADIZs rules may be qualified as a grey zone situation; see on the definition of a grey zone situation, Elizabeth Kiessling, 'Gray Zone Tactics and the Principle of Non-Intervention: Can "One of the Vaguest Branches of International Law" Solve the Gray Zone Problem?' (1 February 2021) Harvard NSJ online. Also with regard to China, Peter Layton, 'China's Gray Zone Air Power' (26 March 2024) https://irregularwarfare.org/articles/chinas-gray-zone-air-power/

CHAPTER 2

Preliminary Considerations: Jurisdiction in International Law

International law sets out rules governing the limits of State authority and governmental functions, in other words, it seeks to regulate jurisdiction. Jurisdiction derives from sovereignty and territory and means the exercise of authority over people, property and circumstances by establishing legal rights and obligations.[1] Sovereignty and jurisdiction are closely interlinked but not synonymous. The Permanent Court of Arbitration ruled on sovereignty in *The Island of Palmas Case* that sovereignty signifies independence among States and defined it as the right to exercise the functions of a State, to the exclusion of any other State.[2] Sovereignty is inseparable from the territory of the State and the powers of the State exercised there.[3] Jurisdiction is part of the authority of the State deriving from its sovereignty and generally describes the relationship between States and individuals within, but also beyond their territory.[4] The general rules on jurisdiction differentiate between types of jurisdiction and principles of jurisdiction.[5] Consequently, three different types of State jurisdiction can be identified:

1. Prescriptive jurisdiction: to make, i.e., to prescribe laws applicable to the activities, relations, or status of persons whether by legislation, by executive act or order, by administrative rule or regulation, or by determination by a court.[6]

---

1 Malcom N Shaw, *International Law* (9th edn, Cambridge University Press 2021) 469.

2 *The Island of Palmas Case* (*Netherlands v USA*) [1928] Permanent Court of Arbitration, Case No. 1925–01 para. 838.

3 Paola Gaeta, Jorge E Viñuales & Salvatore Zappalá, *Cassese's International Law* (3rd edn, OUP 2020) 94.

4 Robert Jennings & Arthur Watts (eds), *Oppenheim's International Law, Volume 1* (9th edn, Longman 1996) 325; Bernhard M Oxman, 'Jurisdiction' in *Max Planck Encyclopedias of Public International Law* (OUP 2007) para. 2; ILC, 'Responsibility of States for Internationally Wrongful Acts, with commentaries' UN Doc A/56/10 (2001) para. 1.

5 Council of Europe, 'Recommendation No. R (97) 11 of the Committee of Ministers to Member States on the Amended Model Plan for the Classification of Documents Concerning State Practice in the Field of Public International Law' (12 June 1997), hereinafter: Council of Europe Rec (97) 11 (12 June 1997).

6 Cedric Ryngaert, *Jurisdiction in International Law* (2nd edn, OUP 2015) 28.

 | DOI:10.1163/9789004721005_004

2. Adjudicative jurisdiction: to establish procedures for identifying breaches of the rules and the precise consequences thereof.[7]
3. Enforcement jurisdiction: to enforce consequences in case of non-compliance.[8]

The question of the different types of jurisdiction in international law revolves around the discussion of whether States can exercise jurisdiction as long as there is no prohibitive rule, or only if there is a permissive rule.[9] According to the second approach, the legal competence of a State to make, apply, and enforce rules needs to be based on the territorial principle, the personality principle, the protective principle, the effects doctrine, or the universal principle.[10]

According to the territorial principle, a State has jurisdiction over an act committed within its territory.[11] A more nuanced form of the territorial principle is the effects doctrine, also known as the objective territorial principle, which focuses on acts committed outside the national territory but completed within it.[12] Under the personality principle (also known as the nationality principle), a State may exercise jurisdiction over its nationals regardless of their current whereabouts.[13] The personality principle is further subdivided into the active and the passive personality principle.[14] In addition, the protective principle allows States to exercise jurisdiction over acts which threaten their sovereignty or political independence.[15] The protective principle grants States extraterritorial prescriptive jurisdiction over criminal conduct committed abroad, threatening national security or other vital States' interests.[16] It is therefore most commonly concerned with acts such as espionage, terrorism,

7 Council of Europe Rec (97) 11 (12 June 1997).

8 Ibid.

9 Cedric Ryngaert, *Jurisdiction in International Law* (2nd edn, OUP 2015) 29.

10 Christoph Staker, 'Jurisdiction' in Malcom D Evans (ed), *International Law* (5th edn, OUP 2018) 291.

11 Jan Klabbers, *International Law* (3rd edn, 2021 Cambridge University Press) 101.

12 Stanley D Metzger, 'The "Effects" Doctrine of Jurisdiction' (1967) 61 AJIL 1016; Jason Coppel, 'A Hard Look at the Effects Doctrine of Jurisdiction in Public International Law' (2009) 6 Leiden J Int'l L 74, 75.

13 Micheal Akehurst, 'Jurisdiction in International Law' (1972) 46 BYIL 156.

14 Geoffrey R Watson, 'The Passive Personality Principle' (1993) 28 Tex Int'l Law Journal 2.

15 Monika B Krizek, 'The Protective Principle of Extraterritorial Jurisdiction: A Brief History and Application of the Principle to Espionage as an Illustration of Current United States Practice' (1988) 6 BU Int'l Law Journal 337.

16 Iain Cameron, 'International Criminal Jurisdiction, Protective Principle' in *Max Planck Encylopedias of Public International Law* (OUP 2012) para. 1.

and drug trafficking.[17] Enforcement jurisdiction under the protective principle is limited to the State's territory.[18] The universality principle can be found in international criminal law and requires no link to the State but "the nature of the act itself" grants the State jurisdiction for crimes so heinous that every State has a legitimate interest in their repression.[19] As a rule of customary international law, States may only exercise jurisdiction based on one of these principles.[20]

The general rules on jurisdiction may be further limited or broadened by a particular field of law such as in the areas of antitrust, international humanitarian, the law of the sea, outer space law, and human rights law.[21] This aspect is discussed under the term "functional" jurisdiction.[22] Jurisdiction can therefore be assessed differently depending on the subject matter,[23] since the specific scope of the treaty determines the applicable principle.[24] The concept of ADIZs includes two types of jurisdiction, the prescription of national air laws on aircraft in national and international airspace and the enforcement of these laws. ADIZs have extraterritorial aspects, which by their very nature require an examination of extraterritorial jurisdiction.

---

17 Cedric Ryngaert, *Jurisdiction in International Law* (2nd edn, OUP 2015) 114.

18 Iain Cameron, 'International Criminal Jurisdiction, Protective Principle' in *Max Planck Encylopedias of International Law* (OUP 2012) para. 4.

19 For example slave trade and piracy on the high seas, Maria Gavouneli, *Functional Jurisdiction in the Law of the* Sea (Martinus Nijhoff 2007) 28, 29.

20 Cedric Ryngaert, *Jurisdiction in International Law* (2nd edn, OUP 2015) 34–36.

21 Cedric Ryngaert, *Jurisdiction in International Law* (2nd edn, OUP 2015); Arron N Honniball, 'The Exclusive Jurisdiction of Flag States: A Limitation on Pro-active Port States' (2016) 31 Int'l J Marine & Coastal Law 503; Sergio Marchisio, 'National Jurisdiction for Regulating Space Activities of Governmental and Non-Governmental Entities' (United Nations/ Thailand Workshop on Space Law, Bangkok, 16–19 November 2010).

22 Christoph Staker, 'Jurisdiction' in Malcom D Evans (ed), *International Law* (5th edn, OUP 2018) 291.

23 Alex Mills, 'Rethinking Jurisdiction in International Law' (2014) 84 British Yearbook Int'l L 187.

24 For example the Convention Against Torture and Other Cruel, Inhuman or Degrading Treatment or Punishment (1984) 1465 UNTS 85, Convention on the Prevention and Punishment of Crimes against Internationally Protected Persons, including Diplomatic Agents (1973) 15410 UNTS 168, the Montreal Convention for the Supression of Unlawful Acts against the Safety of Civil Aviation 1971, the Hague Convention for the Suppression of Unlawful Seizure of Aircraft (1973) 1973 UNTS 106, or the Tokyo Convention on Offences and Certain Other Acts Committed on Board Aircraft ("Tokyo Convention") (1969) 1969 UNTS 220.

1 Extraterritorial Jurisdiction

The principle of extraterritorial jurisdiction is controversial because it determines how far a State's domestic rules can reach.[25] The term "extraterritoriality" derives from the observation that a State regulates matters, which are not exclusively of domestic concern but have a strong connection with another State's domain.[26] Extraterritorial jurisdiction defies universal definition, but can generally be understood as the power of a State to "make, apply and enforce rules of conduct in respect to persons, property or events beyond its territory."[27] Jurisdiction beyond the State's territory either signifies the exercise of jurisdiction in the territory of another State or the exercise of jurisdiction in an area not subject to any State's territory. For the purpose of this discussion, extraterritorial jurisdiction is to be understood as the exercise of jurisdiction beyond any State's territory, such as in international airspace and on the high seas.[28] Furthermore, extraterritorial jurisdiction has to be divided into extraterritorial prescriptive jurisdiction and extraterritorial enforcement jurisdiction. Extraterritorial prescriptive jurisdiction includes national laws targeting an activity beyond the territory of the State and does not necessarily provide for the exercise of jurisdiction beyond the State's territory.[29] Enforcement jurisdiction is limited to the territory of the State.[30] Only in some exceptional cases do treaties or customary international law provide for enforcement jurisdiction beyond any State's territory.[31] National laws therefore may prescribe rules for an activity beyond the State's territory but the enforcement of these rules is dependent on other factors such as the actor entering national territory.[32]

---

25 Frederick A Mann, *The Doctrine of Jurisdiction in International Law* (AW Sijthoff 1964) 15.

26 Karl Meessen (ed), *Extraterritorial Jurisdiction in Theory and Practice* (Springer 1996) 74.

27 Menno T Kamminga, 'Extraterritoriality' in *Max Planck Encyclopedias of Public International Law* (OUP 2012) 2.

28 Extraterritorial jurisdiction is sometimes referred to the power of one State to exercise jurisdiction in the territory of another State. In fact, all principles for jurisdiction that has not territory as connecting point are part of "extraterritorial jurisdiction".

29 For example, flight information regions above the high seas in which national air traffic rules apply.

30 *Lotus Case,* Judgment No. 9 (1927) PCIJ Series A, No. 10 (hereinafter: *Lotus Case*), 18–19.

31 For example, the seizure of pirate ships pursuant to Art. 105 UNCLOS, the right to visit pursuant to Art. 110 UNCLOS, the right of hot pursuit pursuant to Art. 111 UNCLOS or the right to intercept hijacked aircraft pursuant to Art. 4 Convention for the Suppression of Unlawful Seizure of Aircraft.

32 For example, bunkering activities on the high seas and the enforcement of a decree of seizure, see *M/V "Norstar"* (*Panama v Italy*) (Judgment of 10 April 2019) ITLOS Reports 2018–2019. Not part of further deliberations are the rules on international criminal jurisdiction.

Several areas of public international law deal with complex questions on jurisdictional extension, such as international environmental law, human rights protection, competition law, and the prosecution of international crimes.[33] Particularly, the law of the sea establishes a legal framework that allows States to exercise jurisdiction over parts of the sea adjacent to territorial waters, i.e., outside national territory.[34] Four maritime zones with special jurisdictional rights are accepted under customary international law and under the United Nations Convention on the Law of the Sea, namely the contiguous zone, the continental shelf, the Exclusive Economic Zone (EEZ), and the high sea. In its contiguous zone, a coastal State may exercise the control necessary to prevent the infringement of its customs, fiscal, immigration, or sanitary laws and regulations within its territory or territorial sea and punish infringement of those laws and regulations committed within its territory or territorial sea.[35] States also enjoy certain sovereign rights and jurisdiction within their EEZ adjacent to their territorial waters.[36] In certain cases, States can exercise enforcement jurisdiction in areas of the high seas; the most prominent being the right of hot pursuit.[37] Examples of extraterritorial jurisdiction can also be found in the legal body of international air law, namely in the form of Flight Information Regions,[38] or in the Montreal Convention for offences on board an aircraft.[39]

The *Lotus Case* is one of the most prominent cases dealing with the rights of States beyond their national territory not provided by a treaty or customary international law. In the *Lotus Case*, the Permanent Court of International Justice (PCIJ) considered whether a Turkish court had jurisdiction over a French national following the death of Turkish nationals as a result of a collision between a French and a Turkish vessel on the high seas.[40] The PCIJ drew a distinction between enforcement jurisdiction, for which there must be specific authorisation in international law, and extraterritorial prescriptive and adjudicative jurisdiction provided as long as there is no prohibitive rule.[41] Regarding enforcement jurisdiction, the PCIJ stated the following:

---

33 Malcom N Shaw, *International Law* (9th edn, Cambridge University Press 2021) 469–472.

34 Rene-Jean Dupuy, 'The Sea under National Competence' in Rene Jean Dupuy & Daniel Vignes (eds), *A Handbook on the New Law of the Sea, Volume 1* (OUP 1991) 247.

35 Art. 33 UNCLOS.

36 Art. 55 ff UNCLOS.

37 Art. 107, Art. 110 (4) and Art. 111 UNCLOS.

38 Annex 15 Chicago Convention.

39 Christoph Staker, 'Jurisdiction' in Malcom D Evans (ed), *International Law* (5th edn, OUP 2018) 303.

40 *Lotus Case* 4–5.

41 Ibid at 18–19.

> In this sense jurisdiction is certainly territorial; it cannot be exercised by a State outside its territory except by virtue of a permissive rule derived from international custom or from a convention.[42]

Consequently, extraterritorial enforcement jurisdiction may only be exercised if there is a permissive rule. In contrast, the *Lotus* principle pronounces on prescriptive jurisdiction that sovereign States are free in their actions as long as they do not contravene an explicit prohibition.[43] This statement has generated a great deal of legal debate and criticism from the most prominent legal scholars for its permissiveness, and has sparked calls for a more restrictive approach.[44] In particular, its vagueness and generality have been criticised, and the judgment has been described as unhelpful.[45] Nevertheless, it can be argued, that the exercise of extraterritorial enforcement jurisdiction depends on the existence of a permissive rule, whereas extraterritorial prescriptive jurisdiction requires the absence of a prohibitive rule either in a treaty or in customary international law.

The dichotomy between permissive and prohibitive rules for prescriptive jurisdiction persists despite decades of intense legal debate.[46] It is still not clear which of the two approaches prevails.[47] In any event, the prescribing State has to base its action one of the principles of jurisdiction mentioned above.[48]

---

42 Ibid at 18–19.

43 Stephane Beaulac, 'The Lotus Case in Context – Sovereignty, Westphalia, Vattel and Positivism' in Stephen Allen et al (eds), *Oxford Handbook of Jurisdiction in International Law* (OUP 2019) 56.

44 Louis Henkin, *International Law: Politics and Values* (Springer 1995) 216; Rosalyn Higgins, *Problems and Process: International Law and How We Use It* (OUP 1995) 77; Ole Spiermann, '*Lotus and the Double Structure of International Legal Argument*' in Philippe Sands & Laurence Boisson de Chazournes (eds), *International Law, the International Court of Justice and Nuclear Weapons* (Cambridge University Press 1999) 131.

45 James Crawford, *Brownlie's Principles of Public International Law* (8th edn, OUP 2012) 301.

46 Hugh Handeyside, 'The Lotus Principle in ICJ Jurisprudence: Was the Ship ever Afloat?' (2007) 29 Mich J Int'l L 81. The ICJ refers to the *Lotus Case* in two judgements namely the *North Sea Continental Shelf Case* (1969) at 3, 44, and the *Military and Paramilitary Activities in and against Nicaragua* (*Nicaragua v United States of America*) (Merits) [1986] ICJ Rep 14 para. 214 (hereinafter: *Nicaragua Case* (1986)) at 14, 24, and in one advisory opinion namely the *Legality of the Threat or Use of Nuclear Weapons* (Advisory Opinion) [1996] ICJ Rep 226 at 226, 238–239 (hereinafter: *Nuclear Weapons Advisory Opinion*). However, matters of jurisdiction were not addressed in any of the three mentioned cases.

47 Cedric Ryngaert, 'Territorial Jurisdiction over Cross Frontier Offences: Revisiting a Classic Problem of International Criminal Law' (2009) 9 Int'l Criminal L Rev 29.

48 Christopher Staker, 'Jurisdiction', in Malcom D Evans (ed), *International Law* (5th edn, OUP 2018) 296.

Indisputably, States are not entitled to enforce their laws outside their territory, "except by virtue of a permissive rule derived from international custom or from a convention."[49] These fundamental principles are likewise relevant to the discussion on ADIZs.

2 Prescribing ADIZs beyond National Territory

The concept of ADIZs covers two types of jurisdiction. On the one hand, prescriptive jurisdiction, as States prescribe rules for identification procedures in air zones. On the other hand, ADIZs may involve enforcement jurisdiction, as some rules also regulate the consequences of non-compliance with the identification procedures, such as the interception of civil aircraft. In principle, enforcement jurisdiction is limited to the State's own territory unless an international treaty or customary international law provides for the enforcement outside of national territory.[50] The main argument in favour of this approach is consistent with the purpose of rules on jurisdiction, namely to delimit State powers and reduce conflicts between States.[51] However, in practice the traditional principles of jurisdiction (personal, universal, and territorial) are confronted with two problems which are also relevant for the discussion on ADIZs: to identify the location of acts; and to reconcile conflicts when two or more States have concurrent jurisdiction.[52]

ADIZs are all regulated in national legislation that sets the criteria for the requirement to identify beyond national airspace. National law may stipulate the criteria for subjective and objective types of territorial jurisdiction, but this does not automatically imply conformity with international law. The application of national law to matters beyond national territory increases the risk of overlapping and concurrent jurisdiction, which raises the issue of priority.[53]

49 *Lotus Case*; Ibid Staker, at 303.

50 *Lotus Case*; *Alleged Violations of Sovereign Rights and Maritime Spaces in the Caribbean Sea (Nicaragua v. Colombia)* (Merits) [2022] ICJ Rep 2022 at para. 95 regarding enforcement granted to the coastal State within its EEZ to the exclusion of other States in enforcing certain rights within the scope of Art. 56 UNCLOS.

51 James E Ferry, 'Towards Completing the Charm: The Woodpulp Judgment' (1989) EIPLR stating at 21 that "the objective of international law" is to "help reduce conflicts between states".

52 Christopher Staker, 'Jurisdiction', in Malcom D Evans (ed), *International Law* (5th edn, OUP 2018) 308.

53 Alex Mills, 'Rethinking Jurisdiction in International Law' (2014) 84 British Yearbook of Int'l L 187, 188.

Overlapping jurisdiction means that more than one State claims the application of its laws to the same subject matter.[54] The problem of identifying the location of acts particularly arises where there is a connection with areas beyond any territory. *Staker* assessed that there is "no clear theoretical answer" to the problem where national laws target an act beyond any national territory,[55] and further elaborated that the assertion of jurisdiction can be perceived as in conformity with international law if other States do not protest.[56]

The issue of locating acts and conflicting jurisdictional powers is also apparent in the concept of ADIZs in international airspace. ADIZs are a set of national rules dealing with the regulation of airspace beyond national territory for security purposes. As can be seen in the example of the situation in the airspace above the East China Sea, several zones may overlap and create concurrent jurisdiction. However, the problem of concurrent jurisdiction in overlapping ADIZs and the application of multiple national laws on aircraft may be rebutted if the objective territorial principle is applied to foreign aircraft bound to national airspace.[57] The relevant connecting point for extraterritorial prescriptive jurisdiction could indeed be the territory of the concerned State, namely the national airspace to which the aircraft is bound. The objective territorial principle (i.e. the effects doctrine) provides an appropriate concept by distinguishing between prescriptive jurisdiction over acts committed abroad but completed on the State's territory, and the assertion of enforcement jurisdiction limited to the State's territory.[58] The effects doctrine is discussed in other fields such as international criminal law,[59] and competition

54 Christopher Staker, 'Jurisdiction', in Malcom D Evans (ed), *International Law* (5th edn, OUP 2018) 309.

55 Ibid 308 mentioning custom laws applicable for bunkering activities on the high seas. See on this particular discussion also chapter 6 of this book.

56 Ibid 309.

57 For aircraft with the nationality of the State in which they are registered (Art. 17 Chicago Convention), the nationality respectively the personality principle prevails for the application of the ADIZ's rules.

58 In the *Lotus Case* the PCIJ stated, "the courts of many countries (…) interpret criminal law in the sense that offences the authors of which at the moment of commission are in the territory of another, are nevertheless to be regarded as having been committed in the national territory, if one of the constituent elements of the offence, and *more especially its effects*, have taken place there." (emphasis added). Critical on the effects doctrine, David Gerber, 'Beyond Balancing: International Law Restraints on the Reach of National Laws' (1984) 10 Yale Int'l L 185.

59 Stanley Metzger, 'The "Effects" Doctrine of Jurisdiction' (1967) 61 AJIL 1015; Antonio Cassese, 'Is the Bell Tolling for Universality? A Plea for a Sensible Notion of Universal Jurisdiction' (2003) 1 JICL 589.

law,[60] and asserts that activities abroad, even those of foreign citizens, may be regulated because of their impact on interests within the territorial State's domain.[61] Consequently, the ADIZ's rules of a particular State would apply only to aircraft intending to enter the national airspace of that State. The potential harmful act (namely the aircraft used as a weapon to conduct an attack) affects the security interests of the State and is completed upon the entry into national airspace. The difficulty of locating the act in question would be diminished if national laws on the identification in ADIZs did not apply to aircraft traversing the ADIZ in order to reach the national airspace of another State. A similar approach is applied to offences committed on board an aircraft. Art. 4 Tokyo Convention provides that a State other than the State of registration of the aircraft may only interfere with an aircraft in flight and exercise criminal jurisdiction over an offence committed on board only if the offence has an effect on the territory of the State or is against the security of the State.[62]

In addition to the objective territorial principle, the protective or universal principle could be relevant to ADIZs applicable to aircraft not bound for national airspace. Commentators suggest the application of the protective or the universal principle to military activities in the airspace over the EEZ.[63] Similarly, the protective principle could be used as an argument by those States that apply the rules of their ADIZ to aircraft within their EEZ that are not bound for national territory. It is generally accepted that Sates may assert jurisdiction over activities that might pose a threat to them.[64] However, this could have a negative impact on the discussion of overlapping zones and concurrent jurisdiction in cases where the delimitation of the ADIZ between two States has not been resolved and both claim a threat to them. In order to avoid concurrent jurisdiction, a balancing of interests could provide a fair solution to

60 Jason Coppel, 'A Hard Look At The Effects Doctrine Of Jurisdiction In Public International Law' (1993) 4 Leiden J Int'l Law 73; Vaughan Lowe, 'International Law and the Effects Doctrine in the European Court of Justice' (1989) 48 Cambridge J L 9–11.

61 Najeeb Samie, 'The Doctrine of "Effects" and the Extraterritorial Application of Antitrust Laws' (1982) 14 U Miami Inter-Am L Rev 23.

62 Tokyo Convention on Offences and Certain Other Acts Committed on Board Aircraft ("Tokyo Convention") (1969) 1969 UNTS 220.

63 Gbenga Oduntan, *Sovereignty and Jurisdiction in the Airspace and Outer Space* (Routledge 2012) at 139 stating that certain military activities in airspace might have a negative effect on the coastal State's rights pursuant to Art. 56 UNCLOS and can therefore be regulated by the coastal State.

64 Jan Klabbers, *International Law* (3rd edn, 2021 Cambridge University Press) 102.

determine which State has the stronger connection to the matter.[65] The legitimate interest of the State in asserting jurisdiction, such as the State's security concerns, as well as the reasonable exercise of jurisdiction by the State may be decisive criteria for the balancing of interests approach.[66] Reasonable exercise of jurisdiction means that States "are under an obligation to conduct an additional reasonableness analysis and possibly restrain their jurisdictional assertions."[67] An approach that focuses on the nexus between the States interest in regulating the practice and the reasonable exercise of jurisdiction may resolve conflicting jurisdiction. Similarly, Judge *Fitzmaurice* expressed in his Separate Opinion in the *Barcelona Traction Case*:

> (…) international law does not impose hard and fast rules on States delimiting spheres of national jurisdiction (…). It does however (…) involve for every State an obligation to exercise moderation and restraint as to the extent of the jurisdiction assumed by its courts in cases having a foreign element, and to avoid undue encroachment on a jurisdiction more properly appertaining to, or more appropriately exercisable by another State.[68]

States may object to and express their disapproval of the jurisdictional extension, which would accommodate the fundamental principles of sovereign equality and of non-interference in areas beyond the sovereignty of any State.[69] The objection indicates that the jurisdictional claim has gone too far.[70]

---

65 Similar, Andreas Lowenfeld, 'Conflict, Balancing of Interests and the Exercise of Jurisdiction to Prescribe: Reflections on the Insurance Antitrust Case' (1995) 89 AJIL 42.

66 Cedric Ryngaert, *Jurisdiction in International Law* (2nd edn, OUP 2015) 29.

67 Ibid, claiming that it is a rule of international law; contra: Karl Meessen, 'Antitrust Jurisdiction under Customary International Law' (1984) 78 AJIL 783, 802 stating that the reasonable exercise principle is not operable on the level of international law.

68 *Barcelona Traction, Light and Power Company, Ltd* (*Belgium v Spain*) [1970] ICJ Rep 3, 105 Sep Op Fitzmaurice.

69 The ICJ defined the principle of non-intervention as "the right of every sovereign State to conduct its affairs without outside interference", see *Nicaragua Case* para. 202; see also Djamchid Momatz, 'Chapter 7' in René-Jean Dupuy & Daniel Vignes (eds), *A Handbook on the Law of the Sea, Volume* 1 (Martinus Nijhoff 1991) at 399 elaborating on the fundamental idea of equal State rights on the high seas and the absence of individual State sovereignty outside national territory.

70 As for example when the US enacted a law which prohibited the importation of alcohol, State protested the application of the US Prohibition Law to foreign cruise ships entering US ports. Christopher Staker, 'Jurisdiction', in Malcom D Evans (ed), *International Law* (5th edn, OUP 2018) 309. Related to this discussion is the persistent objector rule, see

This practice of objecting to the extension of jurisdiction can also be seen in the case of the ADIZ above the East China Sea. Since China applies its national ADIZ rules also on aircraft not bound for Chinese airspace, several States that have ADIZs themselves protested this practice.[71]

Elias Olufemi, 'Persistent Objector' in *Max Planck Encyclopedias of Public International Law* (OUP 2006) para. 1.

71 See chapter 3 of this book.

CHAPTER 3

An Analysis of ADIZs in State Practice

1 Implications and Current Stand of State Practice regarding ADIZs

Cuadra first commented on the concept of ADIZs in State practice that these

> zones may become a rule of customary international law if unilateral assertions of limited sovereignty in high seas airspace spread to additional States.[1]

Cuadra referred to the initial situation of 1977 when approximately eleven States claimed an ADIZ: Myanmar, Canada, Iceland, India, Japan, Korea, Oman, Philippines, Sweden, United States, and Vietnam.[2] As of 2022, the legal landscape has changed; former ADIZs disappeared and new ADIZs appeared. The current stand amounts to approximately twenty-seven States permanently claiming an ADIZ. Since it is not clear, whether ADIZs are permitted under international law and due to the absence of rules governing ADIZs, the exact scope and content of ADIZs and the methods of publishing information vary quite drastically.[3] The material scope of ADIZs, in general, sets forth the identification requirements applicable to aircraft and the consequences of not properly identifying in accordance with these requirements.[4] In some cases, it proved to be difficult to obtain all necessary information on the ADIZ's rules and their exact scope of application. Some States enclose details on their ADIZs in national laws, while others solely include the ADIZs' details in Aeronautical Information Publications (AIP), and some States indicated the location of their ADIZs in aeronautical maps without any further details on the applicable

1 Elisabeth Cuadra, 'Air Defense Identification Zones: Creeping Jurisdiction in the Airspace' (1977) 18 Virginia J Int'l L 507.
2 Ibid, Appendix 509.
3 Edmund J Burke & Astrid Stuth Cevallos, *In Line or out of Order? – Chinas Approach to ADIZ in Theory and Practice* (Rand 2017) 3.
4 See also, Pai Zheng, 'Justifications and Limits of ADIZs under Public International Law' (2014–15) 144 Issues Aviation L & Pol'y 138, at 195–199.

 | DOI:10.1163/9789004721005_005

identification procedure.[5] Only sufficiently published ADIZs will be described in more detail representing a diverse overview of different World regions.[6]

The unilateral establishment of the Chinese ADIZ above the East China Sea has raised the concern that these zones may have an influence on maritime territorial disputes. Commentators suggested that aerial claims help to strengthen territorial claims in maritime areas by exercising control.[7] Concerning the principle of effectiveness *Cassese* notes that

> [i]nternational law is a realistic legal system. It takes account of existing power relationship and endeavors to translate them into legal rules. It is largely based on the principle of effectiveness (...); it provides that only those claims and situations which are effective can produce legal consequences. A situation is effective if it is solidly implanted in real life.[8]

Closely related is the principle *ex factis ius oritur,* which addresses the interdependence of long and consistent practice and its factual influence on international law.[9] International law is influenced by the actions of powerful States, which are not prohibited *per se,* and for which a pragmatic solution needs to be found. The practice of establishing an ADIZ above the high seas or the EEZ fuelled the debate on their effect on progressive sovereignty claims of the coastal States. Without suggesting that ADIZs follow some political scheme, a territorial expansion may in the first stage be limited to specialized rights and competences, and in the second stage may evolve into stronger sovereignty

5 AIP are a publication issued by an authority of a State and contains information essential to air navigation in line with Annex 15. Section 5.2. Chicago Convention.

6 Excluding Libya and Turkey for which the author could not access the AIP of the respective States; however described by Jinyuan Su, 'The Practice of States on Air Defence Identification Zones: Geographical Scope, Object of Identification, and Identification Measures' (2019) 18 Chinese J Int' L 817. ADIZs which are no longer in force, such as the Austrian ADIZ or the German ADIZ, which were both in force until 1990, are not part of further deliberation, see also https://www.deutsche-digitale-bibliothek.de/item/JVQVW66LLGEUJ4YARJVUAFAFSFUYDMHV (accessed 11 April 2023).

7 Christopher Lamont, 'Conflict in the Skies: The Law of Air Defence Identification Zones' (2014) 39 Air & Space Law; Alex Calvo, 'China's Air Defense Identification Zone Concept, Issues at Stake and Regional Impact' (2013) Naval War College Press Working Paper 3; Zoltan Papp, 'ADIZ in the Light of Public International Law' (2015) Pécs J Int'l & European L 40.

8 Paola Gaeta, Jorge E Viñuales & Salvatore Zappalá, *Cassese's International Law* (3rd edn, OUP 2020) 12.

9 Aaron Fellmeth & Maurice Horwitz, *A Guide to Latin in International Law* (OUP 2011, online version). Critical Lauri Mölksoo, 'Ex Factis Oritur Ius' in Lauri Mölksoo, *Illegal Annexation and State Continuity* (Brill Nijhoff 2003) 171ff; Marten Breuer, 'Effektivitätsprinzip' in Burkhard Schöbener et al (eds), *Völkerrecht: Lexikon zentraler Begriffe und Themen* (Müller 2014) 69.

claims through repeated and generalized actions. The possibility of creeping sovereignty claims include a twofold transition: From functional competence to territorial rights; and from exclusive competence to discretionary competence.[10]

1.1 *Argentina*

Argentina established in 2014 an ADIZ on the North Coast as part of the flexible use of airspace (FUA).[11] The overall purpose of the Argentinean ADIZ is to achieve the safe and efficient use of airspace both for military as well as civil aircraft.[12] According to Argentina, an ADIZ represents a portion of the airspace where special flight restrictions or regulations are established for reasons of national defence.[13] In 2018, Argentina extended the outer limits of the ADIZ on a temporal basis for the occasion of the G-20 summit.[14] In 2020, the Departamento Informacion Aeronautica published an update on the 2018 rules covering extended dimensions.[15] The Argentinian ADIZ coincides with the two Argentinian FIR CBA and FIR SIS and, hence, covers national territory and parts of the Atlantic Ocean. In accordance with the provisions of Decree 1054/18 of the National Executive Power, it is mandatory to present the flight plan before take-off in order to fly in the area established as class "G" airspace in the North ADIZ, or in any other ADIZ established by the competent aeronautical authority.[16] The updated information includes a document ("formulario de información de intención de vuelo") which needs to be filled out before the flight.[17] Additionally, aircraft that carry out aerial activities in class "G"

---

10 See for a similar discussion on the advances of maritime zones René-Jean Dupuy, 'Chapter 5' in Rene Jean Dupuy & Daniel Vignes (eds), *A Handbook on the New Law of the Sea, Volume 1* (1991) 292.

11 Notifying ICAO about the Argentinian Norte ADIZ (ANADIZ), ICAO Doc, SAM ASTRO/6-NI/03 (24 October 2014). On the flexible use of airspace (FUA) see chapter 5, 2.6.2 of this book.

12 ICAO Doc, SAM ASTRO/6-NI/03 (24 October 2014).

13 "Es una "Zona de Identificación de Defensa Aérea" (por sus sigla expresada en inglés, AIR DEFENCE IDENTIFICATION ZONE) que representa una porción del espacio aéreo donde se establecen restricciones o normas de vuelo especiales por razones de defensa nacional." https://www.fuerzas-armadas.mil.ar/cocaes/pesta%C3%B1as/queressabermas.html (accessed 8 June 2022).

14 Jinyuan Su, 'The Practice of States on Air Defence Identification Zones: Geographical Scope, Object of Identification, and Identification Measures' (2019) 18 Chinese J Int'l Law 817, 818, stating that the ADIZ is no longer in force.

15 Argentina AIP (5 November 2020) ENR 5.2.

16 Decreto 1054/18 del Poder Ejecutivo Nacional.

17 Argentina AIP (5 November 2020) ENR 5.2–1. "Todas las aeronaves deben presentar obligatoriamente Plan de Vuelo o Formulario de Información de Intención de Vuelo (FIIV),

airspace must be equipped with surveillance equipment for the purpose of identification under the surveillance and national security system.[18] Failure to comply with the provisions will "make the aircraft subject to the application of Article 3bis of the Convention on International Civil Aviation," which means that aircraft may be intercepted in accordance with the provision of the Argentinean AIP, ENR 1.12.[19]

1.2 *Australia*

The Australian Civil Aviation Act 1988 establishes the regulatory framework for maintaining, enhancing, and promoting the safety of civil aviation.[20] The Civil Aviation Safety Amendment 2018 sets out the general operating and flight rules and mainly comprises the current regulatory provisions contained in the Civil Aviation Act of 1988. Regulation 91.275 sets forth the concept of ADIZ and states that "ADIZ is airspace in which all aircraft must be identified and in which aircraft may be intercepted in the interest of national security".[21] The exact details of the identification requirements are explained in the Australian Aeronautical Information Publication (AIP). The AIP is not generally considered part of the legislative framework, however, some regulations specifically refer to the AIP and therefore "must be followed."[22]

According to ENR 1.12, Section 2.1.2. AIP, ADIZ signifies "airspace of defined dimensions within which identification of all aircraft is required."[23] The Australian ADIZ stretches into international airspace and obliges to "lodge a flight notification covering flight within the ADIZ with the appropriate ATS unit at least 60 minutes before entry into the ADIZ."[24] The rules of the Australian ADIZ do not link the identification obligation with entry to national airspace but with the entry into the ADIZ. It can be assumed that any aircraft traversing through the zone has to comply with the identification rules. Additionally, aircraft are obliged to report their position to ATS when passing each position

---

antes de iniciar el vuelo y mantenerlo hasta su llegada a destino."Also indicating to which email adresse the document and flight has to be sent.

18 Argentina AIP (5 November 2020) ENR 5.2–1.

19 Argentina AIP (5 November 2020) ENR 5.2–1.

20 Civil Aviation Act 1988, Act No 63.

21 Civil Aviation Safety Amendment (Part 91) Regulations 2018 https://vfrg.casa.gov.au/operations/air-defence-identification-zone/general-2

22 Australian Government – Civil Aviation Safety Authority, *Understanding the Legislative Framework* (May 2021) 19.

23 Australia AIP (16 June 2022) available at https://www.airservicesaustralia.com/aip/aip.asp?pg=10.

24 Australia AIP ENR 1.12, Section 2.1.3 (a); "deben presentar obligatoriamente Plan de Vuelo o Formulario de Información de Intención de Vuelo (FIIV), antes de iniciar el vuelo."

reporting point within the ADIZ and at the ADIZ boundary with a geographical reference.[25] Australia's ADIZ additionally obliges aircraft to report their departure if the departure point is within 100 nm of the ADIZ boundary and to report departure if departing from a point in the ADIZ.[26] While traversing through the ADIZ, aircraft have to maintain a continuous listening watch on the communications frequency of the appropriate ATS unit or another frequency as directed.[27] Moreover, aircraft should not deliberately deviate from tracks and altitudes filed in the flight plan unless prior ATS clearance is obtained, or, outside controlled airspace, notification is given to the appropriate ATS unit.[28] When within 100 nm of the ADIZ or when operating within the ADIZ, aircraft have to activate the aircraft transponder.[29] As regards non-compliance with the ADIZ's rules, significant deviations from the requirements for flight in an ADIZ must be reported immediately to ATS, and details and reasons for the deviation must be reported at the first point of landing, for transmission to the Regional Air Defence Commander.[30]

Aircraft that cannot be satisfactorily identified may be intercepted by fighter aircraft in national airspace.[31] The procedure for interception is detailed in ENR 1.2. Section 1 of the Australian AIP. The aircraft has to follow the instructions given by the intercepting aircraft and has to establish radio communication.[32] The interception can lead to three different results. First, the aircraft may be identified as "friendly" and should then proceed according to the flight plan. Second, the aircraft can be labelled as "unknown" and be shadowed, diverted, or instructed to land at a suitable airfield. Third, aircraft identified as "hostile" may be engaged and destroyed.[33]

1.3 *Bangladesh*

Bangladesh established its ADIZ in 2018 and published the respective rules in AIP SUPP 01/18.[34] According to Bangladesh's opinion, the complete and exclusive sovereignty over the airspace above its territory can only be ensured by

25 Australia AIP ENR 1.12, Section 2.1.3 (b).
26 Australia AIP ENR 1.12, Section 2.1.3 (c).
27 Australia AIP ENR 1.12, Section 2.1.3 (e).
28 Australia AIP ENR 1.12, Section 2.1.3 (f).
29 Australia AIP ENR 1.12, Section 2.1.3 (g).
30 Australia AIP ENR 1.12, Section 2.3.1.
31 Australia AIP, ENR 1.2., Section 1.
32 Australia AIP ENR 1.12, Section 1.1.1.
33 Australia AIP (16 June 2022).
34 Bangladesh AIP SUPP 01/18 (1 February 2018).

imposing an ADIZ in accordance with the Chicago Convention.[35] The purpose of Bangladesh's ADIZ is to "form the first line of defence against aerial intrusions into Bangladesh airspace."[36] It covers international airspace "as this is vital to the national security," which is supposedly in line with the Chicago Convention.[37] The zone covers the airspace over the entire territory of Bangladesh as defined by its international border with India and Myanmar, and also extends over the adjoining sea to the South into international airspace as can be seen in the published coordinates.[38] The Bangladesh ADIZ penetrates the airspace of two adjacent Flight Information Regions (FIR) and therefore impacts aircraft under the control of Air Traffic Control units in other States.

All flights, civil or military, Bangladeshi or foreign, originating within the ADIZ and those penetrating the Bangladesh ADIZ shall obtain prior permission and Air Defence Clearance (ADC).[39] The rules of the Bangladesh ADIZ are partly contradictory and lack important information. For example, it states that "all aircraft intending to operate into, through or within the Bangladesh ADIZ shall obtain ADC number from the appropriate ATS unit before takeoff." The next paragraph, however, requires "all aircraft intending to overfly Bangladesh ADIZ or land in any airfield within Dhaka Flight Information Region (FIR) shall obtain ADC 10 minutes before entering the Bangladesh ADIZ." Additionally, "in case of departures from adjacent FIRs, where the prerequisites of 10 minutes advance notice is not feasible, ADC number shall be obtained before departure." It remains equivocal whether an ADC number shall be obtained before take-off or 10 minutes before entering the Bangladesh ADIZ. Moreover, the rules do not prescribe how an ADC number can be obtained and also do not include the dimensions of the ADIZ. This is particularly negative, as any "aircraft flying without a valid ADC number or failing to comply with any restriction or deviating from flight plan will be liable to interception by Bangladesh Air Force Interceptor aircraft according to ICAO Standard Interception Procedure." The uncoordinated ad-hoc establishment of an ADIZ by Bangladesh in 2018 entails negative effects on the civil aviation industry.[40] Particularly, the

35 Ibid.

36 Ibid.

37 Bangladesh AIP SUPP 01/18 (1 February 2018).

38 Bangladesh AIP SUPP 01/18 (1 February 2018) Coordinates.

39 Bangladesh AIP SUPP 01/18 (1 February 2018).

40 ICAO Doc SAIOACG/9 – WP29, 'Civil/Military Update' Ninth Meeting of the South Asia/Indian Ocean ATM Coordination Group (26.03.2019–29.03.2019).

International Air Transport Association (IATA) expressed concerns about the lack of proper details and the unclear procedure for obtaining an ADC.[41]

1.4 *Brazil*

Brazil established an ADIZ in 2016 and regulates the zones under the name ZIDA in the Aeronautical Information Circular (AIC).[42] Art. 1.3.1 defines the ZIDA as "[a]irspace of special designated and defined dimensions, within which aircraft must comply with special identification and notification procedures, in addition to those related to the provision of air traffic services for air defense purposes."[43] The definition of the ZIDA resembles the wording of the Annexes 4 and 15 of the Chicago Convention. In contrast to the Chicago Convention's definition, Brazil requires the compliance with "notification procedures" instead of "reporting procedures."[44] Aircraft have to submit a flight plan in the ZIDA before entering Brazilian airspace.[45] The Brazilian ADIZ overs national airspace applying to all aircraft traveling in the zone and aligns with the FIR Amazonica and FIR Curitiba.[46]

1.5 *Canada*

Canada established its ADIZ in 1950 with the Canadian Aviation Regulation SOr/96–433.[47] The Canadian Aviation Regulation 600.01 applies to all aircraft before entering into and while operating within the ADIZ and defines the zones as "the airspace that extends upward from the surface in those areas of Canada and off the coasts of Canada, the boundaries of which are specified in the Designated Airspace Handbook."[48] As indicated in the *Designated Airspace Handbook* the dimensions cover national as well as international

41 ICAO Doc SAIOACG/8 and SEACG/25 WP 22, 'Imposition Of Military Requirements And Restrictions On International Civil Aviation'(30.03.2018) para. 1.2.

42 Brazil Aeronautical Information Circular, AIC-N 16/17 (4 August 2017). https://publicacoes.decea.mil.br/publicacao/aic-n-1617

43 Art. 1.3.1, Zona De Identificação De Defesa Aérea: Espaço aéreo de designação especial e de dimensões definidas, dentro do qual as aeronaves devem satisfazer procedimentos especi ais de identificação e notificação, além daqueles que se relacionam à prestação dos serviços de tráfego aéreo, para fins de Defesa Aérea.

44 See Annex 4 and 15, Chicago Convention.

45 Art. 2.2.

46 AIP Brazil (09 Mar 2019) ENR 5.2; Jinyuan Su, 'The Practice of States on Air Defense Identification Zones: Geographical Scope, Object of Identification and Identification Measures' (2019) 18 Chinse J Int'l Law 828 referring to Jeppesen JeppView (Cycle 1905).

47 600.01 Canadian Aviation Regulation (SOR/96–433) (last amended 1 January 2017).

48 600.01 Canadian Aviation Regulation (SOR/96–433).

airspace.[49] The prerequisite for entering the ADIZ is to file a flight plan or flight itinerary with an air traffic control unit, a flight service station, or a community aerodrome radio station.[50] Where the point of departure is outside the ADIZ, the flight plan or itinerary shall include the estimated time and point of ADIZ entry.[51] Additionally, the pilot shall, as soon as possible after take-off, communicate by radio to an air traffic control unit, a flight service station, or a community aerodrome radio station, a position report of the aircraft. The position report includes the location, altitude, aerodrome of departure, and the estimated time and point of ADIZ entry.[52] The same applies also to aircraft where the point of departure is within the ADIZ. Interception in the ADIZ is jointly coordinated between Canada and the US under the North American Aerospace Command (NORAD).[53] NORAD employs a layered defence network of radars, satellites, and fighter aircraft to identify aircraft and determine the appropriate response.[54] In case of interception, typically two fighters approach the stern and the intercepted aircraft may have to land.[55] NORAD is a specific example of a jointly administered air defence system in an ADIZ. The joint administration precluded the issue of overlapping zones and jurisdiction.

1.6 *China*

China unilaterally established its ADIZ over the East China Sea by announcement in 2013.[56] Several laws and regulations apply to the ECS ADIZ, namely the Law of the People's Republic of China on National Defense (14 March 1997), the Law of the People's Republic of China on Civil Aviation (30 October 1995), and Basic Rules on Flight of the People's Republic of China (27 July 2001). The purpose of China's ECS ADIZ is to "protect its state sovereignty and territorial and airspace security. It is conducive to maintaining flying safety in international airspace, and is in line with international laws and conventions."[57]

49 Canadian Designated Airspace Handbook, Issue No 289 (12 June 2021) 195.

50 602.145 (2) Canadian Aviation Regulation (SOR/96–433).

51 602.145 (3) (b) Canadian Aviation Regulation (SOR/96–433).

52 602.145 (3) (c) Canadian Aviation Regulation (SOR/96–433).

53 Roncevert Almond, 'Clearing the Air above the East China Sea: The Primary Elements of Aircraft Defense Identification Zones' (2017) 7 Harvard Nat Sec J 135.

54 https://www.norad.mil/About-NORAD/ (accessed 31 May 2022).

55 Aeronautical Information Manual (AIM 2022) Section 5–6–2.

56 Announcement of the Aircraft Identification Rules for the East China Sea Air Defence Identification Zone of the P.C.R. (23 November 2013) http://us.china-embassy.gov.cn/eng/zt_120777/cadiz/201312/t20131205_4911505.htm (accessed 31 May 2022). Chinese NOTAM A1886/13 and NOTAM A1916/13.

57 http://us.china-embassy.gov.cn/eng/zt_120777/cadiz/201312/t20131205_4911505.htm (accessed 31 May 2022). On aspects of national defence for determining boundaries as

The dimensions of China's ADIZ stretch far beyond national airspace into international airspace.[58] To China's perception the ADIZ boundaries and rules "are totally in line with the UN-Charter and other international practices."[59] Moreover, China claims the right to regulate military activities in the airspace above its EEZ and hence the right to restrict the freedom of overflight if States do not pay due regard pursuant to Art. 58 (3) UNCLOS.[60] As regards the inclusion of disputed maritime islands, the Senkaku/Diayou islands, China argues that the islands "are integral parts of China's territory."[61] Aircraft flying in the East China Sea Air Defense Identification Zone "must provide the following means of identification":

1. Flight plan identification. Aircraft flying in the ECS ADIZ should report the flight plans to the Ministry of Foreign Affairs of the People's Republic of China or the Civil Aviation Administration of China.
2. Radio identification. Aircraft flying in the ECS ADIZ must maintain two-way radio communications, and respond in a timely and accurate manner to identification inquiries from the administrative organ of the East China Sea Air Defense Identification Zone or the unit authorized by the organ.
3. Transponder identification. Aircraft flying in the ECS ADIZ, if equipped with the secondary radar transponder, should keep the transponder working throughout the entire course.
4. Logo identification. Aircraft flying in the ECS ADIZ must clearly mark their nationalities and the logo of their registration identification in accordance with related international treaties.[62]

---

part of China's policies, see Byron N Tzou, *China and International Law – The Boundary Disputes* (Prager 1990) 116 mentioning the Sino-Burmese boundary negotiations.

58 33°11'N (North Latitude) and 121°47'E (East Longitude), 33°11'N and 125°00'E, 31°00'N and 128°20'E, 25°38'N and 125°00'E, 24°45'N and 123°00'E, 26°44'N and 120°58'E.

59 Ministry of Foreign Affairs of the People's Republic of China, "Foreign Ministry Spokesperson Qin Gang's Remarks on Japan's Representations About China's Establishment of an Air Defense Identification Zone in the East China Sea," (25 November 2013) https://www.fmprc.gov.cn/mfa_eng/xwfw_665399/s2510_665401/2535_665405/201311/t20131125_696274.html (accessed 3 June 2022).

60 Matthias Vanhullebusch & Wei Shen, 'China's Air Defence Identification Zone: Building Security through Lawfare'(2016) 16 China Review 133; Raul Pedrozo, 'Preserving Navigational Rights and Freedoms: The Right to Conduct Military Activities in China's Exclusive Economic Zone' (2010) 9 Chinese Journal of International Law 11; also, Art. 11 Exclusive Economic Zone and the Continental Shelf Act (1998).

61 Ibid.

62 Chang Ching, 'An Embarrassing Fact: The Legal Basis of the PCR East China Sea ADIZ' (23 November 2015) http://cimsec.org/an-embarrassing-fact-the-legal-basis-of-the-prc-east-china-sea-adiz/19804 (accessed 31 May 2022).

Aircraft flying in the East China Sea ADIZ should follow the instructions of the administrative organ of the East China Sea ADIZ or the unit authorized by the organ even if they do not intend to enter Chinese national airspace. In case of non-compliance, China's armed forces will adopt defensive emergency measures to respond to the aircraft. However, China has not published the details on the defensive emergency measures in the ECS ADIZ leading to legal uncertainty and an increased risk of accidents.[63] One view proposes that the phrase "defensive emergency measures" does not equalize the shooting down of the aircraft.[64] Instead, in Chinese the term "defensive emergency measures" would signify preventive acts, for example tracking and monitoring.[65] Yet, the method of these defensive emergency measures is nowhere explicitly described.[66] In a recent report in 2024, Japanese military pilots describe Chinese communication attempts near the East China Sea ADIZ, which gave warning to prevent the Japanese aircraft from entering the zone. The pilots entered the zone without following the Chinese procedures and did not experience any interference from Chinese side.[67] It seems therefore unlikely that forceful interception would occur if military aircraft do not comply with the identification obligations. According to Chinese official sources, civil aircraft comply with the ECS ADIZ's requirements.[68]

1.7 *Cuba*

Cuba enclosed details on its ADIZ in AIP ENR 5.1.[69] The outer limits of the Cuba ADIZ conform with the Habana FIR, which extends into the Caribbean Sea in

63 Raul Pedrozo, 'The Bull in the China Shop: Raising Tensions in the Asia-Pacific Region' (2014) 90 Int'l L Studies 93–94.

64 Jinyuan Su, 'The East China Sea Air Defense Identification Zone and International Law'(2015) 14 Chinese J Int'l L 285.

65 Newsletter No.0107, Embassy of the PCR in the United States of America, describing the Chinese interception procedure (15 April 2011) https://www.mfa.gov.cn/ce/ceus//eng/sgxx/sggg/sstx/2001/t35019.htm); also Qin L 'U.S Plane Grossly Violated International Law' (3 April 2001) https://www.fmprc.gov.cn/ce/cegv/eng/premade/11437/article040401.html (accessed 31 May 2022).

66 Edmund J Burke & Astrid Stuth Cevallos, *In Line or out of Order? – Chinas Approach to ADIZ in Theory and Practice* (Rand 2017) 7.

67 Kenta Kamimura, 'Tensions Rising Around Maritime Border Claimed by China; Globally Recognized 'Freedom of Overflight' Under Threat', The Japan News (29 January 2024) https://japannews.yomiuri.co.jp/politics/defense-security/20240129-165259/.

68 Jinyuan Su, 'The East China Sea Air Defense Identification Zone and International Law' (2015) 14 Chinese J Int'l L 288. Contrary to that: Hiroyuki Kachi & Yoshio Takahashi, 'Japan asks Airline to Ignore China Flight-Plan Rule' (26 November 2013, Wall Street Journal) https://www.wsj.com/articles/SB10001424052702304281004579221681641322204 (accessed 31 May 2022).

69 Cuba AIP (25 April 2019).

the South and the Atlantic Ocean in the North.[70] All aircraft flying through the ADIZ (Inner FIR) of Cuban airspace must have a Cuban Overflight Permit.[71]

1.8 *Finland*

The coordinates of the Finnish ADIZ can be found in AIP Finland, ENR 5.2.8. of 26 April 2018. The ADIZ aligns with the Helsinki FIR and covers national territory and parts of the Baltic Sea.[72] The Finnish AIP is prepared in accordance with the Standards and Recommended Practices (SARPs) of Annex 15 to the Convention on International Civil Aviation and the Aeronautical Information Services Manual (ICAO Doc 8126).[73] The specific rules on air traffic within Finnish territory also conform with the SARPs of Annexes 2 and 11.[74] It can therefore be concluded that Finland views the concept of an ADIZ as in line with the Chicago Convention and its SARPs. A flight plan shall be submitted for a flight intended to be conducted in the ADIZ or in a prohibited or restricted area.[75] Details on the procedure for filing a flight plan are publicly available.[76] The flight plan needs to include inter alia the identification of the aircraft, route, and departure time.[77]

1.9 *Greece*

In 1931, Greece claimed a 10-nautical-mile air defence zone around its islands based on its presumed sovereignty over this area.[78] The 10-nautical miles delimitation leads to the result that the territorial sea and the sovereign airspace do not align. The situation of the Greece ADIZ presents a particular challenge due to the geographical feature of the Aegean Sea and the many unresolved territorial disputes between Türkiye and Greece in this area.[79] Greece considers the boundaries of the Athens FIR, over which it has authority, as a defence perimeter for its ADIZ and insists that military aircraft conform to the ICAO

70 Cuba AIP (25 April 2019), ENR 5.1.
71 https://www.cubahandling.com/overflight.
72 Details on the Helsinki FIR can be accessed here: https://www.ais.fi/ais/bulletins/efinen-fr.htm; https://xn.ivao.aero/finland (accessed 15 July 2022).
73 Finland AIP (26 April 2018), Gen 0.1.2.
74 Finland AIP (26 April 2018), Enr. 1.1.
75 Finnish Aviation Act (864/2014), Section 5 (21 September 2018), Regulation 4 (15) TRAFI/499813/03.04.00.00/2016 OPS M1–1.
76 https://www.ais.fi/en/pre-flight-information-service-and-flight-plans/fpl-instructions.
77 Ibid.
78 Kateros M Iannou, 'The Greek Territorial Sea' in Theodore Kariotis (ed), *Greece and the Law of the Sea* (Springer 1997) 115, 151.
79 Jon M Van Dyke, 'An Analysis of the Aegan Disputes under International Law' (2005) 36 Ocean Development & Int'L L 85, 86.

reporting procedures within the Athens FIR.[80] Consequently, Greece maintains the view that military aircraft entering into Athens FIR should submit flight plans.[81] Due to the disagreement on maritime boundaries in the Aegean Sea region, Türkiye continuously protests the Greece ADIZ.[82]

1.10 *Iceland*

Iceland established in 1960 an ADIZ in international airspace for aircraft bound for national airspace.[83] The Iceland ADIZ covered land territory and adjacent waters in the Greenland Sea, the Norwegian Sea, and the North Atlantic Ocean.[84] After the Cold War, Iceland dismantled the ADIZ, which is thus no longer in force.[85]

1.11 *India*

The Indian *Manual on Flexible Use of Airspace* regulates the concept of an ADIZ. According to India, the flexible use of airspace must also include airspace over the high seas within the jurisdiction of the FIR, considered without detriment to the rights and obligations of Member States under the Chicago Convention.[86] The FUA Manual takes into consideration the national security situation, the national background on civil-military cooperation, as well as the "current and future requirements, global benchmarks and best practices" in line with the principles of the FUA enshrined in various ICAO Annexes and Documents.[87] It can therefore be assumed that India views the concept of an ADIZ as a legitimate use of international airspace in line with the rules of the Chicago Convention and related ICAO Annexes and documents.

---

80 Michael N Schmitt, 'Aegan Angst – The Greek-Turkish Dispute' (1996) 49 Naval War College Review 61; Alexis Heraclis, *The Greek-Turkish Conflict in the Aegean* (Springer 2010) 214–219.

81 Türkiye Ministry of Foreign Affairs, 'Airspace Related Problems' https://www.mfa.gov.tr/air-space-related-related-problems.en.mfa (accessed 18 June 2022).

82 Philip Chrysopoulos, 'Turkish Fighter Jets Violate Greek Airspace, Again' (17 July 2015) https://greekreporter.com/2015/07/17/turkish-fighter-jets-violate-greek-airspace-again/ (accessed 18 June 2022).

83 Nicholas M Poulantzas, *The Right to Hot Pursuit in International Law* (2nd edn Brill 2002) 342; UNSC, 'Chapter VIII. Maintenance of International Peace and Security' (881st Meeting, July 25 1960) 185, 186.

84 Jinyuan Su, 'The Practice of States on Air Defence Identification Zones: Geographical Scope, Object of Identification, and Identification Measures' (2019) 18 Chinese J Int'l Law 818.

85 Joëlle Charbonneau, Katie Heelis & Jinelle Piereder, 'Putting Air Defense Identification Zones On The Radar' (2015) CIGI Graduate Fellows Series 2.

86 Manual on Flexible Use of Airspace, ATFM/SG/5-WP13 Attachment A (2015) VI.

87 Ibid.

Section 6.1.1. defines ADIZs as "zones established for air defense clearance."[88] Air Defence Clearance (ADC) signifies "authorization of a proposed flight by the ADIA originating from and/or penetrating into an Indian ADIZ during peace and war." It further states that "no flight or aircraft civil/military, Indian or foreign originating within the ADIZ defined above and those penetrating into these ADIZ are permitted without ADC."[89] The Indian ADIZ therefore clearly applies to civil as well as military aircraft intending to enter the zone. The *Manual on Flexible Use of Airspace* also offers an explanation of the purposes of the ADC, namely:

(a) to provide ADIA with advance flight plan data for prompt identification of friendly movements by correlation.
(b) to avoid wastefully flying effort involved in physical recognition of friendly aircraft.
(c) to ensure prompt and appropriate tactical action to investigate unknown flights.
(d) to effectively deal with unauthorized and objectionable intrusion by foreign aircraft.[90]

Section 6.3 includes a detailed procedure for obtaining an ADC and thus offers more legal security compared to the Bangladesh ADIZ's requirement of an ADC.[91] However, some provisions remain ambiguous. On the temporal scope for obtaining an ADC it is stated that "all flights shall obtain ADC before entering the ADIZ from respective FIR ten minutes prior to entering Indian airspace".[92] This raises the question of whether entering of the ADIZ always aligns with entering the Indian airspace within 10 minutes. This seems not likely as India altogether has six ADIZ with different coordinates.[93] It is unclear whether the aircraft shall obtain the ADC when entering the ADIZ or ten minutes prior to entering national airspace. Aircraft flying without an ADC or failing to comply with any restriction or deviation from flight plans will be liable to identification and interception procedures.[94] More details on the ADC procedure would be welcome to avoid interception.

88 Manual on Flexible Use of Airspace, ATFM/SG/5-WP13 Attachment A (2015).
89 Manual on Flexible Use of Airspace, Section 6.2.1.
90 Section 6.2.1.1 Manual on Flexible Use of Airspace.
91 Section 6.3.1–6.3.8.
92 Section 6.3.3.
93 The coordinates of the ADIZ North, West, Central, East, South and South-East can be found in Section 6.1.1–6.1.7.
94 Section 6.2.2. The details on the interception procedure can be found at AIP India ENR 1.12.

1.12 *Indonesia*

The Indonesian ADIZ is currently located in the airspace of a small portion of South Sumatra, Java and Madura, Bali, Lombok, and a small part of western Sumbawa Island and covers only national airspace to an extent of 3sm.[95] This can be explained by the fact that Indonesia first established an ADIZ in 1960, when it was not recognized as an archipelago State, and hence aligned the zone with the width of 3sm of the territorial sea at that time.[96] New attempts aim to re-define the concept of ADIZs and to include detailed rules in national law with regulation No. 4 of 2018 on Airspace Security amended with Law No. 1 of 2009 on Aviation.[97] It was suggested that the legal basis in international law for the Indonesia ADIZ could either be customary international law or the inherent right to self-defence.[98] There is currently no official English translation of the regulation available so that the following analysis is based on the translation offered by *Laksmana*.[99] Art. 9 (a) Regulation No. 4 on Airspace Security defines ADIZ as "specific air spaces above the land and/or waters established to identify aircraft for the purposes of state defense and security." Art. 9 (b) differentiates between "airspace," meaning "sovereign airspace" and, "jurisdictional airspace," meaning "airspace above the exclusive economic zone (EEZ), continental shelf, and contiguous zone, where Indonesia has "sovereign rights prescribed by international law."[100] The future Indonesian ADIZ therefore could share the same boundaries as the Indonesian EEZ. Indonesia bases its ADIZs claim on international custom.[101] Articles 14 and 15 regulate the obligation to identify, namely that unscheduled foreign aircraft flying within the "jurisdictional airspace" would be required to report their identity, destination, and flight plan to air traffic control personnel.[102] Any non-compliance with the obligation to identify may result in interception.[103] The interception within the Indonesian ADIZ is regulated in Art. 6 of Act No. 3 (2002) on national defence and Act No. 34

95 Deni Marsono, 'Determination of Air Defense Identification Zone (ADIZ) in order to Support Sovereignty of National Air Region' (2018) 8 Journal of Defense & State Defense 17.

96 Ibid 18.

97 Regulation No. 4 of 2018 on Airspace Security (Peraturan Pemerintah) (19 February 2018).

98 Deni Marsono, 'Determination of Air Defense Identification Zone (ADIZ) in order to Support Sovereignty of National Air Region' (2018) 8 Journal of Defense & State Defense 15, 16.

99 Evan Laksmana, 'Is an Indonesian Air Defence Identification Zone Forthcoming?' (10 April 2018) https://amti.csis.org/indonesian-adiz-forthcoming/ (accessed 20 May 2022).

100 Ibid.

101 Ibid.

102 Ibid.

103 Art. 28 Regulation No. 4 of 2018 on Airspace Security (Peraturan Pemerintah), (19 February 2018).

(2004) on the Indonesian Armed Forces.[104] The Indonesian Armed Forces may undertake active air defense by detecting, identifying, and forcing the landing of aircraft.[105] Currently, Indonesia has not yet established an ADIZ under the new regime, however, at least a rudimentary legal framework was created.[106] Under the new rules, the Indonesian ADIZ would partly cover international airspace and partly national airspace.[107] This is also due to the fact that there are still disagreements on the borderline between Indonesia and Malaysia.

1.13 *Iran*

Iran established an ADIZ in 2018, and aligned its boundaries with the Tehran FIR.[108] Iran's AIP states under the section "Air Identification Zone (ADIZ) Procedure" that

> (a)ll aircraft entering Iran ADIZ (which coincides with Tehran FIR boundary) shall be at FL 150 or above, Aircraft not to do so shall obtain prior permission. (…) Aircraft not complying with these regulations are subject to interception. All flights before entering Iran ADIZ (Tehran FIR) are required to contact the appropriate air defense radar station on 127.800 MHZ or 135.100 MHZ, at least 10 minutes prior to entering Tehran FIR; if unable to contact, try again utmost 20NM before FIR boundary.[109]

The outer limits of Tehran FIR cover national as well as international airspace and stretch over the Caspian Sea and the Persian Gulf. Interestingly, the obligation to identify becomes not effective when entering the zone but 10 minutes prior to entering the Tehran FIR. Hence, aircraft also need to identify themselves when still traversing through the national airspace of neighbouring countries. Additionally, different radars have to be informed depending on the entry point in the Iran ADIZ.[110] Section 4 includes details on position

104 Harry Purwanto & Levina Yustitianingtyas, 'The Establishment of an Air Defence Identification Zone as an Opportunity in Enforcing the Sovereignty of the State and Law in Indonesia' (2019) 85 J L Pol & Globalization 76, 78.

105 Ibid.

106 Laksmana suspects the lack of available means of enforcement as the main reason for the declaration of an expanded ADIZ, 'Is an Indonesian Air Defence Identification Zone Forthcoming?' (10 April 2018) https://amti.csis.org/indonesian-adiz-forthcoming/ (accessed 20 May 2022).

107 Deni Marsono, 'Determination of Air Defense Identification Zone (ADIZ) in order to Support Sovereignty of National Air Region' (2018) 8 Journal of Defense & State Defense 12.

108 Iran AIP, ENR 1.1–1 WEF 16 (August 2018).

109 Iran AIP, ENR 1.1–1 WEF 16 (August 2018), 2.

110 Tabriz radar when entering from ALRAM, BONAM, DASIS, AGINA, DULAV, MAGRI, and PARSU. Babolsar radar when entering from LALDA, BATEV, ULDUS, PUTMA and SOMAD.

reporting, namely "the aircraft's identification, position, time, level, including passing actual level and cleared level if not maintaining the cleared level, next position and time over, and ensuing significant point."[111]

1.14 *Japan*

The Japanese ADIZ was established in 1956 by the United States during the occupation of the Okinawa islands and Japan has continued this practice from 1969 onwards.[112] Japan regulates its ADIZ under the Defense Agency Directive No. 36, 1969, and concretizes the content in the Japanese AIP.[113] The Japanese AIP defines an ADIZ as "airspace established by the Japan Ministry of Defense to facilitate taking measures against territorial airspace violation."[114] Japan justifies the establishment of the ADIZ and interceptions taking place within the zone with the "the right of policing intended to maintain public order."[115] Moreover, in line with the Japanese Self-Defense Forces Act, ADIZ assist in implementing effective measures against aerial intrusions of Japan's territory.[116] The Japanese ADIZ aligns with the Fukuoka FIR and stretches beyond national airspace up to the north of Japan's coastline. Before entering the Japanese ADIZ, aircraft are asked to submit a flight plan voluntarily. Strictly speaking, there is no obligation to submit a flight plan based on the rules regarding ADIZ.[117] The Japanese Air Self Defence Force (JASDF) receives information on civil aircraft entering the ADIZ from the FIR Fukuoka and compares the data with their own information.[118] JASDF, therefore, does not actively ask the civil aircraft to identify themselves and submit their flight plans before entering the ADIZ. Apart from the ADIZ's rules, Japan in general requests any aircraft planning to enter Japanese national airspace to submit an overflight permit 48 hours prior to departure.

Mashhad radar when entering from GIRUN, DEBER, RIKOP, ORPAB, NAZAR, OTRUZ, and PAMTU. Birjand radar when entering from SOKAM and KAMAR. Zabol radar when entering from PIRAN and DERBO.

111 Iran AIP, ENR 1.1–1 WEF 16 (August 2018), 4.

112 Yurika Ishii, *Japanese Maritime Security and Law of the Sea* (2022 Brill) 169.

113 Japan AIP, ENR 5.1. (1 March 2018).

114 Japan AIP, ENR 5.2.

115 Japanese Ministry of Defense, *Defense White Paper* (2022) 240.

116 Kentaro Serita, *The Territory of Japan* (Springer 2023) 175.

117 Toshimichi Nagaiwa, 'A Technical Aspect of ADIZ' (2014)109 The Japanese Institute of International Affairs, www.jiia.or.jp/en/ajiss_commentary/column-209.html); Kentaro Serita, *The Territory of Japan* (Springer 2023) 167.

118 Ibid.

Even though characterized as non-binding instructions, the JASDF intercept non-complying aircraft on the basis of Art. 84 Self-Defence Law.[119] Alone in 2021, 1004 interceptions, or in the official Japanese military language scrambles, occurred.[120] Scrambles included early warnings, the launch of fighters to approach the intruding aircraft, a warning to leave the territorial airspace, and eventually the forced landing of the aircraft.[121] Moreover, the Japanese government lodged protests through diplomatic channels, for example, regarding an intrusion by a Russian aircraft on 2 March 2022.[122] Considering national legislation as proof for customary international law, what matters more than the actual text is how it has been interpreted and applied.[123] One can hardly speak of a voluntary character if coercive measures are undertaken in case the aircraft does not identify according to the ADIZ's rules. Japan attempts to intercept only aircraft which are likely to invade the country's airspace. However, in practice, if it is uncertain whether the aircraft will enter Japanese territorial airspace, the JASDF will nevertheless intercept the aircraft.[124] Interception need not necessarily be the standard procedure. For example, Japan and South Korea came to agree on a bilateral solution on overlapping ADIZs and military encounters in their ADIZs. Since the Japanese ADIZ partly overlaps with the Korean ADIZ, a hotline has been established to voluntarily inform each other of military activities within the zone including also the voluntary submission of their flight plans.[125] Notification of military activities is made through the Aeronautical Fixed Telecommunication Network or via on-board.[126]

On 21 October 2022, the author visited with support from Professor Dai Tamada (Kyoto University) and Professor Akira Mayama (Osaka University) the National Institute of Defense Studies in Tokyo to conduct an interview with high-ranking air self-defence officials. Accordingly, the Japanese ADIZ is perceived to not violate the freedom of overflight due to the fact that they do not intercept aircraft which are not bound for national airspace and because

---

119 Japanese Ministry of Defense, *Defense White Paper* (2022) 242.

120 Ibid, 722 Chinese military aircraft were intercepted in the East China Sea region near the Senkaku/Diaoyu islands, and 256 Russian military aircraft were intercepted at the Northern boundary of the Japanese ADIZs.

121 Japanese Ministry of Defense, *Defense White Paper* (2022) 240, 241.

122 Ibid 241.

123 International Law Commission, 'Draft conclusions on identification of customary international law' (2018) Yearbook of the International Law Commission, vol II, Commentary

124 Yurika Ishii, *Japanese Maritime Security and Law of the Sea* (2022 Brill) 170.

125 Kentaro Serita, *The Territory of Japan* (Springer 2023) 177.

126 Ibid 250.

commercial aircraft, in general, submit their flight plans in advance to the aviation authority. On the question of whether the establishment of the Chinese ADIZ above the disputed Senkaku/Diaoyu islands had the intent to strengthen China's territorial claim, Japanese officials denied any dispute altogether. Instead, they regarded the Chinese ADIZ as a political symbol and part of China's foreign affairs strategy.[127] The Japanese ADIZ forms a unique example of a set of rules which are theoretically non-binding on foreign aircraft in international airspace but are in fact connected with enforcement measures in case of non-compliance.

1.15 *Myanmar*

Myanmar published details on its ADIZ in the AIP and explicitly states that these rules "conform to Annex 2 and 11" of the Chicago Convention.[128] To Myanmar's assessment, these rules are adopted in the interest of national security to enable identification as early as possible of air traffic entering the ADIZ.[129] Myanmar aligns the ADIZ with the Yangon FIR, and thus covers international airspace.[130]

Prior to entering the ADIZ, aircraft need to obtain an Air Defence Clearance. The procedure for obtaining this clearance is described in Section 3.1.3 AIP. The English text of the Myanmar AIP is to some extent ambiguous. Accordingly, no flight of any aircraft either originating in or penetrating into the ADIZ will be permitted without Air Defense Clearance.[131] In order to obtain an ADC, a flight plan has to be filed 30 minutes before take-off and has to include the route and altitude while within the ADIZ.[132] It is not completely clear if the "30 minutes before take-off" requirement means that the flight plan has only to be filed when departing from Myanmar or if it includes flights from any destination outside of Myanmar. As the purpose of the ADIZ is to identify aircraft entering the ADIZ, it can be interpreted as obliging any aircraft that intends to enter the ADIZ to already file the flight plan before take-off from a destination outside of Myanmar. This becomes more apparent when read with subparagraph (4) which states, that for flights originating within the ADIZ an ADC shall be obtained before departure (from Myanmar).[133] The competent authority

127 For security reasons, the names of the attendees cannot be disclosed.
128 Myanmar General Rules and Procedures https://www.ais.gov.mm/eAIP/2017-08-03-AIRAC/html/eAIP/ENR-1.1-en-GB.html (accessed 2 January 2023).
129 Myanmar AIP (3 August 2017) ENR 3.1.1.
130 Myanmar AIP ENR 3.1.2.
131 Myanmar AIP ENR 3.1.3.
132 Myanmar AIP ENR 3.1.3.
133 Myanmar AIP ENR 3.1.3.

for issuing an ADC is the Air Traffic Control Centre.[134] For flights entering the ADIZ from the west and east, an ADC has to be requested at first contact at the FIR boundary.[135] However, the AIP additionally states that "(i)n respect of all flights conducted of airways, aircraft shall contact ATCC at least 10 minutes before entering the ADIZ giving the ETA over the ADIZ boundary and requesting ATC."[136] Any aircraft penetrating into or flying within the ADIZ without an ADC, or failing to comply with any instructions or deviating from the flight plan or approved airways, will be "liable to interception for identification according to the interception procedures outlined in section ENR 1.12."[137] According to ENR 1.12, the intercepted aircraft has to respond to the visual signals, notify the Air Traffic Service unit and establish radio communication.[138]

1.16 *Pakistan*[139]

Details on the four Pakistan ADIZ, North, East, South, and West, can be found in the Air Navigation Order of 4 December 2009.[140] The term ADIZ is defined as "[s]pecial designated airspace of defined dimensions within which aircraft are required to comply with special identification and/or reporting procedures additional to those related to the provision of air traffic services (ATS)."[141] All aircraft, civil and military, foreign and national, penetrating the ADIZ have to obtain an Air Defence Clearance (ADC).[142] An ADC has to be obtained before take-off, when the departure point is within Pakistani territory.[143] For flights entering the ADIZ, the ADC has to be obtained at "least 15 minutes prior to entering Pakistan airspace/ADIZ."[144] Even though national in nature, the Pakistani ADIZ nevertheless has an extraterritorial effect due to the 15-minute timeframe. Additionally, arriving aircraft must report the estimated entry point.[145] Unclear remains the exact procedure on how to obtain such ADC. Aircraft operating without ADC or failing to comply or deviating from the flight plan will be liable to identification and interception procedures set forth

134 Myanmar AIP ENR 3.1.3.
135 Myanmar AIP ENR 3.1.3.
136 ATC means Air Traffic Control.
137 Myanmar AIP ENR 3.2.1. 'Identification and Interception'.
138 AIP Myanmar ENR 1.12, Section 2.1. (10 November 2016).
139 Pakistan AIP (20 April 2020) https://caapakistan.com.pk/eAIP/01-22/eAIP/index.html.
140 Air Navigation Order (4 December 2009) D5.3.1.1–5.3.1.4.
141 Air Navigation Order (4 December 2009) D1.1.1.
142 Air Navigation Order (4 December 2009) D5.3.2.
143 Air Navigation Order (4 December 2009) D5.3.3.1.
144 Air Navigation Order (4 December 2009) D5.3.3.3.
145 Air Navigation Order (4 December 2009) D5.3.3.6.

in part 2, ENR 1.12 of AIP Pakistan.[146] Pakistan only intercepts aircraft over the territory and the territorial waters, whereby the interception procedure is in line with Annex 2 Chicago Convention.[147]

1.17 *Panama*[148]

The Panama Canal Zone Domestic ADIZ was part of the sovereign airspace of the United State and covered only national airspace per definition.[149] It required position reports and flight plans of civil aircraft operating within or into the ADIZ and in general applied the same rules as of the other US ADIZ. The Panama Canal Zone ceased to exist on 1 October 1979 when the Panama Canal Treaty between Panama and the United States became effective and the territory was returned to Panama.[150] With amendment 99–10 (11 September 1981) of the Federal Aviation Regulation was the Panama Canal Zone Domestic ADIZ revocated.[151] Accordingly, the US federal regulations on the ADIZ were removed and the Panama Canal Zone Domestic ADIZ ceased to exist. Even though Panama included in Art. 2 of the Junta Directiva de la Autoridad Aeronautica Civil of 2017 a definition for an ADIZ, no further details were available on the current scope of a Panama ADIZ.[152]

1.18 *Peru*

Peru established an ADIZ by decree covering only national airspace as part of its sovereignty.[153] Art. 3 of Law No. 27261, Law of Civil Aviation, specified by Law No. 29941, establishes that Peru exercises sovereignty and jurisdiction over the airspace that covers its territory and the adjacent sea. The ADIZ was first established in 1991 by the then General Directorate of Air Transport through Directorial Resolution No. 0090–91-TC/15.12 of 9 October 1991, modified with

146 Ibid.

147 Pakistan AIP (20 April 2020) ENR 1.12.

148 Panama AIP https://www.aeronautica.gob.pa/PAGINA%20NUEVA3/aac/racp/zip/RACP_LIB_XXXI.pdf.

149 US Code of Federal Regulations, Title 14, §99.43 (1 January 1966).

150 US Federal Aviation Regulation, Part 99 (September 1993), P-10.

151 Ibid.

152 La Junta Directiva de la Autoridad Aeronautica Civil, Articulo 2 (16 August 2017), "Zona de identificación de defensa aérea: Espacio aéreo designado especial de dimensiones definidas, dentro del cual las aeronaves deben satisfacer procedimientos especiales de identificación y notificación, además de aquellos que se relacionan con el suministro de servicios de tránsito aéreo (ATS)."

153 Article 2, Decreto Supremo que regula la Zona de Identificación de Defensa Aérea (ADIZ PERÚ), N° 005–2016-DE (3 April 2016).

Directorial Resolution No. 0041–94-MTC /15.12 of 4 August 1994.[154] Given the elapsed time since the establishment of the ADIZ, Peru found it necessary to amend the existing rules. Art. 1 defines the term as "a portion of the national airspace of defined dimensions within which the prompt identification, location, and control of aircraft are required."[155] Within the Peru ADIZ, aircraft have to comply with special identification and notification procedures, in addition to those related to the provision of Air Traffic Services (ATS). Pursuant to Art. 3 (1), all aircraft have to carry activated transponder equipment, establish communication with the Peru ATS Unit, and have to submit a flight plan specifying in it all the planned landing points along its route.[156] The Controlling Authority is the Peruvian Air Force, which will intercept any aircraft not complying with these regulations.[157]

1.19 *Poland*

Poland bases the ADIZ claim on the flexible use of airspace (FUA). In its AIP of 24 February 2022, it is stated under Chapter 5.2. 'Military Exercise And Training Areas And Air Defence Identification Zone (ADIZ)' that "the FUA concept is based on the principle that airspace should no longer be designated as either military or civil airspace but should be considered as a continuum and used flexibly on a day-to-day basis. Consequently, any necessary airspace segregation should be only of a temporary nature." Poland has three ADIZs, namely ADIZ Rosja, ADIZ Bialorus, and ADIZ Ukraina, whereas all only cover national airspace up to 15 km deep into the territory of Poland.[158] ENR 5.2.3 specifies the rules on ADIZ namely that it "is obligatory to file a flight plan including information on the intention to perform an operation within the ADIZ and maintain a two-way radio contact with the territorially competent ATS unit." There is no specific interception procedure within the ADIZ as it aligns with national airspace.

154 https://busquedas.elperuano.pe/normaslegales/decreto-supremo-que-regula-la-zona-de-identificacion-de-defe-decreto-supremo-n-005-2016-de-1363240-2/#:~:text=La%20Zona%20de%20Identificaci%C3%B3n%20de%20Defensa%20A%C3%A9rea%20(ADIZ%20PER%C3%9A)%20es,ubicaci%C3%B3n%20y%20control%20de%20aeronaves.

155 Decreto Supremo que regula la Zona de Identificación de Defensa Aérea (ADIZ PERÚ), N° 005–2016-DE.

156 Ibid.

157 Art. 3.5 & 3.6 Decreto Supremo que regula la Zona de Identificación de Defensa Aérea (ADIZ PERÚ), N° 005–2016-DE.

158 Poland AIP (24 February 2022), ENR 5.2.3.

1.20 *South Korea*

South Korea's ADIZ was unilaterally established by the US Air Force in 1951 in order to halt Chinese attacks through the West Sea (Yellow Sea) and the South Sea (East China Sea) during the Korean War.[159] The zone was established against Soviet-made MIG-15s and Chinese aircraft after the country launched into full-scale combat at the height of the Korean War.[160] In 2013, South Korea extended the limits to cover a submerged rock beyond its territorial sea, the Ieodo rock and published the coordinates of the extended ADIZ in the South Korean AIP from 2015.[161] South Korea claims jurisdiction over the waters surrounding Ieodo as part of its Exclusive Economic Zone.[162] The AIP of South Korea note in ENR 5.2, 2.1.1, that "pilots who want to fly within the KADIZ shall submit a flight plan to the Minister of Defense prior to conducting the flight."[163] Additionally, radio communications, Secondary Surveillance Radar, and position report requirements all apply to aircraft "while operating within the KADIZ."[164] The KADIZ overlaps with the Japanese ADIZ, as well as with the Chinese ECS ADIZ.[165] South Korea intends to solve the conflict of overlapping zones covering disputed islands through diplomatic channels.[166] For this reason, South Korea initiated consultations with neighbouring States in advance and fixed the ADIZs boundaries with its FIR.[167] Interception of foreign military aircraft occur frequently within South Korea ADIZ.[168]

---

159 Min Gyo K, 'China's Proclamation of its Air Defense Identification Zone and South Korea: The International Legal Perspective' (17 December 2013) http://www.eai.or.kr/main/english/search_view.asp?intSeq=8929&board=eng_multimedia.

160 Gil Yun-hyung, The History of Air Defense Identification Zones in Northeast Asia' (27 November 2013), https://english.hani.co.kr/arti/english_edition/e_international/612953.html (accessed 20 October 2022).

161 BMS KTO AIP (2015).

162 Woon J Lee, 'Tension in the Air: The Air Defense Identification Zones on the East China Sea' (2014) 7 J E Asia & Int'l L 276.

163 South Korea AIP (27 September 2018) ENR 5.2, 2.1.1.

164 South Korea AIP (27 September 2018) ENR 5.2, 2.1.3 & 2.2.1.

165 Mercedes Trent, 'Overview of ADIZ in East Asia' in Federation of American Scientists (eds) *Over the Line – The Implications of China's ADIZ Intrusions in North East* (2020) 11, 12.

166 Min Gyo Koo, 'China's Proclamation of its Air Defense Identification Zone and South Korea: The International Legal Perspective' (17 December 2013) available at, http://www.eai.or.kr/main/english/search_view.asp?intSeq=8929&board=eng_multimedia.

167 Woon J Lee, 'Tension in the Air: The Air Defense Identification Zones on the East China Sea' (2014) 7 J E Asia & Int'l L 276.

168 Japantimes, 'South Korea scrambles Jets as Chinese and Russian Warplanes enter Air Defense Zone' (19 November 2021) https://www.japantimes.co.jp/news/2021/11/19/asia-pacific/south-korea-china-russia-aircraft-air-defense-zone/ (accessed 2 January 2023).

1.21 *Sri Lanka*

Sri Lanka established an ADIZ in its national airspace.[169] However, the rules of the Colombo ADIZ require approaching aircraft to comply with the identification requirements before entering the zone. ENR 2.3.1 (a) states that no flight or aircraft shall operate within, *into* or out of ADIZ without valid Air Defence Clearance (ADC). The procedure for obtaining an ADC when entering the Colombo ADIZ requires obtain an ADC number from the Area Control Centre 15 minutes before entering the ADIZ.[170] Interestingly, the Area Controller shall coordinate with the Air Defence Command to obtain an ADC number and pass the ADC number to the pilot before entering the ADIZ.[171] Additionally, the Tower Controller fulfils the same function for departing aircraft and passes the ADC number to the pilot with start-up clearance.[172] Additionally, all aircraft with a departure point within the ADIZ have to submit a flight plan at least one hour before the intended departure time[173] and have to report their position.[174] Contrary, aircraft entering the Colombo ADIZ do not need to submit a flight plan. Instead, the pilot only has to report to the appropriate ATS Unit before penetration "the time, position and altitude at which the aircraft passed the last reporting point before penetration and the estimated time of arrival over the next appropriate reporting point along the flight route."[175] Any aircraft flying without a valid ADC Number is liable for interception by the Sri Lanka Air Force under the interception procedure.[176] However, the method of contacting the Area Controller and Tower Controller is not described. It therefore depends on the Area Controller and Tower Controller whether they pass the ADC number to the Air Force. This bears the inherent risk being intercepted if the ADC number was not properly passed on.

1.22 *Taiwan*

Taiwan issued *Rules of the Air* on its ADIZ in accordance with the provisions of Art. 41 (2) of the Civil Aviation Act.[177] The Taiwan ADIZ covers the whole Taiwan island and adjacent waters, as well as part of Mainland China.[178] Pursuant to

---

169 Sri Lanka AIP (30 January 2015), ENR 2.1.
170 Sri Lanka AIP 2.3.2. (e).
171 Sri Lanka AIP 2.3.1 (c).
172 Sri Lanka AIP 2.3.1 (b).
173 Sri Lanka AIP 2.4.
174 Sri Lanka AIP 2.6 (c).
175 Sri Lanka AIP 2.6. (a).
176 Sri Lanka AIP ENR 2.3.1. & 2.3.2 (c).
177 Rules of the Air //law.moj.gov.tw/ENG/LawClass/LawAll.aspx?pcode=K0090014.
178 AIP Taipei FIR (14 May 2015) ENR 5.2, 5.2.3.

Art. 2 (79) Rules of the Air the term "Air Defence Identification Zone" is defined as "(a)n airspace specified for the purpose of national defence within which the control and swift identification and location of an aircraft is required."

Art. 19 provides the details of an ADIZ, namely that an aircraft entering or within controlled airspace shall be equipped with a two-way radio and an ATC transponder except under conditions prescribed by the appropriate authority.[179] The obligation to identify can be found in Art. 30 Rule of the Air which prescribes the submission of a flight plan for *inter alia*, "any flight within or into designated areas, or along designated routes when so required by the appropriate ATS authority to facilitate coordination with appropriate military units or with air traffic services units in adjacent States in order to avoid the possible need for interception for the purpose of identification."[180] According to Art. 31, the flight plan needs to be submitted at least sixty minutes before departure, or, if submitted during flight, at a time which will ensure its receipt by the appropriate air traffic services unit at least ten minutes before the aircraft is estimated to reach the intended point of entry into a control area or advisory area. Even though Art. 30 does not mention "control areas" as an area, which requires a flight plan, Art. 31 would become a meaningless provision if providing detail for flight plans applicable to areas not requiring a flight plan. Moreover, Art. 19 describes ADIZ as "controlled airspace,"[181] which can be understood as a "control area" in the sense of Art. 31.[182] The exact information to be included in the flight plan is listed in Art. 32 Rules of the Air.[183] As prescribed in Art. 30 (3) an aircraft can be subject to interception for the purpose of identification. The Taiwan Air Force is in charge of any interception within the ADIZ to protect Taiwanese airspace.[184] Appendix 3 to the Rule of the Air regulates the procedure of interception in more detail. Interception

179 Art. 19 Rules of the Air (amended 25 March 2021).

180 Art. 30 lit c Rule of the Air (amended 25 March 2021).

181 Art 2 (32) defines "controlled airspace" as: "An airspace of defined dimensions within which air traffic control service is provided in accordance with the airspace classification, including of Classes A, B, C, D, E and class E surface airspace."

182 Art. 2 (30) defines "control area" as: "A controlled airspace extending upwards from a specified limit above the earth."

183 1. Aircraft identification. 2. Flight rules and type of flight. 3. Number and type(s) of aircraft and wake turbulence category. 4. Equipment. 5. Departure aerodrome. 6. Estimated off-block time. 7. Cruising speed. 8. Cruising level. 9. Route to be followed. 10. Destination aerodrome and total estimated elapsed time. 11. Alternate aerodrome(s). 12. Fuel endurance. 13. Total number of persons on board. 14. Emergency and survival equipment. 15. Other relevant information.

184 Chien Chung, 'Military Culture and Air Force Restructuring' in Martin Edmonds & Michael Tsai (eds) *Taiwan's Security and Air Power* (Routledge 2003) 155.

includes visual signs to which the aircraft has to respond by establishing radio communication. The interception procedure can also be witnessed on multiple occasions when Chinese military aircraft entered the Taiwanese ADIZ. For example on 10. April 2024, six Chinese military aircraft entered Taiwan's southwestern ADIZ and as a response Taiwan employed CAP aircraft, Navy vessels and coastal missile system.[185]

1.23 *Thailand*

Thailand sets forth rules on its ADIZ in the Act on Conduct of Violating Aircraft, B.E.2553 (2010), and concretized the details in the AIP as part of Air Traffic Services.[186] To Thailand's perception, these services are provided in accordance with the provisions contained in several ICAO documents, *inter alia* Annex 2 and Annex 11 Chicago Convention.[187]

The Thailand Air Defense Identification Zone (TADIZ) covers the airspace over the land and partly beyond the territorial sea. Pursuant to Art. 8 (2) AIP, all aircraft destined for an aerodrome within the TADIZ or overflying the TADIZ have to "submit flight plans at the point of departure for relaying to Bangkok Area Control Centre." Additionally, aircraft approaching the TADIZ shall "report the estimated time over TADIZ boundary at least 10 minutes in advance."[188] For that reason, the aircraft has to establish and maintain radio communication. If unable to establish and maintain radio communication with the appropriate ATC agency, the pilot may contact the nearest Ground Control Intercept (GCI) site for positive identification prior to entering the TADIZ.[189]

The inspection and identification system follows an Air Defence Plan stipulated by the Royal Thai Armed Forces.[190] The aircraft will be intercepted by Royal Thai Air Force (RTAF) interceptors if it does not adhere to the *Air Defense Identification Procedures* or the *Air Traffic Control Regulations and Procedures*.[191] Aircraft under interception will be attacked if they fail to obey

185 R.O.C. Air Force, 'PLA activities in the waters and airspace around Taiwan Apr. 10, 2024' (10.04,2024) https://air.mnd.gov.tw/EN/News/News_Detail.aspx?CID=214&ID=56950.

186 Act on Conduct of Violating Aircraft, B.E.2553 (2010); https://aip.caat.or.th/2020-02-27-AIRAC/html/eAIP/VT-GEN-3.3-en-GB.html.

187 Thailand AIP, GEN 3, Air Traffic Services, 1.2. Annex 2 – Rules of the Air, Annex 11 – Air Traffic Services, Doc 4444 – Procedures for Air Navigation Services – Air Traffic Management (PANS – ATM), Doc 8168 – Procedures for Air Navigation Services – Aircraft Operations (PANS-OPS), and Doc 7030 – Regional Supplementary Procedures.

188 Thailand AIP, GEN 3, Air Traffic Services, 8.3.

189 Thailand AIP, GEN 3, Air Traffic Services, 8.4.

190 Act on Conduct of Violating Aircraft, B.E.2553 (2010), Section 7.

191 Thailand AIP, GEN 3, Air Traffic Services, 8.5.

any instructions given by RTAF interceptors.[192] Interception means "operation to identify and control the aircraft to operate under the military official command and shall mean to include the destruction of aircraft in case of necessity in order to maintain internal security and disaster prevention to the public."[193] The rules on interception further state that the authority of the RTAF will not be responsible for any damage caused to aircraft by the interceptors of other devices.[194] Moreover, the owner of the aircraft will be charged for expenditures used by the interceptors sent up to investigate and identify.[195] Thailand, therefore is so far the only country with specific rules on damages and compensation applicable specifically in the ADIZ.

1.24 *The United States of America*

National security is the most fundamental objective of the US ADIZ consistent with the right to self-defence.[196] The United States argues the legitimacy of ADIZ in international airspace with the right to establish reasonable conditions of entry into its national airspace.[197] The purpose of the US ADIZs is to assist in the early identification of aircraft intending to enter US domestic airspace.[198] The Federal Aviation Act of 1958 is the statutory basis for the US ADIZ and the Federal Aviation Administration (FAA) is the responsible agency.[199] In the FAA's opinion the ADIZ's rules "comply with International Civil Aviation Organization (ICAO) Standards and Recommended Practices to the maximum extent practicable."[200] The Federal Aviation Act 14 CFR Part 99 prescribes the rule for security control of air traffic and includes details on ADIZs.[201] Accordingly, an ADIZ is defined as "an area of airspace over land or water, in which the ready identification, location, and control of all aircraft is required in the interest of national security."[202] Four ADIZ have been established during the 1950s,

192 Thailand AIP, GEN 3, Air Traffic Services, 8.7.
193 Act on Conduct of Violating Aircraft, B.E.2553 (2010).
194 GEN 3, Air Traffic Services, 8.8.
195 GEN 3, Air Traffic Services, 8.9.
196 Roncevert Almond, 'Clearing the Air above the East China Sea: The Primary Elements of Aircraft Defense Identification Zones' (2017) 7 Harvard Nat Sec J 138, 141–143.
197 Kirk Davies, Eric Johnson, Laura Desio, Sam Kidd, & Paul Thomasa, *Air Force Operations and the Law* (3rd edn 2014, Maxwell Air Force Base: Judge Advocate General's School) 78.
198 US AIM Section 6, 5-6-1.
199 Roncevert Almond, 'Clearing the Air above the East China Sea: The Primary Elements of Aircraft Defense Identification Zones' (2017) 7 Harvard Nat Sec J 139.
200 69 Federal Register No. 40 (2004) 16754 on the amendment of Civil Aviation Act.
201 Doc. No. FAA-2001-10693, 66 FR 49822 (28 Sept. 2001).
202 Federal Aviation Act 14 CFR §99.3.

namely Alaska ADIZ,[203] Guam ADIZ,[204] Hawaii ADIZ[205] and the Contiguous ADIZ.[206] The Contiguous US ADIZ extends more than 300 nautical miles into the Atlantic Ocean and more than 400 miles into the Pacific Ocean.[207]

The rules target civil as well as military aircraft, national as well as foreign, except for some types of US public aircraft and foreign State aircraft explicitly excluded.[208] According to §99.7 'special security instructions', each person operating an aircraft in an ADIZ must comply with special security instructions issued by the Administrator in the interest of national security.[209] Pursuant to § 99.9 (a) a person who operates a civil aircraft into an ADIZ must have a functioning two-way radio, and the pilot must maintain a continuous listening watch on the appropriate aeronautical facility's frequency. Additionally, lit (b) stipulates that no person may operate an aircraft into, within, or whose departure point is within an ADIZ unless the person files a DVFR flight plan containing the time and point of ADIZ penetration, and the aircraft departs within five minutes of the estimated departure time contained in the flight plan.

Moreover, pursuant to §99.11 no person may operate an aircraft into, within, or from a departure point within an ADIZ, unless the person files, activates, and closes a flight plan with the appropriate aeronautical facility, or is otherwise authorized by air traffic control.[210] The flight plan has to contain the information listed in §91.169 and §91.153(a).[211] Additionally, a foreign civil aircraft has to give a position report at least one hour before entering the ADIZ, if it is not more than two hour average cruising speed from the US.[212] Some exceptions to the general ADIZ identification requirements exist, such as for aircraft operating less than 180 knots in the Hawaii ADIZ.

203 §99.45.

204 §99.47.

205 §99.49.

206 14 CFR §49.43.

207 14 CFR §49.43.

208 Peter Dutton, 'Caelum Liberam: Air Defense Identification Zones Outside Sovereign Airspace' (2009) 103 AJIL 699.

209 Two additional public purposes for ADIZs were suggested by the Federal Aviation Administration namely the benefit for search and rescue services for an overdue aircraft and the curtailing of dangerous flight methods used by drug smugglers, see Roncevert Almond, 'Clearing the Air above the East China Sea: The Primary Elements of Aircraft Defense Identification Zones' (2017) 7 Harvard Nat Sec J 153.

210 § 99.11 'ADIZ flight plan requirements'.

211 ENR 1.4.5. https://www.faa.gov/air_traffic/publications/atpubs/aip_html/part2_enr_section_1.12.html

212 https://www.faa.gov/air_traffic/publications/us_restrictions/airspace/#adiz.

It has to be mentioned that foreign military aircraft can operate freely and without adhering to the ADIZ rules as long as they do not intend to enter US national airspace.[213] This interpretation is also in line with §99.9. b) which connects the requirement of filing a flight plan with the penetration of the ADIZ. A person may "operate an aircraft into, within, or whose departure point is within the ADIZ" without having to comply with the identification requirements as long as they do not enter US national airspace.[214] Thus, the US policy applies the ADIZ conditions only to aircraft entering national airspace.[215] As a result, the United States instructs its military aircraft not to comply with the identification requirements of other States' ADIZ if they do not intend to enter the national airspace of that State.[216]

The interception procedure is detailed in chapter 5 of the US Aeronautical Information Manual. Interception is jointly administered by the FAA and NORAD.[217] If subjected to a military intercept, aircraft have to comply with ICAO standard signals relayed from the intercepting aircraft. Typically, interception has three stages: (1) approach phase whereby two fighter jets approach from the rear, (2) identification phase, (3) post-intercept phase.[218] One fighter flies around to make visual contact with the pilot and initiates a slow, level turn, which the intercepted aircraft has to follow.[219] The use of force against unauthorized aircraft depends on its status as either civil or military aircraft.[220] The US interception procedures for civil aircraft in general follow the rules of the Chicago Convention.[221] Non-compliance may result in the use of force by the interceptor even against a civil aircraft as part of the right to self-defence.[222]

---

213 Edmund J Burke & Astrid Stuth Cevallos, *In Line or out of Order? – Chinas Approach to ADIZ in Theory and Practice* (Rand 2017) 5; Ian Rinehart & Elias Bart 'China's Air Defence Identification Zone' (2015) Congressional Research Service.

214 Differently interpreted by Su, Jinyuan, 'The Practice of States on Air Defence Identification Zones: Geographical Scope, Object of Identification, and Identification Measures' (2019) 18 Chinese Journal International Law 822.

215 US Department of the Navy, *The Commander's Handbook on the Law of Naval Operations* (2008) 2.7.2.3.

216 US Department of the Navy, *The Commander's Handbook on the Law of Naval Operations* (2008) 2.7.2.3.

217 Ian Rinehart & Elias Bart, 'China's Air Defense Identification Zone' (2015) Congressional Research Service 3.

218 US Navy Commander Handbook 5-6-2.

219 Aeronautical Information Manual 5-6-2, https://www.faa.gov/air_traffic/publications/atpubs/aim_html/chap5_section_6.html.

220 US Navy Commander Handbook 4.4.2

221 Roncevert Almond, 'Clearing the Air above the East China Sea: The Primary Elements of Aircraft Defense Identification Zones' (2017) 7 Harvard Nat Sec J 165.

222 US Navy Commander Handbook 4.4.2: „in contrast to its stance on intercepting military aircraft, the United States recognizes that a state may not use weapons against an aircraft with civil markings expect in the exercise of self-defence."

1.25 *Uruguay*

The legal foundation of the Uruguay ADIZ can be found in Regulation Aeronáutico Latinoamericano, LAR 211.[223] The *Advisory Circular on Acceptable Methods of Compliance* (MACs) offers an interpretation of the ADIZ rules to guide all aircraft conducting air operations within ADIZ Uruguay. Accordingly, aircraft have to comply with the provisions of LAR 211 Chapter 211.075 and the rules on the protection of the sovereignty of the Uruguayan airspace.[224] The rules of the ADIZ are seen as part of the flexible use of airspace aligning military and civil air traffic. The outer limits of the Uruguay ADIZ are identified in the respective Aeronautical Charts in line with Doc. PANS/ATM (Doc. 4444). The term ADIZ is defined as "[e]spacio aéreo de dimensiones definidas sobre el territorio y/o las aguas jurisdiccionales del Estado, dentro del cual las aeronaves deben cumplir procedimientos especiales de identificación y notificación con los Servicios de Tránsito Aéreo (ATS)."[225] Uruguay therefore claims an ADIZ over its territory as well as "jurisdictional waters". Even though the term "jurisdictional waters" is not concretized, it can be interpreted as meaning territorial waters since the coordinates of the zone align with Uruguay national territory.[226]

Further information on the ADIZ can be found in the AIP Uruguay ENR 5.2. Accordingly, all aircraft conducting air operations within the ADIZ Uruguay shall submit a flight plan to the ATS unit, specifying the planned landing points along their route by using a flight plan form.[227] Aircraft can either submit the flight plan before the flight or during the flight.[228] The Uruguayan Air Force is in charge of defending and safeguarding the territorial integrity and exercises the function of an Air Police.[229] Any aircraft not complying with the rules will be declared Irregular Air Traffic (Tránsito Aéreo Irregular-TAI) and will be subject to the progressive use of force, through interception, identification, and diversion.[230] An aircraft that incurs in one or more circumstances

223 Reglamento Aeronáutico Latinoamericano, LAR 211 (01 August 2020) Gestión Del Tránsito Aéreo.

224 Circular de Asesoramiento, CA.UY.ANS/ATM/011 (7.5.2021); Reglamento Aeronáutico Latinoamericano, LAR 211 (01.08.2020); Article 112 to 117, Espacio Aéreo Nacional, Law No. 19.889 (9 July 2020).

225 LAR 211, Capitulo A-11, 211–075; Circular de Asesoramiento, CA.UY.ANS/ATM/011 (7.5.2021).

226 Circular de Asesoramiento, CA.UY.ANS/ATM/011 (7.5.2021), MAC (1) 211.075 Reglas Aplicables En La Adiz Uruguay, 1 stating the exterior limits as "línea de costa sobre el Río Uruguay hasta línea de costa sobre Laguna Merín, límite terrestre con Brasil."

227 Circular de Asesoramiento, CA.UY.ANS/ATM/011 (7.5.2021) 4 (a)&(b).

228 Circular de Asesoramiento, CA.UY.ANS/ATM/011 (7.5.2021) 4(b) i, II.

229 Circular de Asesoramiento, CA.UY.ANS/ATM/011 (7.5.2021) 5.

230 Circular de Asesoramiento, CA.UY.ANS/ATM/011 (7.5.2021) 6, in conjunction with ICAO Doc. 9433-AN/926 (Manual on Air Traffic Control) and other applicable standards (Art. 3° Protocol Actuation No. 4-Decree N° 327/2020).

of “Hostile Acts” shall be declared a “Hostile Aircraft” by the Commander-in-Chief of the Air Force and may be subject to the use of force by persuasion or neutralisation.[231]

2 Summary of the State Practice

The analysis of the 25 States’ practices portrays a rather diverse picture. Common characteristics are the purpose of national security, the non-discriminatory application on national as well as foreign aircraft, the identification requirements, and the consequence of non-compliance, namely interception. Divergent State practice exists on the legal basis in international law, the geographic extension, the application on aircraft traversing through the zone without intending to enter national airspace, and the requirement of an Air Defence Clearance number. The application to both civil and military aircraft remains unclear, unless explicitly provided for in the ADIZ’s rules.

2.1 *The Purpose of ADIZs*

In all cases, the main purpose of an ADIZ is the protection of national security. More specifically, national ADIZs above the national territory aim to protect the sovereign airspace and territory from all aerial threats. Similarly, States with an ADIZ beyond the national territory argue that only the international character of the zone can sufficiently protect national security from any approaching threats. In some cases, the secondary objective is to administer and regulate access to national airspace through identification. The safe use of airspace and the regulation of air traffic shall be safeguarded through procedures designed to locate, identify and control aircraft within the zone. Another purpose of ADIZs is to foster the flexible use of airspace (FUA) and to align the use of airspace by civil as well as military aircraft in a safe and efficient manner. There are thus two main purposes: to provide security from air threats and to ensure the safety of air traffic. The US and Canada, for example, combine both approaches to regulate the entrance into national airspace.[232]

2.2 *The Geographic and Temporal Scope of Application*

The analysis of all ADIZs shows that eleven zones are permanently established along the lines of national airspace, while twelve zones are permanently

231 Circular de Asesoramiento, CA.UY.ANS/ATM/011 (7.5.2021) 7.

232 Canadian Designated Airspace Handbook, Issue No 289 (12 June 2021) 195; US AIM Section 6, 5-6-1.

claimed in international airspace. The geographic scope of international ADIZS, i.e. the coordinates, are in most cases published in Aeronautical Charts[233] and vary considerably. Some States with national ADIZS explicitly align their zone with the boundaries of their FIR, which facilitates the identification procedure for civil aircraft. Iran, Japan, and Myanmar align their ADIZS with their FIR also in international airspace. In one case, South Korea, the boundaries of its EEZ determine the boundaries of its ADIZ. Indonesia has announced plans to extend its ADIZ's boundaries to coincide with the outer limits of its EEZ's but has not yet done so. In the case of the US, the aerial boundaries of its ADIZ are drawn without any reference to the FIR or EEZ. This approach can be seen in the majority of ADIZS in international airspace. On some occasions in the past, States have created a temporary ADIZ in the past, namely the Argentinian ADIZ in 2018 for the purpose of the G-20 summit,[234] and the South African ADIZ which was established for the period of 26 July 2012 to 4 August 2012.[235] In all other cases, no end date of the temporal scope of application is indicated.

2.3 *The Personal Scope of Application – "All" Aircraft*

All ADIZS apply indistinctively in a non-discriminatory manner to both national and foreign civil aircraft. However, it is ambiguous if "all aircraft" can be understood to include civil as well as military aircraft. There is no generally accepted international rule defining the term "state aircraft". State practice shows that state aircraft, including military aircraft, are more susceptible to interception.[236] One conclusion drawn from State practice is that ADIZS published in the AIP in line with Annex 2 and Annex 15 Chicago Convention cannot be understood as covering military aircraft *strictu sensu*, since the Annexes to the Chicago Convention apply only to civil aircraft and not to state aircraft.[237] Annex 15 is the method of publishing the information required for civil aviation, and Annex 2 concretized the identification requirements. Annex 15 of the Chicago Convention describes the information required for the safe conduct of flights and related aeronautical information provided by the ICAO

233 Which is also the proposed procedure according to Annex 15 Chicago Convention.

234 Jinyuan Su, 'The Practice of States on Air Defence Identification Zones: Geographical Scope, Object of Identification, and Identification Measures' (2019) 18 Chinese Journal International LawLaw 817, 818.

235 South African Civil Aviation Authority, AIRAC AIP Sup S060/12.

236 Mercedes Trent, 'Appendix A: List of Publicized PLA ADIZ Intrusions from 2016–2020' in Federation of American Scientists (eds), *Over the Line: Implications of China's ADIZ Intrusions in Northeast Asia* (2020) 43–54.

237 Art. 3(a) Chicago Convention.

Members.[238] ADIZs claimed to be in line with the Annexes of the Chicago Convention would only apply to national as well as foreign civil aircraft, but not to military aircraft, unless another source for the ADIZ rules is provided. The Annexes to the Chicago Convention alone do not provide for a sufficient legal basis for the application of the rules to state aircraft. Nevertheless, it can be assumed that if a State applies its ADIZ's rules to civil aircraft, it likely applies them to military aircraft, which generally pose a more serious threat. In general, it is desirable that States consider Annex 15 Chicago Convention for the publication of all the necessary information on their ADIZs,[239] in order to achieve transparency and legal clarity.

The divergent application to aircraft entering national airspace and aircraft only traversing through the ADIZ is particularly relevant for zones established in international airspace.[240] The Australian ADIZ, for example, requires all aircraft to lodge a flight notification and report position while traversing through the ADIZ.[241] The identification requirement is not explicitly dependent on the entry into national airspace. Similar provisions can be found in the ADIZs of China, Iran, Myanmar, and Thailand. In contrast, the ADIZs of Bangladesh, Canada, India, Japan, South Korea, Taiwan, and the United States only apply the obligation to identify aircraft intending to enter national airspace. It is worth noting that the ADIZs of Japan, South Korea, and Taiwan were all first established by the United States in the 1950s, to provide each of the three countries with a role in monitoring the Soviet east coast and mainland China.[242] All three zones were created according to the US concept of a legitimate ADIZ.[243] Therefore, the assertion that the Chinese State practice of applying ADIZ rules to aircraft not intending to enter national airspace is inconsistent

238 The object of the aeronautical information service (AIS) is to ensure the flow of aeronautical data and aeronautical information necessary for the global air traffic management system, see Annex 15 Chicago Convention (2018).

239 Roncevert Almond, 'Clearing the Air above the East China Sea: The Primary Elements of Aircraft Defense Identification Zones' (2017) 7 Harvard Nat Sec J 157.

240 Edmund J Burke & Astrid Stuth Cevallos, *In Line or out of Order? – Chinas Approach to ADIZ in Theory and Practice* (Rand 2017) 8.

241 Australia AIP ENR 2.1.3

242 Gil Yun-hyung, The History of Air Defense Identification Zones in Northeast Asia' (27 November 2013), https://english.hani.co.kr/arti/english_edition/e_international/612953.html (accessed 20 October 2022).

243 Mercedes Trent, *Over the Line: The Implications of China's ADIZ Intrusions in Northeast Asia* in Federation of American Scientists (eds), Over the Line: Implications of China's ADIZ Intrusions in Northeast Asia (2020) 9.

with general State practice cannot be sustained, as there is simply no consistent State practice to support this assertion.[244]

2.4 *Substantive Scope: Identification Requirements*

Of the analysed framework, twenty-one States require to file a flight plan irrespective of the characterization as national or international ADIZ. The wording of the national legislation and AIPs uses terms such as "shall", "must", and "obliged" and can therefore be understood as prescribing an obligatory identification requirement.[245] Only in one case, namely Japan, are the identification rules phrased as voluntary. Yet, there are divergent approaches to the temporal requirements of filing the flight plan. Whereas some States require the flight plan to be filed 10 minutes[246] or 15 minutes prior to entering the zone,[247] others make the filing of the flight plan dependent on the temporal proximity to entering national airspace[248] or to entering their FIR,[249] or on the time of departure.[250] In this respect, they differ from the standards of Annex 2 on the timing of flight plan submission.[251] In addition, the methods of submitting the flight plan to the competent authority are not uniform. The content of the identification requirements varies. In some cases, aircraft additionally have to report their position, establish radio communication and have to be equipped with a transponder with automatic altitude reporting equipment. In other instances, it is not sufficient to file a flight plan but aircraft also have to submit further information such as logo identification and the number of passengers on board the aircraft.[252] Five States require the additional submission of an ADC number,[253] which appears to be problematic due to the non-transparent methods of obtaining an ADC number.

Overall, there is a common State practice on the requirement of a flight plan but not on the procedure for submitting the flight plan.[254] Similar identification

244 See for example Roncevert Almond, 'Clearing the Air above the East China Sea. The Primary Elements of Aircraft Defense Identification Zones' (2017) 7 Harvard Nat Sec J 184.

245 This finding therefore disagrees with Su (2020) who claimed that the identification rules are all voluntarily.

246 Bangladesh, Myanmar and Thailand.

247 Pakistan and Sri Lanka.

248 Australia, China, India, South Korea, USA, and Uruguay.

249 Iran.

250 Argentina, Canada, Taiwan and Pakistan.

251 See on this aspect chapter 5, 2.5.1 of this book.

252 For example, China.

253 Bangladesh, India, Myanmar, Pakistan, and Sri Lanka.

254 Edmund J Burke & Astrid Stuth Cevallos, *In Line or out of Order? – Chinas Approach to ADIZ in Theory and Practice* (Rand 2017) at 8 referring to PRC spokesman Geng.

requirements can be found in FIRs, where the responsible State may require civil aircraft to use identification procedures including flight plans, two-way communication by transponder and radio, and a timely position report.[255] The ICAO standards for flight plans, position reports, and radio communication provide for the basis for similar technical requirements, which are also applied in most ADIZs, and therefore do not impose more stringent conditions than the Chicago Convention.[256] As can be seen from the different national requirements, the procedure for submitting the flight plan is not the same.

2.5 *Enforcement*

In all cases, interception is the method of enforcing the ADIZs' identification requirements in case of non-compliance.[257] In general, interception procedures entail a series of actions and manoeuvres designed to track, identify and communicate with the intercepted aircraft, such as visual signs used by fighter jets. In certain instances, the rules prescribe that the aircraft may be escorted beyond the boundaries of the ADIZ or directed to land at a designated place.[258] In the case of Australia, an aircraft which has intruded national airspace and is identified as hostile might be destroyed. Thailand represents a distinctive case where an intercepted aircraft may be held financially liable for any costs incurred as a result of the interception. However, it is recommended that interception be employed as a last resort, particularly in instances where the use of force is explicitly threatened.[259]

The ADIZs' rules do not always explicitly concretise whether the interception will occur in international airspace or national airspace. Consequently, there is no definitive answer on the extraterritorial enforcement of compliance with the ADIZ's rules. Partly, States may be unable to effectively enforce the ADIZ's rules due to a lack of capabilities and, therefore, limit the interception to national airspace.[260]

---

255 Annex 2, 3.3.1.

256 An ICAO flight plan includes inter alia the flight time, originator, aircraft identification, type of aircraft, equipment, departure and destination aerodrome, time, cruising speed, level, route, number of passengers, aircraft colour and markings, and the pilot in command. See, ICAO Doc 4444, Procedure for Air Navigation Services – Air Traffic Management (15th edn, 2007).

257 For this discussion whether Chinese "defensive emergency measures" can be understood as including intercepting aircraft see above chapter 5, 1.6.

258 See for example Australia, Canada, Indonesia and USA.

259 On the general prohibition to use weapons against civil aircraft see Art. 3bis Chicago Convention.

260 On a very comprehensive list of aerial intrusions into national airspace by military aircraft and the followingly interception (including the reporting of 1,403 written State protests)

Should the suspicion of hostile intent prove to be unfounded and the interception be deemed unnecessary in hindsight, the intercepted civil aircraft could be compensated for any resulting loss or damages. A similar provision can be found in Art. 110 UNCLOS and the right to visit. This article provides for the right to stop and board a ship if there is reasonable ground for suspecting the ship is engaged in piracy, slave trade, engaged in unauthorized broadcasting, is without nationality, or though flying a foreign flag or refusing to show its flag, the ship is, in reality, of the same nationality as the warship.[261] Paragraph 3 explicitly provides that if the suspicions prove to be unfounded, and provided that the ship in question has not committed any act justifying the boarding, it shall be compensated for any loss or damage that may have been sustained.

State aircraft are not subject to ICAO's interception rules and the prohibition to use weapons as stipulated in Art. 3bis Chicago Convention does not apply to them. It is therefore unclear which interception rules cover military aircraft as they are not explicitly mentioned in the Chicago Convention and related ICAO documents.[262] This issue is addressed, for instance, in the *United States and China Memorandum of Understanding on the Rules of Behavior for the Safety of Air and Maritime Encounters* which states that military aircraft that encounter each other in flight should operate in accordance with the Chicago Convention and its Annexes.[263] This legally non-binding Memorandum represents a preliminary step towards the application of interception procedures on military aircraft, despite the fact that it does not address interception in ADIZS. Indeed, the Memorandum states that military aircraft enjoy sovereign immunity and are therefore immune from the jurisdiction of other States.[264] However, the factual situation is different in the absence of such a Memorandum, as evidenced by the numerous interceptions of military aircraft in the ESC region.[265]

---

between 1946–2011, see Gbenga Oduntan, *Sovereignty and Jurisdiction in the Airspace and Outer Space* (Routledge 2012), 151, Appendix I – Chronology of notable military and diplomatic responses to aerial intrusions.

261 Art. 110 UNCLOS.

262 See on the issue of immunity of state aircraft, chapter 4, 3.1.3 of this book.

263 Memorandum of Understanding on the Rules of Behavior for the Safety of Air and Maritime Encounters (Supplement) (15 September 2015).

264 Neither China nor the US have ratified the United Nations Convention on Jurisdictional Immunities of States and Their Property, A/RES/59/38 (2 December 2004). The relevance of this document is diminished as only 23 States are State Parties.

265 Mercedes Trent, 'Appendix A: List of Publicized PLA ADIZ Intrusions from 2016–2020' in Federation of American Scientists (eds), *Over the Line: Implications of China's ADIZ Intrusions in Northeast Asia* (2020) 43–54.

A similar bilateral agreement with direct reference to ADIZs was concluded between India and Pakistan in 1994.[266] The *Agreement Between India And Pakistan On Prevention Of Air Space Violations And For Permitting Over Flights And Landings By Military Aircraft* explicitly states that combat aircraft "will not fly within 10 km of each other's airspace including ADIZ."[267] In the event of a country undertaking flights for military purposes at a distance less than 1000 metres from the other's airspace including the ADIZ, specific information has to be submitted, inter alia the proposed timing of flight and the type of the aircraft.[268] Furthermore, the *Agreement* establishes a method of communication between India and Pakistan.[269]

It is recommendable to publish specific guidance on the interception process for military aircraft.[270] Without clear rules on the interception process, the risk of accidents and miscalculations is increased.[271] A bilateral or multilateral forum discussing the issue of military encounters and interception in international airspace could be an appropriate way of solving this problem. Military confidence-building measures could be another effective soft law mechanism to regulate the application of ADIZs' rules to military aircraft. Confidence-building measures (CBMs) are "planned procedures to prevent hostilities, to avert escalation, to reduce military tension, and to build mutual trust between countries."[272] The voluntary nature of CBMs fosters cooperation as States are free to decide about their commitment. In the case of ADIZs, States so far have refrained from settling the issue in a binding treaty. A case in point for the regulation of military encounters in airspace are the *Nippon Foundation Guidelines*, which regulate military activities in the EEZ.[273] These Guidelines are a set of non-binding, voluntary principles with the aim of avoiding any

---

266 *The Agreement Between India And Pakistan On Prevention Of Air Space Violations And For Permitting Over Flights And Landings By Military Aircraft* (1994) 60 UNTS.

267 Ibid Art. 2.

268 Ibid Art. 3.

269 Ibid Art. 5.

270 The United States for example, published specific rules of engagement for intercepting foreign State aircraft, see US Navy Commander's Handbook, 4.4.2.

271 Raul Pedrozo, 'The Bull in the China Shop: Raising Tensions in the Asia-Pacific Region' (2014) 90 International Law Studies 93.

272 UNODA, 'Military Confidence Building' https://www.un.org/disarmament/cbms/.

273 Guidelines for Navigation and Overflight in the Exclusive Economic Zone (2005) https://nippon.zaidan.info/seikabutsu/2005/00816/pdf/0001.pdf. The Guidelines were designed against the background of military clashes over EEZs in East Asia, see Gbenga Oduntan, *Sovereignty and Jurisdiction in the Airspace and Outer Space – Legal Criteria for Spatial Delimitation* (Routledge 2012) 140 fn 461.

misunderstandings regarding military activities over foreign EEZ.[274] While not directly mentioning ADIZ, part V of the Guidelines provides that

> Warships or aircraft of a State intending to carry out a major military exercise in the EEZ of another State should inform the coastal State and others through a timely navigational warning of the time, date and areas involved in the exercise, and if possible, invite observers from the coastal State to witness the exercise.[275]

A similar provision could be established to apply the ADIZ identification system to military aircraft overflying the EEZ of a foreign State. Part X of the *Nippon Foundation Guidelines* addresses the transparency of legislation; an issue also relevant for the dissemination of information on ADIZS, given that some States do not adequately disclose their ADIZS rules.[276] The recommended method of guaranteeing transparency is to deposit the legislation at the UN-Secretary General.[277] Regarding compliance with the national legislation, part X (d) states that

> Military vessels and aircraft of a State exercising the freedoms of navigation and overflight in the EEZ of another State should observe and comply with the coastal State's legislation on the basis of goodwill, or comply under protest.

A similar practice can be witnessed regarding the compliance of military aircraft with ADIZS' rules. A soft law instrument could thus be an acceptable way to avoid misunderstandings on military actions and can be successful if States strive to reduce tension in areas where the ADIZ covers disputed territories.

2.6 *Compliance*

Prior to the establishment of the Chinese ECS ADIZ in 2013, there was minimal concern regarding the practice of creating a defence zone in international

274 Ibid 1.

275 Ibid 8.

276 Part X (a) states: "Those States with policies and/or legislation regarding military activities in their EEZS should make them as transparent and as widely known as possible, including to the military authorities of other States that are frequently using or navigating their EEZS."

277 Part X (c): "A copy of those laws should also be deposited with the UN Secretary-General, and be made available for easy reference by any interested States, authorities, or persons, with a view to increasing transparency and mitigating any hostile intentions."

airspace applying to civil aircraft. The key issue at stake is the scope of application, which extends to aircraft not intending to enter national airspace and the use of force against civil aircraft. The United States recommended commercial airlines to adhere to NOTAMs issued by foreign countries, including ADIZ rules that differ from those of the US ADIZ. With regard to the ECS ADIZ, the United States emphasized that "operations by US carriers consistent with NOTAMs does not indicate US government acceptance of China's requirement for operation the newly declared ECS ADIZ."[278] The United States view the application of identification requirements on traversing aircraft as unlawful and has therefore taken the step of protesting the Chinese practice. South Korea and Japan have encouraged civil airlines not to follow the Chinese ECS ADIZ rules and advised them not to submit a flight plan.[279] South Korea subsequently modified this statement and now recommends civil airlines to comply with the ECS ADIZ rules. The EU expressed strong concern regarding the "emergency defence measures" in case of non-compliance with the identification requirements within the ECS ADIZ, as it "generally heightens the risk of escalation and raises tension in the region."[280] Furthermore, India criticized China's ADIZ for escalating brinkmanship and regional tensions and emphasized the importance of the freedom of overflight.[281]

As the ICJ stated in the *North Sea Continental Shelf case* "acting or agreeing in a certain way, does not itself demonstrate anything of juridical nature."[282] Consequently, there is no uniform State practice on the application of identification rules on aircraft not bound for national airspace, as it lacks *opinio iuris* in several cases. Conversely, while States issued protests against the establishment of the Chinese ECS ADIZ and its application to traversing aircraft, the same States intercepted aircraft without sufficient proof on their intent of entering national airspace. Japan, for example, launched multiple interceptions against foreign military aircraft that were traversing along the coastline of Japan in international airspace. Considering national legislation as proof for

---

278 US State Department, 'China's Declared ADIZ – Guidance for US Air Carriers' (29 November 2013).

279 Ian Rinehart & Elias Bart, 'China's Air Defense Identification Zone' (2015) Congressional Research Service 16.

280 EU Press Statement, 'Declaration by the High Representative Catherine Ashton on behalf of the European Union on the establishment by China of an "East China Sea Air Defence Identification Zone"' (28 November 2013) 17082/1/13/REV 1.

281 Ann Mary George, 'Constructing the China threat: the Indian strategic community's discursive interpretation of the East China Sea ADIZ' (2021) 59 Commonwealth & Comparative Politics 297.

282 *North Sea Continental Shelf Case* (1969) para. 76.

customary international law, what matters more than the actual text is how it has been interpreted and more importantly, how it has been applied. The example of Japan serves to illustrate the ambiguity between the text and the application of national legislation. It can therefore be concluded that States in general accept the creation of ADIZS in international airspace applicable to civil aircraft with some minor disagreements on the exact scope of application, as can be seen in the reaction of States to the Chinese ECS ADIZ.

Military aircraft tend not to comply with the ADIZ's rules and if so only on the basis of reciprocity or goodwill.[283] There are numerous instances where States send their military aircraft through ADIZS as a form of protest. For example, military aircraft from the US, Japan, and South Korea do not comply with the rules of the Chinese ECS ADIZ as they reject the establishment of the ECS ADIZ altogether.[284] A survey of incidents occurring between 2016 and 2020 lists 81 instances of military aircraft violating the ADIZ rules of Japan, Taiwan, and South Korea by Chinese fighters in the ESC region.[285] Taiwan is the primary target of ADIZ intrusions by Chinese military aircraft. In 2021, Taiwan reported the intrusion of 56 Chinese military aircraft in the Taiwanese ADIZ over a four-day period.[286] While China does not respect the ADIZ's rules of other States, it nevertheless requires other States' military aircraft to comply with its ECS ADIZ's rules[287] and enforces them on foreign military aircraft with fly-by manoeuvres.[288] Occasionally, Russia sends military aircraft into various ADIZS of different States without complying with the identification rules.[289]

283 For example the Japan and South Korea agreed on informing the other State on military manoeuvres conducted within the ADIZ of the other State, see Kentaro Serita, *The Territory of Japan* (JPIC 2018) 250.

284 Ted G Carpenter, 'US Response to China's ADIZ Biased' (23 December 2013) https://www.cato.org/commentary/us-response-chinas-adiz-biased; Kristin Huang, 'US bombers enter Chinese air defence zone as Beijing's navy mounts massive exercises' (17 November 2020) https://www.scmp.com/news/china/military/article/3110262/us-bombers-enter-chinas-adiz-pla-navy-mounts-massive-exercises.

285 Mercedes Trent, 'Appendix A: List of Publicized PLA ADIZ Intrusions from 2016–2020' in Federation of American Scientists (eds), *Over the Line: Implications of China's ADIZ Intrusions in Northeast Asia* (2020) 43–54.

286 Ministry of Foreign Affairs Japan, Press Conference by Foreign Press Secretary Yoshida, 'Situation in Taiwan (Intrusion by Chinese Military Aircraft into Taiwan's Air Defence Identification Zone' (6 October 2021).

287 Reuters, 'China says U.S. should respect China's air defense zone' (23 March 2017) https://www.reuters.com/article/us-china-usa-defence-idUSKBN16U0SB.

288 Ian Rinehart & Elias Bart, 'China's Air Defense Identification Zone' (2015) Congressional Research Service 11.

289 European Leadership Network, 'List of Military Close Encounters Between Russia and the West, March 2014–2015' (2015) 14, 16, 17, 21; David Cenciotti, 'Why the Russian Tu-95

States tend to react differently to military intrusions. In response to the intrusion, the United States deploys fighter jets to intercept the intruding military aircraft and escort them beyond the ADIZ boundaries.[290] Taiwan, on the other hand, attempts to avoid direct confrontation and intercepts intruding military aircraft by closely monitoring the intruders and issuing radio warnings.[291]

The reasoning of the ICJ in the *Right of Passage over Indian Territory* case illustrates that the same right can be granted differently to civil persons and military persons in State practice.[292] The ICJ distinguished between a right to passage granted to civil persons, and the right to passage of armed forces. While the ICJ confirmed such a right for civil persons as a rule of (bilateral) customary international law, it negated the same right to armed forces.[293] The Court found that during the British period up to 1878, passage of armed forces and armed police between British and Portuguese possessions was contingent upon reciprocity, rather than a matter of right.[294] Moreover, Portuguese troops never crossed British territory without permission as the Governor of Bombay protested the crossing.[295] A comparable distinction between civil and military claims on the usage of airspace can be observed in State practice on ADIZ. While States appear to accept the application of ADIZ rules on civil aircraft in national as well as international airspace, the compliance of military aircraft with the international ADIZ rules is mostly based on reciprocity and goodwill.

2.7 *Legitimacy*

The review of State practice reveals a wide range of justifications for ADIZs in international airspace. While the overarching justification for the

---

bombers that intruded US air space weren't intercepted' (4 May 2015), https://www.businessinsider.com/why-the-russian-tu-95-bombers-that-intruded-us-air-space-werent-intercepted-2015-5.

290 NORAD Press Release, 'NORAD intercepts Russian bombers and fighters entering Alaskan Air Defense Identification Zone' (22 May 2019); Luis Martinez, 'Russian bombers intercepted 8 miles from US airspace' (10 June 2020) https://abcnews.go.com/Politics/russian-bombers-intercepted-miles-us-airspace/story?id=71171943.

291 Ministry of Foreign Affairs Taiwan, 'MOFA condemns Taiwan ADIZ intrusions by PLA, urges vigilance against threats' (11 September 2020); Dutch Aviation Society, 'New intercepts in Taiwan ADIZ' (7 December 2020) https://www.scramble.nl/military-news/new-intercepts-in-taiwan-adiz.

292 *Right of Passage over Indian Territory* (*Portugal v India*) (Merits) ICJ Rep 6, 38, 39. See also, Michael Mendelson, 'Right of Passage over Indian Territory' in *Max Planck Encylopedias of International Law* (OUP 2007) para. 8–10.

293 *Right of Passage over Indian Territory* (*Portugal v India*) (Merits) ICJ Rep 6.

294 Ibid 38.

295 Ibid 39.

establishment of these zones is the protection of national security, only in two instances has the right to self-defence been explicitly mentioned. These instances are Indonesia and the United States. The self-defence claim is also closely connected to the argument that States simply have the right to regulate which aircraft may enter national airspace.

Another factor of legitimacy is the safe conduct of air traffic and the general safety of aviation. The flexible use of airspace (FUA) extends this idea by attempting to create a safe and efficient environment for both civil aircraft as well as military aircraft. Even though created in international airspace, some States argue the legitimacy of their ADIZ as being in line with the Chicago Convention and particularly Annex 2 and Annex 11. In the case of Bangladesh, the establishment of an ADIZ was deemed necessary to safeguard national security and sovereignty above its territory and was claimed to be in line with the Chicago Convention. Furthermore, the United States has asserted that it may regulate the entry into national airspace based on the principle of exclusive sovereignty.[296] The extraterritorial extension of sovereignty is not in conformity with the most fundamental principles of public international law.[297] Art. 11 of the Chicago Convention does also not link regulations relating to the admission to the territory of a Contracting State with sovereignty. Instead, Art. 11 Chicago Convention regulates the admission to airspace without requiring any secondary legal base within the principle of sovereignty. Any claim based on sovereignty can only be valid for ADIZs in national airspace. Overall, States accept national ADIZ as a practice in line with the Chicago Convention and its Annexes.

In general, States do not view ADIZs as a violation of the freedom of overflight.[298] However, there seems to be a disagreement on whether the freedom of overflight is infringed when an ADIZ applies to aircraft not intending to enter national airspace. The United States, India, and Japan are advocates

---

296 Roncevert Almond, 'Clearing the Air above the East China Sea: The Primary Elements of Aircraft Defense Identification Zones' (2017) 7 Harvard Nat Sec J 146 stating that "the Chicago Convention codifies the right to exclusive sovereignty and authorizes the establishment of rules for the admission of aircraft into the national airspace".

297 Ruwantissa Abeyratne, 'In Search of Theoretical Justification for Air Defence Identification Zones' (2011) J Transp Secur; *Nicaragua Case* (1986), para. 212 stating that sovereignty only extends to the territorial sea and the airspace above it.

298 See for example the Memorandum of Understanding between the US and China which explicitly states that even though military aircraft should "refrain from interfering" with the activities in a designated area, military aircraft "always enjoy the rights and freedom of navigation, overflight, and other internationally lawful uses of the sea related to those freedoms."

of this argument.[299] Japan commented on the establishment of the Chinese ECS ADIZ that it has no validity whatsoever as it violates the freedom of overflight.[300] In contrast, China asserts that it does not contravene freedom of overflight even if the ADIZ applies to aircraft traversing the area. However, China attempts to restrict certain aerial military activities within the ADIZ, such as "provocative flyover and surveillance activities."[301] Foreign military activities within or above the EEZ are viewed by China as political and security threats, which "undermine China's sovereignty and security interest under the pretext of navigation and freedom of overflight."[302] The discussion on the conduct of military manoeuvres in the airspace above an EEZ will remain a prevailing issue due to conflicting views on the questions of whether such activities can be restricted.[303]

2.8 *The Influence of ADIZs on Disputed Maritime Areas*

The establishment of the ECS ADIZ in international airspace has prompted concerns that it may impact territorial claims on the disputed Senkaku/Diaoyu islands.[304] The status of the inhabited Senkaku/Diaoyu islands is unclear in two aspects. First, it is unclear whether they actually are islands as defined in 121 (2) UNCLOS or whether they qualify as rock in the sense Art. 121 (3) UNCLOS with the consequence of not providing for a claim of an EEZ or continental shelf. Second, it is also not completely resolved whether the islands are part of Japan's territory, China's territory or Taiwan's territory.[305] Japan claims to have administrative control over the Senkaku islands based on the acquisition of ownership through discovery and occupation of *terra nullius* and denies the

---

299 Ian Rinehart & Elias Bart, 'China's Air Defense Identification Zone' (2015) Congressional Research Service 11.

300 Ministry of Foreign Affairs Japan, 'Statement by the Minister for Foreign Affairs on the announcement on the "East China Sea Air Defense Identification Zone" by the Ministry of National Defense of the People's Republic of China' (24 November 2013).

301 Zang Ye, 'Air Defense ID Zone to Deter Those with Designs on China's Territory' (26 November 2013, People's Daily Online) http://en.people.cn/90883/8466523.html (accessed 1 December 2022).

302 Ministry of Foreign Affairs of the People's Republic of China, 'Foreign Ministry Spokesperson Hau Chunying's Regular Press Conference' (25 May 2015).

303 Jinyuan Su, 'The East China Sea Air Defense Identification Zone and International Law'(2015) 14 Chinese Int'l L J (2015) 290; On the discussion of military activities on the high seas and in within the EEZ see chapter 6, 3.2.2 of this book.

304 The "Senkaku islands" is the collective term for the Uotsuri Island, Kitakojima Island, Minamikojima Island, Kuba Island, Taisho Island, Okinokitaiwa Island, Okinominamiiwa Island and Tobise Island, see Kentaro Serita, *The Territory of Japan* (JPIC 2018) 107.

305 For a discussion on the territorial status for the islands see European Parliament Research Service, 'Sino-Japanese controversy over the Senkaku/Diaoyu/Diaoyutai Islands' (2021).

existence of a territorial dispute altogether.[306] Following the Second World War the Senkaku/Diaoyu islands were occupied by the US and in the 1970s they were transferred back to Japan under the Okinawa Reversion Treaty.[307] China in contrast asserts that the island is an "inherent part of Chinese territory since ancient times," and that the islands were part of the territory transferred to China under the San Francisco Peace Treaty.[308] The Senkaku/Diaoyu islands are situated in the EEZ of Japan as well as in the EEZ of China and are at the centre of the dispute over the delimitation of maritime boundaries and access to potential oil reserves in this region.[309] Due to the extension of the ECS ADIZ, the zone now covers the disputed island and creates an overlap with the Japanese ADIZ. This may be seen as an attempt to exercise effective control over the disputed islands and to influence the political landscape in this region.

ADIZS are zones with specialized rights and competences regarding aerial security and safety. In principle, ADIZS' security rights are not territorial rights. However, the theoretical problem of the effect of exercising control over disputed territories is still worth to be analysed. The progressive and unilateral exercise of these rights by States in zones over disputed islands raises concerns about influencing the territorial status.[310] Only a few States have adopted national legislation on ADIZ with territorial implications. Even though established in international airspace, Bangladesh and Myanmar base their claim to establish an ADIZ on the principle of sovereignty. It should be clear that States cannot be granted preferential rights in international spaces based on the principle of sovereignty and territoriality.[311] Bangladesh's and Myanmar's State practice also contradicts the majority of other States' practices, which have unilaterally established an ADIZ beyond any quasi-territorial benchmarks. Furthermore, their national laws do not express any territorial tendencies. The additional practice of aligning an ADIZ with the outer limits of the EEZ

306 Gisela Grieger, 'Sino-Japanese controversy over the Senkaku/Diaoyu/Diaoyutai Islands' (2021) European Parlament Research Service 2. See for the original Chinese statement on the territorial status of the Senkaku/Diaoyu Island translated into English, Kentaro Serita, *The Territory of Japan* (JPIC 2018) 108.

307 Kentaro Serita, *The Territory of Japan* (JPIC 2018) 110.

308 Gisela Grieger, 'Sino-Japanese controversy over the Senkaku/Diaoyu/Diaoyutai Islands' (2021) European Parlament Research Service 2; namely as part of the region around Taiwan, see Kentaro Serita, *The Territory of Japan* (JPIC 2018) 110.

309 Kentaro Serita, *The Territory of Japan* (JPIC 2018) 107.

310 Taisaku Ikeshima, 'Chinas's Air Defence Identification Zone (ADIZ) and its Impact on the Territorial and Maritime Disputes in the East and South China Sea' (2016) 3 Transcommunication 157.

311 On this aspect, see above chapter 1, 1.1. and 1.4.

demonstrates the symbiosis between maritime zones and superjacent airspace. In the current context, the extension of the State's authority requires a generalization and limitation of aerial zones for specific and well-defined purposes.[312]

2.9 *The Recognition of ADIZs by Other States*

Recognition by other States plays an important role if there are long-simmering border conflicts between two States, as it can lead to a change in the territorial status.[313] Compliance with factual requirements of Statehood coupled with the acceptance by other States seems to be at the centre of territorial disputes.[314] Divergent views exist on whether recognition is a constitutive element or only has declarative functions.[315] Recognition, at least, is an important political aspect and indicates acceptance by the international community.[316] Even when viewed as a declaratory act, recognition has a profound impact on the international legal system, and with far-reaching implications for both the international and domestic legal orders.[317] Recognition implies, at the very least, a commitment to respect the newly changed circumstances.[318]

States have to proceed cautiously when recognizing a new situation, as they generally have to refrain from formally recognizing a situation created by an illegal act, and also have to refrain from implicitly doing so.[319] The principle of non-recognition concerns the breach of an international obligation leading to an unlawful situation and has particularly been referred to as the acquisition of territory involving the use of force.[320] The rationale behind the principle of

312 As described in chapter 6, 3 of this book, ADIZ aligning with the EEZ do not create territorial rights.

313 Winston P Nagan & Aitza M Haddad, 'Recognition of Palestinian Statehood: A Clarification of the Interests of the Concerned Parties' (2012) 40 Ga J Int'l & Comp L 341, 362ff.

314 Pasha L Hsieh, 'An Unrecognized State in Foreign and International Courts: The Case of China and the Republic of Taiwan' (2007) 28 Mich J Int'l L 765: On the example of Taiwan, multiple States acknowledge its existence but still deny its recognition as State.

315 Critical on recognition as constitutive element, see James Crawford, 'The Creation of the State of Palestine' (1990) 1 European J Int'l L 309; Jochen Frowein, 'Recognition' in *Max Planck Encyclopedias of Public International Law* (OUP 2010) para. 10, emphasizing the prevailing opinion on the declarative function of recognition.

316 Phillip M Brown, 'The Legal Effects of Recognition' (1950) 44 AJIL 617.

317 James Crawford, *The Creation of States in International Law* (2nd edn, OUP 2007) 22.

318 Recognition can also be understood as the absence of protest to a newly established State practice. It may then contribute also to the emergence of a rule of customary international law. See also, *Fisheries* (*United Kingdom v Norway*) (*Merits*) [1951] ICJ Rep 116, at 139 stating that "the United Kingdom could not have been ignorant of the Decree" issued by Norway.

319 ILC Report, 53rd. Session, GAOR 56th Session, Suppl. No. 10 (A/56/10) 2001, 287, para. 5.

320 Ian Brownlie, 'The Principle of Non-Recognition' in *International Law And The Use Of Force By States* (OUP, 2012) 410; also Friendly Relations Declaration, UNGA Res 2625 (XXV), 1970, UN Doc A/RES/25/2625.

non-recognition is that actions contrary to basic values commonly accepted should not be legitimized.[321] In its 1971 *Namibia Advisory Opinion,* the ICJ affirmed the obligation of non-recognition of the administration of the occupied territory by South Africa.[322] This approach was subsequently reiterated in 2004 with the *Palestinian Wall Advisory Opinion* for the occupied territory of Palestine.[323] The duty of non-recognition under international law aims at preventing the validation of an unlawful situation by third States and is a well-accepted principle concerning territorial changes as a result of an illegal act.[324] This also relates to the principle of *ex injuria non oritur jus*, namely that an aggressive act, i.e. illegal act, cannot be the basis of any legal right.[325] The situation of disputed borders is yet complex and a change of factual circumstances might lead to the crystallizing of the de-facto situation.[326]

The establishment of ADIZs has the potential to create a new environment in international airspace and influence the current international legal order. Some authors have argued that particularly the ECS ADIZ created by China is on the verge of crystallizing into a de-facto situation with an effect on the existing maritime disputes there.[327] Additionally, there has been concern raised that China might advance its territorial claims by exercising exclusive aerial competence in other areas as well, such as the South China Sea region.[328] In this context, it is important to understand the perception of China on international law as "an instrument of bourgeois nations to perpetuate their

---

321 Paola Gaeta, Jorge E Viñuales & Salvatore Zappalá, *Cassese's International Law* (3rd edn, OUP 2020) 341.

322 *Legal Consequences for States of the Continued Presence of South Africa in Namibia* (*South Africa v. Namibia*) *notwithstanding Security Council Resolution 276* (Advisory Opinion) [1971] ICJ Rep 16, 56.

323 Ibid para. 159.

324 UN General Assembly, UN Doc. Res 2734 (XXV) stating at para.5 that "no territorial acquisition resulting from the threat or use of force shall be recognized under international law as legal."

325 Christopher R Rossi, 'Ex Injuria Jus Non Oritur, Ex Factis Jus Oritur, and the Elusive Search for Equilibrium after Ukraine' (2015) 24 Tul J Int'l & Comp L 155.

326 For example, the Canadian Supreme Court found on the secession of Quebec that even though there is no unilateral right of secession, the success of a de-facto secession depends on the recognition of other States, which would also consider the legality and legitimacy of the secession, Canadian Supreme Court [1998] Secession of Quebec, 2 SCR 217.

327 Christopher Lamont, 'Conflict in the Skies: The Law of Air Defence Identification Zones' (2014) 39 Air & Space Law 189; Peter Kreuzer, 'Chinas Luftverteidigungszone und der Konflikt um die Diaoyu/Senkaku Inseln' (2013) 9 HSFK Report 3; Taisuku Ikeshima, 'China's Air Defense Identification Zone (ADIZ) and its Impact on the Territorial and Maritime Disputes in the East and South China Seas' (2016) 3 Transcomm 158.

328 Duc L Ho, 'A South China Sea ADIZ – Vietnam's Next Challenge' (Master Thesis, 2016, Naval Postgraduate School) 2.

favoured position in the world", and a "prejudice of Western nations and tainted by imperialism and colonialism."[329] In general, China rejects the *modi* of territorial acquisition and instead relies on the "adjustment" of territory.[330] Without assuming some Machiavellian scheme, ADIZs might be a good tactic to bolster or strengthen territorial claims. The issue of non-recognition is not relevant for ADIZs as they do not cause the change of territory by force, which would be illegal and other States would need to refrain from recognizing this situation. ADIZs are per se not illegal and State practice even shows a tendency towards accepting or recognizing these aerial defence zones as a rule of customary international law.

In the broader context of geopolitics, ADIZs may provide a rationale for the acceptance of unilateral advances in territorial claims and the potential to influence the geopolitical landscape.[331] Conversely, States may adhere to the ADIZ rules of other States and even formally recognize the existence of a territorial dispute. As the ICJ stated in the case *Coastal State Rights in the Black Sea, Sea of Azov, and Kerch Strait*, the mere recognition of the objective fact of the existence of a dispute with territorial implications does not recognize any alteration of the territorial status.[332] Consequently, the risk of ADIZ's claims hardening into territorial claims by complying with them is thus diminished. Territorial disputes are multi-faceted and they are susceptible to a partial understanding if certain elements are not taken into account. Consequently, they must be assessed in their entirety. The issue of aerial claims is just one factor among many that are relevant to the complex situation.

2.10 *Core Issues of Potential Disputes*

The exercise of State powers in ADIZs gives rise to a number of problems that can be resolved by initiating negotiations on the amendment of the current international legal framework. Four types of disputes can be identified:

---

329 Byron N Tzou, *China and International Law – The Boundary Disputes* (Praeger, Westport 1990) 7, 8.

330 Adjustment includes the right to self-determination, the right of the State to recover ceded territory, and the right to make minor adjustment of their territories with neighbouring States, see ibid at 13.

331 Colin Flint & Zhang Xiaotong, 'Historical – Geopolitical Contexts and the Transformation of Chinese Foreign Policy' (2019) 12 Chinese J of Int'l Politics 300, describing that the driving force of Chinese foreign policy decisions combine territorial, political and economic elements. The main argument focuses on the hypothesis that territorial strategies require economic resources, and economic growth requires creating new territorial arrangements.

332 *Dispute Concerning Coastal State Rights in the Black Sea, Sea of Azov, and Kerch Strait (Ukraine v the Russian Federation)* [2017] PCA, Case No. 2017–16, para. 178.

The first type of dispute relates to the exercise of the freedom of overflight when violated by the State's discretionary powers. This would safeguard that States act in conformity with the freedom of overflight and establishes a balance between the interests of States. Particularly the enforcement of ADIZS rules by interception will be at the center of scrutinized actions. This type of dispute also relates to the much-discussed issue of military activities in international spaces.

The second type of dispute relates to the violation of specific air traffic regulations by the ADIZ-State and the abusive exercise of ADIZ rights. This might be relevant with regard to overlapping zones and competences within a FIR. The method of sharing all necessary details and information on ADIZ can also be challenged under this type of dispute.

The third type concerns the exercise of State power in relation to the jurisdiction of the State, whose nationality the aircraft enjoys. This is also closely related to any matters of criminal jurisdiction and concurrent jurisdiction (if not solved with treaty negotiations).

The most serious difficulties are raised in case the zone is established over disputed territories. States, in general, seem to refrain from solving territorial disputes through dispute settlement, as in some instances, the territorial dispute is denied altogether (f.e. Senkaku/Diaoyu conflict). Good-faith negotiations aimed at concluding a formal agreement could be a suitable alternative to mandatory dispute settlement in this regard.[333]

There exists a risk of abusive litigation initiated by other States and any dispute settlement system should be designed to avoid abusive recourse. There might be a realistic fear that the protection of national security from aerial threats might be seriously affected by legal complaints. The party who initiated the proceedings thus has to present a prima facie well-founded claim. Otherwise, it might form an obstacle for States to agree upon a dispute settlement system that might lead to a challenge of essential security interests. Nevertheless, it is also not implausible that a State may exercise its ADIZ rights in an abusive manner. For both sides, any accusation needs to be based on objective criteria. A compromise can also be to provide for a mandatory conciliation procedure. This would allow States to retain genuine freedom of political decision-making regarding their national security.

333 See on the different types of dispute settlement of territorial disputes, Jorge E Nuñez, *Territorial Disputes and State Sovereignty: International Law and Politics* (Taylor and Francis 2020) 91–116.

3 Conclusion

The premise of this chapter is to offer an understanding of the various ADIZs and their influence on territorial disputes. This part focuses on the State practice of 25 States that have actively claimed an ADIZ. A rule of customary international law might be confirmed, even when States have not established a zone themselves. Inaction as acceptance of a rule of customary international law is widely recognized as only prohibitive rules need affirmative State practice.[334] One can only speak of a uniform State practice with regard to the most basic common ground namely, the general establishment of an ADIZ in either national airspace or international airspace, the requirement of identification and interception in case of non-compliance. Due to the plurality of approaches in the various national legal systems, it is hardly possible though to draw a final conclusion on the exact scope of application of an ADIZ. The inconsistency in State practice on the personal scope of application can be divided into two blocks, each claiming legitimacy and compliance with the freedom of overflight. The extensive geographic scope is the only point of critique when covering disputed islands but otherwise raises not much concern.

States regulate ADIZs in different ways and thus requires the initiation of negotiations on the most pressing issues. These include the publication of all necessary information, matters of concurrent jurisdiction in overlapping zones and the personal scope of application. A common set of key conceptual elements helps to provide legal clarity and diminishes the risk of being wrongfully intercepted. As regards the application to military aircraft, soft law instruments, such as the Nippon Foundation Guidelines, would be the most promising means of achieving an agreement between States and avoiding any escalation of conflict. The delicate problem of unresolved border disputes in maritime areas can act as a stumbling block during negotiations due to the lack of a political will to address them. Therefore, it is recommended that this issue be solved through other means. In particular, the current uncompromising stances in the ESC region do not appear to offer any room for discussion with the goal of achieving a permanent settlement. Overall, international ADIZs seem to have the primary purpose of identifying the intent of aircraft to enter national airspace and only in a second step aim at identifying an armed attack.

334 For example, the surrounding of Earth by the first satellite Sputnik in Outer Space led to the creation of the customary rule of the free use of Outer Space as States remained inactive during its travel.

CHAPTER 4

Defending the Skies: ADIZs and the Inherent Right to Self-Defence

This chapter will analyse the right to self-defence as potential legal basis for the establishment of ADIZs. In scholarly literature, several authors have proposed the idea that ADIZs arise from the inherent right to self-defence pursuant to Art. 51 UN-Charter.[1] Discussions concern the establishment of AIDZs in international airspace as replacing the situational concept of self-defence by a 'spatial' concept.[2] Some compare ADIZs with the situation where the right to self-defence may be claimed for military aggressions that occurs not suddenly but over a long period of time.[3] Another argument is that the right to self-defence may limit the right of overflight in international airspace only in times of war.[4] In peacetime, the right to self-defence "will provide guidance on the circumstances in which an aircraft may be engaged."[5] Some argue in favour of the legality of ADIZs on the basis of the right of anticipatory self-defence and the inherent right of States to make necessary military preparations.[6] The connection between the right to claim an ADIZ and the right to self-defence can be based on safeguarding the State's sovereignty and aerial security against threats from the air.[7] The security purpose of ADIZs is to identify any aircraft and thus achieve enough early-warning time for responsive

---

1 Richard Almond, 'Clearing the Air above the East China Sea: The Primary Elements of Aircraft Defense Identification Zones' (2017) 7 Harvard National Security Journal 136. Christopher Petras,'The Law of Air Mobility-the International Legal Principles behind the U.S. Mobility Air Forces' Mission' (2010) 44 Air Force L Rev 63.

2 Stefan Kaiser, 'The Legal Status of Air Defense Identification Zones: Tensions over the East China Sea' (2016) 63 ZLW 531–533.

3 Alexander Calvo, 'China's Air Defense Identification Zone: Concept, Issues at Stake and Regional Impact' (2013) Naval War College Press 14.

4 Ashley Roach, 'Air Identification Zones' in *Max Planck Encyclopedias of Public International Law* (OUP 2017) para. 10.

5 Ibid para. 9.

6 Jaw W Lee, 'Tension on the Air: The Air Defence Identification Zones on the East China Sea' (2014) 7 J East Asia & Int'l L 278.

7 Justin Bronk, 'China's Air Defence Identification Zone and its Role in Chinese Geo-Strategic Policy' (2013) RUSI Analysis, Royal United Services Institute, https://stage.rusi.institute/explore-our-research/publications/commentary/chinas-air-defence-identification-zone-and-its-role-chinese-geo-strategic-policy.

 | DOI:10.1163/9789004721005_006

measures to maintain security. This chapter posits that ADIZs may qualify as the lawful exercise of pre-emptive self-defence under certain circumstances.

1 The Right to Self-Defence against Aerial Attacks

First, it has to be mentioned that the invocation of forceful measures against civil aircraft as part of self-defence is in line with the rules of the Chicago Convention, which states in Art. 3bis that even though States should, in general, refrain from resorting to the use of weapons against civil aircraft, this "shall not be interpreted as modifying in any way the rights and obligations of States set forth in the Charter of the United Nations."[8]

In general, a State may exercise the right to self-defence under the following conditions: self-defence must be a response to an armed attack, it must be necessary and proportionate.[9] The UN-Charter provides in Art. 51 UN-Charter for the right to self-defence and introduces the first requirement, namely the occurrence of an armed attack. Art. 51 UN-Charter reads as follows:

> Nothing in the present Charter shall impair the inherent right of individual or collective self-defence if an armed attack occurs against a Member of the United Nations, until the Security Council has taken measures necessary to maintain international peace and security (...).[10]

Customary international law adds two additional requirements for the lawful exercise of the right to self-defence, namely necessity and proportionality.[11] It is generally accepted that the right to self-defence is a rule of customary international law.[12]

Vast literature exists on the right of self-defence covering multiple aspects, such as self-defence for institutions,[13] anticipatory self-defence,[14] self-defence

8 Art. 3bis Chicago Convention.

9 Christopher Greenwood, 'Self-defence' in *Max Planck Encyclopaedias of Public International Law* (OUP 2011) para. 8.

10 Art. 51 Charter of the United Nations ("UN-Charter") (1945) 1155 UNTS 331.

11 Ian Brownlie, 'The Use of Force in Self-Defence' (1961) 37 BYIL 279; Judith Gradam, *Necessity, Proportionality and the Use of Force by States* (Cambridge Studies in Int'l and Comp L 2004); Christine Gray, 'The Use of Force and the International Legal Order' in Malcom D Evans (ed), *International Law* (5th edn, OUP 2018) 148ff; *Nicaragua Case* (1986) 94; *Legality of the Threat or Use of Nuclear Weapons, Advisory Opinion* [1996] ICJ Rep 226, 245 (hereinafter: Nuclear Weapons Advisory Opinion).

12 *Nicaragua Case* (1986) 14, 94.

13 Nicholas W Barber, 'Self-Defence for Institutions' (2013) 72 Cambridge LJ 558.

14 Alexandra L Laposi, 'Anticipatory Self-Defence' (2014) Caiete de Drept Penal 107.

against non-state actors,[15] and self-defence against cyber-attacks.[16] This chapter therefore does not divulge too long on the prerequisites of the right to self-defence but will only evaluate if the right to self-defence sustains a claim for ADIZs. Two circumstances seem to create a conflict between the establishment of an ADIZ and the right to self-defence. First, ADIZs are established on a permanent basis irrespective of the imminent occurrence of an armed attack, whereas unilateral self-defence is exceptional and only a temporal right.[17] Second, the obligation to identify, as imposed by the ADIZ, is not a forceful measure and thus might be outside the scope of the right to self-defence overall.

1.1 *The Notion of "Armed Attack" Includes Civil Aircraft Used as a Weapon*

In general, civil aviation is considered to be peaceful, yet the Preamble of the Chicago Convention already recognizes the potential that "its abuse can become a threat to the general security."[18] The UN-Charter prohibits in Art. 2 (4) "the threat or use of force against the territorial integrity or political independence of any State" and the abusive operation of a civil aircraft can amount *prima facie* to a threat in this sense. The right to self-defence is one of the exceptions to the prohibition of the threat or use of force in the event of an armed attack. Even though the UN-Charter does not define the term "armed attack", the character and qualification of the armed attack determine whether a State's response in self-defence is lawful.[19] The notion of armed attack covers two preliminary aspects. First, the characteristic of an armed attack, and second, the temporal preconditions of an armed attack.

In the *Nicaragua Case* the International Court of Justice describes the term "armed attack" as "the most grave forms of the use of force" and customary law determines the context of the term.[20] In contrast, "less grave forms" of the use of force, as reflected in the Friendly Relations Declaration, do not qualify as

15 Mary E O'Conell, Christian J Tams & Dire Tladi (eds), *Self-Defence against Non-State Actors* (Cambridge University Press 2019).

16 Yoram Dinstein, 'Computer Network Attacks and Self-defence' (2001) 76 International Law Studies, Naval War College 96.

17 Christine Gray, *International Law and Use of Force* (4th edn, OUP 2018) 119.

18 Preamble, Chicago Convention.

19 Malcom N Shaw, *International Law* (9th edn, Cambridge University Press 2021) 822.

20 *Nicaragua Case* (1986) para. 191, 195; The Court referred in its argument to the UN General Assembly Resolution 3314 (XXIX) Definition of Aggression as a rule of customary law, UNGA Res 3314 (XXIX) 'Definition of Aggression' (14 December 1974).

an armed attack.[21] A minor incident, therefore, would not qualify as an armed attack.[22] To the Court's conception, an armed attack requires the involvement of the government to a certain degree.[23] However, the Court did not provide a decisive description of the threshold of an armed attack. Hence, the judgment does not contain an exclusive interpretation regarding those forms of force, which are serious enough to constitute armed attacks, and those, which are less grave forms of the use of force.[24]

In the *Oil Platforms Case,* the Court concluded that several minor attacks can reach in their entirety the threshold of an armed attack.[25] In the same judgment, the Court introduced another requirement for an armed attack namely the "specific intention of harming."[26] The invocation of intention was largely rejected in scholarly literature, as the attack itself was already unrebuttable proof of harmful intention.[27] One must take into consideration that the *Nicaragua Case* was decided in 1984 and 1986 and the customary nature of the scope of the right to self-defence might have been modified by subsequent State practice. Also, the subsequent decision in the *Oil Platforms Case* did not offer more clarity on the notion of an armed attack. The current stand of law, therefore, requires a review based on the rule of treaty interpretation.

Pursuant to the rules of treaty interpretation of Art. 31 (1) Vienna Convention on the Law of Treaties, a treaty shall be interpreted in good faith in accordance with the ordinary meaning, to be given to the terms, in their context and in the light of the object and purpose of the treaty.[28] *Tams* defines "armed attack" in its ordinary meaning by relating "attack" to an "aggressive and violent act against a person or place" and "armed" as involving the "use of weaponry or firearms."[29] According to *Constantinou* an armed attack "implies

21 *Nicaragua Case* (1986) para. 191; UNGA Res 2625 (XXV) 'Declaration on Principles of International Law concerning Friendly Relations and Co-operation among States in accordance with the Charter of the United Nations' (24 October 1970).

22 *Nicaragua Case* (1986) para. 195.

23 Christine Gray, 'The Use of Force and the International Legal Order' in Malcom D Evans (ed), *International Law* (5th edn, OUP 2018) 612.

24 Yoram Dinstein, *War, Aggression and Self-Defence* (2nd edn, Cambridge University Press 2012) 195; Greenwood C, 'Self-Defence' in *Max Planck Encyclopedias of Public International Law* (OUP 2011) para. 12.

25 *Oil Platforms Case* para. 64.

26 Ibid para. 64

27 Avra Constantinou, *The Right to Self-Defence under Customary International Law and Article 51 of the UN-Charter* (Sakkoulas Athenes 2000) 62.

28 Vienna Convention on the Law of Treaties (VCLT) (1969) 1155 UNTS 33.

29 Christian J Tams, 'Self-Defence against Non-State Actors: Making Sense of the 'Armed Attack' Requirement' in Mary E O'Conell, Christian J Tams & Dire Tladi (eds), *Self-Defence*

an act or the beginning of a series of acts of armed force of considerable magnitude and intensity (i.e. scale) which have as their consequence (i.e. effects) the infliction of substantial destruction upon important elements of the target State."[30] The ordinary meaning of armed attack includes classical forms of warfare such as an invasion and attacks against a State's military ship or military aircraft.[31] However, an armed attack may not only be understood in its conventional military terms but includes biological and chemical weapons.[32] Weapon in its ordinary meaning signifies an "instrument of any kind used in warfare or in combat to attack and overcome an enemy."[33] An armed attack is therefore not limited to a specific type of weapon but depends on the use of the instrument. This functional approach is also reflected in the 1950 'Peace Through Deeds Resolution' by the UN General Assembly, which condemned the use of force without limiting the use of a specific weapon.[34] Likewise, the International Court of Justice stated in its *Advisory Opinion on the Legality of the Threat or Use of Nuclear Weapons* that Art. 51 UN-Charter does not refer to specific weapons; the right to self-defence applies to any armed attack, regardless of the weapon employed.[35]

The right to self-defence has to be read in the context of the UN-Charter and particularly its embedment in the system of collective security.[36] Art. 51 UN-Charter is situated in 'Chapter VII – Action with respect to Threats to Peace, Breaches of Peace and Acts of Aggression' and provides for the exemption of the general prohibition of the use of force pursuant to Art. 4(2) UN-Charter and the prohibition of the threat or use of force.[37] The contextual interpretation aligns the term "armed attack" within the overall structure of the treaty

---

against Non-State Actors (Cambridge University Press 2019) 112, 113, citing the Oxford Dictionary of English (2nd ed, OUP 2005).

30 Avra Constantinou, *The Right to Self-Defence under Customary International Law and Article 51 of the UN-Charter* (Sakkoulas Athenes 2000) 63–64.

31 Oliver Corten, *The Law against War* (OUP 2010) 403. For example the Security Council declared the attack of North Korean troops as "armed attack" upon the Republic of Korea (UNSC Res 83, UN Doc S/RES/83 (27 June 1950), and encouraged States to act in collective self-defence (UNSC Res 85, UN Doc S/RES/85 (7 July 1950).

32 Ian Brownlie, 'The Use of Force in Self-Defence' (1961) 37 BYIL 255–256.

33 Oxford English Dictionary, 'Weapon' (OUP) online.

34 UNGA Res 380 (V) 'Peace through Deeds Resolution' (17 November 1950): "Whatever the weapon used, any aggression (...) is the gravest of all crimes against peace and security."

35 *Nuclear Weapons Advisory Opinion*, at para. 244.

36 Dire Tladi, 'The Use of Force in Self-Defence against Non-State Actors', UN Lecture Series https://legal.un.org/avl/ls/Tladi_PS.html.

37 Christopher Greenwood, 'Self-defence' in *Max Planck Encyclopaedias of Public International Law* (OUP 2011) para. 1.

and in particular Art. 4(2) UN-Charter. Commentators largely agree that "force" according to Art. 4(2) UN-Charter is a minor form of an armed attack, in the sense that all armed attacks are uses of force but not all uses of forces also amount to an armed attack.[38] An isolated minor incident does not amount to a threat to the safety of the State and thus does not fulfil the requirement of an "armed attack."[39] This favours the interpretation that there are stricter preconditions for the right to self-defence than for violations of the prohibition of the use of force.[40] The criterion of armed attack also has to be seen in the broader context of threats to peace, breaches of peace and acts of aggression. Chapter VII, where Art. 51 is located, and forms part of the Charter's *ius ad bellum*. The rules of Chapter VII permits the use of force which would otherwise violate Art. 4(2) UN-Charter.[41]

The object and purpose of the UN-Charter cover a wide range of different aspects. The telos of the UN-Charter can be found in Art. 1, which sets forth the general purpose of the United Nations namely the maintenance of international peace and security.[42] The Preamble to the UN-Charter supplements Art. 1 UN-Charter which emphasizes again that the utmost goal is to maintain international peace and security. The preservation of peace is thus the 'purpose of all purposes'.[43] This interpretation was also confirmed by the ICJ in its Advisory Opinion on *Certain Expenses* where the Court stated that "[t]he primary place ascribed to international peace and security is natural since the fulfilment of the other purposes will be dependent upon the attainment of that basic condition."[44] In light of the object and purpose, the right to self-defence needs to be interpreted in a narrow way. The renunciation of any use of force is the guiding principle for States, so that disputes should be settled peacefully

38 Christiane Wandscher, *Internationaler Terrorismus und Selbstverteidigungsrecht* (Duncker & Humboldt 2006) 134.

39 Karl Zemanek, 'Armed Attack' in *Max Planck Encyclopedias of Public International Law* (OUP 2013) para. 7.

40 Oliver Corten, *The Law against War* (OUP 2010) at 50 and 402, discussing the difference between military force and other forms of forces such as economical, political and economic forces whereas the later does not provide for the use of self-defence. Also Ralph Janik, *International Law and the Use of Force* (Taylor Francis 2020) 100.

41 James A Green, 'Questioning the Peremptory Status of the Prohibition of the Use of Force' (2011) 32 Michigan J Int'l 229.

42 *Certain Expenses of the United Nations* (Advisory Opinion) [1962] ICJ Rep 151 where the ICJ reiterates the UN goals as mentioned in Article 1.

43 Rüdiger Wolfrum, 'Ch. I Purposes and Principles, Article 1' in Bruno Simma (ed), *The Charter of the United Nations – A Commentary* (OUP 2012) 109.

44 *Certain Expenses of the United Nations* (Advisory Opinion) [1962] ICJ Rep 151, 168.

in the first place.[45] The Charter is concerned with grave breaches of peace and it would be a misreading to apply the right to self-defence to any illegal use of force not constituting an "armed attack".[46]

Military aircraft equipped with weaponry can conduct an armed attack. However, it is also possible for the aircraft itself to be used as a weapon.[47] Shimpu Tokkotai, also commonly known under the name of Kamikaze, is a specific example of an aircraft used as a weapon. During the Second World War, Japanese military pilots carried out suicide attack campaigns in which they used their aircraft as weapons by aiming their aircraft at US military vessels and military bases.[48] To cause harm to US military infrastructure, the military aircraft and their pilots took the role of torpedoes.[49] From a functional point of view, civil aircraft can also be used as weapons to conduct an "armed attack" that reaches a certain scale and effect. An example of an armed attack carried out with a civil aircraft is the terrorist attack of 11 September 2001 in New York. The ICAO Assembly strongly condemned these terrorist attacks and declared that using "civil aircraft as weapons of destruction" constitutes a violation of international law.[50] Moreover, the Security Council characterized the 9/11 terrorist attacks in Resolution 1368 (2001) as a "threat to peace and security", and further recognized in the Preamble of the same resolution "the inherent right of individual or collective self-defence in accordance with the Charter."[51] The inherent right to self-defence against armed attacks involving civil aircraft was additionally reaffirmed by the Security Council in Resolution 1373 (2001).[52] Likewise, the Statement of NATO labelled the terrorist attacks as an attack that validates to resort to the

45 UNGA Res 39/11 (12 November 1984) UN Doc A/RES/39/11.

46 Humphrey Waldock, *The Regulation of the Use of Force by Individual States in International Law* (Collected Course 1952) 496–497.

47 On the discussion whether a device that is intended for peaceful purpose may qualify as a weapon, see David Koplow, 'Legal Aspects of the Use of Nuclear Explosive Devices in Planetary Defence' in Irmgard Marboe & Cordula Panosch (eds), *Legal Aspects pf Planetary Defence* (2021 Brill Nijhoff) 233, 234.

48 Emiko Ohnuki-Tierney, *Kamikaze Diaries: Reflections of Japanese Student Soldiers* (Chicago University Press 2006).

49 The tokkotai pilot Wada Minoru wrote in his diary: "If human torpedoes must appear in Japan (…) there is no other group of people but us who would become pilots." See Emiko Ohnuki-Tierney, *Kamikaze, Cherry Blossoms, and Nationalisms* (University of Chicago Press 2002) 228.

50 ICAO Assembly Res, Doc 9848, VII-1, 'Declaration on Misuse of Civil Aircraft as Weapons of Destruction and Other Terrorist Acts Involving Civil Aviation'.

51 UNSC Res 1368 (12 September 2001).

52 UNSC Res 1373 (28 September 2001).

right to self-defence.[53] In general, civil aircraft may be used as a weapon for an armed attack that reaches the scale and effect necessary to resort to self-defence to counter the attack.[54]

The notion of an armed attack is difficult to determine due to its complexity. The International Court of Justice elaborates in the *Nicaragua Case* that "it seems dangerous to define unnecessarily strictly the conditions for lawful self-defence, so as to leave a large area where both a forcible response to force is forbidden, and yet the United Nations employment of force, which was intended to fill that gap, is absent."[55] This makes it also *a fortiori* difficult to assess the role of ADIZs in relation to the right of self-defence. The exact meaning of armed attack remains contested and a strict understanding of the right to self-defence seems not to be accepted by States.[56] Nevertheless, in support of the argumentation that civil aircraft may indeed be used as a weapon serves the Beijing Convention which includes the criminalization of an act of using civil aircraft in service as a weapon.[57] When the aircraft intends to enter national airspace and it is not clear whether it is used as a weapon the issue of anticipatory self-defence arises. Before reaching airspace above sovereign territory, it is not yet clear whether the aircraft in question may be used for an armed attack. It thus needs to comply with the ADIZ's identification procedures to avoid being intercepted.[58] Non-compliance may result in the use of force, namely the interception of the aircraft or even more drastically the shot down of the aircraft before it reaches national airspace.[59] ADIZs are thus a measure to predict an armed attack.[60]

53 NATO Press Release, 12 September 2001.

54 Robin Geiß, 'Civil Aircraft as Weapons of Large-Scale Destruction: Countermeasures, Article 3bis of the Chicago Convention, and the Newly Adopted German "Luftsicherheitsgesetz"' (2005) 27 Mich J Int'l L 246.

55 *Nicaragua Case* (1986), Dis. Op. Judge Jennings para. 211.

56 Ibid 211.

57 Jiefang Huang, 'Security Regulations' in *Routledge Handbook of Public Aviation Law* (2016) 149, 150; See also, ICAO Res A33–1, 'Declaration on Misuse of Civil Aircraft as Weapons of Destruction and other Terrorist Acts Involving Civil Aviation'.

58 In particular aircraft inbound to the US national airspace will cross the US ADIZ and must upon entering the zone file a flight plan, see US Far Part 99.

59 US Air Traffic Procedures, Chapter 5, Section 6, 5-6-2 (e) "Pilots of aircraft that do not adhere to the procedures in the national security requirements for aircraft operations contained in this section may be intercepted, and/or detained and interviewed by federal, state, or local law enforcement or other government personnel."

60 Woon J Lee, 'Tension in the Air: The Air Defense Identification Zones on the East China Sea' (2014) 7 J E Asia & Int'l 278.

2 Anticipatory Self-Defence Targeting Civil and Military Aircraft

ADIZs are not the response to an armed attack; they anticipate the attack. The use of an aircraft in order to launch an attack shall be halted and repelled and the non-compliance with the identification obligation is for the concerned State reason enough to use force in the form of interception.[61] The role of ADIZs is to identify the potential harmful conduct of an armed attack with an aircraft. For that purpose, any aircraft, national as well as foreign, civil as well as military, needs to submit details on their identification the moment they enter the defence zone. Prior to the aircraft's entry into national airspace, it is uncertain whether the aircraft in question is being utilized for an armed attack and States may adopt a defensive measures to mitigate the risk of becoming the target of an armed attack. The aircraft thus needs to comply with the ADIZ's identification procedures to avoid interception.[62]

The notion of "if an armed attack occurs" becomes particularly relevant if interpreted flexibly as it may allow for anticipatory self-defence.[63] The question of the legality of anticipatory self-defence is highly controversial and sparks plenty of doctrinal discussion.[64] One view submits that the textual interpretation of Art. 51 UN-Charter leaves no room open for anticipatory self-defence.[65] Yet it would not be plausible to ask States not to react to an attack in preparation. This understanding is also in line with Art. 31 VCLT as an interpretation should not be "manifestly absurd or unreasonable".[66]

61 Ibid 278; The notion of halting and repelling an attack is also discussed under the requirement of proportionality, see *Nicaragua Case* (1986), Sep. Op. Judge Ago 69.

62 In particular aircraft inbound to the US national airspace will cross the US ADIZ and must upon entering the zone file a flight plan, see US Far Part 99. US Air Traffic Procedures, Chapter 5, Section 6, 5-6-2 (e) "Pilots of aircraft that do not adhere to the procedures in the national security requirements for aircraft operations contained in this section may be intercepted, and/or detained and interviewed by federal, state, or local law enforcement or other government personnel."

63 *Nicaragua Case* (1986), Dis. Op. Judge Schwebel 347–348.

64 Michael Bothe, 'Terrorism and the Legality of Pre-emptive Force' (2003) 14 EJIL 22; Oliver Corten, *The Law against War* (OUP 2010); Dimitri Kolesnik, 'The Development of the Right to Self-Defence' in William Butler (ed), *The Non-Use of Force in International Law* (Brill 1989); Michael Reisman & Andrea Armstrong, 'The Past and Future of the Claim of Preemptive Self-Defense' (2006) 100 AJIL 525.

65 Oliver Corten, *The Law against War* (OUP 2010) 406 mentioning that neither the UN-Charter nor any other documents mentions the concept of anticipatory self-defence. Also, Dimitri Kolesnik, 'The Development of the Right to Self-Defence' in William Butler (ed), *The Non-Use of Force in International Law* (Brill 1989) 153–55.

66 Marco Roscini, 'Threats of Armed Force and Contemporary International Law' (2007) 54 Netherland Int'l L Rev 273.

Anticipatory self-defence knows two sub categories, namely pre-emptive self-defence and preventive self-defence.[67] According to the famous *Webster* formula, a State may only act pre-emptively if "the necessity of self-defence was instant, overwhelming, and leaving no choice of means, and no moment for deliberation."[68] Some authors propose that if an attack is objectively verifiable and imminent, then pre-emptive self-defence is permissible.[69] The phrase "if an armed attack occurs" suggests that the attack is presently taking place or about to take place.[70] If the attack is, however, only a possible threat in the future, then self-defence is prohibited.[71] For some commentators, self-defence is also allowed in a situation of a latent threat which is discussed under the notion of preventive self-defence.[72] The concept of preventive self-defence, however, is generally rejected as the risk of unilateral actions negatively impacting the global order is too high.[73] The unilateral exercise of preventive self-defence against latent threats in the future is thus unlawful.[74] Often these notions are not applied consistently and uniformly or lack a precise definition,[75] as shown in the example of the United States and its 2002 National Security Strategy.[76]

---

67 Michael Wood, 'The Caroline Incident -1873' in Tom Ruys, Oliver Corten & Alexandra Hofer (eds), *The Use of Force in International Law: A Case-Based Approach* (OUP 2018).

68 Matthew Waxman, 'The 'Caroline' Affair in the Evolving International Law of Self-Defense' (28 August 2018) https://www.lawfareblog.com/caroline-affair (accessed 29 November 2022).

69 Michael Bothe, 'Terrorism and the Legality of Pre-emptive Force' (2003) 14 EJIL 229, 231–232; Jackson Maogoto, 'New Frontiers, Old Problems: The War on Terror and the Notion of Anticipating the Enemy' (2004) 51 NILR 16, 17; Yoram Dinstein, *War, Aggression and Self-Defence* (2nd edn, Cambridge University Press 2012) 165, 166 saying that anticipatory self-defence is a rule of customary international law.

70 Karl Zemanek, 'Armed Attack' in *Max Planck Encyclopedias of Public International Law* (OUP 2013) para. 4.

71 Michael Bothe, 'Terrorism and the Legality of Pre-emptive Force' (2003) 14 EJIL 229, 231–232.

72 Ruth Wedgewood, 'Unilateral Action in the UN System' (2000) 11 EJIL 355; Michael Reisman & Andrea Armstrong, 'The Past and Future of the Claim of Preemptive Self-Defense' (2006) 100 AJIL 525; Ruth Wedgwood, 'The Fall of Saddam Hussein: Security Council Mandates and Preemptive Self-Defense' (2003) 97 AJIL 584.

73 UNGA Res A/59/565, 'A More Secure World: Our Shared Responsibility Report of the Secretary-General's High-level Panel on Threats, Challenges and Change' (2 December 2004) para. 188; NAM 2006/Doc.1, '14th Summit of Heads of State or Government of the Non-Aligned Movement' (16. September 2006, Havana, Cuba) at para. 22.5.

74 Ralph Janik, *International Law and the Use of Force- Cases and Materials* (Routledge 2019) 95.

75 Christopher Greenwood, 'Self-defence' in *Max Planck Encyclopaedias of Public International Law* (OUP 2011) 42.

76 Also known as Bush Doctrine, see Christian Henderson, 'The Bush Doctrine: from Theory to Practice' (2004) 9 J Conflict & Sec L 3; See also, Archive of the Website of the

The United States of America particularly advocated the right to anticipatory self-defence in the 2002 National Security Strategy in response to the terrorist attack of 11 September 2001. The section 'Prevent Our Enemies from Threatening Us, Our Allies, and Our Friends with Weapons of Mass Destruction' first draws a connection between pre-emption and imminent threats by stating that:

> for centuries, international law recognized that nations need not suffer an attack before they can lawfully take action to defend themselves against forces that present an imminent danger of attack. Legal scholars and international jurists often conditioned the legitimacy of preemption on the existence of an *imminent* threat – most often a visible mobilization of armies, navies, and air forces preparing to attack.[77]

As the name of section V indicates, even a mere threat is sufficient for the United States of America to take action under the right to self-defence. Moreover, under section III, 'Strengthen Alliances to Defeat Global Terrorism and Work to Prevent Attacks Against Us and Our Friends' the idea of identifying a threat and acting promptly to prevent the threat from reaching the US borders is formulated. Here the notions of acting pre-emptively and preventively are used in the same line. Terrorist attacks shall be disrupted and destroyed by:

> defending the United States, the American people, and our interests at home and abroad by identifying and destroying the threat before it reaches our borders. While the United States will constantly strive to enlist the support of the international community, we will not hesitate to act alone, if necessary, to exercise our right of self-defences by *acting preemptively* against such terrorists, *to prevent* them from doing harm against our people and our country.[78]

The text of the strategy then further combines preemptive actions to prevent hostile acts and anticipatory actions for defence. It states that:

> The United States has long maintained the option of preemptive actions to counter a sufficient threat to our national security. The greater the threat, the greater is the risk of inaction – and the more compelling the

White House, https://georgewbush-whitehouse.archives.gov/nsc/nss/2002/ (accessed 13 November 2021).

77 Ibid.

78 Ibid.

> case for taking *anticipatory action* to defend ourselves, even if uncertainty remains as to the time and place of the enemy's attack. To forestall or *prevent* such hostile acts by our adversaries, the United States will, if necessary, *act preemptively*.[79]

In 2004, the UN Secretary General Kofi Anan presented the report 'A More Secure World: Our Shared Responsibility Report of the Secretary-General's High-level Panel on Threats, Challenges and Change' which contained 101 recommendations including a statement on the issue of pre-emptive self-defence and the role of the Security Council. The report generally acknowledges the legality of pre-emptive self-defence under the requirement of immanency, necessity and proportionality.[80] Yet the report remarks on preventive self-defence that "if there are good arguments for preventive military action, with good evidence to support them, they should be put to the Security Council, which can authorize such action if it chooses to."[81] A restrictive interpretation of Art. 51 UN-Charter, therefore, does not grant preventive self-defence.[82] Moreover, the notion of preventive self-defence was categorically rejected by the Non-Aligned Movement, and its 116 Member States.[83] The unilateral exercise of preventive self-defence against latent threats in the future is thus unlawful.[84] Only the Security Council can authorise the preventive use of force.[85]

2.1 *The Distinction between a Situation of Preventive Self-Defence and a Situation of Pre-emptive Self-Defence*

The imprecise language in the terminology of pre-emptive self-defence is the spark of disagreement on the lawfulness of the use of force in self-defence in advance. Some authors rely on the notion of an armed attack to determine the lawfulness,[86] yet others solely depend the legality of pre-emptive self-defence

---

79 Ibid.

80 UNGA Res A/59/565 'A More Secure World: Our Shared Responsibility Report of the Secretary-General's High-level Panel on Threats, Challenges and Change' (2 December 2004) para. 188.

81 Ibid para. 190.

82 Ibid para. 191.

83 14th Summit of Heads of State or Government of the Non-Aligned Movement (16. September 2006, Havana Cuba) at para 22.5 "oppose and condemn (…) the adoption of the doctrine of pre-emptive attack."

84 Ralph Janik, *International Law and the Use of Force- Cases and Materials* (Routledge 2019) 95.

85 Ashley S Deeks, 'Taming the Doctrine of Pre-Emption' in Marc Weller (ed), *The Oxford Handbook of the Use of Force in International Law* (OSAIL 2015) 668.

86 Oliver Corten, *The Law against War* (OUP 2010).

on matters of proportionality.[87] It is also difficult to define a situation of pre-emptive self-defence due to the dearth of actual State practice. As a result, the methodological approach that relies stronger on the treaty language comes to a different conclusion than the approach, which focuses on the different types of State practice.[88]

The discussion of pre-emptive and preventive self-defence revolves around the threshold of the threat that needs to be reached in order to qualify as an imminent armed attack.[89] Even though Art. 51 UN-Charter does not explicitly mention "threat", the UN-Charter is familiar with the concept of threat in Art. 2 (4), stating that "all Member States shall refrain in their international relations from the threat (...) of force." In its *Nuclear Weapons Advisory Opinion* the International Court of Justice elaborates on the prohibition of the threat or use of force which has to be considered in the light of other relevant provisions of the Charter, including the right to self-defence.[90] Likewise, the right of self-defence can be considered in light of the prohibition of the threat or use of force. The interpretation of threat of an armed attack may thus be interpreted by referring to the term "threat" in Art. 2 (4) UN-Charter to distinguish between a preventive and a pre-emptive situation of self-defence.

The definition of a 'threat of force' has received far less consideration in legal writings than the phrase 'use of force'.[91] This is due to the fact that in most cases the use of force followed the threat so disputes focused only on the use instead of the threat of force.[92] A threat of force can be defined as "an explicit or implicit promise of a future and unlawful use of armed force against another state, the realization of which depends on the aggressor's will."[93] As mentioned before, the notion of armed attack can be interpreted as covering "the most grave form of the use of force."[94] Similarly, any threat of force that allows for

87 Ralph Janik, *International Law and the Use of Force: Cases and Materials* (Routledge 2019) 104.

88 Sean D Murphy, 'The Doctrine of Preemptive Self-Defence' (2005) 50 Vill L Rev 720–721.

89 See also UNGA Res A/59/565 para. 189 which discusses "proximate threats" and at para. 193 emphasizing the role of the Security Council for taking actions against threats in a more distant future.

90 *Nuclear Weapons Advisory Opinion* para. 38.

91 Oliver Dörr & Albrecht Randelzhofer, 'Purpose and Principles, Art 2(4)' in Simma B et al (eds), *The Charter of the United Nations: A Commentary, Volume I* (3rd edn, OUP 2012) 217.

92 Ibid, mentioning the piling up of armaments and the shaping of alliances; James Green & Francis Grimal, 'The Threat of Force as an Action in Self-Defence under International Law' (2011) 44 Vanderbilt Journal of Transnational Law 285.

93 Marco Roscini, 'Threats of Armed Force' (2007) 54 Netherland Int'l L Rev 276.

94 *Nicaragua Case* (1986) para. 191; *Oil Platforms Case* para. 51.

the right to self-defence only includes threats of "the most grave form" of the use of force.[95] *Green* and *Grimal* identified three different categories of threats:

1. An expressively or implicitly communicated threat, where the threat is directed towards a specific reaction on the part of the target State and failure to comply will result in the use of force;
2. The conclusion of a defensive treaty, whereas this practice does not amount to an unlawful use of threat;
3. An implicit threat.[96]

With regard to the distinction between preventive and pre-emptive self-defence, any response to the first category of threat may be considered a lawful use of pre-emptive self-defence, as this kind of threat is sufficiently imminent. The second category is part of the unlawful exercise of preventive self-defence since it qualifies as a "latent" threat. The third category of an implicit threat cannot so easily be assigned to either preventive or pre-emptive self-defence, as it comprises certain actions that can be perceived as a threat.[97] For example, the build-up of troops along the border of a neighbouring State may qualify as an unlawful threat.[98] Military routine missions or military manoeuvres as part of training missions, in contrast, are no implicit threats.[99] The standard for an implicit threat, which gives rise to the right to self-defence, requires a causal link between a threat and the behaviour of the target State. If the threat is not directed against the State claiming a right to self-defence, then the causal link is not fulfilled. Secondly, it is not sufficient that the State reacts or believes it is reacting to a presumed threat of force. As stated by Judge *Weeramarty* in his Dissenting Opinion on the *Legality of the Threat or Use of Nuclear Weapons*, it additionally needs a "corresponding conduct" and not only the perceived "intent" of the aggressor.[100] Thirdly, reactions to implicit threats need to be in line with the requirements of necessity and proportionality, which is essential to establish the lawfulness of any reaction in self-defence. Proportionality

---

95 Terry Gill, 'The Law of Armed Attack in the Context of the Nicaragua Case' (1988) 1 Yearbook of Int'l L 30, 35.

96 James Green & Francis Grimal, 'The Threat of Force as an Action in Self-Defence under International Law' (2011) 44 Vanderbilt Journal of Transnational Law 11–13.

97 Ibid 12.

98 David Harris, *Cases and Materials on International Law* (7th edn, Sweeth & Maxwell 2010) 725, describing the situation the build-up of troops by the United Kingdom at the Kuwait border.

99 On the debate of military naval mission see chapter 6, 3.2.2 of this book. On the aspect of military routine missions on land see the Report of the Independent International Fact Finding Mission on the Conflict in Georgia (2009), 232.

100 *Legality of the Threat or Use of Nuclear Weapons*, Dis. Op. Judge Weeramarty 541.

cannot be sufficiently assessed in case of vague or future threats.[101] Therefore, a lawful situation of pre-emptive self-defence exists when an imminent armed attack, which causes significant harm, is compellingly proved, and thus requires immediate action that shall halt or forestall the imminent armed attack.

2.2 *The Imminence of an Aerial Attack*

The current stand of the doctrinal debate focuses on the requirement of imminence in relation to the existence and scale of the armed attack or the threat of the armed attack to materialize. However, this approach is accompanied by several problems, which prove to be the main obstacle when it comes to defining a situation of pre-emptive self-defence. Neither the UN-Charter nor the equivalent provision of self-defence in the ILC Articles on Responsibility for Internationally Wrongful Acts mentions in its plain treaty text "imminent". "Imminent" is thus regarded as a prerequisite established by customary international law. Particularly the aspect of imminence becomes relevant when discussing pre-emptive self-defence as it refers to the temporal scope of self-defence in response to an attack and the manifestation of a threat of an attack.[102] Imminence has to satisfy three aspects: there has to be an impending attack, a reasonable level of certainty that the attack will occur or occurs, and the attack needs to be specific and identifiable.[103] *Bethlehem* proposes as concretising criteria for an imminent armed attack the nature and immediacy of the threat, the probability of an attack, the likely scale of the attack and the injury, loss, or damage likely to result therefrom in the absence of mitigating action, and the likelihood that there will be other opportunities to undertake effective action in self-defence that may be expected to cause less serious collateral injury, loss, or damage.[104]

The conceptual purpose of imminence is to distinguish between permissible pre-emptive self-defence and prohibited preventive self-defence.[105] The

---

101 Marco Roscini, 'Threats of Armed Force' (2007) 54 Netherland Int'l L Rev 274.

102 Terry Gill, 'The Temporal Dimension of Self-Defence: Anticipation, Pre-emption, Prevention and Immediacy' (2006) 11(3) Journal of Conflict & Security Law 361; Michael Wood, 'The Caroline Incident -1873' in Tom Ruys, Oliver Corten &Alexandra Hofer (eds), *The Use of Force in International Law: A Case-Based Approach* (OUP 2018) 13.

103 Noam Lubell, 'The Problem of Imminence in an Uncertain World' in Marc Weller (ed) *The Oxford Handbook of the Use of Force in International Law* (OSAIL 2015) 718.

104 Daniel Bethlehem, 'Principles Relevant to the Scope of a State's Right of Self-Defense against an Imminent or Actual Armed Attack by Nonstate Actors' (2012) 106 AJIL 6.

105 See for a general discussion on the purpose of imminence, Marko Milanovic, 'What is an Imminent Armed Attack? A Hopefully Helpful Hypo' (12 January 2017) www.ejiltalk.org

requirement of imminence differs from requirement of necessity. Necessity in relation to the inherent right to self-defence means that no reasonable peaceful alternatives to force are available, whereas imminence relates to the temporal scope of the attack,[106] as well as non-temporal elements of sufficient proof of the attack to occur.[107]

It seems uncontroversial to assume that an aerial attack is imminent even before the first bombs drop.[108] However, when is the exact moment, the aerial attack has begun and thus allows for pre-emptive self-defence? The example of the attacks on Pearl Harbour lead some commentators to suggest that the aerial attack by Japan on the United States did not begin when the first aircraft reached Pearl Harbour but when the Japanese fleet left Japan with orders to launch the attack some three weeks earlier.[109] *Dinstein* draws the scenario in which he assesses the legality of interceptive self-defence by assuming the hypothetical situation in which the Japanese carrier striking force on its way to its point of attack got intercepted and sunk by the US Pacific fleet before any Japanese military aircraft were bound to Pearl Harbour.[110] *Dinstein* concludes that the United States would not be responsible for the opening of fire but that Japan started the armed attack even before the first shot was fired.[111] The criterion introduced by *Dinstein* is that the other side has committed itself to an armed attack in an "ostensibly irrevocable way."[112] Yet, the notion of immanency is difficult to define and tends to blur the boundaries between the ideas of imminent threats, latent threats, and implicit threats.[113] Particularly, when it comes to implicit threats a reasonable interpretation of information available at the moment of decision is necessary.[114] Therefore, it is necessary to provide

/what-is-an-imminent-armed-attack-a-hopefully-helpful-hypo/ (accessed 18 February 2023).

106 Terry Gill, 'The Temporal Dimension of Self-Defence: Anticipation, Pre-emption, Prevention and Immediacy' (2006) 11(3) Journal of Conflict & Security Law 361.

107 Malcom N Shaw, *International Law* (9th edn, Cambridge University Press 2021) stating at 822 that a State that claims that an armed attack is about to occur has thus the burden of proof.

108 Christopher Greenwood, 'Self-Defence' in *Max Planck Encyclopedias of Public International Law* (OUP 2011) para. 42.

109 Ibid para. 42. However, in the case of Pearl Harbour it was in fact Japan who relied on the right to self-defence and justified the attacks as a preventive measures to diminish a threat of attack by the USA, see Oliver Corten , *The Law against War* (OUP 2010) 413.

110 Yoram Dinstein Y, *War, Aggression and Self-Defence* (3rd edn, Cambridge University Press 2001) 172.

111 Ibid 172.

112 Ibid 173.

113 Oliver Corten, *The Law against War* (OUP 2010) 413.

114 Ibid 173.

sufficient evidence of the occurrence of the attack in order to achieve a balance between the interests of States in avoiding an attack and the risk of abuse.[115]

As regards the determination of the imminent attack, a comparison may also be drawn to the powers of the Security Council to determine a "threat to peace". The concept of "threat to peace" in general includes impeding or already initiated armed conflicts but also implies preventative action well beyond situations of imminent attacks.[116] The extent to which the Security Council is empowered to adopt measures of conflict prevention and action on generalized threats rather than particular conflicts remains a matter of contention.[117] In the context of a Security Council whose legitimacy is open to question[118] and whose capacity to identify impending or imminent attacks is disputed,[119] it is arguably even more critical that one State may subjectively determine a future attack. The problem connected with pre-emptive self-defence, in general, is the State resorting to force either controls the available facts, or timely and objective fact-finding mechanisms are not available.[120] The dangers of the subjective assessment of an armed attack can be seen in the shooting down of the civilian Iran Airbus by the *USS Vincennes* in 1988, where the United States mistakenly assumed an imminent attack by a hostile Iranian military aircraft.[121]

2.2.1 The Problem of Identifying an Imminent Aerial Armed Attack in State Practice

Examples of the use of force against civil aircraft can be found on various occasions. The following list provides a non-exhaustive overview of the use of force against civil aircraft. Only one incident was successfully justified by claiming a right to self-defence. These incidents mainly show that forceful measures were based on an *ex-ante* assessment, which in the end, turned out to be erroneous.

---

115 Malcom N Shaw, *International Law* (9th edn, Cambridge University Press 2021) 822.

116 Nico Krisch, 'Ch.VII Action with Respect to Threats to the Peace, Breaches of the Peace, and Acts of Aggression, Article 39' in Bruno Simma et al (eds), *The Charter of the United Nations: A Commentary, Volume 2* (OUP 2012) 1279.

117 Ibid, 1279.

118 Martin Binder & Monika Heupel, 'The Legitimacy of the UN Security Council: Evidence from Recent General Assembly Debates' (2015) 59 Int'l Studies Quarterly 247, 248.

119 Justin Morris & Nicholas J Wheeler, 'The Security Council's Crisis of Legitimacy and the Use of Force' (2007) 44 Int'l Politics 219.

120 Antonio Cassese, *International Law* (2nd edn OUP 2005) 357 (the 3rd edition of this book does not refer to this aspect anymore).

121 Christine Gray, 'The Use of Force and the International Legal Order' in Malcom D Evans (ed), *International* Law (5th edn, OUP 2018) 612; Paula Fischer, *Das Irrtumsrisiko bei den Ausnahmen des völkerrechtlichen Gewaltverbotes* (Nomos 2020) 188ff.

2.2.1.1 *Israel-Bulgaria Incident (1955)*

In 1955, an Israeli operated airliner was shot down by Bulgarian Anti-Air Defense fighters over Bulgarian territory.[122] Bulgaria, inter alia, alleged that it only fired once the aircraft refused to obey orders to land and due to the fact that it was unable to identify the aircraft.[123] Israel strongly condemned the shooting down of the aircraft and subsequently notified the incident to ICAO.[124] Israel also requested the ICJ to decide the issue, however, the Court found that it was without jurisdiction to adjudicate upon the dispute brought before it.[125] The General Assembly adopted a resolution regarding the incident in which it called upon all States "to take the necessary measures to avoid such incidents."[126] Also, the US condemned the incident as a "grave violation of accepted principles of international law"[127] and later initiated proceedings against Bulgaria at the International Court of Justice.[128] Bulgaria admitted that the organs of the Anti-Air Defense displayed haste and did not take all necessary steps to force the aircraft to land.[129] Bulgaria's statement indicates the reasons why it did not justify the shooting down with the right to self-defence namely because of the missing requirement of necessity.

2.2.1.2 *Israel-Libya Incident (1973)*

A Libyan airliner was shot down by Israeli interceptors on route from Tripoli to Cairo over the Israeli occupied Sinai peninsula in 1973.[130] Israel justified its actions by claiming that it was a matter of defence of its national security interests and that "Israel acted in accord with international law."[131] The delegate of Egypt named the shooting down "a flagrant and serious threat to the safety of

---

122 *Case Concerning the Aerial Incident of July 27th 1955 (Israel v Bulgaria)* [1957] ICJ Rep 127.

123 Belinda Hartzenberg, *The Rights and Obligations of a State under Article 3bis of the Chicago Convention pursuant to an Intrusion of its sovereign Air Space by Civilian Aircraft* (LL.M. Thesis 2019) 27.

124 Eugene Sochor, *The Politics of International Aviation* (Springer 1991) 133.

125 Ibid 146.

126 UNGA Res/927 'Question of the safety of commercial aircraft flying in the vicinity of, or inadvertently crossing, international frontiers' (14 December 1955).

127 Andreas Knauth, 'Bulgarian Destruction of El Al Airliner' (1955) 22 J Air L & Comm 356.

128 *Case Concerning the Aerial Incident of 27 July 1955 (United States of America v Bulgaria)* [1960] ICJ Rep 146; Memorial submitted by the Government of the United States of America, at 167. The proceeding was in the end discontinued and removed from the List by an Order of 30 May 1960.

129 Ibid, citing the Bulgarian Home Service at 178.

130 ICAO Council Res, Doc 9790 (4 June 1973).

131 William J Hughes, 'Aerial Intrusions by Civil Airliners and the Use of Force' (1980) 45 J Air L & Comm 611.

international civil aviation" and particularly highlighted that there "had been no warning before the attack."[132] Also, the representatives of the non-aligned Countries strongly condemned these "unwarranted acts of aggression."[133] The ICAO Assembly later likewise condemned Israel's action and emphasized that "this action affects and jeopardizes the safety of international civil aviation."[134]

2.2.1.3 *KAL Flight 007 Incident (1983)*

In 1983, the Soviet Union shot down the Korean aircraft KAL flight 007, which had strayed off into Soviet airspace.[135] During the Security Council's session, the vast majority of the Member States' representatives condemned the shooting down of the aircraft.[136] The President of the Republic of Korea, pointed out that "[t]here is no provision in international law that justifies the use of force against an unarmed civilian airliner under any circumstances;"[137] the US delegate stated that, next to the general rule of the prohibition of the use of force, there are specific rules of international air law, which "do not include shooting down the civil airliner;"[138] the Japanese delegate spoke of "unrestrained use of force" and that the shooting down is "totally unjustifiable for whatever reason and should be strongly condemned;"[139] the Canadian delegate elaborated that "[t]here can be no justification, whatever might have been the circumstances."[140] In contrast, the delegate of the Soviet Union raised the point, that the aircraft could not be identified, that it did not react to radio

132 ICAO, Doc 9061 A19-Res., Min. (Nineteenth Session – Extraordinary; 27 February – 2 March 1973) 31, 32.

133 Non-Aligned Countries, meeting in New York on 21 February 1973.

134 ICAO, Doc 9790 'Assembly Resolutions in Force' (5 October 2001) 1–27.

135 Farooq Hassan, 'A Legal Analysis of the Shooting of Korean Airlines Flight 007 by the USSR' (1984) 49 J Air L & Comm 555; ICAO Doc Ref. LE 4/19.4 93/68 (1993) including *the Report of the Completion of the ICAO Fact-Finding Investigation* (June 1993) on the destruction of the Korean Air Lines Flight 007; also 'Documents Concerning the Korean Air Lines Incident' (1983) 22 ILM 1109.

136 Gerald FitzGerald, 'The Use of Force against Civil Aircraft: The Aftermath of the KAL Flight 007 Incident' (1984) 38 Canadian Yearbook Int'l L 292.

137 UNSC, UN Doc S/PV/.2470 (2470th Meeting, 2 September 1983) para. 15.

138 Ibid para. 38.

139 Ibid para. 58, 59 and at para. 62 stating "the action of the Soviet Union can in no way be justified."

140 Ibid para. 79. Likewise, the Australian delegate at para. 95; the delegate of the Netherlands at para. 110; the delegate of Pakistan at para. 117; the French delegate at para. 124; the UK delegate at para. 133; the delegate of Zaire at para. 144; the delegate of New Zealand at para. 150; and the delegate of the Democratic Republic of Germany at para. 155.

signals, and that the Soviet anti-air defence aircraft first fired warning shots.[141] China abstained from making a declaration.[142] In 1984, ICAO adopted a resolution in which it recognized "that such use of armed force against international civil aviation is incompatible with the norms governing international behaviour and elementary considerations of humanity (...)."[143] Later in the same year, the ICAO Assembly unanimously adopted Art. 3bis Chicago Convention regulating interception and the use of weapons against civil aircraft.[144]

2.2.1.4 USS *Vincennes Incident (1988)*

In 1988, the Iranian civil aircraft, Air Flight 655, was shot down by the warship USS Vincennes duc to a failure of the Vincennes's computer and tracking systems to properly identify the aircraft as a civilian.[145] The USA claimed that the shooting down was due to a reasonable error and still acted in (mistaken) self-defence, and the use of force was justified and lawful.[146] During an open debate at the Security Council's meeting, Iran heavily condemned the shooting down and in particular raised the point that the incident happened outside of the US' national airspace and that "flights inside the flight information region of a country can be directed only by the civil aviation authorities of that country."[147] Moreover, Iran discarded the US's argument of acting in self-defence and elaborated that the shooting down is a "clear violation of the principle of non-use of force.[148] In its Resolution 616 (1988), the Security Council only stressed the need for "a full explanation of the facts of the incident based upon impartial investigation", but remained silent on the matter of

141 Ibid para. 46; the USSR delegate further declared that the intrusion of soviet airspace was a "pre-planned act" by the United States of America and in fact a "dirty game of anti-Soviet policy" and that the US Administration "is looking for yet another pretext to justify its irresponsible policy in the preparation for nuclear war", at para. 48, 49, 52.

142 Ibid para. 127–130.

143 ICAO Doc. S/i5g66/Rev. i

144 Brian Foont, 'Shooting down Civilian Aircraft: Is there an International Law?' (2007) 72 J Air L & Comm 709.

145 Alexander Cockburn & Ken Silverstein, 'The System that Brought Down Flight 655' (1988) HARPERS 64 https://harpers.org/archive/1988/09/the-system-that-brought-down-flight-655/; ICAO Doc AN 13/4.3–897, *Report of ICAO Fact-Finding Investigation: Destruction of Iran Air Airbus A300 in the Vicinity of Qeshm Island, Islamic Republic of Iran on 3 July 1988* (1988); also 'International Civil Aviation Organization: Resolution And Report Concerning The Destruction Of Iran Air Airbus On July 3, 1988' (1989) 28 ILM 896.

146 UNSC, UN Doc S/PV.2818 (3 July 1988) 56.

147 Ibid 22, 23.

148 Ibid 28–30, 32 "What was the USS Vincennes defending itself against? Against the scheduled flight of an Air Bus jetliner filled with 290 passengers and crew, flying within an internationally recognized civilian airway while ascending to the prescribed altitude?."

self-defence and the use of force against civil aircraft in general.[149] Iran later instituted proceedings at the ICJ and once again emphasized that the US illegally invoked the right to self-defence.[150] Although on previous occasions the ICAO Council had condemned the actions of members who had shot down civil aircraft, it took no such action in this case.[151]

2.2.1.5 *Brother of the Rescue Incident (1996)*

In 1996, two civilian aircraft of the Brother to the Rescue mission were shot down in international airspace by the Cuban Air Force, who pursued the aircraft after they penetrated Cuban Airspace.[152] The ICAO Council adopted a resolution in which it condemned the shooting.[153] By 13-0-2 Vote, the Security Council likewise condemned in it Resolution 1067 (1996) the use of weapons against civil aircraft and called upon Cuba to comply with international law.[154] The Security Council used the same words as the ICAO Council in its resolution, namely that the use of weapons against civil aircraft in flight is "incompatible with elementary considerations of humanity, the rules of customary international law as codified in Art. 3bis of the Chicago Convention and standards and recommended practices set out in the annexes of the Convention."[155] The Security Council took the stance that the prohibition of the use of weapons against civil aircraft as enshrined in Art. 3bis Chicago Convention amounts to a rule of customary international law.

2.2.1.6 *Israel–Lebanon Incident (2001)*

On 24 May 2001, a Lebanese civilian aircraft was stolen by an unlicensed pilot who flew through a restricted military zone in Lebanon before illegally

---

149 UNSC Res 616 (20 July 1988).

150 *Case Concerning the Aerial Incident of 3 July 1988 (Islamic Republic of Iran v United States of America)* [1989] ICJ 132, Memorial of the Islamic Republic of Iran, 197ff. The proceedings were subsequently discontinued by Order of 22 February 1996.

151 After completion of the investigation, the ICAO Council adopted on 17 March 1989 a resolution in which it "deeply deplores the tragic incident which occurred as a consequence of events and errors in identification of the aircraft which resulted in the accidental destruction of an Iran Air airliner and the loss of 290 lives", see for reference ICAO Assembly, 'Minutes of the Seventieth Meeting', A27 -Min. P /7 29/9/89 (27 September 1989) 9.

152 Brian Foont, 'Shooting down Civilian Aircraft: Is there an International Law?' (2007) 72 J Air L & Comm 709.

153 ICAO Council Res, Doc/1996/509 (1 July 1996).

154 UNSC Res 1967 (26 July 1996).

155 UNSC Res 1967 (26 July 1996) point 6; and ICAO Council Res, Doc/1996/509 (1 July 1996) point 4.

entering Israeli airspace.[156] Israel established radio contact, made repeated efforts to communicate with the pilot and fired warning shots.[157] The pilot of the Cessna did not identify himself and refused to respond, leading to the assumption of a potential terrorist intent. Israel, therefore, decided to shoot down the Cessna. While Lebanon raised the incident as part of "Israel's aggression" at the 55th session of the General Assembly,[158] the matter remained unresolved.[159] Israel's use of force was not questioned by ICAO.[160] Due to the circumstances surrounding the incident, it is assumed that Israel lawfully shot down the aircraft.[161]

2.2.1.7 *Ukraine Incident* (2011)

In 2011, the aircraft Tupolev Tu-154 en-route from Israel to Siberia was shot down by Ukraine long-range surface-to-air missile. Ukraine first denied the incident but then later took responsibility for its actions.[162] Issues of self-defence did not arise.

2.2.1.8 *Malaysia Airline MH17 Incident* (2014)

Even though the shooting down of the 2014 Malaysia Airlines Flight MH17 on route from Amsterdam to Malaysia over Ukrainian territories in 2014 remarks one of the most tragic incidents in the 21st century, it will not be further discussed at this point as the issue of State responsibility remains uncertain and no State raised the justification of self-defence. [163] It appears that the situation

156 CNN, 'Israel shoots down Lebanese civil plane' (24 May 2001), available at http://edition.cnn.com/2001/WORLD/meast/05/24/israel.plane.02/index.html (accessed 8 January 2022).

157 Ibid.

158 UNGA, Res/55/959 S/2001/531, 'Letter dated 2001/05/29 from the Permanent Representative of Lebanon to the United Nations addressed to the Secretary-General' (29 May 2001).

159 UNSC, Press Release SC/7242 'Security Council Fails To Adopt Resolution On Middle East Situation, To Condemn Use Of Force, Encourage Monitoring Mechanism' (14 December 2001).

160 ICAO Doc 9958 encompasses all ICAO Assembly resolution in force as of October 2010 but no resolution was adopted regarding the shoot down of the Cessna in 2001.

161 Brian Foont, 'Shooting down Civilian Aircraft: Is there an International Law?' (2007) 72 J Air L & Comm 715.

162 Anatoliy Grytsenko, 'Political Irresponsibility and Lack of Transparency in Ukrainian Defence Reform' in Hans Boern et al (eds), *Civil-Military Relations in Europe* (Routledge 2006) 72.

163 Mark Gibney, 'The Downing of MH17: Russian Responsibility?' (2015) 15 Human Rights Law Review 169–178; Ewa Jaisuk et al, 'The responsibility of a State in the shooting down of Malaysian Airlines flight MH17' (2019) 43 Transport Research Procedia 113–118; Sigmar

can be similarly assessed as in the previous cases of a shooting down of a civilian aircraft due to an error.

2.2.1.9 *Ukraine–Iran Incident* (2020)

In 2020, the Ukrainian aircraft Flight PS752 was shot down over Iranian territory after Iranian armed forces mistakenly identified the airliner as a hostile target and 'unintentionally' shot it down.[164] The ICAO Council initiated an investigation following the incident without yet finishing the report.[165] The main reason for the shooting down of the aircraft was also the erroneous identification of the aircraft. A violation of Art. 3bis Chicago Convention can be assumed, as there was no indication of an imminent armed attack.

2.2.1.10 *Short Conclusion*

Even though some cases of the shooting down of aircraft were referred to the ICJ, States preferred to settle the dispute through negotiations. The majority of cases resulted in *ex gratia* payments by the responsible State without the State officially taking international responsibility.[166] A conclusion drawn from State practice shows that States failed to properly identify the aircraft, assumed an armed attack and based their decision to shoot down the aircraft on wrong assumptions.[167] States mostly did not intend to use force against civil aircraft but instead mistook them for military aircraft or for military aircraft in disguise of a civil aircraft. The international reaction also differed on the supposedly perpetrator. Particularly during the Cold War era, there appeared to be a certain bias in place. While the shoot-down of a civil aircraft by the Soviet Union was condemned by almost all States, the shoot-down by a US warship

---

Stadlmeier, 'The Shooting Down of the Malaysian Airlines Flight MH17' in *The Case of Crimea's Annexation under International Law* (Wladislaw Czaplinski et al 2017) 339–347.

164 The Times of Israel, 'Disastrous mistake': Iran admits it mistakenly downed Ukraine plane, killed 176' (11 January 2020) available at https://www.timesofisrael.com/iran-admits-it-unintentionally-shot-down-ukrainian-jetliner/ (accessed 8 January 2022).

165 'ICAO Council urges Iran to complete PS752 accident investigation Final Report' (6 November 2020), available at https://www.icao.int/Newsroom/Pages/ICAO-Council-urges-Iran-to-complete-PS752-accident-investigation-Final-Report.aspx; and 'Statement on Ukraine International Airlines Flight PS752' (8 January 2021) https://www.icao.int/Newsroom/Pages/Statement-on-Ukraine-International-Airlines-Flight-PS752.aspx (both accessed 8 January 2022).

166 Hamid Kazemi & Naser Asiabipourimani, 'Reparation of Aerial Accidents under International Law with Emphasize On 752 Ukrainian Flight' (2021) 24 Legal Research Quarterly 369.

167 Paula Fischer, *Das Irrtumsrisiko bei den Ausnahmen des völkerrechtlichen Gewaltverbotes* (Nomos 2020) 188ff.

only five years later sparked almost no negative reactions. While these cases are of some interest, they are almost irrelevant in the present context.[168] The position of the United States regarding the USS *Vincennes* incident also demonstrates that, despite an error in identifying the aircraft, the United States still asserted that its actions were justified in self-defence. In most cases, the shot down appeared *ex-post* not necessary and the prevailing State practice condemned the use of weapons against civil aircraft in general. In contrast, interception was perceived as the necessary initial step and appeared to be a reasonable alternative to the shot down.

It is also prudent to exercise caution, as it is beyond dispute that warships and military aircraft, when subjected to attack by foreign forces on the high seas or in international airspace respectively, have the right to defend themselves by resorting to military force.[169] The *Oil Platforms Case* demonstrates that even a single attack on a foreign ship outside its territorial waters may theoretically prompt the flag State's right to self-defence.[170] The same problem may also arise when the aim of the purported act of self-defence is a civil aircraft or commercial vessel. In the *Oil Platforms Case*, the ICJ further assessed the evidence regarding the firing of a missile on a commercial vessel.[171] This seems to support the view that even a single attack on a commercial vessel grants the flag State the right to self-defence.[172] However, another view posits that military force against commercial vessels and civil aircraft outside the territory of their home State cannot be equated with attacks on that State itself.

---

168 Charles D Hutchkinson, 'The Air Bridge Denial Program and the Shootdown of Civil Aircraft under International Law' (LL.M. Thesis 2004) 47.

169 Georg Nolte & Albrecht Randelzhofer, 'Ch.VII Action with Respect to Threats to the Peace, Breaches of the Peace, and Acts of Aggression' in Bruno Simma et al (eds), *The Charter of the United Nations: A Commentary, Volume 2* (OUP 2012) 1411.

170 *Oil Platforms Case* para. 72, "The Court does not exclude the possibility that the mining of a single military vessel might be sufficient to bring into play the 'inherent right of self-defence'". Yet in this aspect, the Court contradicted itself as he stated in para. 51 that the United States not only have to show that its actions were necessary and proportional, but also that "the platforms were a legitimate *military target* open to attack" (emphasis added); See also Art. 3(d) of the definition of aggression, UNGA Res 3314 (XXIX). For a critique on this judgement see William H Taft IV, 'Self-Defense and the Oil Platforms Decision' (2004) 29/2 Yale J Int'l L 295.

171 *Oil Platforms Case* para. 78.

172 Georg Nolte & Albrecht Randelzhofer, 'Ch. VII Action with Respect to Threats to the Peace, Breaches of the Peace, and Acts of Aggression' in Bruno Simma et al (eds), *The Charter of the United Nations: A Commentary, Volume 2* (OUP 2012) 1411; Natalino Ronzitti, 'The Expanding Law of Self-Defence' (2006) 11 J Conflict & Security L 350; Tom Ruys, *Armed Attack and Article 51 of the UN-Charter* (CUP 2010) 204–213.

Consequently, the State may not exercise the right to self-defence.[173] Thus, the Security Council's debate on the Israeli interception of a civilian Libyan aircraft within international airspace on 4 February 1986 was confined to the legal rules of international air law rather than to those pertaining to the use of force.[174] it is important to emphasise that the temporal scope of the discussion predates the terrorist attacks on the World Trade Centre and the subsequent paradigm shift in the debate on the right to self-defence involving non-state actors.[175] Considering the underlying idea of de-escalation and the prohibition of self-defence against self-defence,[176] the lawful use of force against a civil or military aircraft appears to be a challenging position. As *Dinstein* put it: "Under no circumstances can the actual use of force by both parties to a conflict be lawful simultaneously."[177]

2.2.2 The Standard of Proof for an "Imminent Armed Attack"

It is of the utmost importance to determine whether there is sufficient evidence on the threat to justify acting pre-emptively.[178] A State claiming the occurrence of an armed attack has the burden of proof.[179] To speak of a standard of proof in public international law is yet to some extent misleading. There is no uniform and specified standard applied by the International Court of Justice.[180] Instead, the threshold of proof required shows a tendency towards the civil law system to apply a flexible standard and an assessment based on the matters of the case.[181] However, the jurisprudence of the International Court of Justice offers good indications for the level of certainty a State should obtain before launching a defensive strike against an imminent armed attack. First,

173 Alfred Verdross & Bruno Simma, *Universelles Völkerrecht: Theorie und Praxis* (3rd edn, Duncker & Humblot) 1984; James A Green, 'The Oil Platforms Case: An Error in Judgment?' (2004) 9 Journal of Conflict & Security Law 380–381, discussing the aspect of necessity.

174 UNSC UN Doc 1986/3, UN Chron 16–19.

175 Dire Tladi, 'The Use of Force in Self-Defence against Non-State Actors', UN Lecture Series https://legal.un.org/avl/ls/Tladi_PS.html.

176 *USA v Von Weizsaecker et al.* (The Ministries Case) [Nuremberg, 1949] 14 NMT. 314, 329.

177 Yoram Dinstein Y, *War, Aggression and Self-Defence* (3rd edn, Cambridge University Press 2001) 162.

178 See also, UNGA Res A/59/565 para. 195.

179 Malcom N Shaw, *International Law* (9th edn, Cambridge University Press 2021) 822.

180 Paola Gaeta, Jorge E. Viñuales & Salvatore Zappalá, *Cassese's International Law* (3rd edn, OUP 2020) at 356 stating that the State acting in self-defence needs to have "compelling evidence" that an attack will be unleashed; Aniruddha Rajput, 'Standard of Proof' in *Max Planck Encyclopedias of Public International Law* (OUP 2021) para. 10.

181 Ana Ridell & Brendan Plant, *Evidence before the International Court of Justice* (British Institute of International and Comparative Law 2016) 132–33.

the Court seems to draw a line between charges of exceptional gravity and charges other than exceptional gravity. For charges of exceptional gravity, such as genocide, the Court requires "proof at a high level of certainty appropriate to the seriousness of the allegation" and applied a standard of "beyond reasonable doubt."[182] In other cases involving less grave forms of the use of force, the ICJ required "sufficient evidence."[183] In cases of less grave allegations, a lower standard of proof is acceptable, namely "the balance of probabilities,"[184] "reasonableness of hypothesis,"[185] or "reasonable conjecture warranted by those facts that are known, and by the probabilities involved."[186]

Assuming that the armed attack is not of exceptional gravity, proof on the threat of the armed attack needs to be sufficiently established.[187] The threatened armed attack needs to be sufficiently clear and serious to justify the use of force.[188] The standard of determining the scale and imminence of the armed attack has to be based on the information reasonably available to decision-makers at the time of the decision-making and cannot be based on post-factum knowledge.[189] The standard is thus an objective *ex-ante* standard that takes into consideration the time for corresponding preparations and avoids the risk of hindsight bias.[190] It also needs to be established that the harm expected must be grave in a quantitative as well as qualitative sense.[191] ADIZs help States gather all necessary information before actually launching an action in self-defence. In this sense, ADIZs align the occurrence of aerial threats and interests of national security with the concept of pre-emptive

182 *Application of the Convention on the Prevention and Punishment of the Crime of Genocide, Bosnia and Herzegovina v Yugoslavia* (Order, Provisional Measures) [1993] ICJ Rep 3 para. 208–211.

183 *Oil Platforms Case*, para. 57, 61 and 76; *Nicaragua Case* (1986), para. 110; *Armed Activities on the Territory of the Congo* (*Congo v Ruanda*) [2005] ICJ Rep 168.

184 *Pulp Mills on the River Uruguay* (*Argentina v Uruguay*) (Merits) [2006] ICJ Rep 156, Sep. Op. Judge Greenwood para. 25–26. Also, *Land, Island and Maritime Frontier Dispute* (*El Salvador v Honduras*) (Merits) [1992] ICJ Rep 351 para. 248.

185 *Sovereignty over Certain Frontier Land* (*Belgium v Netherlands*) (Merits) [1958] ICJ Rep 28, Sep. Op. Judge Spiropoulos para. 232.

186 *Barcelona Traction Case* (*Belgium v Spain*) (Merits) [1970] ICJ Rep 3, Sep. Op. Judge Fitzmaurice para. 58.

187 Noam Lubell, 'The Problem of Imminence in an Uncertain World' in Marc Weller M (ed), *The Oxford Handbook of the Use of Force in International Law* (OSAIL 2015) 704.

188 Also, UNGA Res A/59/565 para. 207.

189 Yoram Dinstein, *War, Aggression and Self-Defence* (2nd edn, Cambridge University Press 2012) 212.

190 Paula Fischer, *Das Irrtumsrisiko bei den Ausnahmen des völkerrechtlichen Gewaltverbotes* (Nomos 2020) 248.

191 See the discussion on the requirements of an imminent armed attack above at 2.2.

self-defence and create an intersection between the academic debate with operational realities.[192]

3 Analysis of Concrete ADIZs' Obligations

As part of customary international law, necessity and proportionality have to be fulfilled for the lawful use of self-defence.[193] Necessity means that no reasonable peaceful alternatives to force are available.[194] Proportionality concerns the relationship between the action and its purpose, namely either halting, repelling, or even preventing the attack.[195] To reach a conclusion on whether ADIZs fulfil the requirements of necessity and proportionality, one has to examine the facts bearing on the issue with regard to the specific obligations of the defence zone, the defensive needs, and related topographical considerations. The deconstruction of obligations within an ADIZ reveals two aspects: 1) civil and military aircraft have the obligation to identify themselves; 2) aircraft will be intercepted in case of non-sufficient identification. Both of these aspects have to be assessed separately and individually on their necessity and proportionality. The multiple cases of erroneous use of force against civil aircraft show that States mostly based their decision on incorrect facts when the aircraft was already in national airspace and the timeframe for taking action was short. Yet, the defensive act needs to be assessed from the point of view of the State at the time it adopted the relevant measures.

3.1 *The ADIZ' Interception Mechanism Analysed under the Right to Self-Defence*

The requirement of temporal proximity means that the State must be in a position where it needs to act at that point in time to avert the risk of harm. Given the speed of aircraft and the potentially devastating effect, if used as a weapon,

192 On the general problem of the academic debate being too distinct from operational realities, see Daniel Bethlehem, 'Principles Relevant to the Scope of a State's Right of Self-Defense against an Imminent or Actual Armed Attack by Nonstate Actors' (2012) 106 AJIL.

193 Christine Gray, 'The Use of Force and the International Legal Order' in Malcom D Evans (ed), *International Law* (5th edn, OUP 2018) 612.

194 Eighth Report on State Responsibility by Mr. Roberto Ago, Special Rapporteur – The Internationally Wrongful Act of the State, Source of International Responsibility (Part 1), Yearbook of the International Law Commission 1980. Vol. II(1) para. 121.

195 Ibid.

these expansive buffer zones in the form of ADIZ provide time and space for appraising hostile intent and the nature of the threat.[196]

3.1.1 The Interception of Aircraft as Forceful Act

The discussion under this point concerns whether an interception *per se* is a forceful act. Even though Art. 3bis Chicago Convention regulates the interception in national airspace, this provision applies wherever civil aircraft are in flight.[197] Generally, a State is entitled to require a civil aircraft to land at a designated airport only over its territory in the exercise of its sovereignty.[198] The wording of Art. 3bis Chicago Convention indicates that the interception of an aircraft may be an act of force because it aligns "the use of weapons against civil aircraft in flight" with the "case of interception".[199] Interception pursuant to Art. 3bis Chicago Convention has a narrower scope of application than interception based on Art. 51 UN-Charter.[200] Unlike the Chicago Convention, Art. 51 UN-Charter is not limited to civil aircraft but also applies to military aircraft.[201]

A prominent example of an unlawful interception of a civil aircraft took place on 23 May 2021 when the Ryanair flight FR4978 was intercepted by Belarus military aircraft and forced to land at the Minsk Airport. Following the incident, the EU imposed sanctions against Belarus because of the "forced

196 Ibid 142.

197 Andrew S Williams, 'The Interception of Civil Aircraft Over the High Seas in the Global War on Terror' (2007) 59 Air Force Law Review 135; confirmed by the Security Council in UN Doc S/Res/1067 (26 July 1996).

198 See Art. 3bis (b) Chicago Convention: "The contracting States recognize that every State, in the exercise of its sovereignty, is entitled to require the landing at some designated airport of a civil aircraft flying above its territory without authority or if there are reasonable grounds to conclude that it is being used for any purpose inconsistent with the aims of this Convention." See for the discussion on sovereignty and territory chapter 5, 3 of this book.

199 Robin Geiß, 'Civil Aircraft as Weapons of Large-Scale Destruction: Countermeasures, Article 3bis of the Chicago Convention, and the Newly Adopted German "Luftsicherheitsgesetz"' (2005) 27 Mich J Int'l L at 243, 244 stating that legal forms of interception would ipso facto involve the use of force to some degree.

200 Andrew S Williams, 'The Interception of Civil Aircraft Over the High Seas in the Global War on Terror' (2007) 59 Air Force Law Review, raising the point at page 98 that an interception over the high seas may be legitimate but can nevertheless interfere with the jurisdiction of the State of registry of the concerned aircraft.

201 Robin Geiß, 'Civil Aircraft as Weapons of Large-Scale Destruction: Countermeasures, Article 3bis of the Chicago Convention, and the Newly Adopted German "Luftsicherheitsgesetz"' (2005) 27 Mich J Int'l L 238.

and unlawful landing."[202] While several States criticized Belarus' action at the United Nations Security Council's meeting, no resolution was achieved due to a veto by Russia.[203] Nonetheless, 6 of the 15 Security Council members, Estonia, France, Ireland, Norway, Britain, and the United States, released a joint statement in which they condemned the interception as "a blatant attack on international civilian aviation safety and European security."[204] The ICAO Council similarly expressed its concerns on the "apparent forced diversion of Ryanair Flight FR4978"[205] and established a fact-finding investigation.[206]

An example of the right to self-defence being used to intercept an aircraft in international airspace occurred in 1985. A US military aircraft intercepted an Egyptian aircraft over the Mediterranean Sea and forced it to land in Italy to seize and prosecute alleged terrorists on board the craft.[207] The US claimed that due to exceptional circumstances a civil aircraft may be intercepted because "the ability to take such action in carefully defined and limited circumstances is an aspect of the inherent right of self-defence recognized in the United Nations Charter."[208] The Security Council was unable to issue a formal condemnation of the incident due to the US veto.[209] This indicates that the

202 Council of the EU, 'Belarus: fourth package of EU sanctions over enduring repression and the forced landing of a Ryanair flight' (21 June 2021) available at https://www.consilium.europa.eu/en/press/press-releases/2021/06/21/belarus-fourth-package-of-eu-sanctions-over-enduring-repression-and-the-forced-landing-of-a-ryanair-flight/ (accessed 9 January 2022).

203 Reuters, 'U.N. Security Council to discuss Belarus plane interception–diplomats' (25 May 2021) available at https://www.reuters.com/article/belarus-politics-un/u-n-security-council-to-discuss-belarus-plane-interception-diplomats-idUSL2N2NC1TU (accessed 9 January 2022).

204 Reuters, 'Six U.N. Security Council members condemn Belarus plane interception' (26 May 2021) available at https://www.reuters.com/world/europe/six-un-security-council-members-condemn-belarus-plane-interception-2021-05-26/ (accessed 9 January 2022).

205 ICAO Council, 'ICAO Council to pursue fact finding investigation into Ryanair FR4978' (27 May 2021) https://www.icao.int/Newsroom/Pages/ICAO-Council-agrees-to-pursue-fact-finding-investigation-into-Belarus-incident.aspx (accessed 9 January 2022).

206 ICAO Council, 'Update on fact-finding investigation on Ryanair flight FR478' (16 June 2021) available at https://www.icao.int/Newsroom/Pages/Update-on-factfinding-investigation-into-Ryanair-flight-FR4978.aspx (accessed 9 January 2022).

207 Antonio Cassese, *Terrorism, Politics And The Law: The Achille Lauro Affair* (S J K Greenleaves 1989); Gerald P McGinley, 'The Achille Lauro Affair-Implications for International Law' (1985) 52 Tenn L Rev 691.

208 UN Security Council, 'Provisional Verbatim Record of the 2655th Meeting', S/ PV.2655 (6 February 1986) at 114.

209 Australia, Denmark, France, and Britain all abstained to vote, see Gergory V Gooding, 'Fighting Terrorism in the 1980's: The Interception of the Achille Lauro Hijackers ' (1987) 12 Yale J Int'l L 176.

interception itself was a forceful act that may only be justified outside the provisions of the Chicago Convention in accordance with the requirements of Art. 51 of the UN Charter and customary international law. Based on an *a argumentum a maiore ad minus* reasoning, if the shooting down of an aircraft can be justified with the right to self-defence, then the same has to be true for the less grave form of using force, namely the interception of an aircraft.

With regard to the interception of an aircraft within an ADIZ, it is also possible to draw a parallel with the concept of "naval quarantines."[210] In 1962, the United States instituted a "naval quarantine" without formally invoking the right to self-defence to stop vessels on the high seas carrying missiles to Cuba.[211] "Naval quarantines" is used to describe a forceful measure that is part of anticipatory self-defence, as the United States acted before any actual firing of weapons.[212] It is widely agreed among commentators that the blockade infringed upon the freedom of the high seas and that the quarantine amounts to a threat of the use of force, which may only be justified under Art. 51 UN-Charter.[213] The interception of vessels on the high seas is a forceful act that may be excused if necessary and proportionate for the purpose of securing the States' defence.[214] Similarly, ADIZs create a "buffer zone" which provides time to determine the hostile intent of the approaching aircraft, thereby enabling the State to take interceptive measures.[215] It can therefore be concluded, that the interception of an aircraft amounts to a forceful act that can *prima facie* be excused under the right to self-defence.

---

210 Quincy Wright, 'The Cuban Quarantine' (1963) 57 Law and Conflict: Changing Patterns and Contemporary Challenges at 9, 10 concluding that the transport of missiles does not amount to an "armed attack" hence the US could not rely on the right to self-defence. Contra: Myres S McDougal, 'The Soviet-Cuban Quarantine and Self-Defense' (1963) 57 AJIL 597.

211 Paola Gaeta, Jorge E Viñuales & Salvatore Zappalá , *Cassese's International Law* (3rd edn, OUP 2020) 355 fn 20; Tom Ruys, 'The Cuban Missile Crisis -1962' in Tom Ruys, Oliver Corten & Alexandra Hofer (eds), *The Use of Force in International Law: A Case-Based Approach* (OUP 2018) 97.

212 Paola Gaeta, Jorge E Viñuales & Salvatore Zappalá, *Cassese's International Law* (3rd edn, OUP 2020) 355 fn 20 explaining the US relied on the legal endorsement by the regional organization OAS and did not formally invoke anticipatory self-defence.

213 Quincy Wright, 'The Cuban Quarantine' (1963) 57 Law and Conflict: Changing Patterns and Contemporary Challenges 10.

214 Myres S McDougal, 'The Soviet-Cuban Quarantine and Self-Defense' 57 AJIL 598.

215 Roncevert Almond, 'Clearing the Air Above the East China Sea: The Primary Elements of Aircraft Defense Identification Zones' (2017) 7 Harvard Nat Sec J 142.

3.1.2 The Requirements of Proportionality and Necessity in Relation to Interception

The act of interception may be justified as a form of self-defence, provided that it is proportionate and necessary. Generally, the protection afforded to intercepted aircraft depend on its status as either civil or state aircraft. While interception may be justified under Art. 51 of the UN Charter or customary international law, it is not independent of the Chicago Convention's rules. Any interception of civil aircraft that is not in line with the specific standards of the Chicago Convention may be considered not necessary and not proportionate. The first step of identification includes the establishment of radio communication between the administrative unit of the State and the intruding aircraft. Without endangering the safety of the passengers, the second stage of measures includes surrounding the civil aircraft with interceptors, using tracers as a warning, conducting visual or radio interrogation, restricting flight paths, and firing warning shots when the aircraft refuses to comply.[216] During the interception of civil aircraft, States should aim to avoid endangering the safety of the aircraft and the passengers on-board. The recommendation of Annex 2 Chicago Convention explicitly provides the details on the interception of aircraft, namely "the interception must be limited to determining the identity of the aircraft."[217] Furthermore, "to eliminate or reduce the need for interception of civil aircraft," States must make "all possible efforts (...) to secure identification of any aircraft which may be a civil aircraft, and to issue any necessary instructions or advice to such aircraft, through the appropriate air traffic services units."[218] Proportionality can be assumed if States adhere to the recommendations set out in Annex 2 and initially attempt to identify the aircraft in a passive manner before resorting to active forceful measures.

In the event that an aircraft fails to respond to any communication and cannot be passively identified, then the level of the implicit threat rises from latent to concrete. Consequently, the interception of the aircraft is necessary when the interception procedure was not complied with and other means of establishing communication have failed. The scale and impact of an armed attack involving civil aircraft in relation to the interception of the aircraft comply with a strict standard of proportionality. The use of force against a civil aircraft

---

216 Attachment A to Annex 2 Chicago Convention; Similiar, Maj Ann De Luca, 'Using the Air Force against Civil Aircraft – From Air Terrorism to Self-Defense' (2012) ASPJ Africa & Francophonie 49.

217 Attachment A to Annex 2 Chicago Convention. ICAO has issued special recommendations in Annex 2 in order to further standardize interception practices through the implementation of "appropriate regulatory and administrative action[s]" by contracting States.

218 Attachment A, 2.2 to Annex 2 Chicago Convention.

should only be undertaken as a last resort and should be aimed at identifying the aircraft and any hostile intent.[219] The same approach of using force against commercial vessels can also be seen in the detention and arrest of ships on the high seas.[220] Likewise, if a trespassing military aircraft shows no hostile intent and enters national airspace due to an error or force majeure, then it would be reasonable to assume that the aircraft should be given the opportunity to establish communication to express its non-hostile intent or change course before the State resorts to the use of force.[221] The actual shooting down of a civil aircraft can only be excused under very limited circumstances, which is also reflected in the reactions of States regarding the use of force involving civil aircraft as previously discussed in this chapter. A comparison may be drawn with the law of armed conflicts, which provides that civil airliners are generally exempt from any attack unless they are making an "effective contribution to military action."[222] If the aircraft was erroneously intercepted, the interception may be deemed an internationally wrongful act, thereby giving rise to compensation.[223]

3.1.3 The Interception of Military Aircraft and Questions of Immunity

The immunity of warships or military aircraft derives from the principle of non-intervention and protects vessels against coercive measures.[224] The term "coercion" is not clearly identified in international law but it is generally understood to involve acts that to some degree "subordinate the sovereign will" of another State.[225] Coercive measures are not strictly limited to military or armed force and can include economic, diplomatic, subversive, and other

---

219 Ibid.

220 *The M/V "SAIGA" (No. 2) (Saint Vincent and the Grenadines v. Guinea)* (Merits) [1999] ITLOS Reports at para. 156 "The normal practice used to stop a ship at sea is first to give an auditory or visual signal to stop, using internationally recognized signals. Where this does not succeed, a variety of actions may be taken, including the firing of shots across the bows of the ship. It is only after the appropriate actions fail that the pursuing vessel may, as a last resort, use force. Even then, appropriate warning must be issued to the ship."

221 Roncevert Almond, 'Clearing the Air above the East China Sea: The Primary Elements of Aircraft Defense Identification Zones' (2017) 7 Harvard Nat Sec J 173.

222 Int'l Institute Of Humanitarian Law, *San Remo Manual On International Law Applicable To Armed Conflicts At Sea* (1994) §40.

223 ILC Articles 31–34.

224 United Nations Convention on Jurisdictional Immunities of States and Their Property, A/RES/59/38 (2 December 2004) is left out of this discussion due to its reduced relevance as only 23 States are State Parties.

225 Maziar Jamnejad & Michael Wood, 'The Principle Of Non-Intervention' (2009) 22 Leiden J Int'l L 381.

types of coercion.[226] In an order of provisional measures in the ARA *Libertad Case*, ITLOS confirmed the immunity of warships and observed that "any act which prevents by force a warship from discharging its mission and duties is a source of conflict that may endanger friendly relations among States."[227]

The Permanent Court of International Justice held in its Advisory Opinion in the *Nationality Decrees Issued in Tunis and Morocco Case* that, "jurisdiction which, in principle, belongs solely to the State, is limited by rules of international law" and thus no longer considered a matter that traditionally falls within the domestic jurisdiction.[228] Military aircraft fall traditionally in the jurisdiction of its State of nationality. However, the immunity of military aircraft does not extend the airspace above it and the sea column below it to the exclusion of existing international regulation.

The ADIZS' interception procedure does not necessarily amount to a coercive measure in the sense of a violation of the principle of non-intervention. Interception is a multi-staged process that includes monitoring the behaviour, giving warning shots, and only where the aircraft is about to enter national airspace will coercive measures be applied, such as the forceful landing or the shooting down of the aircraft. The immunity of the military aircraft does not preclude other foreign military aircraft from approaching it as in the first two steps of interception. Consequently, while a particular vessel may indeed be entirely immune from the jurisdiction of other States, it does not necessarily follow that military aircraft interactions fall solely within the State of nationality's domestic affairs.[229] Where a military aircraft enters national airspace, the

226 Declaration on Friendly Relations, at 123 ("No State may use or encourage the use of economic, political or any other type of measures to coerce another State in order to obtain from it the subordination of the exercise of its sovereign rights and to secure from it advantages of any kind. Every State has an inalienable right to choose its political, economic, social and cultural systems, without interference in any form by another State."); *Nicaragua Case* (1986), para. 205 ("Intervention is wrongful when it uses methods of coercion in regard to such choices, which must remain free ones. The element of coercion, which defines, and indeed forms the very essence of, prohibited intervention."); Philip Kunig, 'Prohibition of Intervention' in *Max Planck Encyclopedias of Public International Law* (OUP 2008) para. 22.

227 *ARA Libertad* (*Argentina v Ghana*) (Provisional Measures, Order of 15 December 2012) ITLOS Reports 2012 para. 94, 97; James Kraska, 'The "ARA Libertad" (Argentina v. Ghana)' (2013) 107 AJIL 404.

228 *Nationality Decrees Issued in Tunis and Morocco* (*France v Great Britain*) (Advisory Opinion) [1923] PCIJ.

229 Elizabeth K Kiessling, 'Gray Zone Tactics and the Principle of Non-Intervention: Can "One of the Vaguest Branches of International Law" Solve the Gray Zone Problem?' (2020) 12 Harvard Nat S J 160.

level of threat rises significantly, that a shooting down can be justified under the right to self-defence.

3.2 *The Obligation to Identify Analysed under the Right to Self-Defence*

3.2.1 The Obligation to Identify is a Non-Forcible Act

The UN-Charter does not prescribe which acts are an invocation of the right to self-defence. As mentioned above, Art. 51 UN-Charter is subject to interpretation according to the general rules on treaty interpretation codified in Art. 31–33 VCLT, which also reflects customary international law.[230] The right to self-defence is inextricably connected with the prohibition of the use of force as it sets the legal justification for unilaterally using military force against another State.[231] In general, the right to self-defence primarily includes forceful acts, as its purpose is to preclude the wrongfulness of an act against an armed attack.[232] In this context, the question arises as to whether there is a threshold of force that needs to be connected with the action in question, or whether non-forcible measures may also be included under the right to self-defence.

Two States have claimed an ADIZ in international airspace based on the right to self-defence so far, namely Indonesia and the United States.[233] In general, both the shooting down and the interception of aircraft exists outside of and independent of the establishment of an ADIZ. In every of the previously mentioned cases involving the use of force against aircraft above, the action was taken due to the specific circumstances of each individual incident. Either because of a sudden and potentially threatening behaviour of the aircraft or sometimes because of the State's erroneous perception. The obligation to identify is a non-forceful measure, which can only be enforced by intercepting the aircraft. Some scholars have indicated that non-forcible self-defence may conceptually be permissible.[234] However, the majority of literature proposes

230 Georg Nolte & Albrecht Randelzhofer, 'Ch.VII Action with Respect to Threats to the Peace, Breaches of the Peace, and Acts of Aggression' in Bruno Simma et al (eds), *The Charter of the United Nations: A Commentary, Volume 2* (OUP 2012) 1400, stressing that because of "the fundamental importance of the right to self-defence for the Charter system of collective security, the conditions for the recognition of any significant reinterpretation of, or superseding exception to, Art. 51 are strict."

231 Georg Nolte & Albrecht Randelzhofer, 'Ch.VII Action with Respect to Threats to the Peace, Breaches of the Peace, and Acts of Aggression' in Bruno Simma et al (eds), *The Charter of the United Nations: A Commentary, Volume 2* (OUP 2012) 1399.

232 Christopher Greenwood, 'Self-defence' in *Max Planck Encyclopaedias of Public International Law* (OUP 2011) para. 4.

233 See chapter 3, 2.7 of this book.

234 James Green & Francis Grimal, 'The Threat of Force as an Action in Self-Defence under International Law' (2011) 44 Vanderbilt Journal of Transnational Law 21; Marco Roscini, 'Threats of Armed Force' (2007) 54 Netherland Int'l L Rev 237.

that self-defence includes inherently forcible measures.[235] Yet, it is still worth examining whether the obligation to identify may be based on the right to self-defence.

One famous example of non-forcible self-defence can be found in the *Palestinian Wall Advisory Opinion*. On the construction of a wall on occupied Palestine territory, Israel's Permanent Representative to the United Nations asserted that "the fence is a measure wholly consistent with the right of States to self-defence enshrined in Art. 51 of the Charter"; and further stated that the Security Council resolutions 1368 (2001) and 1373 (2001), "have clearly recognized the right of States to use force in self-defence against terrorist attacks, and therefore surely *recognize the right to use non-forcible measures* to that end."[236] This led the UN General Assembly to request the ICJ for an advisory opinion on the legal consequences arising from the construction of the wall. During the proceedings, Israel claimed again that the construction of the wall is part of the right of self-defence pursuant to Art. 51 UN-Charter. The Court, however, dismissed Israel's argument on the ground that Israel did not claim that the attacks against it are attributable to a foreign State.[237] Furthermore, the Court concluded that Art. 51 UN-Charter has no relevance as the "threat which it [Israel] regards as justifying the construction of the wall originates within, and not outside, that [Occupied Palestinian] territory."[238] The Court refrained from providing a definitive answer to the question of whether non-forcible measures are covered by Art. 51 of the UN Charter.

Judge *Higgins* remarked in her Separate Opinion that she remained unconvinced that non-forcible measures fall within self-defence under Art. 51

235 Ian Brownlie, 'The Use of Force in Self-Defence' (1961) 37 BYIL 254 (referring to self-defence as being "exercisable through the medium of armed force"); Yoram Dinstein, *War, Aggression and Self-Defence* (3rd edn, Cambridge University Press 2001) 176 (defining self-defence as "a permissible form of armed self-help"); Myra Williamson, *Terrorism, War And International Law: The Legality Of The Use Of Force Against Afghanistan In 2001* (Ashgate 2009) 108 ("[E]ven if the Charter had preserved a right of customary self-defence, the customary right would probably only have entitled states to use force in response to an armed attack from another state."); and ILC, Report of the International Law Commission on the Work of its Thirty-Second Session (5 May–25 July1980) UN Doc. A/35/10, at 54 ("[S]elf-defense almost by its very nature involves the use of armed force.").

236 UNGA Res A/ES-10/PV.21, 'Emergency Special Session' (20 October 2003) 4 (emphasized added).

237 *Advisory Wall Opinion* para. 139. Disagreeing Judge Higgins in her Separate Opinion that the attack need not necessarily be made by a State against another State at para. 33; Similarly, Sep. Op. Judge Kooijmans para. 35.

238 *Advisory Wall Opinion* para. 139.

UN-Charter.[239] Even if the construction of the wall is a measure of self-defence then it would need to be justified as necessary and proportionate, which in the present case seems not to be given as the wall did not resulted in a diminution in attacks.[240] In contrast, Judge *Buergenthal* seemed inclined to accept the construction of the wall as a measure of self-defence and some part of the wall even as necessary and proportionate.[241] Scholarly literature on the *Palestinian Wall Advisory Opinion* mostly addressed the limitation of the Court that self-defence is only permissible against other States.[242] Most debates therefore surrounded the topic of self-defence against non-state actors and requirements of necessity but not the construction of the wall *per se*.[243] It appears that the construction of the wall, even though it does not include the active use of force, was perceived as a measure of self-defence that has to meet the requirement of the self-defence test.[244] The Court, however, did not assess whether the construction of the wall was a proportionate response to the threat of an attack.[245] The Court's failure to address Israel's reliance on the inherent right to self-defence has been met with criticism as the most problematic aspect of the advisory opinion.[246] In any case, the *Advisory Wall Opinion* provides further support for the general viability of non-forcible self-defence.[247] Despite different opinions, it is important to recognise that if other measures than forceful ones are feasible, they would still need to be necessary and proportionate.[248]

239 *Advisory Wall Opinion*, Sep. Op. Judge Higgins para. 35.

240 Ibid para. 35.

241 *Advisory Wall Opinion*, Sep. Op. Judge Buergenthal para. 5, "it is not inconceivable to me that some segments of the wall being constructed on Palestinian territory meet that test".

242 Sean Murphy, 'Self-Defense and the Israeli Wall Advisory Opinion: An Ipse Dixit from the ICJ?' (2005) 99 AJIL 67–70.

243 Christian J Tams, 'Light Treatment of a Complex Problem: The Law of Self-Defence in the Wall Case' (2006) 16 EJIL 963.

244 See for example the arguments of the Palestine delegate why the Wall does not meet the requirements of Art. 51 UN-Charter and in particular because "Article 51 does not allow self-defense against a future armed attack, the construction of the "wall" cannot be justified as a means of preventing such an attack." Advisory Wall opinion, Written Statement Submitted by Palestine 233, para. 531 (30 January 2004).

245 Sean Murphy, 'Self-Defense and the Israeli Wall Advisory Opinion: An Ipse Dixit from the ICJ?' (2005) 99 AJIL 71.

246 Sir Arthur Watts & Remy Jorritsma, 'Israeli Wall Advisory Opinion (Legal Consequences of the Construction of a Wall in the Occupied Palestinian Territory)'in *Max Planck Encyclopedias of Public International Law* (OUP 2019) para. 43.

247 James Green & Francis Grimal, 'The Threat of Force as an Action in Self-Defence under International Law' (2011) 44 Vanderbilt J Trans L 25.

248 Federica Paddeau, 'Self-Defence as a Circumstance Precluding Wrongfulness: Understanding Article 21 of the Articles on State Responsibility' (2015) British Y Int'l L 16, 17 stating that Art. 51 UN-Charter is in general limited to forceful measures only.

This is particularly relevant in cases where it is not clear if the action reaches the threshold of an armed attack in the sense of Art. 51 UN-Charter, so that other proportionate non-forcible measures may be applied.[249] The identification requirements of ADIZ can in fact be a feasible alternative to taking forceful actions of self-defence.

3.2.2 The Obligation to Identify Is Neither Necessary Nor Proportionate

Every situation of self-defence has to be assessed based on the circumstances of the case. Relevant considerations include the nature and severity of the attack, the capacity of the State to respond in time, and the probability that the threat will materialize if action is not taken.[250] The primary objective of ADIZs is to identify potential threats, which requires the collection and analysis of comprehensive information. ADIZs provide information on the temporal proximity of the threat, namely the time at which the aircraft is entering national airspace, and on the nature and seriousness of the attack, namely the source of the threat.

The obligation to identify appears to be ta classic example of the "chicken or egg" problem. Does the ADIZ lead to the identification of the imminent armed attack, or does the potential for an imminent armed attack cause the obligation to identify? ADIZs would require an imminent armed attack to be legal, but are at the same time necessary to gather sufficient proof to identify the armed attack in order to react lawfully. The inherent risk associated with ADIZs is that they may create a *presumptio iuris et de jure*, an irrefutable presumption that exceeds any reasonable limit of defence.[251]

The identification requirement *prima facie* can only be necessary and proportionate when the foreign aircraft is bound for national airspace. It is neither necessary nor proportionate if it addresses aircraft only traveling through the zone without the intent to enter national airspace.[252] If based on Art. 51 UN-Charter, an ADIZ may only be established for defensive purposes, rather

249 *Oil Platforms Case*, Sep. Op. Judge Simma at 331, 332 on proportionate and immediate defensive measures equally of military character.

250 Abraham D Sofaer, 'On the Necessity of Pre-emption' (2003) 14 EJIL 220.

251 Which was the case in the "total exclusion zone" declared by Great Britain during the Falkland Island conflict with Argentina. This zone prohibited any ship and aircraft, whether military or civil to be within this zone. Any ship or aircraft found within this zone was subject to be attacked by the British forces. Great Britain based the establishment of the zone on "its inherent right to self-defence recognized by article 51 of the Charter of the United Nations." See SC, UN Doc. S/15006 (28 April 1982).

252 Ashley Roach, 'Air Identification Zones' in *Max Planck Encyclopedias of Public International Law* (OUP 2017) para. 7.

than for administrative purposes.[253] The administrative control of air traffic is already guaranteed by the existence of Flight Information Regions, so that ADIZs, as an additional administrative zone, are neither necessary nor proportionate. The limitation to security purposes balances the defensive interest of the State with the interest of free and unhindered air traffic of other States. The issue of overlapping zones due to topographical features and concurrent jurisdiction is resolved when the aircraft only has to comply with the identification obligation of the State it intends to enter. Regarding the situation over the East China Sea, for example, an aircraft that intends to enter Japanese airspace would consequently only need to comply with the rules of the Japanese ADIZ but not with the Korean or Chinese ADIZs' rules even if it traverses through these zones. It is not proportionate to require the aircraft to identify itself if it is not bound for either Korean or Chinese airspace. Moreover, in order to avoid exposure to arbitrariness, the State who establishes an ADIZ also needs to publish the procedure for proper identification.[254] The publication of the ADIZ's details minimizes the risk of interception and leads to the assumption that the State attempted to use less drastic means before resorting to interception. In this regard, the Bangladesh ADIZ is a negative role-model as it does not provide clear instructions on how to receive an Air Defence Clearance number, which is necessary to fly within the Bangladeshi ADIZ.

Considering the generally peaceful nature of civil aviation and the involvement of non-State actors, a particular strict test needs to be employed[255] The obligation to identify conceptually falls within the scope of preventive self-defence as it applies on a permanent basis independent of the occurrence of

---

253 See for example the Chinese ECS ADIZ which was also established to regulate air traffic and provide administrative guidance.

254 See for example the rules of the US ADIZ, US Far Part 99. Also in line with Annex 2 Chicago Convention.

255 Since there already exist vast literature on the right to self-defence against non-state actors, this book does not further discuss this topic but assume the legality of self-defence against non-state actors. See for example: Mary E O'Conell, Christian J Tams & Dire Tladi (eds), *Self-Defence against Non-State Actors* (Cambridge University Press 2019); Christopher Greenwood, 'Self-defence' in *Max Planck Encyclopaedias of Public International Law* (OUP 2011) para. 18; Srinivas Burra, 'Use of Force as Self Defence against Non-State Actors and TWAIL Considerations: A Critical Analysis of India's State Practice' (2018) 24 Asian Yearbook Int'l L 116; Daniel Bethlehem, 'Principles Relevant to the Scope of a State's Right to Self-Defence against an Imminent and Actual Armed Attack by Nonstate Actors' (2012) 106 AJIL 769; Leiden Policy Recommendations on Counter Terrorism and International Law (2010) para. 38; Principles of International Law on the Use of Force by States in Self-Defence (2005), Principle 6.

an armed attack.[256] The obligation to identify is useful but not necessary. The situation might be different for a military aircraft bound to foreign national airspace and which is not cooperating with the aviation authority of the respective foreign State. It seems difficult to argue that a lone military aircraft, in contrast to a whole fleet, is a clear and manifest threat of an imminent armed attack.[257] One indicator may be the type of military aircraft in question but it appears that the necessity requirement is not easily met.[258] The determination of proportionality is challenging due to the coexistence of three distinct concepts.[259] A strict standard relates the scale and impact of the initial attack and the reaction.[260] A less strict standard allows the State to exceed the level of force used by the attacker if the State is otherwise unable to defend itself.[261] The third concept applies the reasonable alternatives test by asking whether a State could have achieved the same result – from an *ex-ante* perspective – with less intrusive means.[262] Even if one where to apply a flexible and less strict approach for the proportionality test, the application of the ADIZ's obligation to identify to every single (civil) aircraft traversing through the zone during peacetime seems not proportionate, given that ADIZs are established on a permanent basis and cover vast spaces of international airspace.[263]

---

256 However, it shall be mentioned that in the *Oil Platforms Case* the ICJ rejected the United States' argument of self-defence because the oil platform was of no military importance and also by drawing a distinction between a merchant vessel and a military vessel as legitimate target, see *Oil Platforms Case* para. 74.

257 In the same line of discussion fall automated Missile Defence Systems, such as Israel's Iron Dome, that intercept missiles outside national territory. Whereas the interception of missiles, which a clearly aiming to destroy, is rather unproblematic in contrast to the identification of (supposedly peaceful) military aircraft in international airspace. Francis Grimal, 'Missile Defence Shields: Automated and Anticipatory Self-Defence' (2014) 19 J Conflict & Sec L 317.

258 The most likely aerial threats stem from unmanned aerial vehicles, bombers, fighter-bombers, fighters and close air support aircraft, see United States Army Air Defense Artillery School, 'Small Arms Defense Against Air Attack' (2006) 9.

259 Dapo Akande & Thomas Liefländer, 'Clarifying Necessity, Imminence, and Proportionality in the Law of Self-Defense' (2013) 107 AJIL 563, 566.

260 *Nuclear Weapons Advisory Opinion* para. 40–46.

261 Eight Report on State Responsibility by Mr. Roberto Ago, Special Rapporteur – The Internationally Wrongful Act of the State, Source of International Responsibility (Part 1), Yearbook of the International Law Commission 1980, Vol. II(1), para. 119–123.

262 Ralph Janik, *International Law and the Use of Force- Cases and Materials* (Routledge 2019) 108.

263 Roncevert Almond, 'Clearing the Air above the East China Sea: The Primary Elements of Aircraft Defense Identification Zones' (2017) 7 Harvard Nat Sec J, at 174–177 critical on the extensive temporal scope of ADIZ.

To conclude, it is clear that the primary purpose of ADIZs is to halt or identify a potential threat. However, actions against vague and non-specific threats do not meet the requirement of imminence in order to prevent the excessive use of force. In fact, the obligation to identify represents a peaceful alternative to intercepting the aircraft and thus constitutes a preliminary stage to the use of force and the right to self-defence. ADIZs help to comply with the requirement of imminence as it identifies a concrete threat that is going to materialize into a specific attack. The obligation to identify is a less intrusive means than the interception or the shooting down of the aircraft and may be a reasonable alternative outside the scope of the right to self-defence.[264]

4 ADIZs and Necessity as a Circumstance Precluding Wrongfulness

This sub-chapter aims to discuss the justification of necessity pursuant to Art. 25 (1) (a) ILC Articles in relation to ADIZs and the requirement of "imminence". Outside the scope of this contribution is a discussion of the second condition for invoking necessity, set out in paragraph 1 (b), namely that the conduct in question must not seriously impair an essential interest of the other State or States concerned, or of the international community.

If one considers ADIZs to be a violation of the freedom of overflight or another "undesirable behaviour" violating any other international obligation,[265] these zones may be justified under necessity pursuant to Art. 25 ILC Articles. In general, necessity is not responsive to another State's action but applies to an objective situation.[266] The primary challenge in the context of pre-emptive self-defence is to accurately identify the nature of the threat and to gather evidence regarding the imminent occurrence of an armed attack. ADIZs in fact facilitate the acquisition of information necessary to identify a threat before the foreign aircraft enters national airspace. However, the obligation to identify cannot be excused under the right to self-defence as it is not an act of force, and because it is directed against latent threats in the future.

Art. 25 ILC Articles states:

1. Necessity may not be invoked by a State as a ground for precluding the wrongfulness of an act not in conformity with an international obligation of that State unless the act:

264 On the reasonable alternative test, see Ralph Janik, *International Law and the Use of Force-Cases and Materials* (Routledge 2019) 108. However, defence zones bear the risk of qualifying as an unlawful threat of force if the interception rules include the shooting down of the aircraft.

265 Jan Klabbers, *International Law* (3rd edn, 2021 Cambridge University Press) 138.

266 Ibid 144.

(a) is the only way for the State to safeguard an essential interest against a grave and imminent peril; and
(b) does not seriously impair an essential interest of the State or States towards which the obligation exists, or of the international community as a whole.[267]

In the *Gabcikovo-Nagymaros Case*, the ICJ emphasized the risk of an abusive invocation of necessity and the need to narrowly interpret the term.[268] Necessity is a rule of customary international law according to which a factual situation of a grave and imminent peril for the essential interests of a State would legally justify a breach of an international obligation because it is the only way to safeguard an essential interests.[269] Necessity arises when there is an irreconcilable conflict between an essential interest on the one hand and an obligation of the State invoking necessity on the other. An essential interest depends on the circumstances of the case and addresses the interest of the State and its people as well as the interest of the international community as a whole.[270] The conflict as regards ADIZs is between the interest of the State to safeguard its national airspace and national security, the obligation to not violate the freedom of overflight in international airspace, and the obligation not to intercept aircraft outside the scope of Art. 51 UN-Charter and the Chicago Convention.

Necessity and pre-emptive self-defence share the common characteristic of the requirement of "imminence". However, the level of imminence is different. In contrast to the concept of self-defence, which necessitates the existence of a concrete and imminent threat, the principle of necessity is concerned with the avoidance of future harm.[271] Consequently, it requires States to engage in the process of prediction in order to identify potential future scenarios. The term 'imminent' in the sense of Art. 25 ILC Articles does not require that the risk is about "to materialize (immediacy in temporal terms)," rather it has been interpreted as "harm not yet having (completely) materialized at the time a State act in a situation of necessity."[272] Temporal proximity in the sense of Art. 25

267 Articles on the Responsibility of States for Internationally Wrongful Acts UN Doc (A/56/10) (2001).
268 *Gabcikovo-Nagymaros Project (Hungary v Slovakia)* (Merits) [1997] ICJ Rep 7 para. 102.
269 Attila Tanzi, 'State of Necessity' in *Max Planck Encyclopedias of Public International Law* (OUP 2021) para. 1.
270 ILC, 'Responsibility of States for Internationally Wrongful Acts, with commentaries' UN Doc (A/56/10) (2001) para. 15.
271 Federica Paddeu & Michael Waibel, 'Necessity 20 Years On: The Limits of Article 25' (2022) 37 ICSID Review – Foreign Inv L J 165.
272 ILC, 'Responsibility of States for Internationally Wrongful Acts, with commentaries' UN Doc (A/56/10) (2001) para. 16; *Gabčíkovo-Nagymaros* para. 54. In the literature, see also James Crawford, *State Responsibility: The General Part* (2013 CUP) 310.

ILC Articles refers not to the risk of harm but to the need of the State to act immediately in order to avoid the harm.[273] Uncertainty exists on the temporal scope between the identification of the risk of harm and the materialisation of the harm.[274] *Paddeu* and *Waibel* argue that

> the plea of necessity can be reactive (the triggering event has occurred or is unfolding, and the State acts to prevent the materialisation, or reduce the impact, of its consequences) or prophylactic (the event has not occurred yet, and the State acts to prevent its occurrence or pre-emptively guard against its consequences).[275]

The difference between necessity and self-defence emanates from the fact that self-defence cannot be claimed as preventive act.[276] Nevertheless, both necessity and self-defence require the presence of sufficient evidence of the risk in question.[277] The standard of proof for a situation of necessity is less strict than in the case of self-defence, as it only requires the probability of the harm occurring.[278]

The aspect of acting preventively to avert the risk is the core of the ADIZs' obligation. Necessity can only be invoked if no other means to deal with the imminent peril are available.[279] It is also clear, that questions about the lawfulness of certain uses of force fall outside the law of State responsibility and the justification of necessity. Accordingly, humanitarian intervention and military necessity are not within the remit of Art. 25 as they qualify as primary rules.[280] The plea of necessity has been invoked to protect a wide variety of interests, including safeguarding the environment, preserving the very existence of the State and its people in times of public emergency, or ensuring the safety of a

---

273 Federica Paddeu & Michael Waibel, 'Necessity 20 Years On: The Limits of Article 25' (2022) 37 ICSID Review – Foreign Inv L J 167, "it is not necessary that there is a risk of immediate harm, but there must be a need for immediate action."

274 Ibid 166.

275 Ibid 167.

276 Sean D Murphy, 'The Doctrine of Preemptive Self-Defence' (2005) 50 Vill L Rev 720–721.

277 Federica Paddeu & Michael Waibel, 'Necessity 20 Years On: The Limits of Article 25' (2022) 37 ICSID Review – Foreign Inv L J 167.

278 Ibid 168, 169.

279 *Advisory Wall Opinion* para. 140; James Crawford & Simon Olleson, 'The Character and Forms of International Responsibility' in Malcom D Evans (ed), *International Law* (5th edn, OUP 2018) 438 referring to the Argentina financial crisis.

280 James Crawford, *The International Law Commission's Articles on State Responsibility* (Cambridge University Press 2001) 185–186.

civilian population.[281] It may also be invoked for security aspects amounting to an essential interest.

The obligation to identify is intended to facilitate the prediction whether the aircraft in question is being used for the "peril" of an armed attack. It is in the essential interest of the State to react timely to this kind of peril. The peril has to be established on the basis of the evidence reasonably available at the time.[282] Due to the high speed of an aircraft in flight and the limited time available for reaction, it appears necessary to require the aircraft to identify before it enters the national airspace. Consequently, States need to act by requiring identification before the risk of harm, namely an attack, has materialized. From the standpoint of the State, the establishment of an identification zone correlates with its national security interest in tracking any potential peril stemming from the air. It is important to note that aircraft are not prohibited from flying within the zone but are only obliged to comply with certain rules.[283] The issue of concern is not the requirement to identify aircraft, but rather the interception of aircraft if it is subsequently determined that no actual threat was posed by the aircraft in question.

The plea of necessity can also be applied to situations taking place beyond the State's territory. In the *Torrey Canyon* incident of 1967, a Liberian oil tanker was causing oil pollution on the high seas and was subsequently sunk to limit oil pollution damage threatening the Cornish coast.[284] In the *Fisheries Jurisdiction Case* of 1998, Canada claimed that the boarding and seizure of a Spanish fishing ship by Canadian officials on the high seas was necessary in order stop to the overfishing of straddling fishstock.[285] In the *M/V "Saiga" (No. 2) Case* the seizure of foreign vessels in violation of the UN Convention on the Law of the Sea was examined by the International Tribunal on the Law of the Sea under the plea of necessity.[286]

281 ILC, 'Responsibility of States for Internationally Wrongful Acts, with commentaries' UN Doc A/56/10 (2001) para. 14.

282 Ibid para. 16.

283 See for example *SAIGA (No.2)* case in which ITLOS discussed the prohibition of certain acts in the Exclusive Economic Zone justified under the concept of "public interest", para. 131.

284 Torrey Canyon, P.C.I.J., Series C, No. 87, 141.

285 Fisheries Jurisdiction (Spain v. Canada) (Merits) [1998] ICJ Rep 1998, 432.

286 The M/V "Saiga" (No. 2) (St. Vincent and the Grenadines v. Guinea) [1999] ITLOS Rep 10, paras. 132–36, 38 ILM 1323 (1999).

If the act is regarded as a wrongful act not excused under necessity, reparation can still be claimed under the Articles of State Responsibility.[287] Reparation may take the form of monetary compensation for economically quantifiable damage as well as for non-material damage, depending on the circumstances of the case.[288] If no monetary damage was caused, the most suitable form of reparation would be justification in the form of a formal apology.[289] The same is true for any damages arising out of the creation of the defence zone and the obligation to identify if seen as a violation of the freedom of overflight. Compensation could include any losses related to the reschedule of flight plans, the reorganisation of routes, and the costs of excessive flight times.

5 Conclusion

The right to self-defence allows for the taking of defensive actions in the form of intercepting and, as a last resort, shooting down aircraft in accordance with the strict requirements of Art. 51 of the UN Charter and customary international law. The occurrence of an armed attack does not necessitate that the attack originate from a specific geographical location; thus, the attack may also originate from the high seas and airspace above the high seas. Nevertheless, the establishment of an ADIZ without temporal limitation during peacetime can be classified as an unlawful exercise of preventive self-defence. ADIZs apply not only to military aircraft but also to civil aircraft in their ordinary course of commercial aviation transportation. Any interpretation of the right to self-defence to include non-forcible measures and preventive self-defence might lead to abuse. The legal concept of self-defence shall not deteriorate to the political excuse for dominance. Conversely, ADIZs facilitate the anticipation and identification of aerial armed attacks, thereby reducing the risk of erroneous assessments of the situation. They contribute to the differentiation between pre-emptive and preventive self-defence.

The ADIZs' obligation to identify is conceptually distinct from self-defence measures. Unlike self-defence measures, which are inherently forceful, identification of aircraft is a peaceful alternative. It is only when no peaceful

287 Art. 31 ILC Articles; *Chorzow Factory Case* [1928] PCJI, Series A, No. 17, 47.

288 Malcom N Shaw, *International Law* (9th edn, Cambridge University Press 2021) Art. 36 ILC Articles "(1)The State responsible for an internationally wrongful act is under an obligation to compensate for the damage caused thereby, insofar as such damage is not made good by restitution. (2) he compensation shall cover any financially assessable damage including loss of profits insofar as it is established.

289 Art. 37 ILC Articles.

alternative is available that the interception and shooting down of aircraft can be justified. In the event that an aircraft destined for national airspace cannot be identified, the level of threat rises from latent to specific, thereby allowing for the assumption of an armed attack. Some State actions, such as ADIZs, are not susceptible to being properly defined or fit into prescribed categories. In such instances, a legal legitimation of such actions as actions of self-defence seems inappropriate. Furthermore, the assumption of ADIZs as an internationally wrongful act could be excused under the circumstances of necessity, which would preclude wrongfulness. Without undertaking a comprehensive analysis of the scope and content of necessity, the concept of ADIZs could be more suitable for examination under necessity than under the right to self-defence pursuant to Art. 51 of the UN-Charter and customary international law.

CHAPTER 5

The Legality of ADIZs and Aspects of National Security in International Air Law

In recent years, the absence of a rule on ADIZs within the body of international air law has become a pressing issue, as the number of ADIZs claimed by States in international airspace has increased. While none of the Articles of the Chicago Convention explicitly mentions ADIZs, certain Articles relate to the regulation of entry into national airspace and the establishment of rules in airspace above the high seas, which are more concretized in Annexes. Two of these Annexes in fact include a definition of the term "air defence identification zone". At the international level, treaties include provisions phrased in such a way as to accommodate different political stances and to allow for interpretation.[1] The fundamental principle of a legal system is not to regulate every eventuality in detail, but rather to frame legal norms in a general manner to encompass aspects that were not foreseen at the time of drafting. The Chicago Convention is a prime example of a framework treaty and offers States broad leeway in interpreting its treaty provisions and in stipulating concretizing details in national legislation. ADIZs represent a development that had or could not have been foreseen at the time of the Chicago Convention's adoption, but States may find a legal basis for ADIZs in its text and Annexes. It can be argued that ADIZs are not necessarily in conflict with any pertinent rule of international air law. In other words, the Chicago Convention does not explicitly prohibit the establishment of defence zones for national security.

1 Relevant Principles of International Air Law

The term "international air law" covers provisions on the operation and use of civil aircraft and on international institutions concerned with air law.[2] The legal framework of international air law includes bilateral and multilateral treaties, as well as rules of customary international law relating to civil aviation.

---

1 Tuerk described the divergent interpretation of the law of the sea due to political compromises as "constructive ambiguities", see Helmut Tuerk, 'Some Developments and Issues after the Adoption of UNCLOS' (2021) 9 Korean J Int'l L 2.

2 Chia-Jui Cheng (ed), *Studies in International Air Law* (Brill 2018) 35.

 | DOI:10.1163/9789004721005_007

International air law is generally divided into public international air law, governing the interactions between States and international organisations, and private international air law.[3] Public international air law is based on the premise that the use of airspace shall be governed for the benefit of aviation, the general public and the nations.[4] Most prominently, the Chicago Convention sets forth the fundamental rules for the safe and orderly development of civil aviation and provides the current overall framework, comprehending 96 Articles and 19 Annexes with technical Standards and Recommended Practices (SARPs),[5] supplemented by two additional agreements, the International Air Services Transit Agreement[6] and the International Air Transport Agreement.[7]

The drafting of the Chicago Convention was significantly influenced by the events of the Second World War, which led to an improvement in technical and operational aspects of aircraft with a lasting impact on civil aviation in peacetime.[8] Considerations on the peaceful use of aircraft have influenced and determined the development of international air law with the recognition of the need for an international organisation. Moreover central themes were economic objectives, such as free use of airspace and the simplification of customs procedures, and technical objectives, such as uniform technical standards and navigational services.[9] The conduct of air traffic in a safe manner was another factor that influenced the drafting of the Convention.[10] The overarching objective was to achieve uniformity of aviation regulations, standards, and procedures in order to ensure the safety of air traffic and to establish an international organisation with a mandate to enact and adapt multilateral rules in the form of SARPs included in the Annexes to the Chicago Convention.[11]

---

3 Private international air law covers various aspects such as the financing of aircraft, regulating contractual and non-contractual relations between private parties, in relation to airlines, their passengers, cargo forwarders, and other service providers, and lessors and lessees of aircraft, see Pablo Mendes de Leon, *Introduction to Air Law* (10th edn, Kluwer 2017) 3.

4 Philipina I Diederiks-Verschoor & Pablo Mendes De Leon, *Introduction to Air Law* (9th edn, Kluwer 2012) 1.

5 Chicago Convention, and its Annex 1–18. For example Annex 8 provides technical rules on the airworthiness of aircraft.

6 International Air Services Transit Agreement (1944) 84 UNTS 389 (known as the Two-Freedoms Agreement).

7 International Air Transport Agreement (1944) 502 UNTS 171 (known as the Five-Freedoms Agreement).

8 Ronald Bartsch, *International Aviation Law: A Practical Guide* (2nd edn, Ashgate 2012) 18.

9 Jacob Schenkman, *International Civil Aviation Organization* (Droz 1955) 63.

10 Paul Larsen, Joseph Sweeney & John Gillick, *Aviation Law: Cases, Law and Related Sources* (2nd edn, Martinus Nijhoff 2012) 33.

11 Peter Sand, James Lyon & Geoffrey Pratt, 'An Historical Survey of International Air Law since 1944' (1960) 7 McGill L J 128, 129.

Although the freedom of airspace was presented as a crucial aspect of civil aviation during the negotiations, the Chicago Convention reiterates the principle of absolute State sovereignty over airspace above national territory and emphasises the principle of *aer clausum*.[12] The doctrine of sovereign national airspace can be traced back to Roman times and is based on the maxim *cujus est solum, ejus est usque ad caelum* ("Whose is the soil, to him belongs the sky").[13] This unambiguous assertion of complete and exclusive sovereignty in the Chicago Convention is a consequence of the increased production of military aircraft during the Second World War and the awareness that there are no physical obstacles for aircraft when traversing from the airspace of one country to the airspace of another.[14]

For the following discussion on ADIZs it is necessary to outline the basic principles of international air law which are:

1. Territorial sovereignty and jurisdiction in national airspace;[15]
2. Distinction between national airspace and international airspace;[16]
3. Distinction between civil aircraft and state aircraft;[17]
4. Nationality of aircraft based on the State of registry;[18] and
5. Cooperation on the basis of equality.[19]

Currently, the Chicago Convention is one of the most ratified international treaties with 192 Member States.[20] For comparison, the United Nations counts in total 193 Member States, which underlines the wide acceptance of the Chicago Convention's framework and its importance for civil aviation.[21]

---

12 Art. 1 Chicago Convention; similarly, the Paris Convention as predecessor of the Chicago Convention also stipulated in Art. 1 the principle of sovereignty in national airspace.

13 Yehuda Abramovitch, 'The Maxim "Cujus Est Solum Ejus Usque Ad Coelum" As Applied In Aviation' (1962) 8 McGill L J 247ff. John Cooper, *Roman Law and the Maxim „Cujus est Solum" in International Air Law* (McGill University 1952) 26, 31; A matter of debate was the exact height to which the landowner could control airspace.

14 Philipina I Diederiks-Verschoor & Pablo Mendes De Leon, *Introduction to Air Law* (9th edn, Kluwer 2012) 11.

15 Art. 1, Art. 2 Chicago Convention.

16 Art. 1, Art. 12 Chicago Convention.

17 Art. 3 Chicago Convention.

18 Art. 17 Chicago Convention.

19 Preamble Chicago Convention: "Therefore, the undersigned governments having agreed (…) that international air transport services may be established on the basis of equality of opportunity and operated soundly and economically."

20 https://www.icao.int/MemberStates/Member%20States.Multilingual.pdf (accessed 18 February 2023).

21 http://www.un.org/en/member-states/ (accessed 18 February 2023).

2 Scope of Application: the Distinction between Civil Aircraft and State Aircraft

One of the main purposes of the Chicago Convention is to establish regulations governing the safe and orderly operation of civil aviation.[22] From the outset, the drafting of international air law has been exclusively focused on civil aviation, leading to a distinction between civil aircraft and state aircraft in the Chicago Convention. The Chicago Convention emphasises its applicability to "international civil aviation" in its title and further expressly excludes state aircraft from its scope of application. In this respect, Art. 3 (a) Chicago Convention states that the rules of the Chicago Convention "shall not be applicable to state aircraft."[23] However, some provisions of the Chicago Convention do encompass rules relating to state aircraft,[24] and state aircraft should, in general, cooperate with the ICAO system.[25]

The Chicago Convention does not provide a distinctive definition of the terms "civil aircraft" and "state aircraft".[26] Despite the lack of a definition, Art. 3 (b) specifies that any aircraft used in military, customs, or police services can be regarded as "state aircraft". Conversely, each aircraft that is not a state aircraft in accordance with Art. 3 (b) is deemed to be a civil aircraft.[27] The Chicago Convention does not clarify whether this is an exhaustive list or whether other types of aircraft can also be regarded as state aircraft.[28] Commentators largely agree that Art. 3 (b) formulates a rebuttable presumption and not an

---

22 Preamble Chicago Convention.

23 Ibid.

24 Art. 3 (c) and (d) Chicago Convention; Christopher Petras, 'The Law of Air Mobility-the International Legal Principles behind the U.S. Mobility Air Forces' Mission' (2010) 44 Air Force L Rev 8; also Art. 39 (3) UNCLOS stipulates that "state aircraft will normally comply with such safety measure" meaning the Rules of the Air established by ICAO.

25 Jon M van Dyke, 'An Analysis of the Aegean Disputes' (2005) 36 Ocean Dev & Int'l L 86.

26 Ricardo De Oliveira, 'Does the Current Legal Framework Provide Sufficient Clarity of Law with Regard to Civil and State Aircraft in Relation to Aviation Practicalities?' (2016) 41 Air & Space Law, mentions at 335 that during the proceedings for adopting the Chicago Convention the term was purposely adopted in a vague manner and concretises in fn 46 "In later discussion (which was not recorded), it was suggested that the article be expanded to give a definition of military and state aircraft and defining their status with respect to the Convention. 'After considerable consultations with the military authorities of the United States and United Kingdom', the text was adopted as it appears in Art. 3."

27 Adrianus D Groenewege, *Compendium of International Civil Aviation Organisation* (Intl Air Transport Assn 1999) at 437 stating that civil aircraft can be defined as an aircraft carrying passengers, baggage, cargo and mail, excluding government and military aircraft.

28 Ruwantissa Abeyratne, *Convention On International Civil Aviation – A Commentary* (Springer 2014) 51.

exhaustive list.[29] As a result, Art. 3 (b) does not define the term "state aircraft" but rather highlights three specific, demonstrative services that qualify aircraft as state aircraft. ICAO documents accentuate the three aforementioned types as state aircraft, and concede, that ambiguity exists with regard to the classification of state aircraft as there are other types of activities that might qualify as state-related activities but are not mentioned in Art. 3 (b).[30] Therefore, the defining characteristics of an aircraft are its functions, activities and intended use. These factors provide a preliminary indication of the aircraft's character until further evidence emerges to challenge this assumption.[31] Legal uncertainty remains regarding the definition of state aircraft when it comes to the mixed character of aircraft and flights operated for multifunctional purposes.

A functional approach suggests that the categorisation of aircraft should depend on the purpose for which the aircraft is used, regardless of the official label they may carry.[32] The functional approach was also emphasised by EUROCONTROL which adopted a definition of "state aircraft" that relies on the use of the aircraft irrespective of whether it has been registered as civil or military aircraft.[33] This leads to the conclusion that the status of an aircraft depends on its purpose, use, and function in the specific context.[34] This line of reasoning was exemplified by the case of the civil aircraft Egypt Air Boing 737, MS flight 2843 from Cairo to Tunis, which carried suspected terrorists out of the country under a police escort and was later intercepted by US military jets. The US contended that the aircraft was operating as state aircraft because

---

29 Michael Milde, *Rendition Flights and International Law* (Redress 2008) 18.

30 ICAO Doc LC/36-WP/2–6, 'State/Civil Aircraft Definition and its Impact on Aviation', Legal Committee – 36th Session (29 September 2015).

31 Benjamyn I Scott & Andrea Trimarchi, *Fundamental of International Aviation and Policy* (Routledge 2009) 38.

32 Ruwantissa Abeyratne, *Convention On International Civil Aviation – A Commentary* (Springer 2014) 51.

33 EUROCONTROL, 'The Eleventh Session of the Provisional Council, Composed of Civil and Military Representatives, Endorsed the Principles Used to Identify State Aircraft for ATM Purposes' (12 July 2001), Principle , "Principle 1: For ATM purposes and with reference to article 3(b) of the Chicago Convention, only aircraft used in military, customs and police services shall qualify as State Aircraft. Accordingly: Aircraft on a military register, or identified as such within a civil register, shall be considered to be used in military service and hence qualify as State Aircraft; Civil registered aircraft used in military, customs and police service shall qualify as State Aircraft; Civil registered aircraft used by a State for other than military, customs and police service shall not qualify as State Aircraft."

34 Stefan Kaiser, 'No-Fly Zones Established by the United Nations Security Council' (2011) 60 ZLW 404. Stephan Hobe & Michael L Fremuth, 'No Fly Zones: Connectivity Between International Law and Air Law in the Case of Lybia' (2001) 60 Zeitschrift für Luft- und Weltraumrecht 389.

it was used for an exclusive State purpose.[35] The determining criterion is the usage of the aircraft in question, while other factors such as aircraft registration and markings are a rebuttable presumption.[36]

As state aircraft are not covered by the Chicago Convention's scope of application, the rules of the Chicago Convention and its Annexes do not apply to them. Instead, bilateral or multilateral agreements regulate the authorisation for state aircraft to fly over the territory of another State.[37] In contrast, both civil as well as state aircraft are free to fly over non-state areas, such as the high seas.[38] Any potential legal basis of ADIZ within the legal framework of the Chicago Convention does not affect state aircraft but only applies to civil aircraft. Consequently, the following remarks of this chapter are applicable only to civil aircraft.

3 The Definition and Delimitation of National and International Airspace

State sovereignty is a fundamental principle in international law.[39] It describes the legal personality of a State and the legal competence it enjoys in relation to its territory and in relation to other States.[40] It follows the doctrine "par in parem non habet imperium" and the common understanding of non-interference with the internal affairs of other States. Aerial sovereignty follows the same rules as territorial sovereignty,[41] and refers to the exclusive competence of a State to exercise its legislative, administrative, and judicial powers within its national airspace.[42] The Chicago Convention reproduces the established principle of complete and exclusive sovereignty regarding superjacent airspace in Art. 1 Chicago Convention by stating that every State has complete and exclusive sovereignty over the airspace above its territory. The term "territory"

35 ICAO Doc LC/29-WP/2–1, Secretariat Study on 'Civil/State Aircraft'(1994) 12.
36 Ibid 5.
37 Art. 3 (c) Chicago Convention.
38 As part of the freedom of the high seas set forth in Art. 87 UNCLOS; see also, Ricardo De Oliveira, 'Does the Current Legal Framework Provide Sufficient Clarity of Law with Regard to Civil and State Aircraft in Relation to Aviation Practicalities?' (2016) 41 Air & Space Law 333.
39 UN-Charter, Art. 2.1. "The Organization is based on the principle of the sovereign equality of all its Members."
40 James Crawford, *Brownlie's Principles of Public International Law* (8th edn, OUP 2012) 204.
41 Malcom N Shaw, *International Law* (9th edn, Cambridge University Press 2021) 404.
42 ICAO Doc ATConf/6-WP/80 'Airspace Sovereignty' Sixth Meeting of the Worldwide Air Transport (18.3–21.3.2013) 1.

is defined in Art. 2 Chicago Convention and encompasses "the land areas and territorial waters adjacent thereto under the sovereignty suzerainty, protection or mandate of such State." The principle of exclusive sovereignty over the airspace above the territory is also accepted as declaratory of customary international law.[43] The concept of sovereignty in airspace above the State's territory as a rule of international air law was also recognized by the ICJ in the *Benin/Niger Case*. The ICJ found that "a boundary represents the line of separation between areas of state sovereignty, not only on the earth's surface but also in the subsoil and in the superjacent column of air."[44] Even though the Chicago Convention follows the approach that airspace is split into national airspace where States enjoy full sovereignty and international airspace as the airspace adjacent to national airspace,[45] it is silent on the geographical scope and dimensions of airspace. The Chicago Convention does not delineate the boundaries between national airspace and international airspace; in other words it does not contain a delimitation and a definition of the term "airspace."[46]

Due to the fact that airspace is part of the legal regime of the subjacent territory, including the sea, one cannot regard the status of airspace without considering the status of the territory and the sea beneath.[47] The delimitation of airspace is dependent on the provisions of the United Convention on the Law of the Sea (UNCLOS) since the horizontal delimitation of airspace is drawn along the national border including territorial waters under the coastal State's sovereignty.[48] The ICJ recognises in the *Nicaragua Case* a connection between the Chicago Convention and UNCLOS and emphasises that the prescription of treaty law on territorial sovereignty in airspace above the territorial sea is a recognition of firmly established customary international law.[49] Even though the territorial waters are part of the territory of States, there is no such right as

43 Robert Jennings & Arthur Watts (eds), *Oppenheim's International Law, Volume 1* (9th edn, Longman 1996) 523: John Cooper, *Roman Law and the Maxim „Cujus est Solum" in International Air Law* (McGill University 1952) 55.

44 *Frontier Dispute (Benin vs. Niger)* (Merits) [2005] ICJ Rep 90, para. 124.

45 Stephan Hobe, 'Airspace' in *Max Planck Encyclopedias of Public International Law* (OUP 2019) para. 2.

46 John Cooper, 'Legal Problems of Upper Space' (1965) 23 J Air L & Comm 311.

47 Art. 1, Art. 2 Chicago Convention, determining national airspace as including territorial waters. Art. 12, stating that "Over the high seas, the rules in force shall be those established under this Convention."

48 Chicago Convention, Art. 2; for an in depth discussion on the interpretation of international air law by taking into account the law of the sea, see chapter 5, 1.2 and 3.1. of this book.

49 *Nicaragua Case* (1986) para. 212.

innocent passage in national airspace.[50] Art. 3 UNCLOS determines territorial waters as not exceeding 12 nautical miles. Therefore, national airspace can be defined as the airspace above the State's territory including the territorial sea and thereby delimitated as not exceeding 12 nautical miles. In contrast, international airspace is airspace which is not national.

4 Jurisdiction in International Air Law

The principle of sovereignty under international law gives rise to the fundamental exclusivity of State sovereignty over the entire territory.[51] Based on the principle of sovereignty, States enjoy territorial jurisdiction over the national territory including the airspace above it as well as personal jurisdiction over nationals and quasi-personal jurisdiction over ships, aircraft and spacecraft.[52] The coexistence of territorial jurisdiction on the one hand and personal and quasi-personal jurisdiction on the other hand may lead to overlaps in the exercise of jurisdiction. It is therefore important to differentiate between abstract jurisdictional powers and specific jurisdictional powers enabling States to exercise or enforce specific tasks in particular in areas beyond national jurisdiction.

The Chicago Convention follows a three-fold approach. In general, Art. 1 Chicago Convention provides for the territorial jurisdiction of States over the airspace above their territory. Additionally, Art. 17 Chicago Convention establishes quasi-personal jurisdiction over aircraft having the nationality of the State in which they are registered. Even though quasi-personal jurisdiction hinges upon the nationality of the aircraft, the Chicago Convention does not define the term of "nationality".[53] Only certain consequences connected with

50 Paul Larsen, Joseph Sweeney & John Gillick, *Aviation Law: Cases, Law and Related Sources* (2nd edn, Martinus Nijhoff 2012) 96. A special case was the *Right of Passage over Indian Territory*, where the ICJ ruled that a State may acquire a right of overflight over foreign territory to reach an enclave due to bilateral customary international law, see *Right of Passage over Indian Territory* (*Portugal v India*) (Merits) [1960] ICJ Rep 6, 39. Art. 25 Chicago Convention stipulates that States have to provide assistance to aircraft in distress, however this does not qualify as "innocent passage" but this obligation is rather based on elementary considerations of humanity, see Gbenga Oduntan, *Sovereignty and Jurisdiction in the Airspace and Outer Space* (Routledge 2012) 152.

51 Cedric Ryngaert, *Jurisdiction in International Law* (2nd edn, OUP 2015) 35.

52 Art. 17 Chicago Convention on the nationality of aircraft, Art. 94 UNCLOS on the flag State jurisdiction; Art. VIII Outer Space Treaty on the jurisdiction of the State of registry of a space object.

53 In this regard, Art. 18 Chicago Convention says that an aircraft cannot be registered in more than one State.

the nationality of the aircraft are mentioned in several other articles of the Chicago Convention, such as Art. 20 on the display of marks and Chapter V regarding the conditions to be fulfilled with respect to aircraft. The Chicago Convention hence creates a co-existence of territorial and quasi-personal jurisdiction when an aircraft enters the airspace of a State different from its State of registry. An aircraft in foreign airspace is subject to the laws of the State of registry and shall also comply with the national laws of the State overflown. States are responsible for implementing measures to ensure that all aircraft bearing their nationality mark comply with the relevant rules and regulations relating to the flight and manoeuvre, *wherever such aircraft may be.*[54] As a consequence, States also have to ensure that their national aircraft comply with certain rules in international airspace.

This leads to the third aspect of jurisdiction, namely the jurisdiction of ICAO to establish rules in airspace above the high seas pursuant to Art. 12 Chicago Convention. This type of functional jurisdiction directly relates to the flight and manoeuvre of aircraft in international airspace. In contrast, the Rome Convention on Damages Caused by Foreign Aircraft to Third Parties on the Surface stipulates in Art. 23 that aircraft on the high seas shall be regarded as part of the territory of the State in which it is registered and hence provides for quasi-territorial jurisdiction in international airspace.[55] Similar, the Tokyo Convention explicitly provides for the jurisdiction of the State of registry regarding certain offences and crimes on board an aircraft in international airspace.[56] Additionally, Art. 4 of the Tokyo Convention sets forth five exception to the registry State's criminal jurisdiction: when the offence has effect on the territory, has been committed by or against a national or permanent resident, is against the security, consists of a breach of any rules or regulations relating to the flight or manoeuvre of aircraft in force or is necessary to ensure the observance of any obligation of the State under a multilateral international agreement. Consequently, the Chicago Convention does not provide for the complete and exclusive jurisdiction of the State in which the aircraft is registered. Instead, there is a variety of rules on jurisdiction depending on the applicable regime.

International air law is therefore characterized by a functional division. Rules on civil aviation result from the quasi-legislative function of ICAO, other

---

54 Art. 12 Chicago Convention.

55 Rome Convention on Damages Caused by Foreign Aircraft to Third Parties on the Surface (9 September 1958) 310 UNTS 181.

56 Tokyo Convention on Offences and Certain Other Acts Committed on Board Aircraft (Tokyo Convention) (1969) 1969 UNTS 2.

international organizations and also to a large extent from bilateral aviation agreements.[57] Other rules relating to international air law, in particular rules on national security relating to threats emanating from the air and State aircraft, are part of the prescriptive jurisdiction of States. This interplay between different forms of jurisdiction may result in the creation of (harmful) concurrent jurisdiction in areas beyond national jurisdiction. This can only be alleviated through methods of treaty interpretation based on the common understanding that, in general, States may not use coercive powers to enforce rules outside their territory unless a treaty or customary international law explicitly provides for enforcement jurisdiction. The abstract principles of jurisdiction, namely the territorial, personal, universal and protective principles, do not necessarily lead to the exercise of State powers for specific competences but in most cases a treaty or a rule of customary international law provides for specific prescriptive or enforcement jurisdiction.[58] Particularly the aspect of State function exercised by State officials in areas beyond national jurisdiction or in foreign territory requires careful assessment.[59] In the context of international air law, the issue of enforcement jurisdiction is closely connected with the powers of the aircraft commander or pilot during a flight. While the Chicago Convention does not list any specific powers of pilots, the Tokyo Convention provides for extensive powers of the aircraft commander in relation to certain offences taking place on board an aircraft in foreign airspace.[60] In international airspace, national law regulates the actions of the aircraft commander for offences and acts committed on board a civil aircraft in flight.[61]

Following the traditional differentiation between *acta iure imperii* and *acta iure gestionis*, the question also arises whether a State could rely on immunity while carrying out functions in civil aviation.[62] One opinion suggests that interception actions qualify as *acta iure imperii*, while air traffic management

---

57 On the role of EUROCONTROL, A Majid, 'Legal Capacity of Eurocontrol to Ensure Smooth Aviation in Europe' (1991) 16 Air Law 267.

58 See for the discussion on the Lotus principle, above chapter 2.

59 For example, the Vienna Convention on Diplomatic Relations (1961) 500 UNTS 95 on certain functions of diplomats on foreign State territory and chapter VII of the UN-Charta on coercive measures authorised by the UN-Security Council.

60 Chapter III of the Tokyo Convention.

61 Art. 5 Tokyo Convention reads: The provisions of this Chapter shall not apply to offences and acts committed or about to be committed by a person on board an aircraft in flight in the airspace of the State of registration or over the high seas or any other area outside the territory of any State unless the last point of take-off or the next point of intended landing is situated in a State other than that of registration, or the aircraft subsequently flies in the airspace of a State other than that of registration with such person still on board.

62 Pablo Mendes de Leon, Introduction to Air Law (10th edn Kluwer 2017) 33.

can be characterized as *acta iure gestionis*.[63] For reasons of completeness, it shall also be mentioned that the UN Convention on Jurisdiction Immunity of States and their Property provides for the immunity of aircraft operated by States. Even though the Convention is not yet in force, it shows that State aircraft in general are immune from the jurisdiction of courts of other States.[64] Additionally, the UN Convention on the Law of the Sea provides for the sovereign immunity of State aircraft regarding the provisions on the protection and preservation of the marine environment.

5 Overview of Aerial Zones

The following part illustrates three different forms of no-fly zones and their distinction from ADIZs. As can be observed, international air law is familiar with the concept of aerial zones imposing certain limitations on aircraft in both national and international airspace. The three unique forms of no-fly zones will be described in a cursory manner for the sake of completeness, but will not be subjected to a comprehensive examination of their legal aspects:

1. Territorial no-fly zone or "special use airspace": States can prohibit or restrict flights of all aircraft with and without a temporal limit inside their national airspace pursuant to Art. 9 Chicago Convention.[65]
2. Extraterritorial no-fly zone: States can impose national laws which prohibit national aircraft to fly inside certain areas in foreign airspace.[66]
3. Supranational no-fly zone: The Security Council can create a no-fly zone over foreign territory applicable to all aircraft.

5.1 *Territorial No-fly Zones*

Pursuant to Art. 9 Chicago Convention, a contracting State may "for reasons of military necessity or public safety, restrict or prohibit uniformly the aircraft of

63 Ibid.

64 Art. 3 (3) United Nations Convention on Jurisdictional Immunity of States and their Property (2004).

65 For example, India has several no-fly zones, one of them is located over the Kalpakkam nuclear installation. No aircraft may fly up to the height of 10,000 ft. over the area within a radius of 10 kms, see order No.9/38/77-IR Vol.II, retrieved from http://dgca.nic.in/aic/aic14_2008.pdf. Also in US airspace, many no-fly zones can be found, see https://www.faa.gov/uas/recreational_fliers/where_can_i_fly/airspace_restrictions/. The majority prohibited areas are located above military infrastructure.

66 The Federal Aviation Administration of the US provides a list of all restricted an prohibited areas worldwide, see https://www.faa.gov/air_traffic/publications/us_restrictions/ (accessed, 06.02.2019).

other States from flying over certain areas of its territory."[67] The prohibition of overflight in national airspace is not discriminatory, as there is no distinction made between aircraft belonging to the State whose territory is involved in international scheduled airline services and those belonging to other contracting States engaged in the same activities.[68] Annex 15 of the Chicago Convention further concretizes Art. 9 and distinguishes between a prohibited area and a restricted area. Accordingly, a prohibited area is defined as

> An airspace of defined dimensions, above the land areas or territorial waters of a State, within which the flight of aircraft is prohibited.[69]

Whereas a restricted area can be defined as

> An airspace of defined dimensions, above the land areas or territorial waters of a State, within which the flight of aircraft is restricted in accordance with certain specified conditions.[70]

In the event that prohibited and restricted areas are not subject to temporal limitations, they may not encompass the entirety of the State's territory. Areas that are prohibited and restricted without temporal limitations must satisfy certain criteria in order for them to be considered legally valid:

- Reason of military necessity or public safety;
- No distinction between foreign aircraft and national aircraft;[71]
- Reasonable extent and location;
- No unnecessary interference with air navigation; and
- Publication of description.[72]

In contrast, temporary prohibition zones do not require the existence of military necessity, but rather exceptional circumstances or a period of emergency pursuant to Art. 9 (b) Chicago Convention. Moreover, in contrast to no-fly zones pursuant to Art. 9 (a), temporary prohibition zones may extend over the entire territory.[73]

---

67 Art. 9 Chicago Convention; Oliver Lissitzyn, 'The Treatment of Aerial Intruders in Recent Practice and International Law' (1953) 47 AJIL 568.

68 Nicolas M Matte, *Treatise on Air-Aeronautical Law* (McGill University 1981) 173.

69 Chicago Convention, Annex 15, 1-8.

70 Ibid, p 1-9.

71 *Appeal Relating to the Jurisdiction of the ICAO Council (Paksitan v India)* (Merits) (1972) ICJ Rep 1974.

72 Art. 9 (a) Chicago Convention.

73 Peter Keenan, Anthony Lester & Peter Martin, *Shawcross and Beaumont on Air Law* (3rd edn, Butterworths 1966) 206.

Not all States act in conformity with these requirements. For instance, Hong Kong established a prohibition zone over Hong Kong Disneyland to avoid noise and visual disturbances.[74] Consequently, there was no military necessity or public safety rationale for the temporarily unrestricted zone. Another significant conflict arising from Art. 9 (a) of the Chicago Convention occurred in 1967 when Spain declared a prohibited area in the vicinity of Gibraltar for fundamental reasons of national security, which prompted protest from the United Kingdom.[75] The dispute was brought before the ICAO Council but was subsequently deferred *sine die*.[76] An example of a violation of Art. 9 Chicago Convention on the grounds of discrimination was India's suspension of overflights over its territory by Pakistani civil aircraft only. The suspension of overflights by Pakistan arose out of a hijacking incident of an Indian aircraft.[77] In the ensuing dispute, India denied the ICAO Council's competence and turned to the ICJ. The dispute was ultimately resolved in 1976 through a joint statement by the parties announcing the cessation of proceedings.[78]

Some authors have proposed that Art. 9 Chicago Convention may provide for a possible legal foundation for ADIZs in national airspace.[79] The underlying rationale for both ADIZs and territorial no-fly zones is the principle of sovereignty in airspace above national territory. However, Annex 4 and Annex 15 explicitly differentiate between ADIZs and prohibited and restricted areas. ADIZs serve a specific purpose: to identify aircraft for defence reasons. They do not require a reason of military necessity or public safety. As long as aircraft comply with the identification obligations of ADIZs, they may freely traverse through national airspace freely. In contrast, prohibited and restricted areas exclude all aircraft from traversing through national airspace over a certain part of the territory. Aircraft cannot evade the blockade of airspace by identifying themselves. It can be seen that Art. 9 Chicago Convention does not provide for advanced notification and identification requirements. Moreover, Annex 4

74 https://www.cad.gov.hk/english/flight_prohib_area.html (accessed 06.02.2019).

75 ICAO Doc 8724 A16-P/3 'Annual report of the Council to the Assembly for 1967' (1968) 116.

76 ICAO Doc 8869 A18-P/2 'Annual Report of the Council to the Assembly for 1969' (1970). Another dispute concerned the relations between Pakistan and India after establishing prohibited areas between 1918 and 1947, see D Bhatti, H Drion, & P Heller 'Prohibited Areas in International Civil Aviation' (1953) U.S. and Canadian Aviation Reports 109.

77 *Appeal Relating to the Jurisdiction of the ICAO Coucil* (*India v Pakistan*) (Merits) [1972] ICJ Rep 1974 64. The case was brought forward to the ICJ, who ultimately dismissed the appeal.

78 Paul S Dempsey, *Public International Air Law* (2nd edn, McGill University 2017) 709.

79 Stefan Kaiser, 'The Legal Status of Air Defense Identification Zones: Tensions over the East China Sea' (2016) 63 ZLW 534.

regulates prohibited, restricted and danger areas under paragraph 7.9.2 and ADIZs under 7.9.3 separately.[80] Consequently, Art. 9 Chicago Convention does not serve as a legal basis to claim an ADIZ neither in either national or international airspace.

5.2 *Extraterritorial No-fly Zones*

The second form of no-fly zones, extraterritorial no-fly zones, have their legal basis in national legislation and affect solely aircraft registered on the respective State's registry. Based on national law, States can declare prohibition and restriction zones to prevent national aircraft from flying over an as dangerous for aviation determined area in foreign territory.[81] For instance, in the aftermath of the downing of the civilian aircraft Malaysian Airlines Flight MH17, the United States established a no-fly zone over Ukraine and prohibited certain US flight operations in the Simferopol Flight Information Region (FIR UKFV) and Dnipropetrovsk Flight Information Region (FIR UKDV).[82] In contrast to Art. 9 Chicago Convention, States are only permitted to impose restrictions on national aircraft. These restrictions must not affect any other aircraft and must not infringe upon the sovereignty of the affected State. Extraterritorial no-fly zones serve a specific purpose, namely to prevent national aircraft from flying in risk-induced airspace. ADIZs and extraterritorial no-fly zones are therefore two separate concepts.

5.3 *The Security Council's No-fly Zones*

The third form of no-fly zones is the so-called "no-fly order" of the Security Council.[83] A "no-fly-zone" is a legal measure to prohibit a State from exercising effective control over its entire airspace, or parts thereof, while another State, groups of States or international organisations are authorised to exercise the same control.[84] In the context of the Arab Spring in 2011, the Security Council adopted Resolution 1973 and imposed a no-fly zone on all flights in

---

80 Chicago Convention, Annex 4, 11th ed. (2005).

81 For example: 49, US Code, Subtitle I, sections 106(f) and (g) in accordance with 49, US Code, Subtitle VII, Part A, subpart III, section 44701.

82 Rule, 83 FR 52954, 14 CFR 91; Prohibited and restricted areas under US Law are listed here https://www.faa.gov/air_traffic/publications/us_restrictions/.

83 Michel Bourbonniere & Louis Haeck, 'Military Aircraft And International Law: Chicago Opus' (2000) 66 J Air L & Com 956.

84 Stefan Kaiser, 'No-Fly Zones Established by the United Nations Security Council' (2011) 60 ZLW 402.

Libyan airspace in order to protect civilians and diminish aerial aggression.[85] In doing so, the Security Council relied on the Responsibility to Protect Principle (R2P),[86] and first authorised intervention for the protection of civilians against the will of a State with an intact government.[87] It is important to note that the no-fly zones created by the Security Council cannot be regarded as ADIZs. Firstly, ADIZs can only be claimed by States but not by the Security Council. Secondly, no-fly zones are not established for identification procedures but for the protection of civilians and hence serve a different purpose.[88] Moreover, no-fly orders adopted by the Security Council also restrict States to regulate airspace above their territory. This is in line with Art. 103 UN-Charter, which stipulates that in the event of a conflict between obligations under the UN-Charter and obligations under any other international agreement, the obligations under the UN-Charter prevail.[89] The priority of obligations under the UN-Charter also encompasses the binding decisions of the Security Council.[90]

6 The Legality of ADIZs in National Airspace

As previously stated, each State is entitled to regulate its national airspace as part of its sovereignty.[91] Sovereign airspace includes two main elements namely the use and control of national airspace without any interference

---

85 UN Security Council S/RES/1973 (2011) invoking S/RES/1970 (2011); Michael N Schmitt, 'Wings over Lybia – The No Fly Zone in Legal Perspective' (2011) 36 Yale J Int'l L online 46, 47.

86 On the topic of Responsibility to Protect, see: ICISS Report, *The Responsibility to Protect* (2001); Alan J Kuperman, 'Rethinking the Responsibility to Protect' (2008) 19 Whitehead J Diplo & Int'l Rel 19–28; Julia Hoffmann & Andre Nollkaemper, *Responsibility to Protect: From Principle to Practice* (Pallas Publication 2012); Peter Hilpold (ed), *Responsibility to Protect: A new Paradigm of International Law?* (Brill Nihjoff 2015).

87 Alex Bellamy, 'Libya and the Responsibility to Protect: The Exception and the Norm' (2011) 25 Ethics & Int'l Affairs 263, 264.

88 UN Security Council S/RES/1973 (2011) which reads: "Considering that the establishment of a ban on all flights in the airspace of the Libyan Arab Jamahiriya constitutes an important element for the protection of civilians as well as the safety of the delivery of humanitarian assistance and a decisive step for the cessation of hostilities in Libya".

89 Johann R Laeiae & Andreas Paulus, 'Ch. XVI Miscellaneous Provisions, Article 103' in Bruno Simma et al (eds), *The Charter of the United Nations: A Commentary, Volume 2* (OUP 2012) 2136.

90 *Question of Interpretation and Application of the 1971 Montreal Convention Arising from the Aerial Incident at Lockerbie* (*Libyan Arab Jamahiriya v United Kingdom and the United States*) (Provisional Measures) [1992] ICJ Rep 3, 114.

91 Jean Ritchie, *Prohibited Areas in International Air Law* (LL.M. Thesis 1969) 40.

from other States. This also correlates with the principle of non-intervention, which signifies that other States cannot exercise power within another State's territory.[92] The Friendly Relations Declaration further emphasises that any form of intervention violates the spirit and letter of the UN-Charter and creates situations, which threaten international peace and security.[93] The passage through national airspace and landing rights on the territory are hence subject to the control of the State whose territory is to be overflown.[94] This principle of exclusive control is also reflected in the provisions of the Chicago Convention. Pursuant to Art. 6 Chicago Convention, a scheduled international air service, namely commercial airline services, may not be operated over or into the territory of a contracting State without that State's special authorisation.[95] Similarly, Art. 3 (c) requires that a special authorisation be obtained for state aircraft to fly over the territory of another State.[96] Consequently, flights may be restricted unilaterally at the discretion of the State within its in national airspace and aircraft have to comply with the national air law of the respective State therein.[97]

While the exclusive sovereignty of States over their national airspace is an indisputable fact,[98] the principle of complete sovereignty is qualified by various multilateral and bilateral conventions that provide for exemptions to cross

92 *Nicaragua Case* (1986) para. 202, 251 "The effects of the principle of respect for territorial sovereignty inevitably overlap with those of the principles of the prohibition of the use of force and of non-intervention."; Maziar Jamenjad & Michael Wood, 'The Principle of Non-Intervention' (2009) 22 Leiden J Int'l L 347.

93 UN General Assembly, 'Declaration on Principles of International Law concerning Friendly Relations and Cooperation among States in accordance with the Charter of the United Nations' A/RES/2625(XXV) 24 October 1970.

94 Gbenga Oduntan, *Sovereignty and Jurisdiction in the Airspace and Outer Space* (Routledge 2012) 65.

95 Art. 6 Chicago Convention. However, Art. 5 Chicago Convention contains an exemption for non-scheduled airflights from requesting prior authorisation, granting them right to fly over contracting States and to stop for non-traffic purposes. On the right of scheduled flights to cross the territory of contracting States without landing and to land for non-traffic purposes see the two-Freedoms Agreement.

96 Chicago Convention, Art. 3: "No state aircraft of a contracting State shall fly over the territory of another State or land thereon without authorization by special agreement or otherwise, and in accordance with the terns thereof."

97 Sigmar Stadlmeier, 'Luftverkehr' in August Reinisch (ed), Österreischisches Handbuch des Völkerrechts (5th edn, Manz 2013) 509.

98 *Nicaragua Case* (1986) para. 212, 251, "The basic legal concept of State sovereignty in customary international law [...] extends to the internal waters and territorial sea of every State and to the airspace above its territory. The principle of respect for territorial sovereignty is also directly infringed by the unauthorized overflight of a State's territory."

and land in the territories of the States parties.[99] The Chicago Convention encompasses in Art. 5 the right to fly through national air space of all contracting parties for non-scheduled flight.[100] The right under Art. 5 can be restricted "as each contracting State nevertheless reserves the right, for reasons of safety of flight, to require aircraft desiring to proceed over regions which are inaccessible or without adequate air navigation facilities to follow prescribed routes, or to obtain special permission for such flights." Furthermore, the majority of international air traffic is comprised of scheduled flights, which are primarily operated by commercial airlines.

A State may establish an ADIZ in its own airspace based on the principle of sovereignty and may require foreign aircraft to comply with the ADIZ's identification procedures when traversing sovereign airspace.[101] National law can set forth details on the identification procedures of ADIZ in sovereign airspace. National airspace aligns with the territorial sea and thus extends to 12 nautical miles measured from baselines determined in accordance with UNCLOS.[102] Therefore, national ADIZs are also delimited by the territorial sea. In contrast to the law of the sea, there is no right of innocent passage in national airspace that might preclude the creation of an ADIZ.[103] The disagreement between States on the inclusion of the freedom of overflight and innocent passage above States' territory in the text of the Chicago Convention led to a separate agreement.[104] The International Air Service Transit Agreement of 1944 provides for the "freedoms of the air" in Art. 1, namely the "privilege to fly across its territory without landing", and "the privilege to land for non-traffic purposes."[105] These two privileges only apply to scheduled international air services but not non-scheduled or military aircraft. However, the Transit Agreement is of almost no significance as only 11 States have signed it. Outside

---

99 Oliver Lissitzyn, 'The Treatment of Aerial Intruders in Recent Practice and International Law' (1953) 47 AJIL 559. Christopher Petras, 'The Law of Air Mobility-the International Legal Principles behind the US Mobility Air Forces' Mission' (2010) 44 in Air Force L Rev 57.

100 Art. 5 Chicago Convention.

101 Ruwantissa Abeyratne, 'In Search of Theoretical Justification for Air Defence Identification Zones' (2011) J Transp Secur 87.

102 Art. 3 UNCLOS.

103 Jaw Woon Lee, 'Revisiting Freedom of Overflight in International Air Law: Minimum Multilateralism in International Air Transport' (2013) 38 Air and Space Law 355; Gbenga Oduntan, *Sovereignty and Jurisdiction in the Airspace and Outer Space* (Routledge 2012) 151. See on the right to innocent passage through the territorial sea, Art. 17 UNCLOS.

104 Jaw Woon Lee, 'Revisiting Freedom of Overflight in International Air Law: Minimum Multilateralism in International Air Transport' (2013) 38 Air and Space Law 360.

105 International Air Services Transit Agreement 84 UNTS 389.

the scope of the Transit Agreement, foreign commercial aircraft cannot freely fly across the territory of other States without its prior permission.[106] Even if the Air Service Transit Agreement is applicable, the establishment of an ADIZ would be a legitimate practice in line with the agreement, as aircraft can "fly across its territory without landing" as long as they comply with the identification requirements. National ADIZs are not in conflict with the provisions of the Chicago Convention nor any (non-existing) innocent passage regime. Art 1. Chicago Convention provides for the legal basis to establish an ADIZ in national airspace.[107] As previously stated, Art. 9 (b) Chicago Convention outlines the conditions and requirements for the restriction of overflight in certain areas. It could be argued that the conditions and requirements for the establishment of restricted areas pursuant to Art. 9 Chicago Convention could be applied to ADIZs. The criteria of non-discrimination and reasonableness in extent and location, should be equally applicable to ADIZs in national airspace in order to avoid undue interference with air navigation.[108]

7 The Legality of ADIZs in International Airspace

The following sub-chapter examines the Chicago Convention and its Annexes as potential the legal basis for ADIZs in international airspace. It aims to discuss the authority of the State to prescribe rules applicable to aircraft in international airspace in relation to ICAO's quasi-legislative powers. The discussion will first illustrate certain examples of extraterritorial jurisdiction granted by the Chicago Convention, before turning to an in-depth analysis of relevant provisions for the creation of an ADIZ in international airspace and the rule-making system of the Chicago Convention.

106 Paul P C Haanappel, 'The Transformation of Sovereignty in the Air' in Chia-Jui Cheng (eds), *The Use of Air and Outer Space Cooperation and Competition* (Martinus Nijhoff 1998) at 24 stating that innocent passage needs to be negotiated bilaterally.

107 Jinyuan Su, 'The East China Sea Air Defense Identification Zone and International Law'(2015) 14 Chinese J Int'l L 276.

108 The „temporal" criterion could be omitted as a restricted area affect air transport more severely, whereas ADIZ only require the identification of aircraft and therefore can be permanently established. See also Andrew Williams, 'The Interception of Civil Aircraft over the High Seas in the Global War on Terror' (2007) 59 A F L Rev at 96: "International law permits states to establish reasonable conditions of entry into their territorial airspace, ... [provided] the conditions are applied to the aircraft of all contracting states 'without distinction' as to their nationality."

7.1 *The Administration of International Airspace: Flight Information Regions*

Airspace is divided into Flight Information Regions (FIR), which are defined in Annex 11 as "an airspace of defined dimensions within which flight information service and alerting service are provided."[109] The Chicago Convention's Annex 11 thus governs the regime of FIR, ensuring unproblematic and smooth air traffic. FIR are certain areas over land and waters in which the civil air navigation services providers (ANSP) of a contracting States have administrative functions and the responsibility for providing air traffic control.[110] These regions are established by States parties to the Chicago Convention, which provide flight information services in national as well as international airspace. The safe conduct of air traffic has been the central point since the early beginnings of negotiations on an international framework dealing with civil aviation and FIR serve to sustain this purpose. FIR aim to prevent collisions between aircraft, maintain an orderly flow of air traffic, and provide advice and information useful for the safe and efficient conduct of flights.[111] Three principal functions can be discerned: the provision of flight information services, alerting services and air traffic control services.

The general flight rules of Annex 2 apply to FIR and encompass *inter alia* visual flight rules and instrument flight rules.[112] A well-functioning FIR system is of utmost importance and requires a well-established air traffic management service and communication systems because the safety of the whole air traffic industry depends on reliable air services. For example in Austria, Austro Control Ltd. is the responsible air traffic service provider for the safe conduct of civil aviation inside the FIR Vienna.[113] Air service providers are responsible for the administration of air traffic, which involves the provision of information for the safe and efficient conduct of flights, the alerting of aircraft in distress, and the determination of air traffic routes, landings, and take-offs.

The dimensions of each FIR may vary considerably, encompassing vast oceanic areas within international airspace or merely the airspace above a single State. In the event that the FIR is situated above the high seas, the International Civil Aviation Organization delegates the responsibility for providing

109 Chicago Convention, Annex 11; ICAO Doc 4444 PANS-ATM 'Air Traffic Management' (16th edn, 2016).

110 Ruth Marlin, *Understanding Air Traffic Control Financing* (National Air Traffic Controllers Association 2005) 5.

111 Chicago Convention, Annex 11.

112 Chicago Convention, Annex 2.

113 See for more information, https://www.austrocontrol.at/ (accessed 6.9.2022). The boundaries of the Vienna FIR coincides with the borders of Austria.

navigational information to certain States.[114] In international airspace, States provide services based on regional air navigation agreements between neighbouring States and air navigation plans (ANPs), which serve as a repository document for the assignment of responsibilities to States for the provision of air navigation facilities and services.[115] The air navigation service of the respective contracting States is responsible for concluding a regional air navigation agreement following a Regional Air Navigation Meeting, which has to be subsequently approved by ICAO.[116] It is not within the purview of States to establish a FIR outside their national airspace without the express permission of ICAO. In the majority of cases, coastal States provide air traffic services in airspace above the high seas approved by ICAO, thereby exercising administrative jurisdiction beyond the boundaries of their national territory.

ADIZ and FIR are two different concepts.[117] During the Cold War, FIRs were deemed inadequate to prevent the unannounced incursion of national airspace.[118] For this reasons, ADIZs were established as an early warning system to detect such incursions and initiate defensive measures in the event of non-compliance with identification procedures for security reasons.[119] In general, ADIZs and FIR differ significantly in their purpose. ADIZs are buffer zones dedicated to the identification of intruding aircraft for the purpose of national security, whereas FIRs aim to provide air services and ensure safe air traffic.[120] Since States may exercise jurisdiction in areas beyond national territory in the form of FIRs in international airspace, a discussion on the establishment of ADIZs as part of extraterritorial jurisdiction is possible.[121] It is important to

114 Such as in the case of Japan and the Fukuoka FIR, see ICAO Doc RASMAG/15–WP/2101–05/08/2011, 'Safety Assessment of RVSM within the Fukuoka FIR' (2011); on the diameters of the Fukuoka FIR, see Civil Aviation Bureau (Japan), https://www.mlit.go.jp/common/001132162.pdf (accessed 6.9.2022).

115 ICAO Doc 9750, 'Global Air Navigation Plan (GANP)'; Art. 28 (c) Chicago Convention.

116 Ruwantissa Abeyratne, *Convention On International Civil Aviation – A Commentary* (Springer 2014) 182.

117 Annex 11 describes FIR as being different from ADIZ and includes also different definitions for each concept.

118 Alex Calvo, 'China's Air Defense Identification Zone Concept, Issues at Stake and Regional Impact' (2013) Naval War College Press Working Paper 10.

119 Demetri Sevastopulo, 'Q&A: What is an air defence identification zone?' Financial Times (29 November 2013).

120 Taisaku Ikeshima, 'China's Air Defense Identification Zone (ADIZ) and its Impact on the Territorial and Maritime Disputes in the East and South China Seas' (2016) 3 Tanscommunication 156.

121 According to the foreword of Annex 11: „The standards and recommended practices in Annex 11 apply in those parts of the airspace under the jurisdiction of a Contracting State within Air Traffic Services are provided and also wherever a Contracting State accepts

note that FIRs above the high seas do not amount to an extension of sovereignty to these areas.[122] This insight is equally relevant for the establishment of ADIZs in international airspace, as they do not necessarily imply a change of sovereignty or an extension of sovereignty.[123]

7.2 *The Flexible Use of Airspace* (*FUA*)

Even though the Chicago Convention applies solely to civil aircraft, ICAO nevertheless strives to coordinate the use of airspace by civil as well as military aircraft.[124] Under the concept of the flexible use of airspace (FUA), airspace is no longer categorised as exclusively "civil" or "military" airspace; rather airspace is regarded as "one continuum and allocated according to user requirements."[125] Under the FUA concept airspace shall be managed to accommodate both civil and military requirements on the use of airspace.[126] The concept describes the availability of airspace for military purposes, whereby airspace can be temporarily segregated based on real-time usage within a specific time frame.[127] EUROCONTROL specified the concept even more:

> Airspace allocation is dynamically updated and information is constantly being shared to all affected participants. An example of this is informing airspace users when their desired trajectory is impacted by the request for airspace reservation made by a military user. The trajectory can then

---

the responsibility of providing Air Traffic Services over the high seas or in airspace of undetermined sovereignty. A Contracting State accepting such responsibility may apply the standards and recommended practices in a manner consistent with that adopted for airspace under its jurisdiction."

122 Benjamyn I Scott & Andrea Trimarchi, *Fundamental of International Aviation and Policy* (Routledge 2009) 35.

123 See ICAO Doc SAIOACG/9 – WP 29, para. 2.16. stating that ADIZ cannot be established in International airspace based on sovereignty.

124 Also under the Single European Sky, Commission Regulation (EC) No 2150/2005 of 23 December 2005 lays down common rules for the flexible use of airspace by stating that "(f)lexible use of airspace is an airspace management concept described by the International Civil Aviation Organisation (ICAO) and developed by the European Organisation for the Safety of Aviation (Eurocontrol), according to which airspace should not be designated as either purely civil or purely military airspace, but should rather be considered as one continuum in which all users' requirements have to be accommodated to the maximum extent possible."

125 ICAO, Manual on the Flexible Use of Airspace; EUROCONTROL, *Flexible Use of Airspace* (*FUA*) *– AMC/CADF Operations Manual* (2022).

126 ICAO, 'Civil and Military ATM Cooperation (CMAC) and Flexible Use of Airspace (FUA)', https://www.icao.int/APAC/APAC-RSO/Pages/Civil-Mil-Coordination.aspx.

127 EUROCONTROL, *The EUROCONTROL Concept of the Flexible Use of Airspace* (2002) 2.

> be updated accordingly. Military users are to be informed of the impact of their request on the planned trajectories so that they may choose a solution that keeps the impact of reservation to a minimum.[128]

The overarching objective is to utilise airspace in a dynamic manner, thereby enhancing flexibility and minimising the impact on civil aviation while satisfying the needs of military airspace users.[129] Under the ICAO system, specific civil-military cells can be established to address the requirements of both civil and military air traffic. The joint civil-military cell is responsible for establishing the procedures and measures required for implementing the flexible use of airspace. The establishment of the joint civil-military cell is agreed upon between ICAO and the civil aviation authority of the respective States. The idea of the FUA is relevant for the discussion on ADIZS, as some States base the legitimacy of their zones on the need to align military and civil uses within the ADIZ.[130] It can be seen that a close collaboration between ICAO and States effectuates new concepts for the use of airspace.

7.3 *Article 11: Regulating the Admission to National Airspace*

One potential legal basis for the establishment of ADIZS in international airspace could be found in Article 11 of the Chicago Convention, which reads:

> Subject to the provision of this Convention, the laws and regulations of a contracting State relating to the admission to or departure from its territory of aircraft engaged in international air navigation, or to the operation and navigation of such aircraft while within its territory, shall be applied to the aircraft of all contracting States without distinction as to nationality, and shall be complied with by such aircraft upon entering or departing from or while within the territory of that State.

Art. 11 Chicago Convention expressly recognises the right of each Contracting State to apply national laws to aircraft upon entering national airspace, such as national aviation acts regulating the overflight of the territory as well as rules of the air and technical standards.[131] Art. 11 Chicago Convention permits

---

128 EUROCONTROL, 'Advanced Flexible Use of Airspace', https://www.eurocontrol.int/publication/advanced-flexible-use-airspace-afua-concept.

129 EUROCONTROL, *European Action Plan for Airspace Infringement Risk Reduction* (2022) 5.

130 See chapter 3 of this book.

131 Ashley Roach, 'Air Identification Zones' in *Max Planck Encyclopedias of Public International Law* (OUP 2017) para.4. See for example §8 of the Austrian Aviation Act (Federal

the implementation of national aeronautical procedures with binding effect on foreign aircraft engaged in international air navigation bound for national airspace, even if they are still in the national airspace of another State or in international airspace.[132] The possibility of imposing certain operational rules on the access and departure of aircraft to and from a State's territory is not limited to any specific reasons.[133] While no specific reason is required for the applicability of national air regulations on aircraft intending to enter national airspace, some States based entry conditions on operational as well as environmental reasons. Germany, for example, prohibits overflight over its territory below a certain altitude at specified times in order to reduce the noise of air traffic.[134] In accordance with law of the European Union in conformity with Art. 11 Chicago Convention, restrictions imposed must be interpreted narrowly and subject to considerations of proportionality and necessity.[135]

Art. 11 Chicago Convention is directly relevant for ADIZs, as it allows for the regulation of the admission of national as well as foreign aircraft into national airspace.[136] However, a conceptual problem remains regarding the actual scope of the entry conditions. It is unclear whether Art. 11 of the Chicago Convention provides for the establishment of a specific reporting point or for a wide-ranging reporting zone of designated airspace.[137] There is no indication of the geographical scope of application of Art. 11 Chicago Convention whatsoever, leaving the reach of its application unresolved.[138] Nevertheless, it seems

Law Gazette Nr. 253/1957) prescribing whether and under what conditions a permit from Austro Control GmbH is required for entry into and departure from the territory of Austria.

132 Stefan Kaiser, 'The Legal Status of Air Defense Identification Zones: Tensions over the East China Sea' (2016) 63 ZLW 530.

133 Lisa Tomas, 'Air Law' in *Max Planck Encyclopedias of Public International Law* (OUP 2008) para. 52.

134 *Swiss Confederation v European Commission*, European Court of Justice, Case C-547/10 P (7 March 2003). As a result the landing approached from Swiss territory were no longer possible during a specific period of time.

135 Art. 15, Art. 20, Regulation (EC) No 1008/2008 of the European Parliament and of the Council of 24 September 2008 on common rules for the operation of air services in the Community (Current consolidated version: 28/05/2020).

136 Roncevert Almond, 'Clearing the Air above the East China Sea: The Primary Elements of Aircraft Defense Identification Zones' (2017) 7 Harvard Nat Sec J 149. Also, Kirk Davies et al, *Air Force Operations and the Law* (3rd ed., Maxwell Air Force Base, Ala.: Judge Advocate General's School, 2014) 78.

137 Stefan Kaiser, 'The Legal Status of Air Defense Identification Zones: Tensions over the East China Sea' (2016) 63 ZLW 530.

138 Edmund J Burke & Astrid Stuth Cevallos, *In Line or out of Order? – Chinas Approach to ADIZ in Theory and Practice* (Rand 2017) at 5, stating that based on the right to establish reasonable entry condition, States may require aircraft to give a position report at least

reasonable to assume that Art. 11 Chicago Convention grants States the extension of State powers beyond national airspace to some extent.[139]

The ICAO Council discussed the actions taken by States for the non-compliance with national aeronautical regulations based on Art. 11 Chicago Convention, but did not reach a definitive conclusion.[140] This primary discussion on the admission to national airspace formed the basis of Annex 17 Chicago Convention and established a link between the security aspects of Annex 17 and Art. 11 Chicago Convention.[141] Even though not explicitly mentioned in the treaty text of the Chicago Convention, the term "security" can be understood as "a combination of measures and human and material resources intended to safeguard civil aviation against acts of unlawful interference."[142] According to Annex 17, Recommended Practice 6.1.2, each ICAO Member State should require the operators of aircraft of to conform to the international civil aviation security requirements of the States into which they operate.[143] Annex 17 reflects the importance of preventive measures, especially with regard to the involvement of civil aircraft used as part of a terrorist attack.[144]

The aspect of preventing threats is also relevant to the discussion on ADIZS. Annex 17, 6.1.2 indicates compliance with the national regulations on ADIZS as it encourages each Member State to require the operators of aircraft to conform with security requirements. Some States apply their ADIZS' rules only to aircraft intending to enter national airspace, while other States impose identification procedures also on aircraft traversing through the ADIZS not bound for national airspace.[145] It is therefore clear that the reasonable entry conditions as promulgated in Art. 11 Chicago Convention may only be applied to aircraft that are actually intending to enter national airspace.[146] Consequently,

one hour prior to ADIZ penetration and file the estimated time of penetration at least 15 minutes prior to entering the ADIZ.

139 Ruwantissa Abeyratne, *Convention on International Civil Aviation* (Springer 2014) at 155, speaking of "sovereignty extended".

140 ICAO Doc 7367, A7-P/1 (16 June–6 July 1953).

141 Ruwantissa Abeyratne, *Convention on International Civil Aviation* (Springer 2014) 155.

142 Chicago Convention, Annex 17.

143 Chicago Convention, Annex 17; Ruwantissa Abeyratne, *Aviation Security Law* (Springer 2010) discussing in particular the importance of Annex 17 with regard to the threat of cyber attacks at 17ff.

144 Jiefang Huang, 'Security Regulations' in Paul S Dempsey & Ram Jahku (eds), *Routledge Handbook of Public Aviation Law* (Taylor Francis 2016) 161.

145 See on this discussion chapter 3, 2.2.

146 Matthew Stubbs & Dale Stephens, 'Dredge Your Way to China? The Legal Significance of Chinese Reclamation and Construction in the South China Sea'(2017) 2 Asia-Pacific Journal Of Ocean Law And Policy 43.

Art. 11 Chicago Convention may therefore only serve as a legal basis for ADIZs applicable on aircraft entering national airspace, while Annex 17 provides for the compliance mechanism, particularly with national aviation security rules.

7.4 *Article 12: Rules of the Air in International Airspace*

In the context of the ongoing debate surrounding the legal status of ADIZs in international airspace, it is particularly pertinent to consider Art. 12 Chicago Convention, which reads as follows:

> Each contracting State undertakes to adopt measures to insure that every aircraft flying over or manoeuvring within its territory and that every aircraft carrying its nationality mark, wherever such aircraft may be, shall comply with the rules and regulations relating to the flight and manoeuvre of aircraft there in force. Each contracting State undertakes to keep its own regulations in these respects uniform, to the greatest possible extent, with those established from time to time under this Convention. Over the high seas, the rules in force shall be those established under this Convention.

Accordingly, Art. 12 regulates three aspects:

1. Any aircraft flying over or manoeuvring within the territory of a contracting State shall comply with the rules and regulations relating to flight and manoeuvre of aircraft there in force,
2. Contracting States shall apply regulations uniformly to the greatest possible extent, and
3. Over the high seas, the rules in force shall be those established under this Convention.[147]

The third facet of Article 12 of the Chicago Convention, namely that over the high seas, the rules in force shall be those established under the Chicago Convention, is of particular relevance to the discussion on a possible legal basis for ADIZ in international airspace. This phrase raises two fundamental questions. First, who can establish the respective rules in force over the high seas? Second, what is the legal value of these rules?

To determine the exact meaning of this phrase, the Chicago Convention must be interpreted in accordance with the rules on treaty interpretation contained in Art. 31 VCLT.[148] According to Art. 31 (1) VCLT, a treaty shall be interpreted in good faith in accordance with the ordinary meaning to be given to

147 Art. 12 Chicago Convention.

148 Vienna Convention on the Law of the Treaties ("VCLT") (1980) 1155 UNTS 331.

the terms of the treaty in their context and in the light of its object and purpose. Although the VCLT cannot be applied retroactively (the VCLT came into force in 1980, whereas the Chicago Convention came into force in 1947), the principles of treaty interpretation represent customary international law and therefore also apply to treaties that pre-date the VCLT.[149]

First of all, the use of the term "shall", in its ordinary meaning, does not envisage a possibility but an obligation. Accordingly, the verb "shall" does not suggest the option to act in accordance with the rules established under the Chicago Convention but the duty.[150] Taken as such, in its most ordinary meaning, that expression requires States to act accordingly and proscribes any contrary behaviour as a violation of the Chicago Convention.[151] That interpretation is reinforced both by the form of the words and by the context of the whole treaty. The Chicago Convention itself uses "shall" in multiple other articles always as an obligation and does not imply the existence of an option to choose.[152] The object and purpose of the whole Chicago Convention would be undermined, if "shall" is used synonymously with "may".

7.4.1 Different Rules of the Air in National and International Airspace

The Chicago Convention does not specify the exact connotation and meaning of the phrase "rules (…) established under this Convention", leaving the interpretation open as to whether it encompasses only specific Articles or Annexes of the Chicago Convention. Regarding international airspace, the penultimate sentence of Art. 12, "rules" appears to include rules of the air with direct effect on air flights above the high seas. This is also supported by the logical implication of the phrase "over the high seas", which constitutes the other component of the phrase. The question arises as to whether there are different rules of air dependent on the status of airspace, namely either national or international airspace.

---

149 *Maritime Delimitation and Territorial Questions between Qatar and Bahrain* (*Qatar v Barain*) (Merits) [1994] ICJ Rep 112 para. 33; *LaGrand* (*Germany v United States*) (Merits) [2011] ICJ Rep 466 para. 99; *Sovereignty over Pulau Case* (*Indonesai v Malaysia*) (Merits) [2002] ICJ Rep 625; Mark E Villiger, *Commentary On The 1969 Vienna Convention On The Law Of Treaties* (Brill 2009) 439, 440; Matthias Herdegen, 'Interpretation in International Law' in *Max Planck Encyclopedias of Public International Law* (OUP 2020) para.7–8, 16–17; Lori Damrosch et al, *International Law – Cases And Materials* (5th edn, West Academic Publishing 2009) 124–126.

150 Ruwantissa Abeyratne, 'The Legal Status of the Chicago Convention and its Annexes' (1994) XIX Air & Space Journal 117.

151 Ibid 115.

152 Art. 2, Art. 3, Art. 5, Art. 7, Art. 8 Chicago Convention.

In general, the ICAO Council has legislative powers to establish rules under the Chicago Convention.[153] Hence, the rules in force in airspace over the high seas in the sense of Art. 12 Chicago Convention are considered to be rules established by the ICAO Council.[154] While Art. 37 Chicago Convention obliges States to "collaborate in securing the highest practicable degree of uniformity in regulations (...)", States still enjoy the power to prescribe rules within their national airspace based on the principle of sovereignty pursuant to Art. 2 Chicago Convention and Art. 38 Chicago Convention.[155] The principle of sovereignty in national airspace enables States to impose rules and adopt measures divergent from the rules established by the ICAO Council. The capacity of States to regulate national airspace is also restated in Art. 12 Chicago Convention which refers in the first sentence to the rules and regulations within the territory of the contracting State. States may impose different national rules and regulations relating to the flight and manoeuvre of aircraft in national airspace provided that they are kept to the greatest possible extent uniform with those rules established under the Convention and that they are immediately notified to ICAO in the event of any deviations.[156]

Pursuant to Art. 32 VCLT, the preparatory work of the treaty and the circumstances of its conclusion can be taken into consideration as supplementary means of interpretation.[157] The intention of the drafters was to include any provision with binding and regulatory character under the terms "rules" and "regulations".[158] Therefore, the Convention uses the terms "rules" and "regulations" throughout its text with the same significance. Consequently, it is possible for a single set of rules of the air to be established by States for application

153 Art. 54 (l) Chicago Convention; Ruwantissa Abeyratne, 'Law Making and Decision Making Powers of the ICAO Council – A Critical Analysis' (1992) 41 ZLW 387, 388.

154 Art. 39 (3) (a) UNCLOS regulates the duty of aircraft to observe the Rules of the Air established by the International Civil Aviation Organization while transiting through straits used for international navigation between one part of the high seas or an exclusive economic zone and another part of the high seas or an exclusive economic zone.

155 Art. 38 Chicago Convention enables States to deviate from an "international standard or procedure" if they find it "impracticable to comply in all respects" with such rule. Moreover, Art. 38 Chicago Convention addresses the States' "own regulations or practices" and hence indicates a separate set of regulations created by the States.

156 Art. 38 Chicago Convention.

157 Odile Ammann, 'Chapter 6 The Interpretative Methods of International Law: What are they and Why Use Them?' in Odile Ammann (ed), *Domestic Courts and the Interpretation of International Law* (Brill 2020) 208.

158 Jean Carroz, 'International Legislation On Air Navigation Over The High Seas' (1959) 26 J Air L & Comm 163, stating that "such variation might easily be the consequence of hasty drafting."

to national airspace, while another set of rules of the air may be established by the ICAO Council for application to international airspace.[159] Nevertheless, it is recommended that States endeavour to maintain uniformity between their respective rules of the air and those established by ICAO.[160] With regard to the substance of the respective rules, the treaty text suggests that only those rules established by ICAO that relate to the flight and manoeuvre of aircraft are covered and apply to the airspace above the high seas.[161]

7.4.2 Limitation to Rules relating to the Flight and Manoeuvre of Aircraft

Art. 12 Chicago Convention contains a limitation to specific rules of the air, namely rules relating to the flight and manoeuvre of aircraft. The penultimate sentence of Art. 12 Chicago Convention aims to encourage States to apply the same rules relating to the flight and manoeuvre of aircraft established under the Convention. This argument hinges upon the interpretation of the first part of Art. 12 that "(…) each aircraft shall comply with the rules and regulations relating to the flight and manoeuvre of aircraft there in force" which precedes the reference "[o]ver the high seas, the rules in force shall be those established under this Convention". The fact that Art. 12 Chicago Convention is not subdivided into paragraphs leads to the conclusion that the penultimate sentence cannot be considered in isolation. Instead the phrase "rules established under this Convention" has to be interpreted as rules relating to the flight and manoeuvre of aircraft, as indicated by the first part of Art. 12 Chicago Convention.[162] The overall context of Art. 12 Chicago Convention leads to the logical assumption that the rules referred to are meant to be the same throughout the article.

A review of the preparatory work reveals that Art. XXXII of the Canadian draft to the Paris Convention referred to "rules as to lights and signals, Air traffic rules". This was replaced by the more descriptive phrase "rules relating to the flight and manoeuvre of aircraft" in the text of the Chicago Convention.[163] On 15 April 1948, the ICAO Council adopted Annex 2 to the Chicago Convention and explicitly emphasized the Annexe's character as rules relating to the

159 Art. 54 Chicago Convention.
160 Chicago Convention, Annex 2, 5th edn (2005) 2–1; Chicago Convention, Art. 37.
161 Jean Carroz, 'International Legislation on Air Navigation over the High Seas' (1959) 26 J Air L & Comm 162.
162 Ibid 162.
163 Proceedings of the International Civil Aviation Conference, Department of State, Publication 2820 Vol I, 585; The Drafting Committee of the Chicago Convention also amended the title of Art. XXXII "Rules of the Air etc." to omit the "etc."

flight and manoeuvre of aircraft within the meaning of Art. 12 Chicago Convention.[164] With regard to Annex 11, the ICAO Council similarly determined that certain standards constitute rules relating to the flight and manoeuvre of aircraft,[165] as there is no limitation to these two Annexes.[166] Instead "rules relating to the flight and manoeuvre of aircraft" is a descriptive phrase. It can be seen from the intention of the drafters that Art. 12 Chicago Convention is limited in its scope to rules relating to the flight and manoeuvre of aircraft, which can be further specified by the Annexes to the Convention.

7.4.3 Annexes are Rules within the Meaning of Art. 12 Chicago Convention

The general legal framework of the Chicago Convention is heavily reliant upon Annexes and their Standards and Recommended Practices (SARPS), which provide greater detail regarding the content of the Convention's Articles. A prime example is Art. 12 Chicago Convention, which itself does not state any specific rule of the air but needs to be concretised in more detail in Annexes. Without appropriate implementation in the respective Annexes, Article 12 of the Chicago Convention would be a hollow and meaningless provision.[167] Consequently, the term "rules established under this Convention" is understood to encompass the rules relating to the flight and manoeuvre of aircraft set forward in Annexes.

It appears that the use of such descriptive and general terminology is intended to preclude any specific reference to any particular Annex, thereby including rules relating to the flight and manoeuvre of aircraft within the scope of any given Annex. Consequently, the rules set out in Art. 12 Chicago Convention do not extend to all parts of the Annexes, but only to those provisions that address the flight or manoeuvre of aircraft.[168] The general rule of aircraft being free to fly wherever they want in international airspace is limited by the regulations of Art. 12 Chicago Convention and its Annexes.[169] The legal value and character of the Annexes are different than those of the Articles of the Chicago Convention, they are nonetheless intended to influence and regulate States' actions in airspace.

164 ICAO Doc 7037–2, C/814–2, para 81.
165 Ibid para. 71.
166 Ibid para. 81.
167 Michael Milde, 'The Chicago Convention – After Forty Years' (1984) 9 Annals Of Air & Space Law 126.
168 ICAO Doc 7037–2, C/814–2, para. 81.
169 Alex Calvo, 'China's Air Defense Identification Zone Concept, Issues at Stake and Regional Impact' (2013) Naval War College Press Working Paper 5.

7.4.4 The Legal Character of Annexes and Their Relevance in the International Legal System

The difficulty of formulating and enacting binding treaties on technical advances has resulted in the creation of Annexes. In total, ICAO has adopted eighteen Annexes, which consist of broad range of SARPs.[170] The purpose of Annexes is to provide technical rules on the clarification and specification of air traffic, which are considered too detailed for the incorporation in Articles. The greatest advantage of Annexes lies in their flexibility to be frequently amended to adjust to new technical developments and innovations.[171] Even though they cover a broad range of topics related to air navigation, they all share the common purpose of maintaining and ensuring safe air navigation. The ICAO Council is the exclusive body for establishing rules and can designate these rules as Annexes to the Convention.[172] The quasi-legislative function of the Council of ICAO on Annexes is provided in Art. 54 (l) Chicago Convention. Pursuant to Art. 37 (c) Chicago Convention, the ICAO Council can adopt and amend from time to time, as may be necessary, International Standards and Recommended Practices (SARPs) with regard to rules of the air and air traffic control practice.[173] The procedures for adopting and amending Annexes are set forth in Art. 90 Chicago Convention and are a rare example of international rule making by majority decision. Annexes generally require a two-thirds vote of the Council for their adoption and need to be submitted to the Contracting States before they become effective.[174] One exemption are amendments, which require only a majority vote.[175]

---

170 The full list of Annexes is as follows: Annex 1 – Personal Licensing, Annex 2 – Rules of the Air, Annex 3 – Meteorology, Annex 4 – Aeronautical Charts, Annex 5 – Units of Measurement to be used in Air-Ground Communications, Annex 6 – Operation of Aircraft -International Commercial Air Transport, Annex 7 – Aircraft Nationality and Registration Marks, Annex 8 – Airworthiness of Aircraft, Annex 9 – Facilitation, Annex 10 – Aeronautical Telecommunications, Annex 11 – Air Traffic Services, Annex 12 – Search and Rescue, Annex 13 – Aircraft Accident Inquiry, Annex 14 – Aerodromes, Annex 15 – Aeronautical Information Services, Annex 16 – Environmental Protection, Annex 17 – Security: Safeguarding International Civil Aviation Against Acts of Unlawful Interference, Annex 18 – The Safe Transport of Dangerous Goods by Air, Annex 19 – Safety Management.

171 Ludwig Weber, 'The Chicago Convention', in Paul S Dempsey & Ram S Jakhu (eds), *Routledge Handbook of Public Aviation Law* (Routledge 2017) 19.

172 Thomas Buergenthal, *Law Making in the International Civil Aviation Organization* (Syracuse Univ Press 1969) 57.

173 Art. 37 Chicago Convention.

174 Art. 90 Chicago Convention; Annexes and Amendments to Annexes become effective after three months.

175 Jean Carroz, 'International Legislation On Air Navigation Over The High Seas' (1959) 26 J Air L & Comm 165.

Following the rules of treaty interpretation, Art. 12 Chicago Convention has to be interpreted in the context of the treaty, and thus, has to be read in conjunction with Art. 37, 54 (1), and 90 Chicago Convention.[176] *Prima facie*, only the ICAO Council can establish rules over the high seas in the sense of Art. 12 Chicago Convention. In general, contracting States are obliged to secure "the highest practicable degree of uniformity in regulations, standards, procedures, and organisation."[177] Nevertheless, pursuant to Art. 38 Chicago Convention, States may deviate from the ICAO SARPs when they find it impracticable to comply in all respects with any Standard. The historical development of the legal body of international air law demonstrates that the most significant distinction between the Paris and the Chicago Convention was that the latter abandoned the concept of universal standards and practices with binding character.[178] Annexes to the Paris Convention constituted an integral component and possessed the same legally binding effect as Articles.[179] In contrast, the Chicago Convention's Annexes permit States to deviate from them due to considerations of practicability.[180]

7.4.4.1 *Difference between Standards and Recommended Practices*

Annexes are divided into two categories: Standards and Recommended Practices. Each category bears a different legal significance. It is therefore worth examining whether both categories share the status of "rules" in the understanding of Art. 12 Chicago Convention. It is suggested that both provisions are to be regarded as "rules" for they constitute provisions with regulatory character within the meaning of Art. 12 Chicago Convention. Even though Recommended Practices constitute only desirable conduct, they nevertheless refer to aspects relevant for civil aviation.[181]

A number of ICAO materials include a definition of the terms "Standard" and "Recommended Practice". Accordingly, Standard is defined as:

> Any specification for physical characteristics, configuration, matériel, performance, personnel or procedure, the uniform application of which

---

176 Ibid 161.

177 Ibid 161.

178 Peter Keenan, Anthony Lester & Peter Martin, *Shawcross and Beaumont on Air Law* (3rd edn, Butterworths 1966) 213.

179 Ibid 58, 59.

180 One exemption is the mandatory character of Annex 2, see for guidelines on reporting differences, ICAO Doc 7600/3 'Standing Rules of Procedure of the Assembly of the International Civil Aviation Organization' (1977).

181 ICAO Doc AN-Conf/11-WP/142, A-1. 'SARPS "Notification of Differences" Procedures and PANS Status', Eleventh Air Navigation Conference (8.9.2013).

> is recognized as necessary for the safety or regularity of international air navigation and to which Contracting States will conform in accordance with the Convention; in the event of impossibility of compliance, notification to the Council is compulsory under Art. 38.[182]

Whereas Recommended Practice denotes:

> Any specification for physical characteristics, configuration, matériel, performance, personnel or procedure, the uniform application of which is **recognized as desirable** in the interest of safety, regularity or efficiency of international air navigation, and to which Contracting States will endeavour to conform in accordance with the Convention.[183]

Generally, States should comply with the rules set forward in Annex and act accordingly, regardless of their classification as "Standard" or "Recommended Practice".[184] States are generally obliged to implement Standards in their national law to ensure secure, safe, and regular air services.[185] However, there is a loophole as States can avoid implementing standards if compliance would be impracticable. The distinction between Standard and Recommended Practice is that States are generally bound by Standards in case they do not file any alternative in accordance with Art. 38 Chicago Convention.[186] The binding effect of Standards arises from their mandatory nature if States fail to notify non-compliance in national legislation.[187] States are invited but not obliged to extend such notification to any differences from the Recommended Practices. This obligation of notification is not obligatory for Recommended Practices; it is only desired.[188] Recommendations are subject to eventual acceptance by

---

182 ICAO Assembly Resolution A15–6, Appendix E (1965); ICAO Doc AN-Conf/11-WP/142, A-1.

183 Ibid.

184 Ruwantissa Abeyratne, 'The Legal Status of the Chicago Convention and its Annexes' (1994) XIX Air & Space Journal 117.

185 Michael Milde, *International Air Law and ICAO* (4th edn Eleven International Publishing 2023) 175–180.

186 Zoltan Papp, 'ADIZ in the Light of Public International Law' (2015) Pécs J Int'l & European L 36, 37.

187 Paul S Dempsey, 'Compliance & Enforcement in International Law: Achieving Global Uniformity in Aviation Safety' (2004) 30 North Carolina J of Int'l L and Commercial Regulation 5.

188 Eugen Pepin, 'ICAO and Other Agencies Dealing with Air Regulation' (1952) 19 J Air Law and Commerce 153. One reasons is that States may lack the necessary human or financial resources to comply with the ICAO standards, see: Paul S Dempsey, *Public International Air Law* (2nd edn, McGill University 2017) 71.

each Contracting State.[189] Therefore, Recommended Practices provide general guidance to be applied to the fullest extent practicable, although states are not obliged to notify ICAO in the event of non-compliance.[190] Even though States may depart from SARPs and apply different rules, SARPs on the flight and manoeuvre of aircraft can be understood as rules within the meaning of Art. 12 Chicago Convention.[191] In the context of Art. 12, the term 'rules' is understood to encompass both binding and non-binding provisions.

7.4.4.2 *The Classification of Annexes as Non-binding Rules*

Annexes do not have the same legally binding effect as the Articles of the Chicago Convention due to the fact that Annexes are not subject to ratification.[192] The opting-out possibility of Art. 38 Chicago Convention for Annexes qualifies SARPs as "soft law", i.e. non-binding norms.[193] Conceptual differences in the exact notion of soft law can be found in scholarly literature and can be categorised in two ways.[194] The first approach focuses on the non-binding character of soft law, whereas the second approach draws a difference between precise "rules" with commitments (hard law) and more general phrased "principles" (soft law).[195] Under both approaches, soft law is a significant contributor to the development of international law, such as declarations and resolutions adopted by States.

The concept of soft law is not easily defined but can be generally understood as "principles, rules, and standards governing international relations which are not considered to stem from one of the sources of international law

189 Nicolas M Matte, *Treatise on Air-Aeronautical Law* (McGill University 1981) 185.

190 Bin Cheng, *The Law of International Air Transport* (Stevens 1965) 25. It has to be noted, that Standards may incorporate Recommended Practices by reference, making the Recommended Practice part of the Standard, see Chicago Convention, Annex 15, 16th ed. (2018).

191 Nicolas M Matte, *Treatise on Air-Aeronautical Law* (McGill University 1981) at 195: "only the standards in relation to the air medium above the High Seas are binding ipso jure upon member States".

192 Ludwig Weber, 'The Chicago Convention', in Paul S Dempsey & Ram S Jakhu (eds), *Routledge Handbook of Public Aviation Law* (Routledge 2017) 20.

193 Paul S Dempsey, 'Compliance & Enforcement in International Law: Achieving Global Uniformity in Aviation Safety' (2004) 30 North Carolina J of Int'l L and Commercial Regulation 14.

194 Christine M Chinkin, 'The Challenge of Soft Law: Development and Change in International Law' (1989) 38 Int'L and Comp L Quarterly 850, 851.

195 Alan Boyle, 'Soft Law in international Law-Making', in Malcom D Evans (ed), *International Law* (5th edn, OUP 2018) 120.

enumerated in Art. 38 (1) ICJ Statute."[196] This definition follows the traditional positivist approach which submits that soft law was deliberately not listed as binding source in Art. 38 (1) ICJ Statute and thus does not enjoy legally binding force.[197] As indicated by the name, soft law is in contrast to hard law a legally not binding instrument.[198] The main difference to "hard law" is that its violation does not entail the State's international responsibility with its inevitable legal consequences, primarily the duty of "full reparation,"[199] and the right of the injured state(s) to enact "countermeasures."[200] Non-binding instruments have become increasingly popular as a potential means of global governance,[201] not only in the area of international air law,[202] but also in outer space law,[203] and with respect to environmental protection.[204] Even though soft law is considered to be not binding, it nevertheless contributes to the corpus of international law in many facets. The effect of such norms may then well resemble that of legally binding norms, thus blurring the difference between "hard" and "soft" law.

The Chicago Convention's SARPs purport to specify technical standards for unanimous application. They do not emanate from the traditional sources of international law as specified in Art. 38 (1) ICJ Statute. However, some authors

196 Daniel Thürer, 'Soft Law' in *Max Planck Encyclopedias of Public International Law* (OUP 2009) para. 5.

197 Steven Freeland, 'The Role of 'Soft Law' in Public International Law and its Relevance to the International Legal Regulation of Outer Space', in Irmgard Marboe (ed), *Soft Law in Outer Space* (Böhlau 2012) 20; Daniel Thürer, 'Soft Law' in *Max Planck Encyclopedias of Public International Law* (OUP 2009) para. 5; Statute of the International Court of Justice (1945) 1155 UNTS 331 (hereinafter: ICJ Statute).

198 Wolfgang Reinicke & Jan Martin Witte, 'Interdependence, Globalization, and Sovereignty: The Role of Non-binding International Legal Accords', in Dinah Sheldon (ed), *Commitment And Compliance: The Role Of Non-Binding Norms In The International Legal System* (OUP 2000) 75, 76.

199 Art. 31 ILC Articles on Responsibility of States for Internationally Wrongful Acts, A/56/10 (2001).

200 Ibid Art. 49.

201 Wolfgang Reinicke & Jan Martin Witte, 'Interdependence, Globalization, and Sovereignty: The Role of Non-binding International Legal Accords', in Dinah Sheldon (ed), *Commitment And Compliance: The Role Of Non-Binding Norms In The International Legal System* (OUP 2000) 75–76.

202 Ruwantissa Abeyratne, 'The Legal Status of the Chicago Convention and its Annexes' (1994) XIX Air & Space Journal 117.

203 Irmgard Marboe (ed), *Soft Law in Outer Space – The Importance of Non-Binding Rules in International Space Law* (Böhlau Verlag 2012).

204 Friedrich Jürgens, *International Environmental "Soft Law": The Functions and Limits of Nonbinding Instruments in International Environmental Governance and Law* (Springer 2013).

argue that due to the wording of Art. 12 Chicago Convention there is little room for interpretation that the law-making authority of ICAO forms SARPs in international airspace into hard law.[205] This is true for the rules of Annex 2 as they are mandatory, but as regards other Annexes with reference to the flight and manoeuvre of aircraft a general obligation to comply cannot be deduced. The argument regarding the obligatory nature of any Annexes in international airspace can be countered by pointing out that the predecessor ICAN (International Commission for Air Navigation), which was replaced by ICAO, had the power to enact definitive decisions on technical Annexes, a right that was deliberately denied to ICAO.[206] Thus, a member State of ICAO may decide not to comply with a given international standard or recommended practice incorporated into an Annex without any temporal limitation.[207] Moreover, the assumption that SARPs in international airspace are hard law seems to be in conflict with Art. 38 Chicago Convention as there is no opting-out restriction in international airspace. Annexes are not self-executing and therefore depend on the good-will of each State to be implemented in their national legal order and to be complied with in international airspace.[208] The rules of Annexes enjoy binding character from the moment States have accepted and actively implemented them in the national legal order.[209]

As described above at 6.1, if States take the responsibility to provide FIR according to Annex 11 in international airspace, they are allowed to apply the same (national) rules used in national airspace to international airspace.[210] Annex 11 (Air Traffic Services) mentions in its Preamble the possibility for States to deviate from the rules of Annex 11 when providing air traffic services

205 Paul S Dempsey, 'Compliance & Enforcement in International Law: Achieving Global Uniformity in Aviation Safety' (2004) 30 North Carolina J of Int'l L and Commercial Regulation 18.

206 Nicolas Matte, *Treatise on Air-Aeronautical Law* (McGill University 1981) 187; Art. 34 Paris Convention of 1919 describes the competency of ICAN and explicitly mentions that Annexes need not be adopted by the contracting States to become effective: "All such modifications of the articles of the convention (but not of the provisions of the annexes) must be formally adopted by the contracting states before they become effective." See Convention for the Regulation on Aerial Navigation, reprinted in 17 American Journal of International Law (1923), 195–212.

207 John Cooper, 'The Chicago Convention – After Twenty Years', in Ivan A Vlasic (ed), *Explorations in Aerospace Law* (1968) 439.

208 Paul S Dempsey, *Public International Air Law* (2nd edn, McGill University 2017) 74.

209 Nicolas Matte, *Treatise on Air-Aeronautical Law* (McGill University 1981) 185.

210 Chicago Convention, Annex 11, 13th ed (2011), 2–1.

over the high seas or airspace of underdetermined sovereignty.[211] The Council and the Air Navigation Commission shared the view that States may deviate from certain principles of Annex 11 when providing air traffic services over the high seas. Instead of two sets of air traffic regulations States may apply only one set of air traffic services both for national airspace as well as for international airspace.[212] Moreover, the Council mentions in the foreword of Annex 11 that States are not bound by ICAO SARPs in areas above the high seas, and can apply the same rules as applicable in their national airspace.[213]

Yet, there seems to be one exemption to this rule, as those Annexes with direct effect on manoeuvre and navigation of aircraft over the high seas are mandatory and not open for opting out in the first place.[214] Annex 2 indisputably counts as Annex with mandatory character over the high seas, whereas all other Annexes fall under the flexibility of Art. 38 Chicago Convention unless they fulfil the specific criteria of Art. 12 Chicago Convention.[215] It has to be mentioned, that some authors also claim SARPs as customary international law with the effect of legally binding norms and the power of ICAO to not only make rules but also to enforce them.[216]

Even though soft law is considered to not impose legally binding obligations on States, legal implications are nevertheless connected with it. Firstly, soft law can be an indicator of the existence of a rule of customary international law or serves as purposive interpretation of international law.[217] The law-shaping potential of soft law relevant for creating custom may not be underestimated.

---

211 ICAO Doc 7037–2, C/814–2 para.77; Chicago Convention, Annex 11, 13th ed. (2001), p (VII): "The Standards and Recommended Practices in Annex 11 apply in those parts of the airspace under the jurisdiction of a Contracting State wherein air traffic services are provided and also wherever a Contracting State accepts the responsibility of providing air traffic services over the high seas or in airspace of undetermined sovereignty. A Contracting State accepting such responsibility may apply the Standards and Recommended Practices in a manner consistent with that adopted for airspace under its jurisdiction."

212 ICAO Doc. 7037–2, C/814–2, para. 77 ff. Jean Carroz, 'International Legislation On Air Navigation Over The High Seas'(1959) 26 J Air L & Comm 162.

213 Chicago Convention, Annex 11, 13th ed (2011), 2–1, Note 2: "A Contracting State accepting the responsibility for providing air traffic services over the high seas or in airspace of undetermined sovereignty may apply the Standards and Recommended Practices in a manner consistent with that adopted for airspace under its jurisdiction."

214 Ruwantissa Abeyratne, *Convention On International Civil Aviation – A Commentary* (Springer 2014) 178.

215 Ibid 179.

216 Ruwantissa Abeyratne, 'The Legal Status of the Chicago Convention and its Annexes' (1994) XIX Air & Space Journal 117, 119.

217 Daniel Thürer, 'Soft Law' in *Max Planck Encyclopedias of Public International Law* (OUP 2009) para. 26, 28.

The general importance of soft law lies within its function of strengthening and complementing the international legal order.[218] Secondly, the emergence of new applications makes it necessary to refer to soft law instruments to keep track with rapid technological developments which could not wait for lengthy negotiations on a multinational level and which also require the inclusion of expert knowledge.[219] As regards the "non-binding character" approach, most notably, General Assembly resolutions may be of non-binding character, yet their importance results from serving as interpretation of the UN-Charter.[220] Even though UN General Assembly resolutions are non-legislative acts, they nonetheless bear legal relevance and contribute to the development of law.

Most importantly, soft law is not law *per se* but it constitutes evidence of the opinions of governments on what they consider at least as politically or morally desirable behaviour (*opinio iuris*) and is also a formative of State practice, the two elements that generate customary international law. A State, which acts in accordance with the recommendations contained in a non-binding instrument is presumed to act lawfully. Therefore, out of such behaviour a "presumption of legality" of that behaviour emerges.[221] Such a "presumption of legality" may have further consequences to gradually develop into the conviction that such behaviour is not only recommended but even "required", which is the classical definition of *opinio iuris*, an element of customary international law.[222] If then, secondly, respective state practice follows – i.e. behaviour of states in accordance with that rule – an unwritten norm of international law has developed, namely customary international law, which is a source of international law according to Art. 38 of the ICJ Statute. With respect to UN General Assembly Resolutions, it is frequently emphasised that despite their recommendatory nature, they have the potential to emerge into a rule of customary international law.[223] The ICJ appoints the purpose of soft law instruments as a

218 Ibid para. 34.

219 Steven Freeland, 'The Role of Soft Law in Public International Law and its Relevance to the International Legal Regulation of Outer Space', in Irmgard Marboe (ed), *Soft Law in Outer Space* (Böhlau 2012) 19.

220 Alan Boyle, 'The Choice of a Treaty: Interaction between Hard Law and Soft Law in the United Nations Law-Making', in Simon Chesterman, David Malone & Santiago Villalpando (eds), *Oxford Handbook of UN Treaties* (OUP 2018) 102, 103.

221 James Crawford, *Brownlie's Principles of Public International Law* (8th edn, OUP 2012) 40.

222 *Military and Paramilitary Activities in and against Nicaragua* (*Nicaragua v United States of America*) (Jurisdiction and Admissibility) [1984] ICJ Rep 392, confirming the general possibility of soft law crystallizing into hard law.

223 *South West Africa Cases* (*Ethiopia v. South Africa; Liberia v. South Africa*) (Merits) [1966] ICJ Rep 6 para. 172; Malcom N Shaw, *International Law* (9th edn, Cambridge University Press 2021) 85–87.

means to codify or assist in the development of international law.[224] Furthermore, soft law provisions have been important first steps in the formulation of international treaties.[225] As the forms and types of non-binding instruments vary significantly, it follows that they will also have different legal significance, as well as different degrees of effectiveness. Declarations, resolutions, guidelines, codes of conduct, and other forms of soft law all are carefully drafted statements, and despite their non-binding form are at any rate an element of good faith commitment.[226]

The Chicago Convention's Annexes provide for technical rules subject to constant revision due to rapid technological advances. As technical development may happen swiftly, future scientific and technical uncertainties and unpredictabilities can be better approached by referring to soft law.[227] Due to cumbersome negotiation processes, hard law can significantly lag behind technology.[228] Yet, not only hard law may lag behind but also States may not have the resources to be up to date with the latest technological development. The preamble of the Chicago Convention points out "that international air transport services may be established on the basis of equality of opportunity," and thus refers to the concept of air space and civil aviation equally accessible to all States. Formulating technical standards as hard law would lead to the exclusion of parts of the State community from participating in certain air transport services. The technical rules of the Chicago Convention's Annexes provide orientation for national legislation on the conduct of aviation. These Annexes aim to influence, harmonise and provide guidance on topics that belong to the domestic sphere of States namely the regulation and the technical requirements of conducting air traffic within national as well as international airspace. Additionally, the SARPs enshrined in Annexes are also to be followed in international airspace, if States take the responsibility to provide services but

224 *Gabcikovo-Nagymaros Case (Hungary v Slovakia)* (Merits) [1997] ICJ Rep 1997, para. 140.

225 In the area of human rights the groundbreaking Universal Declaration on Human Rights is generally referred to as the most important example. See Bertrand G Ramcharan, 'The Foundations', in Carla Ferstman et al (eds), *Contemporary Human Rights Challenges: The Universal Declaration of Human Rights and its Continuing* Relevance (Routledge 2019) 9.

226 *Voting Procedure on Questions relating to Reports and Petitions concerning the Territory of South West Africa* (Advisory Opinion) 1[955] ICJ Rep 67, Se. Op. Judge Lauterpacht 118.

227 Daniel Thürer, 'Soft Law' in *Max Planck Encyclopedias of Public International Law* (OUP 2009) para. 6.

228 The last amendment of the Chicago Convention to its 9th edition took place in 2006 (ICAO Doc. 7300/9), whereas Annex are continuously amended. See for example Annex 6 (11th ed, 2018).

only those rules relating to the flight and manoeuvre of aircraft in Annex 2 are mandatory in international airspace and are binding on all contracting States.

With regard to ADIZs, differences in financial and technological capabilities for establishing and maintaining ADIZs, as well as the essential military nature of ADIZs have prevented States from reaching a legally binding agreement over the decades. As ADIZs are not a treaty concept, the Annexes are important for the purposive interpretation of international air law. As will be described later, some Annexes already encompass SARPs on ADIZ, which may indicate the first step in the formulation of a rule of customary international law.

7.4.4.3 *Procedures for Air Navigation Services* (PANS)

To be distinguished from Standards and Recommended Practices (SARPs) are Procedures for Air Navigation Services – Air Traffic Management (PANS-ATM).[229] PANS stem from practical necessity and comprise operating procedures, which have not attained a sufficient degree for adoption as SARP.[230] They are considered to either have not reached the necessary level of maturity for being adopted as SARP or lack permanent character for being adopted as SARP.[231] PANSs are complementary to the SARPs and specify in greater detail the actual procedures to be applied by air traffic services.[232] The characterization of PANS as general guidance without mandatory function leads to a different legal value in comparison to SARPs.[233] While the SARPs are *adopted* by Council in pursuance of Art. 37 Chicago Convention and are subject to the full procedure of Art. 90, PANS are *approved* by the Council and recommended

229 Procedures for Air Navigation Services – Aircraft Operations, ICAO Doc. 8168 (6th ed. 2018).

230 The Procedures for Air Navigation Services – Aircraft Operations (PANS-OPS) consists of three volumes and establish specific rules for Air Navigation Services outside the scope of SARPs. Volume I – *Flight Procedures* describes the operational requirements for flying, inter alia departure procedures and en-route procedures. Volume II – *Construction of Visual and Instrument Flight Procedures* provides the guidance of procedures specialists and aims for the achievement of safe, regular instrument flight operations. It establishes the basic guidelines on instrument flight charts to States, in order to achieve uniform practices at all aerodromes where instrument flight procedures are carried out. Volume III – *Aircraft Operating Procedures* describes operational procedures recommended for the guidance of flight operations personnel and flight crew, see ibid, (vii).

231 Paul S Dempsey, *Public International Air Law* (2nd edn, McGill University 2017) 72.

232 Paul S Dempsey & Ram S Jakhu (eds), *Routledge Handbook of Public Aviation Law* (Routledge 2017) 33.

233 Eugen Pepin, 'ICAO and Other Agencies Dealing with Air Regulation' (1952) 19 J Air Law and Commerce 155; Procedures for Air Navigation Services – Aircraft Operations, ICAO Doc. 8168 (6th ed. 2018), p. (ix).

to Contracting States for worldwide application.[234] Each Contracting State is responsible for implementing PANS and can elect to enforce PANSs on actual operations.[235] In case States do not wish to comply with PANS, they do not have to notify the ICAO Council pursuant to Art. 38 Chicago Convention.[236] However, States are advised to publish significant differences between their procedures and the related ICAO procedures in their Aeronautical Information Publications in accordance with Annex 15.

7.4.4.4 *The Hybrid System of the Chicago Convention as a Framework Treaty*

The Chicago Convention contains a three-tier norm hierarchy: legally binding Articles, partly binding SARPs, and legally not-binding PANS. The first layer consist of binding Articles adopted by the ICAO Council under the framework of the Chicago Convention. The second layer includes SARPs from which States can deviate in accordance with Art. 38 Chicago Convention. As described above, States should strive to harmonise national law in accordance with the ICAO SARPs but they may opt-out of SARPs if they find it impracticable to comply with them.[237] The third layer encompasses non-binding PANS with their complementary and concretising function. Additionally, national rules apply in national airspace as well as international airspace in specific cases.[238]

The legal body of international air law contains basic principles and core rules that are concretised through non-binding guidelines in the form of Annexes. The Chicago Convention is an example of a framework treaty laying down broad and general principles that are further substantiated through soft law. On the one hand, basic provisions provide for a binding regulatory system and legal certainty in international air law. On the other hand, more detailed regulations on technical aspects is left to non-binding instruments. Thus a hybrid system of binding provisions and non-binding principles exists. Such hybrid systems already exist in other fields of international law, such as the international law of the sea. The UN Convention on the Law of the Sea[239]

---

234 AN-Conf/11-WP/142, A-2.

235 Ibid, A-3.

236 Procedures for Air Navigation Services – Aircraft Operations, ICAO Doc. 8168 (6th ed. 2018) (ix).

237 Michael Milde, 'The Chicago Convention – Are Major Amendments Necessary Or Desirable 50 Years Later?' (1994) 19 Annals Of Air & Space Law 425. Excluded from the opting-out possibility are the mandatory rules of the air in the sense of Art. 12 Chicago Convention, namely rules related to the flight and manoeuvring of aircraft.

238 As in the example of air traffic services in FIRs provided over the high seas by States, see Chicago Convention, Annex 11, 13th ed (2011), 2–1.

239 United Nations Convention on the Law of the Sea ("UNCLOS") (1994) 1833 UNTS 397.

can also be qualified as "framework convention,"[240] since it is complemented and implemented by binding conventions and non-binding codes developed by the International Maritime Organization (IMO).[241] A similar system can be found in international air law, where the Chicago Convention establishes core responsibilities of States to ensure the safety of air transport operation and complementary SARPs developed by ICAO.[242] Thus, international air law and the law of the sea have established a system in which a legally binding "framework convention" sets forth the main obligations of States, that are then further developed by a dedicated international organisation which adopts common standards through legally binding and non-binding instruments. The nature of the Chicago Convention as framework treaty can be seen on the wording of Art. 12, which stipulates a hard law principle that gives rise to soft law requirements.

7.4.5 Short Conclusion

ICAO has regulatory powers on the high seas with regard to the rules of the air relating to the flight and manoeuvre of aircraft. Even though Annexes may generally characterized as non-binding rule, Annex 2 is an exemption as it contains mandatory rules to which the opt-out mechanism of Art. 38 Chicago Convention does not apply. This leads to the conclusion that State do not have regulatory competence on the high seas with regard to rules relating to the flight and manoeuvre of aircraft. However, it needs to be clarified whether the ADIZs' rules qualify as "rules relating to the flight and manoeuvre of aircraft". Moreover, the reference to ADIZ's rules in the Annexes of the Chicago Convention may lead to a progressive development of a rule of customary international law. The Annexes contribute to the enrichment of the international legal body of international air law. They may therefore also influence the concept of ADIZs.

7.5 *Relevant Annexes for the Operation of ADIZs*

Articles, Standards as wells as Recommended Practices are included under the phrase "rules established under this convention" and are relevant in national as well as in international airspace. However, only rules relating to the flight and manoeuvre of aircraft are obligatory in international airspace pursuant

240 Malcom N Shaw, *International Law* (9th edn, Cambridge University Press 2021) 637.

241 Tullio Treves, 'Law of the Sea' in *Max Planck Encyclopedias of Public International Law* (OUP 2011) 44.

242 Brian F Havel & Gabriel S Sanchez, *The Principles and Practice of International Air Law* (Cambridge University Press 2014) 58–64.

to Art. 12 Chicago Convention.[243] In accordance with Art. 31 (2) VCLT, the preamble and Annexes can be taken into consideration for the purpose of treaty interpretation.[244] With regard to ADIZS, rules can particularly be found in Annex 2 (Rules of the Air), Annex 4 (Aeronautical Charts), and Annex 15 (Aeronautical Information Services) of the Chicago Convention.

7.5.1 Annex 2 – The Application of Universal Air Rules to an ADIZ

Upon initial examination, Annex 2 seems to be the most pertinent Annex for the interpretation of Art. 12 Chicago Convention, as they share the same heading of "Rules of the Air". The rules of the air apply to aircraft in all locations, including airspace above the high seas.[245] The ICAO Council confirmed with amendment 1 to Annex 2 that the Standards pursuant to Annex 2 constitute "rules" within the meaning of Art. 12 Chicago Convention.[246] Furthermore, the ICAO Council stated that "rules of the air" pursuant to Art. 12 Chicago Convention are not confined to those set forward in Annex 2.[247] Annex 2 establishes the requirements and obligations for conducting air flights in a safe and efficient manner,[248] and contains only Standards, not Recommended Practices.[249]

Annex 2 encompasses Standards on the protection of persons and property, the avoidance of collisions, flight plans, aircraft control services, and interception procedures.[250] Annex 2 refers to certain aspects of aerial navigation reflect to some extent inthe identification procedures of ADIZS. For example, Annex 2 includes the requirement of informing the air traffic control services about the aircraft's position while being assigned a precise route and altitude. Moreover, aircraft engaged in commercial operations and those intending to cross international borders have to file a flight plan prior to operation. A flight plan provides information on the aircraft's identity and equipment, the point and time of departure, the route and altitude to be flown, the destination and the estimated time of arrival, as well as the alternate airport to be used should landing at the destination be impossible.[251] Annex 2 also contains rules on interception procedures of civil aircraft. Various national legislations stipulate

243 Nicolas M Matte, *Treatise on Air-Aeronautical Law* (McGill University 1981) 177.

244 VCLT, Art. 31.

245 Annex 2, 2.1.1.

246 RAC Division, Fourth Session, Amendment 1 (1950).

247 ICAO Doc. 7037–2, C/814–2, 81.

248 Chicago Convention, Annex 2, 5th ed. (2005).

249 AIS-AIMSG/3-SN No. 7, Appendix A, (iv).

250 For example, if an aircraft flies under instrument flight rules, it has to operate with suitable instruments and navigation equipment appropriate to the route to be flown.

251 Chicago Convention, Annex 2.

the same requirements for properly complying with the ADIZs' identification obligations.[252] The fundamental aspect of the majority of ADIZs is that aircraft are required to file a position report, submit a flight plan, and in the event of non-compliance, may be intercepted.

However, Annex 2 does not explicitly refer to ADIZs, nor does it contain a definition of the term.[253] The ICJ has repeatedly stated that treaty interpretation must be conducted as laid down in the treaty text or the preamble as a secondary means of interpretation, which can lead to an evolutionary interpretation of concepts.[254] Given the Convention's safety-oriented approach,[255] the exclusion of ADIZ from the rules of the air pursuant to Annex 2 cannot be the intent of the contracting States. Although ADIZs were not considered by the contracting States at the time of drafting, it can be assumed by the means of an evolutionary interpretation, that if a State claims a right to establish an ADIZ, then the Standards of Annex 2 apply within the ADIZ. Annex 2 always applies to aircraft in international airspace irrespective of whether an ADIZ has been established or not. Consequently, the rules of airspace as set out in Annex 2 remain valid and applicable to civil aircraft traversing ADIZs, regardless of whether a State has established an ADIZ in international airspace.

The applicability of the rules of the air set forth in Annex 2 in ADIZs means that the identification and position reporting of ADIZs do not impose any additional burdens on civil aircraft. Regardless of whether an ADIZ has been established, aircraft must identify themselves by submitting a flight plan when they intend to cross a border.[256] The term "flight plan", as defined in Annex 2, encompasses comprehensive information on all elements included in the flight plan description and covers the complete route of a flight. The flight plan has to contain all information necessary for identifying aircraft, including the type of aircraft, the route to be followed, and the destination.[257] The submission of flight plans is required when directed by the appropriate air traffic

---

252 On a detailed description of the different national legislations on ADIZs see chapter 3 of this book.

253 Christopher Lamont, 'Conflict in the Skies: The Law of Air Defence Identification Zones' (2014) 39 Air & Space Law 195.

254 *Aegean Sea Continental Shelf Case* (1978), para. 77; *Gabcikovo-Nagymaros Case* (1997), para. 142; *Navigational and Related Rights Case* (2009), para. 63; *Pulp Mills Case* (2010), para. 204; see also Eirik Bjorge, 'The Vienna Rules, Evolutionary Interpretation and the Intentions of the Parties, Interpretation in International Law' in Andrea Bianchi et al (eds), *Interpretation in International Law* (OUP 2015) 190.

255 Peter Sand, James Lyon & Geoffrey Pratt, 'An Historical Survey of International Air Law since 1944' (1960) 7 McGill L J 128, 129; Chicago Convention, Preamble.

256 Annex 2, 3.3.1 (e).

257 Annex 2, 3.3.2.

service (ATS) authority. A flight plan may be submitted prior to departure or during the flight.[258] Flight plans shall be submitted at least sixty minutes before departure, or, if submitted during flight, at a time which will ensure its receipt by the appropriate air traffic services unit at least ten minutes before the aircraft is estimated to reach the intended point of entry into a control area or advisory area.[259] Annex 2 therefore not only establishes the obligation of aircraft to submit flight plans but also for the right of the contracting States to require the submission of flight plans. The purpose of submitting the flight plan in a designated area is to facilitate coordination with military units or with air traffic services units in adjacent States in order to avoid the possible need for interception for the purpose of identification.[260] These two aspects, namely the crossing of borders, or in other words, entering national airspace, and the facilitation of air traffic are also the main reasons for the identification requirements in ADIZS.

7.5.2 Annex 4 – the Identification of ADIZS in Aeronautical Charts

Annex 4 (Aeronautical Charts) and Annex 15 (Aeronautical Information Services) are the only Annexes with a direct reference to ADIZS.[261] Both of the Annexes encompass a definition of the term "ADIZ". Such definition forms an essential part of each Standard and Recommended Practice and has to be read in the context of the respective Annex, as any change to the term would also affect the specification. Accordingly, Annex 4 and Annex 15 define an ADIZ as:

> Special designated airspace of defined dimensions within which aircraft are required to comply with special identification and/or reporting procedures additional to those related to the provision of air traffic services (ATS).[262]

This definition draws a clear distinction between ADIZS and FIRS by stating that the identification and reporting procedures of an ADIZ are additional to

258 Annex 2, 3.3.1.3.
259 Annex 2, 3.3.1.3.
260 Annex 2, 3.3.1. (d).
261 Even though Annex 4 speaks of "the obligations of States to make available certain ICAO aeronautical chart types", one cannot speak of an obligation on the sense of a binding provision due to the possibility to opt-out, see on the legal character of Annexes Chapter II, 6.4.4; at https://www.icao.int/safety/airnavigation/nationalitymarks/annexes_booklet_en.pdf (accessed 18 January 2023).
262 Chicago Convention, Annex 4, 9th ed (2009) 1–1 and Annex 15, 18th ed (2018).

the identification and reporting procedures of other ATS,[263] such as FIRS pursuant to Annex 11.[264] The definition of an ADIZ shows that certain identification procedures may be required in addition to the submission of flight plans under Annex 2.

In accordance with Annex 4, aeronautical charts are maps of airspace designated to assist in air navigation and are used additionally to radio-navigational aids.[265] Each Contracting State provides a specific chart for each phase of flight.[266] Each type of chart includes information necessary for the respective phase of flight to ensure the safe and expeditious operation of the aircraft. The information presented in these charts needs to fulfil certain requirements such as accuracy, absence of distortion and clutter, clarity, and readability under all normal operating conditions.[267] For Enroute Charts, Annex 4 para. 7.9.3. (air traffic service systems) stipulates that where appropriate, components of air traffic service systems should be depicted. These components should include, inter alia, "air defence identification zone (ADIZ) properly identified." As an apposition, para. 7.9.3 notes that ADIZ procedures may be described in the chart legend.

Additionally, ADIZS are mentioned in several other sections of Annex 4, but with a slightly different subject matter. In three additional provisions of Annex 4 it is stated that "where appropriate, ADIZ shall be shown and properly identified", indicating that the publication and identification of ADIZS are also dependent on reasons of appropriateness.[268] This pertains to World Aeronautical Charts, Aeronautical Charts, and Aeronautical Navigation Charts.[269] Nevertheless, all paragraphs describe ADIZS as supplementary means to air traffic services.[270] Consequently, if a State establishes an ADIZ, it has to properly identify the zone, where appropriate, and may publish specifications and procedures in its aeronautical chart to enable aircraft to act accordingly. Annex 4 does not provide specific details on the exact scope and content of ADIZS

263 Chicago Convention, Annex 4, 9th ed (2009) 1–1.

264 On this discussion see above 1.

265 Jeffrey Price & Jeffrey Forrest, *Practical Airport Operations, Safety and Emergence Management* (Butterworth-Heinemann 2016) 244.

266 Ronald Bartsch, *International Aviation Law: A Practical Guide* (2nd edn, Ashgate 2012) 76.

267 Chicago Convention, Annex 4, 9th ed (2009), para. 2.1.

268 Chicago Convention, Annex 4, 9th ed (2009), para. 16.9.5.2, para. 17.9.5.2, para. 18.8.4.

269 Between these three types of Charts, Aeronautical Navigation Charts are the only form of Chart where the provision on ADIZ is formulated as a recommendation and not as a standard.

270 An ATS is a generic term meaning variously, flight information service, alerting service, air traffic advisory service, air traffic control service (area control service, approach control service or aerodrome control service), see. Annex 4, para. 1–1.

but contains the correct publication method of ADIZs rules in Aeronautical Charts. To summarize, Annex 4 recognises the concept of ADIZs but does not impose any obligations on States to identify these zones, because the duty to identify an ADIZs is emasculated by matters of appropriateness.

7.5.3 Annex 15 – the Publication of ADIZs' Details as part of Aeronautical Information Services

The SARPs in Annex 15 of the Chicago Convention regulate the application of the Procedures for Air Navigation Services for worldwide use[271] and the Regional Supplementary Procedures.[272] The objective of aeronautical information services is to ensure the information flow essential for the safety, regularity, and efficiency of international air navigation by collating, collecting, editing, and publishing information for global air traffic management.[273] Annex 15 aims at achieving uniformity and consistency of aeronautical information for operating procedures carried out by international civil aviation. For this purpose, Annex 14 defines the manner in which an aeronautical information service should handle specified aeronautical information. The underlying philosophy of Annex 15 is that each State is responsible for making all information available relevant to and required for the operation of aircraft engaged in international civil aviation.[274]

Generally, aeronautical data and information should be kept up to date and distributed in accordance with a regulated system called AIRAC.[275] AIRAC stands for a system for advancing notification of circumstances that necessitate significant changes in operating practices.[276] This notification of information includes the horizontal and vertical limits, regulations, and procedures applicable to ADIZs.[277] Para. 6.2 of Annex 15 establishes a direct reference to ADIZs by requiring States to publish all relevant details on their ADIZs necessary for the safe operation of aircraft. Given that Annex 15 explicitly applies to aircraft engaged in international air navigation, it could be argued that ADIZ could be established in international airspace. However, once again, Annex 15 does not prescribe the geographical details or content of an ADIZ. The ICAO Council could have included specific details on ADIZs in the Annexes but it

271 ICAO, Doc 10066.

272 ICAO, Doc 7030.

273 Ronald Bartsch, *International Aviation Law: A Practical Guide* (2nd edn, Ashgate 2012) 77.

274 Chicago Convention, Annex 15 18th ed. (2018), (vii).

275 Chicago Convention, Annex 15 18th ed. (2018), para. 6.1, para. 6.2.

276 Ibid pp. 1–2

277 Ibid para. 6.2.1 (a), (6).

deliberately refrained from doing so.[278] Instead, it is for each State to define the scope and content of ADIZs. Annexes 4 and 15 solely aim to ensure that the relevant information on ADIZs is published under the AIRAC system (pursuant to Annex 15) and in Aeronautical Charts (pursuant to Annex 4).

7.6 *The Legality of ADIZs in International Airspace*

The ICAO Secretariat issued a statement in which it explains that national law had no effect in international airspace, and hence ADIZs could not have a legal basis under international law in international airspace.[279] This statement is too general as it fails to address the issue of extraterritorial jurisdiction. It may be that the statement only refers to the prohibition of exercising sovereignty in the sense of Art. 1 Chicago Convention outside the States' territories, but as illustrated above, States' powers beyond their borders can also be based on the principles of jurisdiction.[280] There is a clear distinction between sovereignty and the right to exercise jurisdiction. As long as ADIZs do not amount to a claim of sovereignty of international airspace, other States need not necessarily object to the practice.[281] It is important to note that the Chicago Convention does not contain a provision on the freedom of overflight over the high seas.[282] Instead, international airspace is subject to international traffic management rules, such as in the case of FIR,[283] which impose certain limitations on the conduct of overflight.

7.6.1 International Air Law does not prohibit ADIZs in International Airspace

ADIZs in international airspace represent a form of limited jurisdiction exercised outside the territory of States. The Annexes to the Chicago Convention encompass rules, pertaining to the conduct of ADIZs, do not expressly state the legal basis for the establishment of identification zones in international

278 Jinyuan Su, 'The East China Sea Air Defense Identification Zone and International Law' (2015) 14 Chinese Jl Int'l L 278.

279 ICAO Doc ATMSG/6 WP 26, para. 2.5.

280 Malcom N Shaw, *International Law* (9th edn, Cambridge University Press 2021) 504.

281 A Similar argument was raised in connection with "keep-out-zones" in outer space, see Kenneth Schwetje, 'Protecting Space Assets: A Legal Analysis of "Keep-Out Zones"' (1987) 15 Journal of Space Law 134.

282 Roncevert Almond, 'Clearing the Air above the East China Sea: The Primary Elements of Aircraft Defense Identification Zones' (2017) 7 Harvard National Security Journal 138. For a more detailed discussion on the freedom to overflight see chapter 3 of this book.

283 Christopher Lamont, 'Conflict in the Skies: The Law of Air Defence Identification Zones' (2014) 39 Air & Space Law 195.

airspace. It is well established that the coastal States enjoy jurisdiction over parts of the sea adjacent to the territorial sea.[284] It can also be argued, that the same coastal States also enjoy jurisdiction in the airspace adjacent to national airspace.[285] The discussion on jurisdiction in international airspace mostly concerns criminal offences conducted on board an aircraft. In the legal body of international air law, the Tokyo Convention on Offences and Certain Other Acts Committed on Board Aircraft stipulates in Art. 4 that when an offence has been committed on board an aircraft, States other than the State of registration may interfere with aircraft in flight.[286] Interference with an aircraft is possible if the offence has been committed while that aircraft is in flight or on the surface of the high seas or of any other area outside the territory of any State. In order for an offence to be considered to have been committed in this way, it must also have an effect in the territory of the intercepting State; have been committed by or against a national or permanent resident of such State; be against the security of the State; or consist of a breach of any rules or regulations relating to the flight of aircraft.[287] The Tokyo Convention, therefore, provides for the jurisdiction of States in international airspace when there is a link to their territory or security interests. A similar connection can be seen between the interest of States to prevent aerial threats from materializing in their territory and identifying such threats. Another example of an air law treaty providing for the application of national law outside the State's territory is the 1971 Montreal Convention.[288] The Montreal Convention defines in Art. 1 offences on board an aircraft in flight and requires contracting States to make these offences punishable by severe penalties when the alleged offender is found within the State's territory regardless of the place where the offence was committed pursuant to Art. 3 Montreal Convention.[289] As previously stated, FIRs represent an additional example of the conduct of treaty-based

284 Dolliver Nelson, 'Maritime Jurisdiction' in *Max Planck Encyclopedias of Public International Law* (OUP 2010) para. 2.

285 Robert D Hayton, 'Jurisdiction of the Littoral State' (1964) 111 Philippine Int'l L J 374.

286 Tokyo Convention on Offences and Certain Other Acts Committed on Board Aircraft ("Tokyo Convention") (1969) 1969 UNTS 220.

287 Tokyo Convention, Art. 4; Sami Shubber, *Jurisdiction over Crimes on Board Aircraft* (Martinus Nijhoff, 1973) 48; Iryna Sopilko & Yevhenii Shevchuk, 'Jurisdiction Over Crimes Committed On Board Aircraft In Flight Under The Tokyo Convention 1963' (2016) 69 National Aviation University 121–125.

288 Convention on the Suppression of Unlawful Acts against the Safety of Civil Aviation (Montreal Convention), 974 UNTS 177 (adopted 23 September 1971, entered into force 26 January 1973).

289 Christopher Staker, 'Jurisdiction', in Malcom D Evans (ed), *International Law* (5th edn, OUP 2018) 303.

extraterritorial jurisdiction in international air law. ICAO may assign jurisdictional functions for monitoring air traffic in FIRs in international airspace.[290] If States assume the responsibility for providing air traffic services in the designated FIRs, then they may also apply the same national rules in international airspace as they do in national airspace for FIRs.[291]

The nature and scope of States entitled to exercise criminal jurisdiction and extend their criminal laws to cover events extraterritorially in the absence of a treaty or custom were subject of intensive debate.[292] As discussed above, under the Lotus principle, the issue of extraterritorial jurisdiction can be resolved if the jurisdiction to prescribe laws and the jurisdiction to enforce laws are separated.[293] There is no rule of international law that prohibits States from prescribing laws that address events outside national territory, provided that States do not enforce them extraterritorially.[294] Particularly the separation of prescriptive and enforcement jurisdiction in areas beyond national territory may be helpful for sustaining a claim on ADIZs in international airspace.[295] The same approach was applied to offences committed on board an aircraft. While ADIZs do not require an offence to be committed on board the aircraft, the concept of extraterritorial jurisdiction does not necessarily only concern criminal offences but can also relate to other aspects.[296] States have already taken unilateral acts to temporarily restrict the use of a portion of international airspace while conducting military drills in international waters or even

---

290 Wybo Heere, 'Problems of Jurisdiction in Air and Outer Space' (1999) XXIV Air & Space Law 76; Jean Carroz, 'International Legislation On Air Navigation Over The High Seas'(1959) 26 J Air L & Comm 162.

291 Jonathan Odom, 'A "Rule-Based Approach" to Airspace Defense: A U.S. Perspective on the International Law of the Sea and Airspace, Air Defense Measures, and the Freedom of Navigation' (2014) Revue Belge de Droit International 73.

292 Chia-Jui Cheng (ed), *Studies in International Air Law – Selected Works of Bing Cheng* (Brill 2018) 9.

293 Ole Spiermann, '*Lotus and the Double Structure of International Legal Argument*' in Philippe Sands & Laurence Boisson de Chazournes (eds), *International Law, the International Court of Justice and Nuclear Weapons* (Cambridge University Press 1999) 131.

294 Chia-Jui Cheng (ed), *Studies in International Air Law – Selected Works of Bing Cheng* (Brill 2018) 10.

295 The general rule of interception of civil aircraft can be found in Art. 3(bis) Chicago Convention. A more detailed discussion on enforcement in State practice can be found in chapter 3, 2.7 of this book.

296 The issue of extraterritorial application of national law has been discussed in the field of antitrust and competition law, see ICAO Doc 9470 AT-Conf/3-WP/71, Third Air Transport Conference (22.10.-7.11.1985) at 3–11.

testing nuclear weapons.[297] For this purpose, States have declared a "safety zone" or "warning area" of limited dimensions and issued "general warnings to shipping and aircraft not to enter when the activity is being carried out."[298] Safety zones do not prevent aircraft from entering the respective airspace, they serve to warn them about the possible dangers.[299] Similarly, ADIZs do also not constitute a blockade, but only require aircraft to identify themselves. It is not uncommon for states to exercise jurisdiction outside their territory in accordance with the legal framework of international air law.

7.6.2 ADIZs are outside the Scope of ICAO's Regulatory Competence

In essence, ADIZs are a security measure with the underlying purpose of defending national airspace and preventing strategic aerial attacks against national airspace. These two fundamental reasons, which originated from the era of the Cold War, have been supplemented with the aim of detecting hijacked aircraft used for an attack.[300] Furthermore, the rationales for ADIZs have been further expanded with the administrative need to control air traffic in highly congested skies.[301] The forms of ADIZs have varied due to differing interpretations of their purposes and the absence of an international legal framework.[302] The different justifications for the establishment of ADIZs have led to discussions on the precise scope of jurisdiction of ICAO and its regulatory authority over international airspace. While ICAO's mandate is limited to the safety and facilitation of air transport, its authority does not extend to economic matters or national security.[303] Moreover, States have retained powers falling within the field of the Chicago Convention, including those relating to

297 Ashley Roach, 'Air Identification Zones' in *Max Planck Encyclopedias of Public International Law* (OUP 2017), para. 4.

298 Anthony Aust, *Handbook of International Law* (Cambridge University Press 2005) 348; Kenneth Schwetje, 'Protecting Space Assets: A Legal Analysis of "Keep-Out Zones"' (1987) 15 Journal of Space Law, stating at 135 that "between 1946 and 1954, the United States established warning areas of from 30,000 to 400,000 square miles in the Pacific."

299 Kenneth Schwetje, 'Protecting Space Assets: A Legal Analysis of "Keep-Out Zones"' (1987) 15 Journal of Space Law 135.

300 Christopher Lamont, 'Conflict in the Skies: The Law of Air Defence Identification Zones' (2014) 39 Air & Space Law 190.

301 As can be seen on the example of the ECS ADIZ established by China.

302 Christopher Lamont, 'Conflict in the Skies: The Law of Air Defence Identification Zones' (2014) 39 Air & Space Law 190.

303 Amir Majiel, 'Impact of Current U.S. Policy On International Civil Aviation' (1983) 32 Zeitschrift für Luft- und Weltraumrecht 295, 315; Paul S Dempsey, 'The Role of the International Civil Aviation Organization on Deregulation, Discrimination, and Dispute Resolution' (1987) 52 J Air L & Comm noting at 539 that the Preamble suggests ICAO's jurisdiction over economic matters. On the general structure of an international organisation see

the award of traffic rights, the setting of airport charges, and to the determination of prohibited areas in their territory which may not be flown over.[304]

Art. 44 Chicago Convention delineates the objectives of ICAO by stating that "the aims and objectives of the Organization are to develop the principles and techniques of international air navigation and to foster the planning and development of international air transport." Art. 44 lit. (a) to (i) enumerates specific objectives, including "to ensure the safe and orderly growth of international civil aviation throughout the world,"[305] or to "promote generally the development of all aspects of international civil aeronautics."[306] None of the enumerated aims refers to matters of national security but only to the safety of air traffic operations. With regard to the interpretation of the constituent instrument of an international organisation, the ICJ stated in the *Nuclear Weapons Advisory Opinion* that "the very nature of the organization created, the objects which have been assigned to it by its founders, the imperatives associated with the effective performance of its functions" need to be taken into consideration.[307] Matters of national security are not within the competence of ICAO, as the organization's mandate is limited to the safety and facilitation of air transport and potentially economic matters. ICAO's regulatory authority with regard to security matters is limited to specific cases, such as national security audit programs.

In the wake of the events of 11 September 2001, there was a pressing need to address the issue of security within the purview of ICAO.[308] This led to the convening of the High-level Ministerial Conference on Aviation Security held in February 2002,[309] which resulted in the adoption of a Universal Aviation Security Programme.[310] This was further complemented by the ICAO Security

---

Dapo Akande, 'International Organizations' in Malcom D Evans (ed), *International Law* (5th edn, OUP 2018) 235 ff.

304 Court of the European Union, ECLI:EU:C:2011:864 (21 December 2011) at para. 70, on the application of the Chicago Convention on the European Union.

305 Art. 44 lit (a) Chicago Convention.

306 Art. 44 lit (i) Chicago Convention.

307 *Nuclear Weapons Advisory Opinion* para. 19.

308 Jimena Blumenkron, 'International Safety Requirements', in Paul S Dempsey & Ram S Jakhu (eds), *Routledge Handbook of Public Aviation Law* (Routledge 2017) 47.

309 ICAO Doc 9800, High-level, Ministerial Conference on Aviation Security (Montreal, 19–20.2.2002); For the Declaration issued, XXVI Ann ASL (2001), 441.

310 ICAO Assembly Resolution A35–9, Appendix E, "The ICAO Universal Security Audit Programme".

Audit Reference Material[311] and the ICAO Aviation Security Plan of Action.[312] ICAO's efforts in regulating security aspects have been further concretised in Annex 17 which sets out the basis for the ICAO civil aviation security program and seeks to protect civil aviation and its facilities against acts of unlawful interference.[313] The Security Audit Reference Material, the Aviation Security Plan of Action as well as Annex 17 collectively aim to prevent and surpress all acts of unlawful interference against civil aviation.[314] The aforementioned materials are primarily concerned with administrative and coordination tasks, as well as with adopting technical measures for the protection of the security of international air transport. However, they do not curtail the States' regulatory competence in matters of national security.

The ICAO documents on security measures do not purport to impose regulations on how to administer national security of the Contracting States.[315] Even though States are required to establish their own national aviation security program, they are free to decide the exact content of the security measures.[316] While the preamble of the Chicago Convention considers threats stemming from non-state actors, the actual vulnerability of civil aviation and the accompanying threat to national security has not been much regarded until the events of 11 September 2001.[317] It could therefore be argued that the regulatory

311 ICAO Doc 9807 (2002).

312 ICAO Council C-MIN 166/5, 166th Session (June 2002).

313 Chicago Convention, Annex 17 "Security – Safeguarding International Civil Aviation against Acts of Unlawful Interference" (11th ed, 2020).

314 Act of unlawful interference are defined in Annex 17, 1–1, as: Acts or attempted acts to jeopardize the safety of civil aviation, not limited to: unlawful seizure of aircraft, destruction of an aircraft in service, hostage-taking on board aircraft or an aerodromes, forcible intrusion on board an aircraft, at an airport or the premise of an aeronautical facility, introduction on board an aircraft or at an airport of a weapon or hazardous device or material intended for criminal purposes, use of an aircraft in service for the purpose of causing death, serious bodily injury, or serious damage to property or the environment, communication of false information such as to jeopardize the safety of an aircraft in flight or on the ground, of passengers, crew, ground personnel or the general public, at an airport or on the premise of a civil aviation facility.

315 For example, the justification of the US ADIZ pursuant to 14 C.F.R. §99.9 is based on the need to ensure national security, to control illicit drug activities, to minimize unnecessary intercept and search-and-rescue operations, and to decrease the risk of midair collisions and other public hazards, see Security Control of Air Traffic, 66 Fed. Reg. 49,819 (Sept. 28, 2001).

316 ICAO Doc 8973 'Aviation Security Manual'; Annex 17 "Foreword", p. viii.

317 Robin Geiß, 'Civil Aircraft as Weapons of Large-Scale Destruction: Countermeasures, Article 3bis of the Chicago Convention, and the Newly Adopted German "Luftsicherheitsgesetz"' (2005) 27 Michigan J Int'l L 230.

scope of ICAO does not contain matters of national security and consequently, ICAO cannot adopt corresponding rules. This limitation of ICAO's jurisdictional competence may explain the lack of elaborated provisions on ADIZs in the Annexes, as these zones concern national security and are thus not within ICAO's regulatory competence. It is also important to recall the definition of "Standard" encompassed in the Annexes as they are dedicated to the safety or regularity of international air navigation but are not dedicated to regulating aspects of national security. In light of the aforementioned considerations, it can be argued that ADIZs, as a means of safeguarding national security, may be within the State's right to claim the identification of aircraft attempting to enter national airspace.[318] This argument is also supported by Art. 11 Chicago Convention and the right of States to regulate the admission of aircraft to national airspace.

The Chicago Convention neither explicitly prohibits nor permits the establishment of ADIZs.[319] The Annexes of the Chicago Convention provide for rules on ADIZs but do not include detailed preconditions nor an explicit legal basis for the creation of ADIZs. In addition, the enforcement of identification obligations remained unresolved.[320] The existing SARPs on ADIZs are rudimentary technical specifications for the safe conduct of air transport, but do not concern the legal basis for ADIZs as a matter of national security. Annex 4 regulates the identification of ADIZs in Aeronautical Charts and states that ADIZ procedures may be described in the chart legend.[321] Annex 15 provides that relevant and specific ADIZ information and data need to be notified to AIRAC. Both Annex 4 and Annex 15 presume the existence of an ADIZ, yet neither contains

---

318 Michel Bourbonniere & Louis Haeck, 'Military Aircraft And International Law: Chicago Opus' (2000) 66 J Air L & Com at 954 arguing that ADIZ "are not based upon any specific treaty dispositions, [but] ... are nonetheless consistent with the Chicago Convention."

319 Robert Beckman & Hao D Phan, 'Air Defence Identification Zones: Implications For Freedom Of Overflight And Maritime Disputes' in Truong T Tran, John B Welfield & Thuy T Le (eds), *Building a Normative Order in the South China Sea* (Edward Elgar Publishing 2019) 156; Jinyuan Su, 'The East China Sea Air Defense Identification Zone and International Law'(2015) 14 Chinese J Int'l L 278. Li Juqian, 'Air Defense Identification Zone: The Restriction On The Free Sky Due To The Residual Right Principle'(2014) 2 China Legal Science 17; US Department of the Navy, *Commander's Handbook on the Law of Naval Operations, U.S. Naval Warfare Publication* (2007), para. 2.7.2.3; For the discussion on Art. 12 Chicago Convention as a prohibitive rule, see: Zoltan Papp, 'ADIZ in the Light of Public International Law' (2015) Pécs J Int'l & European L 40, 41.

320 Edmund J Burke & Astrid Stuth Cevallos, *In Line or out of Order? – Chinas Approach to ADIZ in Theory and Practice* (Rand 2017) 3.

321 Chicago Convention, Annex 4, 9th ed (2009), para. 7.9.3. l.

any SARPs or written procedures for the establishment and operation of an ADIZ.[322] There is no explicit reference to any geographical position of ADIZs, leaving it open whether States may create them above the high seas or exclusively in national airspace. Annex 15 only stipulates that the horizontal and vertical limits should be notified, but leaves the parameter of the zone to be determined by States. The Annexes of the Chicago Convention acknowledge the existence of ADIZs and partly also contain regulations on the identification and notification of ADIZs. However, they do not mention which regulations and procedures apply to ADIZs nor do they prescribe the horizontal and vertical limits. This leads to the conclusion that a legal gap exists in the establishment of ADIZs. This legal gap needs to be filled as a logical requirement for a reasonable application of the Annexes in international airspace. As *Cuadra* noted:

> When ICAO is silent on a given topic, States are not precluded from formulating rules on that topic, nor is it mandatory that States notify ICAO of rules they have adopted on such topics.[323]

It can be argued that Annex 4 and Annex 15 do not explicitly refer to either national or international airspace. Consequently, they can be interpreted in the overall context of the Chicago Convention and the two aforementioned Annexes as covering national as well as international airspace.[324] In particular, Annex 15 applies to the worldwide use of aeronautical information and, thus, also covers aircraft traversing in international airspace. This assumption does also not contradict Art. 12 Chicago Convention and the general structure of the Chicago Convention. Pursuant to Art. 12 Chicago Convention, any rule relating to the flight and manoeuvre of aircraft in airspace above the high seas needs to be established under this Convention. However, the rules pertaining to ADIZs do not relate to the technical aspects of flight and manoeuvre, but rather to the most fundamental concerns of States in relation to the protection of national security. It can therefore be assumed that the concept of ADIZs can be further concretised by States in line with the rules of the Chicago Convention and its Annexes.

---

322 Jonathan Odom, 'A "Rule-Based Approach" to Airspace Defense: A U.S. Perspective on the International Law of the Sea and Airspace, Air Defense Measures, and the Freedom of Navigation' (2014) Revue Belge de Droit International 74.

323 Elisabeth Cuadra, 'Air Defense Identification Zones: Creeping Jurisdiction in the Airspace' (1977) 18 Virginia J Int'l L 491.

324 This is also in line with the content of Annex 11, see above chapter 2, 6.3; See also, Jinyuan Su, 'The East China Sea Air Defense Identification Zone and International Law' (2015) 14 Chinese J Int'l L 278.

8 Conclusion

The principal findings of this chapter indicate that the legal basis for the establishment of an ADIZ varies according to the spatial scope, that is to say, whether the zone in question is established in national or international airspace. In the case of national airspace, the legal basis for ADIZs can be found in Art. 1 of the Chicago Convention and the customary principle of sovereignty in the airspace over the territory. While ICAO has expressed concerns about the establishment of ADIZs over the high seas, some details regarding the dissemination of information on ADIZs have been included in Annexes 4 and 15. The Chicago Convention generally encourages States to apply uniform rules to air traffic, but States are free to deviate from ICAO SARPs if they find it impracticable to comply with them. The most convoluted issue in the context of the Chicago Convention and ICAO's quasi-legislative powers is the defensive and military nature of ADIZs. Although Art. 12 of the Chicago Convention provides for ICAO's limited competence to establish rules of the air regulating the flight and manoeuvre of aircraft over the high seas, ADIZs do not have the primary purpose of providing technical flight rules. Instead they are designed to identify potential threats. These defence zones are inextricably linked to the protection of national security, and ADIZs necessarily apply to both civil and military aircraft. Apart from the fact that the Chicago Convention does not apply to military aircraft, ICAO's regulatory powers do not cover matters of national security under which ADIZs would fall. Where States apply their ADIZ rules only to aircraft intending to enter national airspace, Art. 11 of the Chicago Convention could provide a legal basis. However, there are conceptual difficulties with regard to the precise scope of Art. 11 Chicago Convention, as it is unclear whether a wide-area zone or rather the establishment of a reporting point or reporting line in international airspace may be established. Furthermore, the provisions of the Chicago Convention and its Annexes do not explicitly provide for the right to claim an ADIZ in international airspace. Nevertheless, as long as the establishment of ADIZs in international airspace is not based on the principle of sovereignty, it can be assumed that these zones are not contrary to international law.

CHAPTER 6

Impact of the Law of the Sea on Defining ADIZs

International airspace and the high seas share the common characteristic of not being subject to any sovereignty claims. The coherence between these two areas is based on the fact that the legal character of air space is determined by the legal character of the subjacent land or water.[1] A close interrelation, therefore, exists between developments in the law of the sea and international air law. With the adoption of the UN Convention on the Law of the Sea in 1982 (UNCLOS), the law of the sea has undergone significant changes driven by State practice prior to its adoption. UNCLOS brought significant changes and legal security to the international legal landscape as regards the enlargement of the territorial sea, the development of the Exclusive Economic Zone (EEZ), and the exploitation of resources on the high seas and the deep seabed.[2] While the law of the sea has been in a state of flux for several decades prior to the adoption of UNCLOS in 1982, with ongoing effect until the present day,[3] the core rules of international air law on the delimitation of airspace have not undergone much change since the adoption of the Chicago Convention in 1944.[4]

This chapter aims to highlight the role of State practice in the development of jurisdictional competences in maritime zones and the assertion of freedoms over the high seas culminating in the adoption of a treaty. These developments might have had an impact on international air law and new forms of aerial zones in international airspace. A historical overview shows that emerging maritime zones granting jurisdictional competences beyond national territory have their roots in State practice. The establishment of ADIZs as special jurisdictional zones in international airspace may likewise emerge from State practice. Furthermore, this chapter will illustrate that the freedom of the high seas, specifically the freedom of overflight, does not necessarily conflict with the

1 Malcom N Shaw, *International Law* (9th edn, Cambridge University Press 2021) 410; Rothwell and Stephens, *The International Law of the Sea* (2nd edn, OUP 2016); Yoshifumi Tanaka, *The International Law of the Sea* (3rd edn, Cambridge University Press 2019).

2 Malcom N Shaw, *International Law* (9th edn, Cambridge University Press 2021) 411.

3 See for example the ongoing process regarding the legal regime of marine areas beyond national jurisdiction Vito De Lucia, Alex Oude Elferink, & Lan Ngoc Nguyen (eds), *International Law and Marine Areas beyond National* Jurisdiction (Brill 2022).

4 One amendment concerns Art. 3bis and the use of weapons against civil aircraft in 1984, Protocol Relating to an Amendment to the Convention on International Civil Aviation, UN Doc 9436.

 | DOI:10.1163/9789004721005_008

establishment of ADIZs. Moreover, the concept of the EEZ has eroded the strict division between the territorial sea and the high seas. The creation of new maritime zones and new forms of jurisdictional competence co-existing alongside the territorial sea and the high seas, may have had effect on the traditional distinction between national airspace above the territorial sea and international airspace above the high seas. The concept of the EEZ lays the foundation for a similar discussion on new jurisdictional competence in airspace within a special designated zone. The law of the sea is relevant for the evaluation of aerial zones, particularly regarding aerial military activities, which are outside the scope of the Chicago Convention.[5]

1 Introduction to Similar Conceptual Problems of ADIZs and Maritime Zones

The fundamental principle of the law of the sea is the balancing of competing interests in the utilization of maritime areas, which might provide insights into similar problems arising from the competing usage of airspace by States. Historically, the sea was divided between the territorial seas, as part of State territory, and the high seas, which are free to use by all States and not subject to any territorial claims.[6] The concept of *mare liberum* dates back to Roman times.[7] Since that time, the traditional understanding of *mare liberum* has undergone significant changes as a result of the creation of new maritime zones of functional and resource-oriented jurisdiction and sovereign rights.[8] The former principle of free governance of the sea was adjusted to include new, complex realignments of jurisdictional competences and to address the problem of overlapping maritime zones, their delimitation, and competing claims.[9] The

5 Jinyuan Su, 'The East China Sea Air Defence Identification Zone and International Law' (2015) 14 Chinese J Int'l Law 290.

6 Hugo Grotius, *The Freedom of the High Seas: Or, the Rights which Belong to the Dutch to Take Part in the East Indian Trade* (translated by R van Deman Magoffin, OUP 1916); Douglas Guilfoyle, 'Article 87- Freedom of the High Seas' in Alexander Proelß (ed), *United Nations Convention on the Law of the Sea: A Commentary* (Nomos 2017) 678; Douglas Guilfoyle, 'The High Seas' in Donald R Rothwell et al (eds), *Oxford Handbook of the Law of the Sea* (OUP 2015) 203.

7 Bo J Theutenberg, 'Mare Clausum et Mare Liberum' (1984) 37 Arctic 481.

8 Malcom D Evans, 'The Law of the Sea' in Malcom D Evans (ed), *International Law* (5th edn, OUP 2018) 635.

9 Malcom N Shaw, *International Law* (9th edn, Cambridge University Press 2021) 439–451. "Maritime delimitation" can be defined as "the process of establishing lines separating the spatial ambit of the coastal State jurisdiction over maritime spaces where the legal

combination of the diverse types of jurisdiction for the manifestation of State powers' ultimately led to the emergence of an intricate interplay of mutually exclusive, concurrent or parallel, and overlapping varieties of jurisdiction.[10] In numerous cases before the ICJ, as well as ad-hoc tribunals, overlapping claims in maritime areas were subject matter.[11]

The classical concept of sovereignty and jurisdiction form the building blocks of the law of the sea, yet shaped and adapted to align with the interests of States' in the utilization of the sea.[12] Competing interests and entitlements in areas beyond national territory provide for a complex situation that requires the balancing of States' interests. The derogation of the earliest doctrinal division between the territorial sea and the high seas was initiated by factual circumstances. Coastal States simply extended their jurisdiction over resources beyond the territorial sea. In the *North Sea Continental* Shelf *Case*,[13] and the *Fisheries Jurisdiction Case*,[14] the ICJ acknowledged the emergence of the continental shelf and exclusive fisheries zones as areas beyond the territorial sea based on State practice. As the international community could no longer ignore the factual exercise of new forms of jurisdictional competences beyond State territory, negotiations for the adoption of a new maritime regime were initiated.[15] The lengthy negotiation process led to the adoption of the United Nations Convention on the Law of the Sea in 1982, which finally abandoned the "rigidity of the territorial/high sea dichotomy."[16] There are currently

---

title overlaps with that of another State" and needs to be distinguished from "maritime limits" which refers to the maritime space of one single State not in contact with another States' maritime space, see Yoshifumi Tanaka, *The International Law of the Sea* (3rd edn, Cambridge University Press, 2019) 237.

10 Maria Gavouneli, *Functional Jurisdiction in the Law of the Sea* (Brill 2007) 32.

11 Stephen Fietta & Robin Cleverly, *A Practitioner's Guide to Maritime Boundary Delimitation* (OUP 2016); James Crawford, *Brownlie's Principles of Public International Law* (8th edn, OUP 2012) 288–289. For example, *Delimitation of Maritime Boundary in the Gulf of Maine Area (Canada v United States of America)* (Merits) [1984] ICJ Rep 240; *Dispute concerning Delimitation of the Maritime Boundary between Bangladesh and Myanmar in the Bay of Bengal (Bangladesh/Myanmar)* ITLOS Rep 2002, 4.

12 Malcom D Evans, 'The Law of the Sea' in Malcom D Evans (ed), *International Law* (5th edn, OUP 2018) 635.

13 *North Sea Continental Shelf (Federal Republic of Germany v Denmark; Federal Republic of Germany v Netherlands)* (Merits) [1969] ICJ Rep 3.

14 *Fisheries Jurisdiction (United Kingdom v Iceland)* (Merits) [1974] ICJ Rep 3.

15 Rene-Jean Dupuy, 'The Sea under National Competence' in Rene Jean Dupuy & Daniel Vignes (eds), *A Handbook on the New Law of the Sea, Volume 1* (1991).

16 Malcom D Evans, 'The Law of the Sea' in Malcom D Evans (ed), *International Law* (5th edn, OUP 2018) 636, 637.

168 State Parties to UNCLOS,[17] and most provisions reflect customary international law.[18]

The process of introducing new delimitations of the sea by creating special maritime zones and overcoming the distinction between territorial sea and high seas within the law of the sea serves as an important benchmark for similar developments within international air law.[19] The emergence of new forms of maritime zones and their influence on the division of the sea necessitates reflection on the traditional concept of limiting States' powers to national airspace. The introduction of ADIZs to the legal landscape has undermined the classical division of airspace between national and international airspace. The creation of ADIZs also shows analogous conceptual issues, namely the emergence of a novel type of aerial jurisdiction, the coexistence of aerial zones, and the challenge of aerial delimitation. An underlying tension can thus be identified within both areas of law: balancing competing demands of access to areas beyond national territory whilst recognizing the need to preserve good governance and legal security.

1.1 *The Emergence of Maritime Zones and New Forms of Maritime Jurisdiction*

The Chicago Convention in its present form continues to reflect the division of the sea between the territorial sea and the high seas adjacent to the territorial sea, as was the prevailing understanding at the time of its adoption in 1944, a time when no codification of the law of the sea has yet existed.[20] The development of international air law and the law of the sea proceeded in different ways as a result of changing circumstances and evolving State practice. This eventually led to the establishment of a new, functional, division of the sea into the territorial sea, the exclusive economic zone, and the high seas.[21] Part II, V, and VI of UNCLOS contain provisions on the boundaries of maritime zones and set out the respective rights and obligations of coastal and other

17 United Nations Treaty Collection, United Nations Convention on the Law of the Sea https://treaties.un.org/pages/ViewDetailsIII.aspx?src=TREATY&mtdsg_no=XXI-6&chapter=21&Temp=mtdsg3&clang=_en.

18 Ashely Roach, 'Today's Customary International Law of the Sea' (2014) 45 Ocean Development & International Law 239.

19 Jaw Woon Lee, 'Tension on the Air: The Air Defence Identification Zones on the East China Sea' (2014) 7 J East Asia & Int'l L 277.

20 Tullio Treves, 'Historical Development of the Law of the Sea', in Donald R Rothwell et al (eds) *Oxford Handbook of the Law of the Sea* (OUP 2015) 7–9.

21 Peter Dutton, 'Caelum Liberam: Air Defense Identification Zones Outside Sovereign Airspace' (2009) 103 AJIL 2.

States therein.[22] Maritime zones, and in particular the EEZ, are not addressed in the Chicago Convention. However, if there is a change in the law of the sea, then international air law might change likewise.[23]

Over the past few decades, the traditional understanding of the division between the territorial sea and the high seas has been eroded.[24] New maritime zones with special exclusive rights and jurisdiction of the States were embedded in treaty law or created by customary international law, and, while marking a diminution of the freedoms of the high seas, it ensured that the increase of the territorial sea remained limited to 12 nautical miles.[25] In total, five different maritime zones of functional jurisdiction can now be identified: internal waters, territorial sea, contiguous zone, exclusive economic zone, and the high seas.[26] Each of these zones grant maritime jurisdiction or sovereign rights differing in their scope and content. In general, sovereign rights address situations where States enjoy 'functional sovereignty' connected to maritime resources based on particular grounds established by international law.[27] In contrast, maritime jurisdiction can be understood as "the exercise – in conformity with international law – of legislative, executive, and judicial functions over the sea and over persons and things on or under the sea."[28] Maritime jurisdiction can be characterized as functional jurisdiction extending beyond the State's territory. This is because UNCLOS does not explicitly refer to the traditional forms of jurisdiction, but rather focuses on the role of States.[29] The State performs as either "flag State", "coastal State" or "port State", whereas each form opens a different range of functions.[30]

This sub-chapter does not seek to provide a comprehensive overview of the historical development of the law of the sea. Instead, it aims to identify the key legal stages that led to the emergence of the EEZ and the States' jurisdictional powers within this zone. As will be demonstrated, State practice was a pivotal factor in the development of maritime zones ultimately leading to the

22 Robin R Churchill, 'The 1982 United Nations Convention on the Law of the Sea' in Donald R Rothwell et al (eds) *Oxford Handbook of the Law of the Sea* (OUP 2015) 28.

23 Alex Calvo, 'China's Air Defense Identification Zone: Concept, Issues at Stake and Regional Impact' (2013) Naval War College Press 8, 13.

24 Malcom D Evans (ed), *International Law* (5th edn, OUP 2018) 649.

25 Ibid 655.

26 Dolliver Nelson, 'Maritime Jurisdiction' in *Max Planck Encyclopaedias of Public International Law* (OUP 2010) para. 2.

27 Rosalyn Higgins, *Problem & Process, International Law and How we use it* (OUP 1999) 131.

28 Dolliver Nelson, 'Maritime Jurisdiction' in *Max Planck Encyclopaedias of Public International Law* (OUP 2010) para. 1.

29 Maria Gavouneli, *Functional Jurisdiction in the Law of the Sea* (Brill 2007) 33.

30 Ibid, 33, 34.

adoption of a treaty text on rights and duties within these zones. A comparable process can be observed with regard to ADIZs, as State practice likewise indicates the emergence of aerial zones in airspace beyond States' territory.[31]

1.1.1 The Continental Shelf: Ipso Facto and Ab Initio

The concept of the Continental Shelf is only mentioned for reasons of completeness, but the rules on the Continental Shelf do not provide sufficient reasons for a comparison with ADIZs. In its judgment in the *North Sea Continental Shelf Cases*, the ICJ examined the legal regime of the continental shelf and related delimitation problems.[32] In the absence of a binding treaty provision and a rule of customary international law, the ICJ acknowledged that the continental shelf existed *ipso facto* and *ab initio* as a natural prolongation of land territory. The rights of the coastal State over the continental shelf exist by virtue of the State's sovereignty, and "as an extension of it in an exercise of sovereign rights for the purpose of exploring the seabed and exploiting its natural resources."[33] It is the inherent right of each coastal State to declare the existence of the continental shelf, a process that does not require the any special legal act.[34] In contrast, ADIZs cannot be regarded as natural given and are not based on State's sovereignty. As will be discussed later in this chapter, the existence of an ADIZ depends on the actual claim of the zone by a State.

1.1.2 The Fishery Zone as *Tertium Genus*

The concept of extending jurisdiction over areas adjacent to the coast has its roots in State practice that gradually hardened into claims of "exclusive fishery zones."[35] Even though States exercised jurisdiction relating to the exploitation of fishery resources outside the territorial sea, exclusive fishery zones were not seen as appropriating parts of the high seas.[36] As fishery zones did not amount to sovereignty claims, they were not considered to be contradictory to the freedom of the high seas. In the *Fisheries Jurisdiction Case*, the ICJ was concerned with the extension of the limits of Iceland's exclusive fisheries jurisdiction

31 See chapter 3.

32 *North Sea Continental Shelf (Federal Republic of Germany v Denmark; Federal Republic of Germany v Netherlands)* (Merits) [1969] ICJ Rep 3.

33 Ibid para. 19.

34 Ibid para. 19.

35 Donald R Rothwell, 'Fishery Zones and Limits' in *Max Planck Encyclopaedias of Public International Law* (OUP 2008) para. 10.

36 Ibid para. 4.

from a distance of 12 to a distance of 50 nautical miles.[37] In the judgment of 25 July 1974, the ICJ found that the Icelandic regulations, constituting a unilateral extension of exclusive fishing rights to a limit of 50 nautical miles, were not opposable to the United Kingdom. In the same breath, the ICJ stated that Iceland was not entitled to unilaterally exclude other States' fishing vessels from the fisheries jurisdiction zone or to unilaterally impose restrictions on their activities in such area.[38] The rules on jurisdiction within fisheries zones were not codified at the time of the judgment.[39] The first United Nations Conference on the Law of the Sea (UNCLOS I) had adopted a Convention on the High Seas, in which the principle of the freedom of the high seas was declared, nonetheless, the breadth of the territorial sea and extent of the coastal State's jurisdiction were not settled.[40] In addition, the second UN Conference (UNCLOS II) in 1960 left the issue of the territorial sea's breadth and the growing demands for access to resources unresolved.[41] For the evaluation of exclusive fishery zones, the Court, therefore, referred to the evolution of international law through State practice.[42] The ICJ assumed that the concept of a fisheries zone is independent from the territorial sea and that the concept of enjoying rights within these zones had crystallized into a rule of customary international law.[43] The Court distinguished between the scope of exclusive fishery zones as "as a *tertium genus* between the territorial sea and the high sea" and the scope of preferential rights in a situation of special dependence on coastal fishery within the exclusive fishery zone.[44] While the ICJ did not explain the term *tertium genus*, it can be understood as an unknown or indefinite third class (fishery zone) related to two known or definite classes (territorial sea and high seas).[45] However, the fact that Iceland was entitled to claim preferential rights did not

---

37 *Fisheries Jurisdiction* (*United Kingdom v Iceland*) (Merits) [1974] ICJ Rep 3 [hereinafter: *Fisheries Jurisdiction* (1974)].

38 Ibid.

39 The 1958 Convention on Fisheries and Conservation of the Living Resources of the High Seas (adopted 29 April 1958) 559 UNTS 285 only counted 39 State parties and did not gain much international support.

40 Malcom D Evans (ed), *International Law* (5th edn, OUP 2018) 636.

41 Ibid.

42 Peter Tomka, 'Fisheries Jurisdiction Cases (United Kingdom v Iceland; Federal Republic of Germany v Iceland)' in *Max Planck Encyclopaedias of Public International Law* (OUP 2007) para. 13.

43 *Fisheries Jurisdiction* (1974) para. 52, limiting the exclusive fisheries zone to 12 nautical miles.

44 Ibid para. 54.

45 Patrick Hanks (ed), *Collins Dictionary of the English Language* (Collins 1960).

suffice to unilaterally exclude British fishing vessels from all fishing within the limit of the exclusive fisheries zone. The Court concluded:

> A coastal State entitled to preferential rights is not free, unilaterally and according to its own uncontrolled discretion, to determine the extent of those rights. The characterization of the coastal State's rights as preferential implies a certain priority, but cannot imply the extinction of the concurrent rights of other States.[46]

The aspect of extended jurisdiction beyond the territorial sea, and its effect on other States, is likewise relevant for ADIZs. ADIZs first appeared in 1950 when the United States unilaterally declared parts of airspace above the high seas as defence identification zone to exercise security rights, approximately at the same time when States started to claim preferential fishery rights.[47] At the initial stage of States claiming an aerial zone beyond the national airspace, ADIZs may have been regarded as *tertium genus*, namely *tertium genus* between national and international airspace, in which the interests of the coastal State and the interest of other States' aircraft in their freedom of overflight are balanced.[48] The difference between preferential rights on certain resources, and the preferential right to identify intruding aircraft bound for national airspace may address two separate kinds of jurisdictional powers, but they share the common basis of the right of the coastal State to create a special zone. The right of the coastal State to regulate offshore fishery resources within the fishery zone formed the basis for further debates on their recognition at UNCLOS III, and eventually evolved into the Exclusive Economic Zone.[49] As will be elaborated further below, ADIZs might have developed one step further, from a *tertium genus* to a *sui generis* zone, similar to the concept of the EEZ.

1.1.3 The Contiguous Zone as Zone with Limited Jurisdiction

According to Art. 33 UNCLOS, a coastal State may exercise control in the zone contiguous to its territorial sea. A contiguous zone may extend up to 24 nautical miles from the baselines from which the breadth of the territorial sea is

---

46 *Fisheries Jurisdiction* (1974) para. 63.

47 Christopher Lamont, 'Conflict in the Skies: The Law of Air Defence Identification Zones' (2014) 39 Air & Space Law 178.

48 See on a similar discussion on straits qualifying as *tertium genus*, distinct from both the internal waters and the territorial sea, Tullio Scovazzi, 'Management regimes and responsibility for international straits' (1995) 19 Marine Policy 138.

49 Gemma Andreone & Guiseppe Cataldi, 'Sui Generis Zones' in *Max Planck Encyclopaedias of Public International Law* (OUP 2014) 221.

measured.[50] Within such a zone, States may only exercise control if necessary to prevent or punish infringement of its customs, fiscal, immigration or sanitary laws and regulations within its territory or territorial sea. In contrast to the territorial sea, States enjoy the freedom of navigation and overflight in the contiguous zone in the same way as in the EEZ. The contiguous zone is hence not subject to the coastal State's sovereignty, and civil as well as military vessels and aircraft may traverse there.[51] The contiguous zone may overlap with other maritime zones such as the EEZ and the continental shelf, creating a variety of distinctive coastal State jurisdiction and sovereign rights.[52] As a result, the contiguous zone of one State may also overlap with the EEZ of adjacent coastal States. This was also recognized by the ICJ in *Alleged Violations of Sovereign Rights and Maritime Spaces in the Caribbean Sea*.[53]

Similar to the EEZ, States have to actively claim a contiguous zone, and by 2019 a total of 101 States have done so.[54] The exact scope of enforcement jurisdiction and the nature of the coastal State's jurisdiction are subject to controversy. While the restrictive view advocates for enforcement jurisdiction in the contiguous zone only regarding offences committed in the territory or the territorial sea of the State,[55] the liberal view supports the enforcement of national law in the contiguous zone.[56] In order to prevent excessive claims or "jurisdiction creep", State may protest other State's claims or may refer the matter to international organisations to stop or minimize any excessive exercise of jurisdiction.[57] It may also be argued that ADIZS share similar characteristics as the contiguous zones pursuant to Art. 33 UNCLOS. This idea is based on considerations of time and due to the fact that State enjoy only limited jurisdiction. A vessel passes through the contiguous zone in approximately the same time it takes an aircraft to pass through an ADIZ. They also share the characteristic as

50 Art. 33 (2) UNCLOS.

51 Ashley Roach, *Excessive Maritime Claims* (4th edn Brill 2021) 143.

52 Donald R Rothwell & Tim Stephens, *The International Law of the Sea* (3rd edn Hart Publishing 2023).

53 *Alleged Violations of Sovereign Rights and Maritime Spaces in the Caribbean Sea* (*Nicaragua v. Colombia*) ICJ Rep 2022 para 161–164, stating at para 164 that "the provisions of Article 33 of UNCLOS reflect customary international law and that a coastal State is entitled to a contiguous zone which may overlap with the exclusive economic zone of another State."

54 Donald R Rothwell & Tim Stephens, *The International Law of the Sea* (3rd edn Hart Publishing 2023).

55 Gerald Fitzmaurice, 'Some Results of the Geneva Conference on the Law of the Sea' (1959) 8 ICLQ 114.

56 Daniel P O'Connell, International Law of the Sea (Clarendon Press 1982) 1060.

57 John Noyes, 'The Territorial Sea and Contiguous Zone' in Donald Rothwell et al (eds), *The Oxford Handbook of the Law of the Sea* (OUP 2015) 110–112.

of a zone of limited jurisdiction and both zones do not confer upon the coastal State sovereignty or sovereign rights over this zone. It could be argued that, States may regulate the violation of its national ADIZ rules also in airspace contiguous to its national airspace.

1.1.4 Exclusive Economic Zone (EEZ) Characterisation as *Sui Generis* Zone

The concept of the EEZ and the rights of the coastal States within the EEZ were accepted as customary international law during the negotiation process of the third UN Conference on the Law of the Sea (UNCLOS III).[58] The claim for a 200 nautical mile zone traces back to State practice of Latin American States after World War II.[59] The Declaration of Santiago from 1952,[60] the Montevideo Declaration on the Law of the Sea from 1970,[61] and the Lima Declaration from 1970[62] were first attempts to codify the right of coastal States to regulate the exploitation of resources in areas beyond the territorial sea. At the same time as the emergence of State powers to areas beyond national territory, States emphasized the importance of the freedom of navigation and overflight within these zones.[63] This approach was also the centre of a proposal submitted to the UN Seabed Committee, in which it was emphasized that an economic zone can coexist with the freedom of the high seas.[64] In addition, international jurisprudence recognized the value of EEZ and their legal status

58 Robin Churchill & Vaughan Lowe, *The Law of the Sea* (Manchester University Press 1999) 161, 162; *Continental Shelf* (*Libyan Arab Jamahiriya v Malta*) [1984] ICJ Rep 3.

59 Yoshifumi Tanaka, *The International Law of the Sea* (3rd edn, Cambridge University Press 2019) 149, 150.

60 Chile, Ecuador and Peru – Declaration of Maritime Zones [1952] claiming "exclusive sovereignty and jurisdiction over the sea along the coast of their respective countries to a minimum distance of 200sm."

61 Montevideo Declaration on the Law of the Sea [1970] providing for "the right to establish the limits of their maritime sovereignty and jurisdiction in accordance with their geographical and geological characteristics and with the factors governing the existence of marine resources and the need for their rational utilization."

62 Declaration Of The Latin American States On The Law Of The Sea [1970] "right of the coastal State to establish the limits of its maritime sovereignty or jurisdiction in accordance with reasonable criteria, (…) and the need to make rational use of its resources."

63 The Montevideo Declaration specifies: "The right to adopt, for the aforementioned purposes, regulatory measures applicable in areas under their maritime sovereignty and jurisdiction, without prejudice to freedom of navigation by ships and overflying by aircraft of any flag." The text is accessible in the American Journal of International Law, vol.64 (1970) 1021–1023.

64 Kenya: Draft Articles on the Concept of an Exclusive Economic Zone Beyond the Territorial Sea' (1973) 12 International Legal Materials 33–35.

as customary international law. Judge *Oda* stated in his Dissenting Opinion in the *Tunisia/Lybia Continental Shelf Case* on the impact of the EEZ that, "[t]hroughout the history of international law, scarcely any other major concept has ever stood at the threshold of acceptance within such a short period."[65] Judge *Oda's* statement proved to be true, as only three years later the ICJ confirmed in the *Lybia/Malta Continental Shelf Case* that, "[t]he institution of the exclusive economic zone, with its rules on entitlement by reason of distance, is shown by the practice of States to become a part of customary law."[66] In 1982, UNCLOS III eventually established the EEZ as a matter of treaty law. The main provisions of the concept of the EEZ as set forward in UNCLOS are hence recognized as a rule of customary international law, which the ICJ confirmed in a recent judgment in 2022.[67]

The EEZ is an area up to 200 nautical miles beyond the territorial sea and covers waters previously regarded as high seas.[68] In general, EEZ are characterized as sui generis zones.[69] The term "sui generis zone" was first used by the Chairman of the Second Committee of UNCLOS III,[70] and the terminology is also accepted in scholarly literature.[71] EEZ are primarily dedicated to the exploration, exploitation, conserving, and managing of living and non-living natural resources.[72] States do also enjoy jurisdictional rights with regard to the establishment and use of artificial islands, installations and structures, marine scientific research, and the protection and preservation of the marine environment.[73] The EEZ's special sovereign rights and jurisdictional rights coexist with the traditional freedoms of the high seas and include pursuant to Art. 58 UNCLOS the freedom of navigation, overflight, and the freedom of laying submarine cables and pipelines. In contrast, the construction of artificial islands and installations, fishing, and scientific research, are part of the predominant

65 *Continental Shelf* (*Tunisia v Lybian Arab Jamahiriya*) (Merits) [1982] ICJ Rep 18, Dis. Op. Judge Oda, para. 120.

66 *Continental Shelf* (*Lybian Arab Jamahiriya v Malta*) (Merits) [1984] ICJ Rep 3 para. 34.

67 *Alleged Violations of Sovereign Rights and Maritime Spaces in the Caribbean Sea* (*Nicaragua v Colombia*) (Merits) [2022] ICJ Rep 155 para. 56, 57, namely "including Art. 56, 58, 61, 62 and 73."

68 Art. 55 and Art. 57 UNCLOS.

69 Donald R Rothwell & Tim Stephens, *The International Law of the Sea* (Hart Publishing 2023) 84.

70 UNCLOS III, Official Records, Vol. V (1976) 153.

71 Edward D Brown, *The International Law of the Sea, Volume I* (Dartmouth Publishing 1994) 218; Robin R Churchill & Vaughan Lowe, *The Law of the Sea* (Manchester University Press 1999) 166.

72 Art. 56 (1) (a) UNCLOS.

73 Art. 56 (1) (b) UNCLOS.

control of the coastal State within its EEZ and are not covered by the freedom of the high seas.[74] Ambiguities remain as regards the customary nature of the rights and obligations of coastal States.[75] Whether characterized as sovereign rights or jurisdictional rights, coastal States shall pay due regard to the rights and duties of other States in their use of the sea.[76]

The next part of this chapter discusses the relationship of ADIZs with the law of the sea. The main argument revolves around the concern of fragmentation of international law and possible conflicts of laws regarding the attribution of rights and jurisdiction in airspace beyond national territory. Fragmentation may be the result of the fundamental changes in the law of the sea and the concept of EEZ whilst international air law remained unchanged.

1.2 *Regime Interaction between International Air Law and the Law of the Sea*

The isolated development of specialized fields of international law could lead to serious conflicts of laws within the international legal system.[77] Under the prevailing issue of fragmentation of international law and the absence of an overarching legislature promoting consistency, legal fields tend to develop disparately.[78] The notion of fragmentation is linked to the diversity of international law and the rise of specialized rules.[79] As regards the potential negative effects of fragmentation, *Hafner* pointed out

> This diversity of applicable regulations necessitates complex arguments about which regulation to apply, and may give rise to more conflicts than were solved by the creation of each individual legal regime.[80]

---

74 Malcom D Evans (ed), *International Law* (5th edn, OUP 2018) 659.

75 Gemma Andreone, 'The Exclusive Economic Zone' in Donald R Rothwell et al (eds), *Oxford Handbook of the Law of the Sea* (OUP 2015) 162.

76 Art. 56 (2) UNCLOS, see also Gemma Andreone, 'The Exclusive Economic Zone' in Donald R Rothwell and others (eds), The Oxford Handbook of the Law of the Sea (OUP 2015) 165; Tullio Scovazzi (ed), *Marine Specially Protected Areas. The general aspects and the Mediterranean regional system* (Kluwer Law International 1999) 3–43.

77 Campbell McLachlan, 'The Principle of Systemic Integration and Article 31(3)(c) of the Vienna Convention' (2005) 54 Int'l and Comp L Quarterly 284.

78 Margaret A Young, 'Introduction: The Productive Friction between Regimes' in Margaret A Young (ed), *Regime Interaction in International Law: Facing Fragmentation* (Cambridge University Press 2012) 4.

79 Joost Paulweyn, 'Fragmentation of International Law' in *Max Planck Encyclopaedias of Public International Law* (OUP 2006) para 1.

80 Gerhard Hafner, 'Pros and Cons Ensuing from Fragmentation of International Law' (2004) 25 Mich J Int'l L 856.

'Regime' can be understood in the sense of international law being subdivided into functionally defined issue-areas.[81] Accordingly, regimes are "a set of norms, decisions-making procedures and organisations coalescing around functional issue-areas."[82] Fragmentation, between and within regimes, bears the inherent risk of conflicting norms constraining legal certainty and predictability.[83] Fragmentation could lead to mutually exclusive obligations exposed to frictions and contradictions.[84] One of the main causes for fragmentation lies in the decentralized method of norm creation, which can lead to conflicting results if different regimes are applied to one situation.[85] Regime interaction is relevant for new negotiations on treaties and the development of new norms.[86] The overall goal should be not to create a conflict between rules in the first place but to take into account other relevant rules of international law when developing new legal concepts.

Systemic integration can serve as a guiding line to avoid conflicts when adapting a new treaty or amending an existing treaty. As stated by the International Law Commission:

> The principle of systemic integration, however, looks beyond the individual case. By making sure that the outcome is linked to the legal environment, and that adjoining rules are considered – perhaps applied, perhaps invalidated, perhaps momentarily set aside – any decision also articulates the legal-institutional environment in view of substantive preferences, distributionary choices and political objectives.[87]

---

81 Joost Paulweyn, 'Fragmentation of International Law' in *Max Planck Encyclopaedias of Public International Law* (OUP 2006), para. 2.

82 Nele Matz-Lück, 'Norm Interpretation across International Regimes: Competences and Legitimacy' in Margaret A Young (ed), *Regime Interaction in International Law: Facing Fragmentation* (Cambridge University Press 2012) 204–205.

83 ILC 'Report of the Study Group on Fragmentation of International Law', UN Doc A/CN.4/L.682 (2006), 491–492; Joost Paulwelyn, *Conflict of Norms in Public International Law* (Cambridge University Press 2003) 50.

84 Gerhard Hafner, 'Pros and Cons Ensuing from Fragmentation of International Law' (2004) 25 Mich J Int'l 851.

85 Gerhard Hafner, 'Pros and Cons Ensuing from Fragmentation of International Law' (2004) 25 Mich J Int'l 854.

86 Margaret A Young, 'Introduction: The Productive Friction between Regimes' in Margaret A Young (ed), *Regime Interaction in International Law: Facing Fragmentation* (Cambridge University Press 2012) 1.

87 ILC, 'Report of the Study Group on Fragmentation of International Law', UN Doc A/CN.4/L.682 (2006), para. 488.

The systemic nature of international law and its common governing principles do not prevent conflicts between norms from disparate legal regimes in a situation of concurrent activities.[88] The principle of 'systemic integration' addresses situations where there is an inconsistency, a conflict, or an overlap between norms, and serves as a last resort when no other interpretative means may solve the conflict.[89] When several norms bear on a single issue, they should be interpreted so as to give rise to a single set of compatible obligations.[90] This is especially true for situations where one norm assists in the interpretation of another and where the application of two norms would lead to incompatible decisions.[91] The Vienna Convention on the Law of Treaties offers in Art. 31 (3) (c) an interpretation rule for potential conflicts as "any relevant rules of international law applicable in the relations between the parties" have to be taken into account.

Several areas have already been identified as exposed to conflicts and fragmentation, namely between humanitarian law and human rights conventions, immunity and human rights obligations, international trade regulations and international environmental regulations, and the law of the sea convention and international fishery treaties.[92] This book proposes an additional area of concern namely international air law and the law of the sea.

The ICJ acknowledged in its famous *Nicaragua Case* the connection between the Chicago Convention and UNCLOS.[93] The ICJ stated that sovereignty of the coastal State extends not only to the territorial sea but also to the airspace above the territorial sea as part of State territory and confirmed with its judgment long-standing customary international law that relates the status

88 On the discussion on the interpretation of the term 'regime' see Margaret A Young, 'Introduction: The Productive Friction between Regimes' in Margaret A Young (ed), *Regime Interaction in International Law: Facing Fragmentation* (Cambridge University Press 2012) 4–12.

89 Christopher J Borgen, 'Resolving Treaty Conflicts' (2005) 37 George Washington Int'l L Rev 573, 640.

90 ILC, 'Conclusions of the Work of the Study Group on the Fragmentation of International Law: Difficulties arising from the Diversification and Expansion of International Law' Yearbook of the International Law Commission, Vol II (2006) UN Doc A/61/10, para. 251 (4).

91 ILC, 'Fragmentation of International Law: Difficulties arising from the Diversification and Expansion of International Law. Conclusion (2)' Yearbook of the International Law Commission, Vol II (2006) UN Doc A/CN.4/L.702, 7–8.

92 Gerhard Hafner, 'Pros and Cons Ensuing from Fragmentation of International Law' (2004) 25 Mich J Int'l 851–853.

93 *Nicaragua Case* (1986) para. 212.

of airspace with the status of the sea.[94] Not only customary international law highlights the connection between airspace and the sea, but the link between these two areas is also recognized in the framework of the Chicago Convention. As mentioned in chapter 5, the Chicago Convention does not define the term 'national airspace' in which States enjoy sovereignty, but relies for its determination on the territory, namely "land areas and territorial waters adjacent."[95] The legal status of airspace is thus subject to the legal status of the subjacent territory including territorial waters, which is regulated and defined in UNCLOS.[96] Therefore, the Chicago Convention is heavily dependent on the rules of UNCLOS as regards the definition of airspace. Another reference to the close relationship between airspace and the sea can be found in Art. 12 Chicago Convention, which regulates the rules of the air above the high seas. Once again, the Chicago Convention does not contain a definition for the term 'high seas' leaving it open to be specified by the provisions of the law of the sea.

But not only international air law relates for its definition to the law of the sea. UNCLOS includes so called "rules of reference" which creates an interplay between the law of the sea and other international agreements relating to maritime aspects.[97] These provisions require States parties to observe provisions of other treaties or standards adopted by international organizations, which includes standards created by IMO,[98] but also ICAO's SARPs on the rules of the air above the high seas. UNCLOS includes in several provisions a direct reference to the Chicago Convention and airspace in general. Art. 39 UNCLOS deals with the rights and duties of aircraft during transit passage, and explicitly refers to the rules of the air established by ICAO to be followed by transiting aircraft. Art. 47 UNCLOS encompasses rules of the legal status of the air space over archipelagic waters, whereas Art. 54 UNCLOS further concretizes the duties of aircraft for certain activities above archipelagic waters. Moreover, Art. 78 UNCLOS regulates the legal status of the air space above the continental shelf. Likewise, there are several provisions dealing with aircraft activities above the high seas.[99]

---

94 Ibid.

95 Art. 2 Chicago Convention.

96 Art. 2 UNCLOS regulates the legal status of the territorial sea, of the air space over the territorial sea and of its bed and subsoil and stipulates in paragraph 2 that: "This sovereignty extends to the air space over the territorial sea as well as to its bed and subsoil."

97 Gerhard Hafner & Helmut Tuerk, 'The United Nations Convention on the Law of the Sea, 1982: Reflections after 40 Years' (2022) 36 Ocean Yearbook 6.

98 Helmut Tuerk, 'Some Developments and Issues after the Adoption of UNCLOS' (2021) 9 Korean J Int'l L 3.

99 Art. 87, 102–107 UNCLOS.

Under this premise, the law of the sea constitutes one functionally defined regime, and international air law constitutes another regime, while both regimes interact. Due to the interaction between these two areas of law, external developments of the law of the sea might have had an impact on international air law. A potential conflict or at least an inconsistency may arise with regard to the classification of airspace, namely international airspace above the high seas and national airspace above the territorial waters, following the establishment of the EEZ and its influence on the airspace above it. Moreover, ADIZs have developed prior to the concept of the EEZ. An emphasis on the convergence of principles and norms accommodates legal developments at different stages. A flexible understanding of the different stages of legal development suits emerging practices and attempts to understand the dimensions of fragmentation.[100] In the past, the concern was also expressed that ADIZs might create a conflict with the freedoms of the high seas.[101] The interpretation mechanism of ADIZs requires a flexible approach due to the convergence between regulating air traffic with the freedom of overflight. Particularly in the case of ADIZs, where no definite solution was yet achieved by the international community, the method of systemic interaction can effectively contribute to the discussion.

2 ADIZs and the Freedom of the High Seas

The legal regime of UNCLOS is of paramount importance for the free conduct of air navigation as it encompasses the core rule on the freedom of overflight. In contrast, the Chicago Convention does not expressly contain a related right providing for the freedom of overflight. Some authors have expressed concerns about extended jurisdiction restricting the movement of aircraft in international airspace and its effect on the freedom of overflight.[102] Yet this book argues that ADIZs and related jurisdictional rights do not necessarily create a normative conflict and do not hamper the freedom of overflight under certain requirements. For this reason, it is necessary to scrutinise the impact of ADIZs on the freedom of overflight.

100 Tomer Broude & Yuval Shany (eds), *Multi-Sourced Equivalent Norms in International Law* (OUP 2011) 45.

101 ICAO Doc SAIOACG/9 – WP29 para. 2.16.

102 Elisabeth Cuadra, 'Air Defense Identification Zones: Creeping Jurisdiction in the Airspace' (1977) 18 Virginia J Int'l L 491; Kay Hailbronner, 'Freedom of the Air and the Convention on the Law of the Sea' (1983) 77 AJIL 493; Alex Calvo, 'China's Air Defense Identification Zone: Concept, Issues at Stake and Regional Impact' (2013) Naval War College Press 15.

2.1 *Introduction to the General Theory of the Freedom of the High Seas*

Hugo Grotius described the concept of the freedom of the high seas in his famous treatise *Mare Liberum* in 1609.[103] The freedom of the high seas is understood as verbalism of free navigation across the oceans but also as the prohibition to appropriate any parts of the oceans by States.[104] The principle of freedom of the high seas is without any doubt a rule of customary international law that has found its way into codification, namely in Art. 87 UNCLOS and in Art. 58 UNCLOS for its application within the EEZ.[105]

The term "freedom of the high seas" is not defined in the treaty text of UNCLOS and hinges upon the definition of "high seas".[106] The geographical notion of "high seas" is negatively defined namely as covering all areas of the oceans which are not subject to a national legal order.[107] The principle of freedom of the high seas, in general, means that the high seas may not be subject to the sovereignty of a State.[108] *Grotius* also expressed a similar formula: "whatever therefore cannot be seized or enclosed is incapable of being made subject of property."[109] While the size and vastness of the oceans renders it impossible to control and possess them, *Grotius* admitted that coastal States might exercise jurisdiction over them.[110] Fundamental to the freedom of the high seas is the fact that no State was in the past able to effectively exercise claims of sovereignty over the sea. This was also discussed in the *Lotus Case* where the Permanent Court of International Justice held that the principle of the freedom of the seas is nothing more than the absence of any territorial

---

103 Edward Gordon, 'Grotius and the Freedom of the Seas in the Seventeenth Century' (2008) 16 Willamette J Int'l L & Disp Res 252; Antony Anghie, 'Asia in the History and Theory of International Law' in Simon Chesterman et al (eds), *The Oxford Handbook of International Law in Asia and the Pacific* (OUP 2019) 74ff.

104 Albert J Hoffmann, 'Freedom of Navigation' in *Max Planck Encyclopaedias of Public International Law* (OUP 2011) para. 2.

105 Malcom D Evans (ed), *International Law* (5th edn, OUP 2018) 649.

106 John E Noyes, 'Interpreting the 1982 Law of the Sea Convention and Defining it Terms' in Georg E Walker (ed), *Definitions for the Law of the Sea* (Martinus Nijhoff 2012) at 48 explaining that some words and phrases in UNCLOS were intentionally left ambiguous as no agreement could be reached during the negotiation process and that delegates "doubtless thought that some of the (…) differences would be resolved later, through subsequent international agreements, state practice or judicial decisions."

107 Gerhard Hafner & Helmut Tuerk, 'The United Nations Convention on the Law of the Sea, 1982: Reflections after 40 Years' (2022) 36 Ocean Yearbook 7.

108 Art. 89 UNCLOS reads: "No State may validly purport to subject any part of the high seas to its sovereignty."

109 Hugo Grotius, *The Freedom of the High Seas: Or, the Rights which Belong to the Dutch to Take Part in the East Indian Trade* (translated by R van Deman Magoffin, OUP 1916).

110 Jan Klabbers, International Law (3rd edn, 2021 Cambridge University Press) 257.

sovereignty upon the high seas.[111] Technological advances undermined the general understanding that the sea cannot be taken into physical possession, and socio-economic reasons are an additional cornerstone of the freedom of the high seas.[112] The term "freedom" can therefore be understood as "economic liberalism", namely the free economic exploitation of the oceans by States.[113] The two components, the absence of sovereignty claims and equal rights of all States on the high seas, constitute the ideological fundament of the different categories of freedoms.

Even though certain activities are recognized as freedom of the high seas in the treaty text of UNCLOS, this list of freedoms is not exhaustive and a *numerus clausus* of freedoms does not exist.[114] The six components of freedoms as enumerated in Art. 87 UNCLOS are: navigation, overflight, laying submarine cables and pipelines, constructing artificial islands and other installations permitted under international law, fishing, and scientific research.[115] Related rights can also be subsumed under the traditional freedoms, for example the conduct of military activities,[116] or protests at sea as part of the freedom of navigation.[117] Even though not limited to the enumerated activities, the freedom of the high seas per se is subject to certain limitations found in several other provisions of UNCLOS and other treaties. Art. 58 UNCLOS already limits the freedom of the high seas in the EEZ to three aspects, namely navigation, overflight, and laying cables and pipelines. Freedoms within the EEZ are therefore more narrowly constructed than the freedoms granted on the high seas. Additionally, the freedoms of the high seas within the EEZ are insofar limited where they are not incompatible with the regime of that zone.[118] The list of freedoms applicable in the EEZ is therefore exhaustive.[119] Without any doubt, sovereignty claims on

111 *Lotus Case* 25.

112 Djamchid Momatz, 'Chapter 7', in René-Jean Dupuy & Daniel Vignes (eds), *A Handbook on the Law of the Sea, Volume 1* (1991 Martinus Nijhoff) 389.

113 Gerhard Hafner & Helmut Tuerk, 'The United Nations Convention on the Law of the Sea, 1982: Reflections after 40 Years' (2022) 36 Ocean Yearbook 9.

114 Malcom N Shaw, *International Law* (9th edn, Cambridge University Press 2021) 453.

115 *M/V "SAIGA" (No. 2) (Saint Vincent and the Grenadines v. Guinea)* (Merits) [1999] ITLOS Reports 1999, Sep. Op. Judge Laing, 165, para. 19.

116 Albert J Hoffmann, 'Freedom of Navigation' in *Max Planck Encyclopaedias of Public International Law* (OUP 2011) para. 5, which is, yet, an issue of discussion.

117 *'Arctic Sunrise' (Netherlands v. Russia)* (Merits) [2017] PCA Case No. 2014–02, para. 227.

118 *Alleged Violations of Sovereign Rights and Maritime Spaces in the Caribbean Sea (Nicaragua v. Colombia)* (Merits) [2022] ICJ Rep 2022, paras. 62, 94, 100.

119 Tullio Treves, 'Chapter 17' Rene Jean Dupuy & Daniel Vignes (eds), *A Handbook on the New Law of the Sea, Volume 2* (1991) 845.

parts of the high seas and parts of the EEZ, including the airspace above them, are invalid.[120]

2.2 *The "Freedom of Overflight"*

Neither the Paris Convention, the Madrid Convention, the Havana Convention, nor the Chicago Convention mention the right to freedom of overflight over the high seas. Despite the fact that UNCLOS provides for the freedom of overflight, it does not define the phrase and does not explicitly include in any other provisions jurisdictional rights of the coastal State related to the freedom of overflight.[121] Consequently, the phrase "freedom of overflight" can be considered to be an approximate indication of its definition. It could even be argued that "airspace above the high seas" and "high seas" can be interpreted differently.[122]

2.2.1 Historical Overview on the Freedom of Overflight

The drafting history of UNCLOS reveals that its predecessor, the Geneva Convention on the High Seas, was based on the report of the International Law Commission on maritime law.[123] The Yearbook of the International Law Commission from 1955 was the first attempt to provide a concretization of the freedom of the high seas for a codification of the law of the sea. The concept of the freedom of overflight initially emerged under the designation "freedom to fly through the superjacent air-space", which refers to airspace situated above the high seas.[124] However, the International Law Commission refrained from any further specification of this freedom:

> Freedom to fly over the high seas is mentioned in this article because the Commission considers that it follows directly from the principle of the freedom of the sea. The Commission has refrained from formulating

---

120 Douglas Guilfoyle, 'The High Seas' in Donald R Rothwell et al (eds), *Oxford Handbook of the Law of the Sea* (OUP 2015) 208.

121 George K Walker, *Definitions for the Law of the Sea – The Terms not Defined by the 1982 Convention* (Martinus Nijhoff 2012) 160, 161, however also not offering a definition on "freedom of overflight".

122 Gerhard Hafner & Helmut Tuerk, 'The United Nations Convention on the Law of the Sea, 1982: Reflections after 40 Years' (2022) 36 Ocean Yearbook at 8 stating it is an unresolved issue whether airspace above the high seas is included in the high seas.

123 Gordon W Paulsen, 'An Historical Overview of the Development of Uniformity on International Maritime Law' (1983) 57 Tul L Rev 1067.

124 Report of the ILC, Yearbook of the International Law Commission, Vol. II (1955) A/CN.4/SER.A/1955/ADD.L 21.

> rules on air navigation (…) since the task it set itself for this phase of its work is confined to the codification of maritime law proper.[125]

In the 1956 Yearbook of the International Law Commission, the issue of overflight was once again raised but discussion on this topic was indefinitely postponed to a later date. Israel expressed the concern that the current set of rules does not deal with the right to fly over the high seas. In response, the International Law Commission stated that it had "decided, however, not to go into the details of aerial law. This will have to be dealt with later."[126] And further elaborated:

> Probably a distinction has to be made between the rules of air navigation which are to a great extent regulated by the Convention on Civil Aviation (…) and the general international law governing the right to air navigation over the high seas. Clearly, the first aspect is better dealt with by the International Civil Aviation Organization, but that does not preclude the Commission from laying down what are the general rules of international law concerning such rights of navigation, since it is of opinion that, in so far as concerns the high seas, freedom to fly over the high seas follows directly from the principle of the freedom of the sea. The omission of any further mention of this aspect may have an additional consequence in that it might open the way to the argument that this right is different in kind from other rights and freedoms. But such an interpretation would be completely false and it should be made clear that the right to aerial navigation exists wherever there is freedom of navigation on the sea without any exception.[127]

The International Law Commission stated in its commentaries on the articles concerning the law of the sea from 1956 that:

> [it] has, however, refrained from formulating rules on air navigation, since the task it set itself in the present phase of its work is confined to the codification and development of the law of the sea.[128]

---

125 Ibid 22.

126 Ibid 13.

127 Report of the ILC, Yearbook of the International Law Commission, Vol. II (1956) A/CN.4/SER.A/1956/ADD.L 56.

128 Ibid 278.

The rules of air navigation were indeed regulated by ICAO through extensive Annexes, which also partly apply to navigation above the high seas. However, ICAO had not provided further elaboration on the right of overflight in general. The Annexes represent a restriction on the absolute freedom of overflight by regulating aircraft movements and prescribing certain air routes.[129]

In 1958, the Secretary-General invited several independent experts to submit studies on a specific subject for the first conference on the law of the sea. The right to overflight was more extensively discussed in Pepin's 'The Law of the Air and Draft Articles Concerning the Law of the Sea adopted by the ILC in its 8th Session' at the request of the Secretariat of the United Nations.[130] The preparatory document on the Draft Articles by *Pepin* depicted the freedom to fly over the high seas as an absolute freedom, not limited or restricted in any way.[131] The ICAO's rule-making power relating to the flight and manoeuvre of aircraft over the high seas was described as one exemption to that general rule.[132] The document also identified the establishment of off-shore identification zones extending into the high seas, i.e. ADIZ, as a problematic issue concerning the freedom to fly over the high seas.[133]

ICAO submitted a preparatory document to the ILC enunciating the principle of freedom to fly over the high seas and pointed out that "(t)he existence of such freedom would not be denied if its exercise were subject to international regulations concerning the safety of air navigation."[134] Moreover, ICAO specified that the Annexes constitute rules relating to the flight and manoeuvre of aircraft within the meaning of Art. 12 of the Chicago Convention and that, therefore, those rules apply without exception over the high seas. However, ICAO refrained from any further comment on the notion of the freedom to fly over the high seas. In light of the extensive scope of the work, the first law of the sea conference established five main committees, and the second was conferred with the general regime of the high seas.[135] The report of the Second

---

129 See for example Annex 2, Chicago Convention.

130 United Nations Conference on the Law of the Sea, UN Doc A/CONF.13/4, 'The Law of the Air and the Draft Articles Concerning the Law of the Sea Adopted by the International Law Commission at its Eight Session' by Pepin (4 October 1957).

131 Ibid 68.

132 Ibid 68.

133 Ibid at 70, stating that "(...) it is doubtful, however, whether they (reading: ADIZ) are compatible with the articles of this draft."

134 United Nations Conference on the Law of the Sea, UN Doc A/CONF.31, 'Comments by the International Civil Aviation Organization on the Draft Articles Concerning the Law of the Sea Adopted by the International Law Commission at Its Eighth Session' 337.

135 First Committee (territorial sea and contiguous zone); Second Committee (high seas: general regime); Third Committee (high seas: fishing and conservation of living resources);

Committee on a general regime regarding the high seas showed that the vast majority of States emphasized the importance of the freedom of the high seas, but none made any specific comment on the right to fly over the high seas.[136] Some States expressed the view that the freedom of the high seas is not unlimited.[137] As a result of the first UN conference on the law of the sea, the draft articles on the regime of the high seas were adopted in the 1958 Geneva Convention on the High Seas.[138] This Convention initially, articulated the high seas freedom in a binding treaty, including the "freedom to fly over the high seas."[139] This phrase was subsequently superseded in the 1982 UN Convention on the Law of the Sea, where it was replaced with "freedom of overflight" in Art. 87.[140] The impetus for the negotiations during the conference on UNCLOS was twofold. First, there was concern among traditional maritime powers that navigational rights and freedoms might be restricted through excessive coastal State claims over the oceans.[141] Second, there was a desire to guarantee access to living and non-living natural resources waters beyond the territorial sea ought to be guaranteed to all countries. The general idea was that limitations or restrictions on the freedom of the high seas would be in conflict with the basic purpose of Art. 87 UNCLOS, namely of safeguarding the exercise of its provisions in the interest of the entire international community.[142]

Fourth Committee (continental shelf); and Fifth Committee (question of free access to the sea of land-locked countries).

136 United Nations Conference on the Law of the Sea, A/CONF.13/40, 'Volume IV: Second Committee (High Seas: General Regime) Geneva 24 February – 27 April 1958, 37–39. See also, 'Comments by Governments on the Provisional Articles Concerning the Regime of the High Seas and the Draft Articles on the Regime of the Territorial Sea adopted by the International Law Commission at its Seventh Session', UN Doc. A/CN.4/99 and Add. 1–9, 37ff.

137 United Nations Conference on the Law of the Sea, A/CONF.13/40, at.40 the statement of the Peruvian delegation.

138 The United Nations Conference on the Law of the Sea met at Geneva from 24 February to 27 April 1958, resulting in the adoption of four separate conventions: the Convention on the Territorial Sea and the Contiguous Zone 516 UNTS 205, Convention on the High Seas 459 UNTS 11; Convention on Fishing and Conservation of the Living Resources of the High Seas (1958) 559 UNTS 285, and Convention on the Continental Shelf (1958) 499 UNTS 311. All these conventions have been superseded by the 1982 United Nations Convention on the Law of the Sea.

139 Art. 2 Convention on the High Seas (1968) 459 UNTS 11.

140 In accordance with Art. 331 (1) UNCLOS the 1982 Convention shall prevail over the 1958 Geneva Conventions between State Parties.

141 James Kraska & Raul Pedrozo, *International Maritime Security Law* (Brill Nijhoff 2013) 196.

142 ILC, 'Commentary to the ILC Articles concerning the Law of the Sea' (1956)Yearbook of the International Law Commission, Vol II, UNGOAR UN Doc A/3159, 253.

The debate then shifted to another aspect of overflight, namely to the international liability for injurious consequences arising out of acts not prohibited by international law.[143] The general obligation under the Chicago Convention to allow overflight, transit through a strait or passage over its territory was discussed as a circumstance precluding wrongfulness.[144] However, no connection was made to the right of overflight in the sense of Art. 87 UNCLOS. The freedom of overflight above the high seas was removed from the agenda and was not included in any further elaboration of the ILC.[145] The freedom of overflight resumed being omitted from any further concretisation by any *travaux préparatoires* of UNCLOS.

As a concluding remark, the competence of ICAO to establish rules applicable to aircraft above the high seas relates to air traffic management and aviation safety rules. Likewise, the International Maritime Organisation (IMO) may create standards for the safety of traffic on the high seas. Both organisations regulate technical standards on the safety of navigation, communications methods, and the construction of vessels or aircraft, thereby restricting the freedoms of the high seas to some extent.[146]

2.2.2 The Definition of the Freedom of Overflight

Despite the absence of a definition in UN materials, the term "overflight" can be understood as a flight commenced by an aircraft outside the airspace of its State of nationality.[147] Overflight therefore occurs either when the aircraft flies through the national airspace of another State or international airspace. This interpretation is also in line with the Chicago Convention which conferred on all States parties the right of "flights over the territory of contracting States".[148] The term "freedom of overflight", in the sense of Art. 87 in connection with

143 ILC, 'Fifth Report on International Liability for Injurious Consequences arising out of Acts not prohibited by International Law, by Mr. Robert Quentin Baxter, Special Rapporteur', Yearbook of the International Law Commission, Vol II (12 and 19 June 1984) UN Doc A/CN.4/383, 155FF.

144 ILC, 'Second Report on State Responsibility by Mr. James Crawford, Special Rapporteur' UN Yearbook of the International Law Commission, Vol II (30 April 1999), UN Doc. A/CN.4/498/ADD.2, 14, 36, 52.

145 The ILC lists on its websites the topics completed, including under point 8.1. 'Law of the Sea- Régime of the high seas', whereas the last work was submitted in 1958 at its 8th session. At https://legal.un.org/ilc/guide/8_1.shtml (accessed 31 May 2021).

146 Robert Jennings & Arthur Watts (eds), *Oppenheim's International Law, Volume 1* (9th edn, Longman, 1996) 743.

147 Jan Wouters & Bruno Demeyere, 'Overflight' in *Max Planck Encyclopaedias of Public International Law* (OUP 2008), para. 1.

148 Art. 5 Chicago Convention.

Art. 58 UNCLOS, encompasses any flight of an aircraft above maritime areas outside the territorial sea, i.e. above the EEZ and the high seas. The "freedom of overflight" does not extend to the right to fly over the territory of other States, as the wording of the treaty text clearly limits the application to the EEZ and the high seas. The freedom of overflight is of significant importance in the event that an aircraft does not obtain consent to fly through national airspace or is not registered in a State that is a party to the Chicago Convention.[149] In such cases, only international airspace remains for the aircraft to fly across.

Moreover, significant economic and strategic interests are connected with the right of overflight. The idea of "economic liberalism" is equally true for the freedom of overflight. From a defensive-strategic point, military aircraft necessarily need free access to the airspace above the high seas to reach military installations outside the sovereign territory. The general prohibition of overflight in national airspace as part of State sovereignty faces the general right of overflight in international airspace. The freedom of overflight in Art. 87 UNCLOS applies to all categories of aircraft, including civils as well as state aircraft, in contrast to the regime of the Chicago Convention, which only applies to civil aircraft. Despite the general rule of freedom of overflight, the airspace is regulated and no unlimited right of overflight exists. The gradual extension of the coastal States' jurisdiction by State practice, customary international law but also new codifications influence the freedoms of the high seas.[150] Particularly, *Hafner* and *Tuerk* elaborated on the "waning freedom of the high seas" and the tendency of "freedoms" evolving into a "right of usage" that needs to invoked by States.[151]

2.3 *Limitations of the Freedom of the High Seas*

At the centre of regulating activities on the high seas is the concept of flag State jurisdiction.[152] As a primary rule, all vessels must be registered according to the laws of the State whose flag they fly. The principle of the exclusivity of the flag State purports to attribute a ship to the legal system of the State under

149 Art. 6 Chicago Convention.

150 Albert J Hoffmann, 'Freedom of Navigation' in *Max Planck Encyclopedias of Public International Law* (OUP 2011) para. 4.

151 Gerhard Hafner & Helmut Tuerk, 'The United Nations Convention on the Law of the Sea, 1982: Reflections after 40 Years' (2022) 36 Ocean Yearbook 11 stating that "the former understanding of the freedom of the high seas only required proof of the absence of any restriction" while "the present tendency is moving towards the need to invoke a certain right of usage attributed to a certain State."

152 Malcom D Evans (ed), *International Law* (5th edn, OUP 2018) 649; Art. 94 UNCLOS.

whose sails it flags.[153] Some exceptions exist to the general rule of exclusive jurisdiction, which allows other States to interfere with the free use of the high seas of other States' ships. For instance, in the event that a vessel is stateless or flies more than one flag so that the true State of registry is obscured, any State may exercise jurisdiction over it.[154] Moreover, there is an increasing number of international conventions regulating jurisdiction over foreign ships with respect to specific matters, such as pollution control and resource management. It is important to note that although the freedom of overflight is placed within the framework of UNCLOS, the majority of provisions relate to ships and the concept of the exclusivity of the flag State for jurisdiction.[155] However, aircraft do not have a "flag State" per se, but they bear the mark of nationality of the State of registry.[156] No provision of UNCLOS refers to the nationality mark of aircraft for the purpose of attributing jurisdiction over aircraft.[157] Furthermore, the term "ship" cannot be applied to aircraft, as "ship"/"vessel" means "any object or device found in the seas and connected to a State by a link such that the State claims to exclude interference by other States."[158] Nevertheless, in the absence of clarity on even the basic nature of the freedom of overflight in UNCLOS' text, much less the issues of coastal States' jurisdiction related to air traffic above their EEZ, it is necessary to discuss the broader background of the limitations of the freedom of the high seas and in particular the freedom of navigation as a supplementary means of interpretation.

2.3.1 Particular Examples of Limitations of the Freedom of the High Seas Relevant for the Discussion on ADIZ

Even though States have equal rights on the high seas, they may exercise forms of authority on the high seas over foreign ships.[159] In general, limitations to

153 Djamchid Momatz, 'Chapter 7', in René-Jean Dupuy & Daniel Vignes (eds), *A Handbook on the Law of the Sea, Volume 1* (Martinus Nijhoff 1991) 407.

154 *Naim Molvan v. Attorney General for Palestine (The "Asya")*, [1948] 81 Ll L Rep 277, United Kingdom: Privy Council (Judicial Committee) 351.

155 Tullio Treves, 'Chapter 17' in Rene Jean Dupuy & Daniel Vignes (eds), *A Handbook on the New Law of the Sea, Volume 2* (Martinus Nijhoff 1991) 836.

156 Art. 17 Chicago Convention.

157 Art. 17 Chicago Convention stipulates: "Aircraft have the nationality of the State in which they are registered." And Art. 20 Chicago Convention provides for the display of marks: "Every aircraft engaged in international air navigation shall bear its appropriate nationality and registration mark."

158 Tullio Treves, 'Chapter 17' in Rene Jean Dupuy & Daniel Vignes (eds), *A Handbook on the New Law of the Sea, Volume 2* (Martinus Nijhoff 1991) 842.

159 Djamchid Momatz, 'Chapter 7', in René-Jean Dupuy & Daniel Vignes (eds), *A Handbook on the Law of the Sea, Volume 1* (Martinus Nijhoff 1991) 395; Robert Jennings & Arthur Watts (eds), *Oppenheim's International Law, vol. 1* (9th edn, Longman 1996) 727.

the freedom of the high seas derive from two different kinds of categories. The first category emanates from the co-existence of other freedoms exercised by other States as well as the exercise of rights of the coastal State.[160] The second category concerns fundamental interests, either the interest of the international community or the interest of an individual State, which justify an exception to the freedom of the high seas.[161] In their enjoyment of the right of freedom of navigation and overflight, States have the obligation to comply with the laws and regulations adopted by the coastal State in accordance with UNCLOS and other rules of international law. The following paragraphs discuss certain examples of limitations found in different sources.[162]

2.3.1.1 *Safety Zone around Artificial Islands and Other Installations*

Safety zones provide a good point of comparison with ADIZs, as they share the common characteristic of regulating the safety or security within a zone beyond national territory. Art. 60 UNCLOS encompasses the exclusive right of the coastal State to construct, operate, and use artificial islands, installations, and structures within their EEZ and to create safety zones around them. Pursuant to Art. 60 (2) UNCLOS, the coastal State has exclusive jurisdiction over artificial islands, installations, and structures in terms of Article 60 (1).[163] Jurisdiction in the sense of Art. 60 (2), however, does not address the issue of construction and authorization of the objects concerned, but solely refers to the prescription and enforcement of rules and regulations applicable on and to them.[164] The list of jurisdiction, namely with regard to customs, fiscal, health, safety, and immigration, is not exhaustive, but the coastal State may prescribe and enforce also other aspects, such as environmental standards.[165]

---

160 Tullio Treves, 'Chapter 17' in in Rene Jean Dupuy & Daniel Vignes (eds), *A Handbook on the New Law of the Sea, Volume 2* (Martinus Nijhoff 1991) 847.

161 Ibid 847.

162 Not part of the discussion will be considerations of environmental protection pursuant to Part XII UNCLOS, enforcement of laws relating to living resources in the EEZ pursuant to Art. 73 UNCLOS, the interference of exploitation installations with minor routes of international navigation pursuant to Art. 60 (7) UNCLOS, and exceptional measures for interception such as regulation of illicit traffic in narcotic drugs, see for a list of relevant treaties Yoshifumi Tanaka, *The International Law of the Sea* (3rd edn, Cambridge University Press 2019) 207.

163 Art. 60 (2) UNCLOS.

164 *'Arctic Sunrise' (Netherlands v. Russia)* (Provisional Measures) [2013] PCA, 2014–02, Dis. Op. Golitsyn, para. 23.

165 Alexander Proelß, 'Article 60 – Artificial Islands, Installations and Structures in the Exclusive Economic Zone' in Alexander Proelß (ed), *United Nations Convention on the Law of the Sea: A Commentary* (Nomos 2017) 473.

Firstly, the freedom of the high seas is constrained by the physical reality of the artificial island, which blocks certain parts of the sea due to their existence. As a result, no ship can use that part of the sea for navigation. Yet, the coastal State has to pay due regard when creating artificial islands, installations and structures, including safety zones around them, so that they do not cause interference with the use of recognized sea lanes essential for international navigation.[166] Secondly, UNCLOS provides for several counter-balancing rights of the coastal State to establish a maritime zone for the safety of navigation. According to Art. 60 (4) UNCLOS the coastal State may "where necessary, establish reasonable safety zones around such artificial islands, installations and structures in which it may take appropriate measures to ensure the safety both of navigation and of the artificial islands, installations, and structures." All ships have to respect these safety zones pursuant to Art. 60 (5) UNCLOS. The inclusion of the wording "where necessary" indicates that safety zone needs to serve the purpose of ensuring the safety of navigation and the objects concerned.[167]

In accordance with Art. 60 (1) UNCLOS, coastal States possess a considerable degree of discretion regarding the necessity of the zones.[168] Safety zones represent a restriction to the freedom of the high seas, yet they may be established unilaterally by the coastal State, as they do not need prior authorisation from the International Maritime Organization (IMO).[169] Nevertheless, the coastal States may only extend the safety zone up to 500m around the artificial island, if generally accepted international standards established by IMO provide for an extension or if explicitly recommended by IMO.[170] There is a lack of clarity regarding whether other ships and vessel flying the flag of another State only have to respect the generally accepted international standards regarding navigation or whether the coastal State can also demand compliance with domestic laws within the safety zone.[171] A similar issue arises in the context of

166 Art. 60(7) UNCLOS; Albert J. Hoffmann, 'Freedom of Navigation' in *Max Planck Encyclopaedias of Public International Law* (OUP 2011) para. 15.

167 Alexander Proelß, 'Article 60 – Artificial Islands, Installations and Structures in the Exclusive Economic Zone' in Alexander Proelß (ed), *United Nations Convention on the Law of the Sea: A Commentary* (Nomos 2017) 476.

168 Ibid 476.

169 James Kraska & Raul Pedrozo, International *Maritime Security Law* (Brill Nijhoff 2013) 75, 76.

170 Art. 60 (5) UNCLOS; International Maritime Organisation, 'General Provisions on Ships Routeing', Res A.572/14 (20 January 1985).

171 In favour of the coastal States authority to enact domestic laws within the safety zone: Rainer Lagoni, 'Die Errichtung von Schutzgebieten in der ausschließlichen Wirtschaftszone aus völkerrechtlicher Sicht' (2002) 24 Natur und Recht 124; Contra: Alexander Proelß, 'Article 60 – Artificial Islands, Installations and Structures in the Exclusive

discussions surrounding ADIZs, where States attempt to apply their respective national laws to aircraft of other States.

2.3.1.2 *The Arctic Sunrise Case*

The *Arctic Sunrise Case,* which was decided by ITLOS on 22 November 2013, concerned the enforcement actions of Russian authorities on a ship flying the flag of the Netherlands in the Russian safety zone around the oil platform "Prirazlomnaya" in the EEZ of Russia. The Russian safety zone prohibited any access to that zone without prior permission of the operator of the platform. As the ship did not stop when requested by Russian authorities, it was arrested, brought to a Russian port and 30 crew members were detained.[172] The *Arctic Sunrise Case* is the first case in which the Tribunal was requested to issue the release of a vessel and its crew from detention for alleged violations of a coastal State's maritime regulations applicable to its EEZ.[173] Despite the fact that the Tribunal voted in favour of the order to release the *Arctic Sunrise* and its crew, it did not discuss the distinction between the limited enforcement jurisdiction of a coastal State in its EEZ and the exclusive jurisdiction of the coastal State in the safety zones around its artificial islands pursuant to Art. 60 (2) UNCLOS.[174] However, three judges appended separate/dissenting opinions to the Order taking into account Art. 60 UNCLOS.

Judge *Wolfrum* and Judge *Kelly* expressed their opinion on a broad understanding of the coastal State's authority within the safety zone and stated that:

> [t]he situation is different in respect of artificial islands and installations where the coastal State according to article 60, paragraph 2, of the Convention enjoys exclusive jurisdiction and in the safety zones around such

---

Economic Zone' in Alexander Proelß (ed), *United Nations Convention on the Law of the Sea: A Commentary* (Nomos 2017) 474.

172 An illustration of the events leading to the detention of the "Arctic Sunrise" and its crew, and for the diplomatic actions undertaken after the detention of the ship, can be found in the annexes to the Request of the Netherlands for the prescription of provisional measures. Especially the Statement of Claim from 4 October 2013, included in the diplomatic note of the Ministry of Foreign Affairs of the Kingdom of the Netherlands to the Embassy of the Russian Federation in the Hague, illustrates the institution of the proceedings before the arbitral tribunal (Annex 1); and the Statement of Facts, from 19 October 2013, provided by Greenpeace International (Annex 2), at https://www.itlos.org/en/main/cases/list-of-cases/case-no-22/ (accessed 19 April 2021); *'Arctic Sunrise' (Netherlands v. Russia)* (Provisional Measures Order, 22 November 2013) ITLOS Reports 2013.

173 Eustathia Laina, 'The Arctic Sunrise Case – Provisional Measures Ordered ' (2015) 45–46 Envtl Pol'y & Law 268.

174 *'Arctic Sunrise' (Netherlands v. Russia)* (Provisional Measures, Order of 22 November 2013) ITLOS Reports 2013.

> artificial islands or installations. This includes legislative jurisdiction as well as the corresponding enforcement jurisdiction.[175]

And further, Judge *Golitsyn* expressed in his dissenting opinion that:

> [r]eference in article 60, paragraph 4, to the right of the coastal State to take appropriate measures means that under the Convention the coastal State has the authority to take appropriate measures to ensure compliance with its regulations governing activities within safety zones, in other words to take the necessary enforcement measures.[176]

The issue of enforcement measures and prescriptive jurisdiction within a safety zone was therefore not finally settled by ITLOS but a tendency to a broader understanding of the coastal State's powers within its safety zone can be seen. In the subsequent award on the merits by an arbitral tribunal of the Permanent Court of Arbitration in 2015, the matter of concern was whether Russia's seizure of the vessel had been unlawful.[177] Consequently, the arbitral tribunal discussed the relationship between the right of hot pursuit pursuant to Art. 111 UNCLOS and the coastal State's jurisdiction over artificial islands pursuant to Art. 60 UNCLOS.[178] The tribunal stated with regard to Art. 60 (4) UNCLOS that:

> (…) this provision allows the coastal State to take, in the safety zone, appropriate measures in the nature of the enactment of laws or regulations, and of the enforcement of such laws and regulations, provided that such measures are aimed at ensuring the safety of both navigation and the artificial islands, installations, or structures. These rights of the coastal State go beyond its rights in the EEZ at large.[179]

Therefore, within a safety zone, the coastal State may enact and enforce safety laws and regulations.[180] Safety zones are embedded in the conventional provision of UNCLOS with jurisdictional rights clearly attributed to the coastal

175 *'Arctic Sunrise' (Netherlands v. Russia)* (Provisional Measures, Order of 22 November 2013) Joint Sep. Op. Wolfrum & Kelly) ITLOS Reports 2013, para. 12.

176 *'Arctic Sunrise' (Netherlands v. Russia)* (Provisional Measures, Order of 22 November 2013) Dis. Op. Golitsyn) ITLOS Reports 2013, para. 25.

177 *'Arctic Sunrise' (Netherlands v Russia)* [2015] PCA, 2014–02.

178 Eugene Kontorovich, 'Arctic Sunrise (Netherlands v. Russia); In re Arctic Sunrise (Netherlands v. Russia)' (2016) 110 AJIL 96.

179 *'Arctic Sunrise' (Netherlands v. Russia)* [2015] PCA, 2014–02, para. 211.

180 In the present case, the Tribunal decided that no safety zone beyond the 500 metres was established due to the recommendatory nature of the Notice to Marines, at para. 212, 219.

State. Even though ADIZs are not regulated in any treaty text, safety zones offer an idea for similar conceptual constructions of zones in international airspace. The reasoning in the *Arctic Sunrise Case* addresses a very specific situation that bears a resemblance to the situation of ADIZ. While the *Arctic Sunrise Case* concerned the requirement of requesting permission before entering the safety zone, otherwise the ship would be prohibited from entering, ADIZs require a less drastic obligation, namely to identify before entering. In the event of non-compliance, aircraft are not prohibited from flying through the ADIZ, however interception procedures could be commenced. With regard to enforcement jurisdiction, a different approach will be necessary for ADIZs. In contrast to safety zones which limit jurisdiction to a radius of 500m, ADIZs cover a much larger area of up to 200sm. A more cautious solution would therefore be required.

2.3.1.3 *The Right of Visit*

The freedom of navigation is subject to the right of visit exercised by a warship or a military aircraft in order to intercept a foreign ship pursuant to Art. 110 UNCLOS. The wording of Art. 110 UNCLOS is as follows:

> Except where acts of interference derive from powers conferred by treaty, a warship which encounters on the high seas a foreign ship, (…) is not justified in boarding it unless there is reasonable ground for suspecting that:
> (a) the ship is engaged in piracy;
> (b) the ship is engaged in the slave trade;
> (c) the ship is engaged in unauthorized broadcasting and the flag State of the warship has jurisdiction under article 109;
> (d) the ship is without nationality; or
> (e) though flying a foreign flag or refusing to show its flag, the ship is, in reality, of the same nationality as the warship.[181]

The right of visit marks an exception to the general rule that a ship on the high seas is only subject to the exclusive jurisdiction of its flag State. The underlying ratione for the right of visit can be traced back to the maintenance of a minimum standard of public order on the high seas. This necessarily entails that States also have some general policy-making powers.[182] The right of visit is comprised of two distinct rights: boarding the ship and inspecting papers. The right of visit clearly limits the freedom of navigation and may therefore only be exercised with regard to the subject matters covered by Art. 110

181 Art. 110 UNCLOS.

182 Douglas Guilfoyle, 'Article 110 – Right of Visit', in Alexander Proelß (ed), *United Nations Convention on the Law of the Sea: A Commentary* (Nomos 2017).

(1) (a)-(e).[183] This restriction is explained by the general importance of the freedom of navigation, as only certain reasons were regarded as justifying a limitation of the freedom of navigation.[184]

Art. 110 UNCLOS clearly offers no legal basis for a right to identify aircraft. However, in comparison with the powers of States enjoyed in an ADIZ, the right of visit is considerably more restrictive on the freedom of navigation. ADIZS encompass the duty of aircraft to identify, but do not include the right of States to force the aircraft to land outside national airspace. This would be analogous to the effect of "boarding," which also forces the ship to stop. For comparison, the US naval forces employs specific visit, board, search, and seizure (VBSS) teams to intercept vessels.[185] However, no analogous interception method can be applied to an ADIZ. The duty to identify in an ADIZ represents a minimal intrusion on the aircraft's right to overflight.

2.3.1.4 *The Right of Hot Pursuit*

The right of hot pursuit pursuant to Art. 111 UNCLOS limits the freedom of the high seas to some extent. The right of hot pursuit can be defined as the right of a coastal State to pursue outside of territorial waters, and take enforcement action against, a foreign ship that has violated the laws and regulations of that State.[186] The right of hot pursuit "balances the coastal State's interest in the efficient enforcement of its laws with the general interest in high seas freedom of navigation".[187] The scope and content of the right of hot pursuit exemplifies a restriction of free navigation by the coastal States' enforcement actions of domestic law in areas beyond its sovereignty.[188] As the right of hot pursuit amounts to a restriction of the exclusive jurisdiction of flag States on the high seas, several conditions have to be met. Accordingly, hot pursuit of a foreign ship may only be undertaken when the competent authorities of the coastal State have good reason to believe that the ship has violated the laws

---

183 Craig H Allen, 'The Peacetime Right of Approach and Visit and Effective Security Council Sanctions Enforcement at Sea' (2019) 95 International Law Studies 410.

184 Myron H Nordquist, Satya N Nandan & Shabtai Rosenne (eds), *United Nations Convention on the Law of the Sea 1982: A Commentary, Volume III* (Brill 1995) 241.

185 US Navy, US Coast Guard & US Marine Corps, NTTP3–07.11M/CGTTP3–93.3/MCIP3–33.04, 'Visit, Board, Search, And Seizure Operations' (2013) 1–2.

186 *'Arctic Sunrise' (Netherlands v. Russia)* [2013] PCA, 2014–02, para. 245.

187 Craig H Allen, 'The Doctrine of Hot Pursuit: A Functional Interpretation Adaptable to Emerging Maritime Law Enforcement' (1989) 20 Ocean Dev & Int'l L 311–312.

188 Douglas Guilfoyle, 'Article 111- Right of Hot Pursuit', in Alexander Proelß (ed), *United Nations Convention on the Law of the Sea: A Commentary* (Nomos 2017) 774.

and regulations of that State, both in the EEZ as well on the high seas.[189] Moreover, the pursuit has to be conducted uninterrupted after leaving the territorial sea,[190] a signal to stop has been given,[191] and the pursuit has to cease if the pursued vessel enters another State's territorial sea.[192] All these requirements have to be fulfilled cumulatively.[193] The right of hot pursuit applies in all waters over which the coastal State has sovereignty or jurisdiction, including maritime zones beyond the territorial sea.[194] Hot pursuit may not only be effected by a ship but also by an aircraft as in this case the provisions of Art. 111 paragraphs 1 to 4 shall apply *mutatis mutandis*. As a result, the foreign ship can be ordered to stop and subsequently arrested and escorted to the port of that State for the purposes of an inquiry.[195] If these requirements are not fulfilled, the right to hot pursuit may cause an infringement of the freedom of navigation.[196]

It could also be imagined that hot pursuit could be applied to a foreign aircraft in the airspace above the EEZ and the high seas.[197] An aircraft may be "escorted" and brought to the airport of that State if the State has reasonable grounds to believe that the foreign aircraft poses a threat to security before entering national airspace and has violated the State's identification rules. Unauthorized entry of foreign aircraft into the air space of a State, i.e. intrusion, is usually considered a serious infringement.[198] Art. 111 (6) UNCLOS explicitly stipulates that the rules for hot pursuit "shall apply *mutatis mutandis*" where the hot pursuit is effected by an aircraft. Pursuant to Art. 111 (6) (b) UNCLOS "[i]t does not suffice to justify an arrest outside the territorial sea that the ship was merely sighted by the aircraft as an offender or suspected offender" but it additionally needs to be ordered to stop and pursued by the aircraft. Likewise, any intruding aircraft shall first be pursued and ordered to identify on the condition of being

189 Art. 111 (1) UNCLOS.
190 Art. 111 (1) UNCLOS.
191 Art. 111 (4) UNCLOS.
192 Art. 111 (3) UNCLOS.
193 *M/V "SAIGA" (No. 2)* (*Saint Vincent and the Grenadines* v. *Guinea*) (Judgment of 1 July 1999) ITLOS Reports 1999, 10 at para. 146.
194 Douglas Guilfoyle, 'Article 111- Right of Hot Pursuit', in Alexander Proelß (ed), *United Nations Convention on the Law of the Sea: A Commentary* (Nomos 2017) 774.
195 Art. 111 (7) UNCLOS.
196 *M/V "SAIGA" (No. 2)* (*Saint Vincent and the Grenadines* v. *Guinea*) (Judgment of 1 July 1999, Sep. Op. Wolfrum) ITLOS Reports 1999, 110, para. 51.
197 Similar, Art. 4 Tokyo Convention.
198 Nicholas M Poulantzas, *The Right to Hot Pursuit in International Law* (2nd edn, Brill 2002) 339.

otherwise forced to land.[199] There is no reason why such a pursuit should not occur within the area of an ADIZ if the pursuing aircraft does not report to the competent authorities according to the regulations existing in this zone. Since enforcement measures in international airspace, including interception of foreign aircraft, seem not to be generally accepted, the forced landing is limited to national airspace. If the foreign aircraft was wrongly intercepted, it can bring forward claims for compensation, as similarly stated in Art. 111 (8) UNCLOS.[200]

2.3.1.5 *The Prohibition of Dumping Waste*

Outside the realm of UNCLOS, aircraft above the high seas can be subject to restrictions, as it is within the capacity of the coastal State's legislation to prohibit the dumping of waste.[201] The London Convention aims to achieve antipollution of the marine environment including in its scope the offshore activities of aircraft. Limitations of the right of overflight emerge as States may take effective measures to prevent pollution of the marine environment caused by dumping at sea including the deliberate disposal at sea of wastes from aircraft.[202] Excluded from the scope of application are State aircraft.[203] The Protocol to the London Convention includes a precautionary approach which implies that all dumping is prohibited unless explicitly permitted.[204] The prohibition of dumping waste by aircraft is a very rare example of conventional restriction of the freedom of overflight. Yet it proves shows that States may impose laws also on foreign aircraft in international airspace.

2.3.1.6 *The Chicago Convention's Flight Rules*

Extensive regulations with impact on the freedom of overflight can be found in the Annexes of the Chicago Convention, which contain technical rules on

199 Kay Hailbronner, *Der Schutz der Luftgrenzen im Frieden* (1972) 81; Nicholas M Poulantzas, *The Right of Hot Pursuit in International Law* (2nd edn, Brill 2002) 344, 345.

200 Art. 111 (8) UNCLOS reads: "Where a ship has been stopped or arrested outside the territorial sea in circumstances which do not justify the exercise of the right of hot pursuit, it shall be compensated for any loss or damage that may have been thereby sustained."

201 The Convention on the Prevention of Marine Pollution by Dumping of Wastes and Other Matter (1972) 1046 UNTS 120 [hereinafter London Convention], was replaced in March 2006 with the entry into force of the Protocol to the Convention on the Prevention of Marine Pollution by Dumping of Wastes and Other Matter (1996) and has currently 53 Parties.

202 Arts. I and II of the London Convention; Article 2 of the Protocol to the London Convention.

203 Arts. 1(4), 10(4) Protocol to the London Convention.

204 https://www.imo.org/en/OurWork/Environment/Pages/London-Convention-Protocol .aspx.

the conduct of air traffic including traffic above the high seas.[205] Pursuant to Annex 2 Chicago Convention, the rules of the air apply to aircraft "wherever they may be" as long as they do not conflict with the rules published by the State having jurisdiction over the territory overflown.[206] The ICAO Council resolves that the Annex constitutes rules relating to the flight and manoeuvre of aircraft within the meaning of Art. 12 of the Convention and therefore these rules apply without exception over the high seas.[207] According to Annex 2 Chicago Convention, flight rules prescribe certain limitations on the conduct of the flight, for example aircraft shall not be operated in a "negligent or reckless manner"[208] or "be flown acrobatically."[209] Also, flight plans have to be submitted in order to provide relevant flight information to the air traffic service unit.[210] Only after submitting flight plans obtain aircraft an air traffic control clearance.[211] Where a regional air navigation agreement exists between one State and the ICAO Council, in which the State has accepted the responsibility to provide air traffic service, the same national air traffic rules are applicable in national as well as international airspace pursuant to Annex 11 Chicago Convention. National air traffic control authorities can thus extend their services to the airspace above the high seas for reasons of practicability as otherwise, each State would have two sets of air traffic regulations. Moreover, Annex 15 Chicago Convention contains rules on aeronautical information services whose objective is to "ensure the flow of information/data necessary for the safety, regularity, and efficiency of international air navigation." In an event of operational significance to civil aviation, a notice to airmen (NOTAM) shall be issued. NOTAMs are defined as notices "concerning the establishment, condition or change in any aeronautical facility, service, procedure or hazard (…)" affecting flight operations.[212] As mentioned in chapter 5, the Annexes of the Chicago Convention include a definition of the term "ADIZ". They do not specify whether ADIZ can only be established in national airspace or also in

205 Art. 12 Chicago Convention in connection with Annex 2 and Annex 11 Chicago Convention.

206 Art. 2.1.1. Annex 2 Chicago Convention.

207 Amendment 1 to Annex 2 (November 1951).

208 Art. 3.1.1. Annex 2 Chicago Convention.

209 Art. 3.1.7 Annex 2 Chicago Convention.

210 Art. 3.3.1 Annex 2 Chicago Convention.

211 Art. 3.6.1 Annex 2 Chicago Convention.

212 Art. 2.5. Annex 15 Chicago Convention. Such even may include manoeuvring areas, hazards affecting air navigation (e.g. military exercises) or prohibited, restricted, or danger areas, see James Kraska & Raul Pedrozo, *International Maritime Security Law* (Brill Nijhoff 2013) 104.

international airspace. Yet the inclusion of ADIZ in Annexes demonstrates that the concept of identifying aircraft for safety and security reasons has reached the doorstep of treaty regulations.

2.4 *Case Analysis on Violations of the Freedom of the High Seas*

2.4.1 Current Stand of International Jurisprudence and Decisions

Hardly any jurisprudence of the International Court of Justice exists with regard to limitations of the freedom of overflight and violations thereof. In total, six cases on aerial incidents were submitted by the United States to the ICJ, but in all these cases the Court found that it did not to have jurisdiction to adjudicate.[213] These cases all concerned the seizures of an US American aircraft and its crew but were eventually removed from the list of cases. Similarly, three further cases arising from the destruction of an aircraft belonging to an Israeli airline by Bulgarian anti-aircraft defence forces never reached the merits phase due to a lack of jurisdiction.[214] Furthermore, the destruction of the Iran Air Airbus A-300B, resulting in the deaths of its 290 passengers and crew, was ultimately removed from the Court's list, as this incident was settled by diplomatic negotiations.[215] Other cases involving aerial incidents were not resolved in the merits stage, or only concerned the appeal relating to the ICAO Council's jurisdiction.[216]

The most relevant case for the current discussions is the *Nicaragua Case*, in which the ICJ addressed the freedom of navigation and violations thereof. In general, the freedom of navigation for the purpose of entering and leaving internal waters, i.e. the right to innocent passage, is a rule of customary

---

213 *Aerial Incident of 7 October 1952* (*United States of America v Union of Soviet Socialist Republics*) (Order) [1952] ICJ; Treatment in Hungary of Aircraft and Crew of the United States of America (United States of America v Hungarian People's Republic) (Order) [1954] ICJ; *Aerial Incident of 10 March 1953* (*United States of America v Czechoslovakia*) (Order) [1953] ICJ; *Aerial Incident of 4 September 1954* (*United States of America v Union of Soviet Socialist Republics*) (Order) [1954] ICJ; *Aerial Incident of 7 November 1954* (*United States of America v Union of Soviet Socialist Republics*) (Order) [1954] ICJ.

214 *Aerial Incident of 27 July 1955* (*Israel v Bulgaria*) (Order) [1955] ICJ; *Aerial Incident of 27 July 1955* (*United Kingdom v Bulgaria*) (Order) [1955] ICJ; and *Aerial Incident of 27 July 1955* (*United States of America v Bulgaria*) (Order) [1955] ICJ.

215 *Aerial Incident of 3 July 1988* (*Islamic Republic of Iran v. United States of America*) (Order) [1988] ICJ.

216 *Aerial Incident of 10 August 1999* (*Pakistan v India*) (*Questions of Jurisdiction and Admissibility*) [2000] ICJ Rep 12; *Appeal Relating to the Jurisdiction of the ICAO Council under Article II, Section 2, of the 1944 International Air Services Transit Agreement* (*Bahrain, Egypt and United Arab Emirates v Qatar*) (Merits) [2020] ICJ Rep 172; *Appeal Relating to the Jurisdiction of the ICAO Council under Article 84 of the Convention on International Civil Aviation* (*Bahrain, Egypt, Saudi Arabia and United Arab Emirates v Qatar*) (Merits) [2020) ICJ Rep 81.

international law.[217] Accordingly, the right to freedom of navigation, *in concreto* the freedom of communication and of maritime commerce, was hindered by the laying of mines in internal waters, preventing ships from accessing the port of the coastal State.[218] The Court further elaborated that innocent passage necessarily presupposes the freedom of navigation in the EEZ and on the high seas.[219] The ICJ concluded that "[i]t is certain that interference with navigation in these areas prejudices both the sovereignty of the coastal State over its internal waters, and the right of free access enjoyed by foreign ships."[220] However, in contrast to the law of the sea, there is no such right of innocent passage in airspace above the territorial sea and internal waters in the Chicago Convention.[221] Consequently, there is no connection between the freedom of overflight and access to airports. The International Air Services Transit Agreement with currently 134 State parties may provide for "the privilege to fly across the territory" of a foreign State without landing, however subject to the provisions of the Chicago Convention.[222] As mentioned in chapter 4, the Chicago Convention provides in Art. 11 the right to regulate the admission to national airspace. Moreover, the wording of the International Air Services Transit Agreement already indicates that flying across the territory of a foreign State is not a right but a privilege. If established in national airspace, the possible denial of entrance to national airspace due to non-compliance with the ADIZ's rules does not violate the freedom of overflight.

In its function as "the governing board of ICAO", the ICAO Council not only performs legislative and administrative functions, but also judicial functions and is endowed with the authrotiy to adjudicate disputes between the Member States relating to the interpretation and application of the Convention.[223] The Council has been called upon to resolve a select number of international

---

217 *Nicaragua Case* (1986) para. 214.

218 Ibid.

219 Ibid stating that "since freedom of navigation is guaranteed, first in the exclusive economic zones which may exist beyond territorial waters (Art. 58), and secondly, beyond territorial waters and on the high seas (Art. 87), it follows that any State which enjoys a right of access to ports for its ships also enjoys all the freedom necessary for maritime navigation."

220 *Nicaragua Case* (1986) para. 214.

221 Kay Hailbronner, 'Freedom of the Air and the Convention on the Law of the Sea'(1983) 77 AJIL 491; on the issue of innocent passage of space objects in foreign national airspace see Jinyuan Su, 'The Delineation Between Airspace and Outer Space and the Emergence of Aerospace Objects' (2013) 78 J Air L & Com 369ff.

222 Arts. 1 and 2 International Air Services Transit Agreement (30 January 1945) 84 UNTS 389.

223 Richard N Gariepy & David L Botsford, 'The Effectiveness of the International Civil Aviation Organization's Adjudicatory Machinery' (1976) 42 J Air L & Commerce 353.

aviation disputes. Four cases involved restrictions of overflight rights under the Chicago Convention and the related International Air Services Transit Agreement. These were India/Pakistan (1952), United Kingdom/Spain (1967), Pakistan/India (1971), and Cuba/United States (1998).[224] One case concerned airplane noises (United States/Fifteen European States, 2000), and another case addressed flight restrictions above State territory (Bahrain Egypt and United Arab Emirates/Qatar, 2017).[225] The majority of cases were either settled by negotiations or were deferred indefinitely at the request of the parties.[226] Three cases were adjudicated by ICAO and appealed to the ICJ.[227] To date, none of the cases yet referred to the freedom of overflight in connection with aerial jurisdiction in concreto, or the freedom of the high seas in general, due to the lack of any reference to these terms in the framework of the Chicago Convention. So far, also no case has concerned the establishment of ADIZS.

The International Tribunal of the Law of the Sea (ITLOS) has as addressed the issue of freedom of the high seas in a more comprehensive manner than any other court or tribunal. To date, twenty-nine cases have been settled by ITLOS, whereas in four cases the freedom of the high seas has been discussed in more detail.[228] The freedom of overflight has never been part of any order or merit decided by ITLOS. The following *tour d horizon* aims to illustrate the most relevant decisions pertaining to the freedoms of the high seas.

2.4.2 Violations of the Freedom of the High Seas in ITLOS Case Law

2.4.2.1 *M/V "SAIGA" (No. 2) (Saint Vincent and the Grenadines v. Guinea)*

In *M/V "SAIGA" (No. 2) (Saint Vincent and the Grenadines v. Guinea)* the Tribunal discussed whether custom laws on bunkering amount to an infringement of the freedom of navigation. The bunkering occurred in Guinea's EEZ and in order to enforce the custom laws, Guinea patrol boats fired on, boarded, and arrested the M/V *SAIGA* beyond the EEZ as part of hot pursuit.[229] Guinea argued that Art. 1 of its national law L/94/007, which prohibits the unauthorized import, transport, storage, and distribution of fuel in the Republic of Guinea, "can be

224 Haris Huremagic & Fritz Kainz, 'COVID 19, China and International Aviation Law: A ticket to The Hague?' (2020) https://www.ejiltalk.org/covid-19-china-and-international-aviation-law-a-ticket-to-the-hague/>.

225 Ibid.

226 Richard N Gariepy & David L Botsford, 'The Effectiveness of the International Civil Aviation Organization's Adjudicatory Machinery' (1976) 42 J Air L & Commerce 353.

227 Cecily Rose, 'Appeal Relating to the Jurisdiction of the ICAO Council' (2021) 115 AJIL 301.

228 Stand 24 April 2021.

229 Bernard Oxman & Vincent Bantz, 'The M/V "Saiga" (No. 2) (Saint Vincent and the Grenadines v. Guinea), Judgment (ITLOS Case No. 2)' (2000) 94 AJIL 140.

applied for the purpose of controlling and suppressing the sale of gas oil to fishing vessels in the customs radius according to Art. 34 of the Customs Code." The customs radius amounted to 250 kilometres.

First, the Tribunal declined to determine whether bunkering in the EEZ constitutes an exercise of the freedom of navigation, and whether bunkering is subject to the coastal State's jurisdiction. An in-depth discussion emerged on the question of whether bunkering is part of the freedom of the high seas with some Judges advocating against it,[230] and others in favour.[231] Second, the Tribunal concluded that the application of custom laws and regulations on the activity of bunkering is in conformity with the freedom of navigation as long as they are applied in respect of artificial islands, installations, and structures pursuant to Art. 60 (2) UNCLOS.[232] However, the Tribunal also found that the Convention does not empower a coastal State to apply its customs laws in respect of any other parts of the exclusive economic zone than those mentioned in Art. 60 UNCLOS.[233] The Tribunal also rejected Guinea's argument that necessity or public interest justified the extension of its customs laws in this situation.[234]

The Tribunal summarized that Guinea's customs and related laws provided no legal basis for the hot pursuit and *M/V SAIGA's* arrest in relation to its activities in the exclusive economic zone. *In concreto*, the procedure of the hot pursuit was not in conformity with Art. 111 UNCLOS as Guinea could have had no more than a suspicion of illegal activity, the tanker was too distant to be given visual or auditory signals to stop, the pursuit was interrupted, and the custom laws provided no basis for the pursuit in the first place.[235] Accordingly, the arrest and detention of the *M/V SAIGA*, the prosecution and the confiscation of the cargo, and the seizure of the ship were contrary to UNCLOS.[236] As a consequence, the custom regulations and hot pursuit in order to subject the vessel *M/V SAIGA* to Guinea's jurisdiction violated the freedom of navigation.[237]

---

230 Ibid para. 2.

231 *M/V "SAIGA" (No. 2) (Saint Vincent and the Grenadines* v. *Guinea)* (Judgment of 1 July 1999, Sep Op Anderson) ITLOS Reports 1999, 137; *M/V "SAIGA" (No. 2) (Saint Vincent and the Grenadines* v. *Guinea)* (Judgment of 1 July 1999, Sep Op Vukas) ITLOS Reports 1999, 148, para. 15.

232 *M/V "SAIGA" (No. 2) (Saint Vincent and the Grenadines* v *Guinea)* (Judgment of 1 July 1999) ITLOS Reports 1999, 54, para. 128–35.

233 Ibid para. 127.

234 Ibid para. 136.

235 Ibid paras. 147–149.

236 Ibid para. 136.

237 Ibid para. 136.

As previously discussed, a reversed right of aerial hot pursuit within an ADIZ and the forced landing of an aircraft can only be enforced in national airspace. This argument is in line with the reasoning of ITLOS in the *MV/SAIGA (No. 2) Case*, as the arrest of the ship on the high seas was the issue at stake and not the application of national custom laws on bunkering. In contrast to the law of the sea and particularly Art. 60 UNCLOS, the Chicago Convention neither expressively authorizes nor limits the application of national laws to specific areas. Consequently, national security rules of aircraft identification *prima facie* do not violate the freedoms of the high seas but any enforcement of these rules in international airspace could be regarded as such a violation.

2.4.2.2 *M/V "Louisa" (Saint Vincent and the Grenadines v. the Kingdom of Spain)*

In *M/V "Louisa" (Saint Vincent and the Grenadines v. the Kingdom of Spain)* the Tribunal discussed whether the denial to leave the port is a restriction of the freedom of navigation.[238] The *M/V Louisa* was detained in the context of criminal proceedings relating to the alleged violations of Spanish laws on "the protection of the underwater cultural heritage and the possession and handling of weapons of war in Spanish territory."[239] Saint Vincent and the Grenadines argued that because of the detention of the *M/V Louisa* in the port of Cadiz the vessel was denied access to the high seas and that this detention violates the freedom of vessels to navigate on the high seas as provided for in Art. 87 UNCLOS.[240] In response, Spain pointed out that the detention did not take place on the high seas but while the *M/V Louisa* was docked voluntarily in a Spanish port.[241] The Tribunal concluded that Art. 87 UNCLOS cannot be interpreted in such a way as to grant the *M/V Louisa* a right to leave the port and gain access to the high seas notwithstanding its detention in the context of legal proceedings against it.[242] Judge *Paik* emphasized in his Declaration the evolutive character of the freedoms of the high sea namely that the "freedom of the high seas is subject to change, and indeed has evolved over time"; but emphasized that the freedom of the high seas limited to the high seas and not applicable to the territorial sea.[243] Furthermore, Judge *Paik* clarified that to "extend the freedom of the high seas to include a right of the State to have access to the

238 *M/V "Louisa" (Saint Vincent and the Grenadines* v *Kingdom of Spain*), (Judgment of 28 May 2013) ITLOS Reports 2013, 36.

239 Ibid para 115.

240 Ibid para 106.

241 Ibid para 107.

242 Ibid para. 109.

243 Ibid para. 28.

high seas to enjoy that freedom is warranted neither by the text of the relevant provisions or the context of the Convention nor by established State practice on this matter."[244] A similar train of thought can be applied to the right of entry to national airspace. The freedom of overflight certainly does not grant such right and any denial of entry due to non-compliance with the ADIZ's regulations does not amount to a violation of the freedom of overflight.[245]

2.4.2.3 *M/V "Virginia G" (Panama v. Guinea-Bissau)*

In *M/V "Virginia G" (Panama v. Guinea-Bissau)* the Tribunal was again concerned with bunkering services provided in the EEZ of a coastal State and the question of whether States may restrict bunkering. The question addressed by the Tribunal was whether Guinea-Bissau, in the exercise of its sovereign rights in respect of the exploration, exploitation, conservation, and management of natural resources in its EEZ, had the competence to regulate bunkering of foreign vessels fishing in its zone. In contrast to its previous judgment in the case *M/V "SAIGA"* the Tribunal found that the charging of fees for bunkering activities in the EEZ is within the scope of the coastal State's sovereign rights and therefore does not violate the freedom of navigation.[246] Moreover, the Tribunal found that States can also impose the obligation to request authorization for bunkering activities in the EEZ:

> With reference to the question of the procedure for obtaining an authorization for bunkering, the Tribunal holds that this – if properly followed – is not unduly burdensome for an applicant. In particular, the Tribunal does not consider it an undue burden for bunkering vessels to obtain such authorization in writing.[247]

This reasoning is likewise relevant for the argument on the right to establish an ADIZ and the application of identification procedures. In the sense of *arugmentum a maiore ad minus*, authorization in general puts a stronger restriction on the free use of the high seas than the identification requirement of ADIZs. If States do not request or comply with the authorization requirement, they cannot conduct bunkering as part of the freedom of the high seas in the EEZ of coastal States. As a corollary, the enjoyment of the right of overflight, as part

244 Ibid para. 29.

245 See on this discussion, *Nicaragua Case* (1986), at 43, 44, on innocent passage.

246 *M/V "Virginia G" (Panama v Guinea-Bissau)* (Judgment of 14 April 2014) ITLOS Reports 2014, para. 208.

247 Ibid para. 235.

of the freedom of high seas, can also be restricted. The obligation to identify the aircraft before entering national airspace is also no undue burden or at least not more burdensome than obtaining authorization for bunkering activities. Moreover, the consequence of non-compliance with the identification requirement is not as drastic as in the case of failing to obtain authorization for bunkering activities because aircraft may still continue their flight through international airspace.

2.4.2.4 *M/V "Norstar" (Panama v. Italy)*

From all decided cases so far, the *"M/V Norstar" (Panama v. Italy)* shows more clearly than any other the lack of coherent jurisprudence on violations of the freedom of the high seas.[248] The tribunal found that Italy had violated Panama's right to freedom of navigation on the high sea and based its decision on an expansive understanding and interpretation of the flag State's jurisdiction. The tribunals' reasoning on the jurisdictional exclusivity of the flag State which covers prescriptive as well as enforcement jurisdiction prompted a joint dissent by seven of its twenty-three judges. A more in-depth analysis of the *Norstar* case and the aspect of prescriptive jurisdiction of the coastal State is necessary, illustrating both the majority's decision as well as the arguments of the dissenting judges.

The *Norstar Case* concerned the bunkering activities of the *Norstar* vessel, which bought tax-exempt fuel in Italy and sold it to other vessels in international waters. Under Italian law, bunkering qualifies as criminal conduct, namely tax evasion and smuggling.[249] Consequently, a Decree of Seizure was issued by Italian authorities, resulting in the arrest of *Norstar* while it was anchored in Spanish internal waters. One might inquire as to how the freedom of the high seas can be violated if the arrest of the ship did occur while it was on the high seas. The tribunal also intensively considered whether Italy had violated UNCLOS Art. 87(1) (a) in regulating the activity of a foreign flagged vessel on the high seas via the Decree of Seizure. The tribunal relied in its reasoning on the *Lotus Case* citing the Permanent Court of International Justice that due to "the absence of any territorial sovereignty upon the high seas, no State may exercise any kind of jurisdiction over foreign vessels upon them."[250] The tribunal established a connection between this maxim and Art. 92 UNCLOS, which outlines the exclusive jurisdiction of the flag state over its fleet when it is

248 *M/V "Norstar" (Panama v Italy)* (Judgment of 10 April 2019) ITLOS Reports 2018–2019.

249 Cameron Miles, 'The MV "Norstar" Case (Panama v. Italy)' (2020) 114 AJIL 116.

250 *M/V "Norstar" (Panama v Italy)* (Judgment of 10 April 2019) ITLOS Reports 2018–2019, para. 216.

on the high seas.[251] The tribunal dismissed Italy's argument – that the Decree of Seizure did not take effect until the *Norstar* was seized in Spain's internal waters – and found that, the Decree of Seizure "concerns" and "targets" the vessel's bunkering activities on the high seas.[252] The tribunal concluded that flag State jurisdiction as set forth in Art. 92 UNCLOS applies to prescriptive as well as enforcement jurisdiction:

> Contrary to Italy's argument, even when enforcement is carried out in internal waters, article 87 may still be applicable and be breached if a State extends its criminal and customs laws extraterritorially to activities of foreign ships on the high seas and criminalizes them. This is precisely what Italy did in the present case. The Tribunal, therefore, finds that (…) Italy, by extending its criminal and customs laws to the high seas, by issuing the Decree of Seizure, and by requesting the Spanish authorities to execute it – which they subsequently did – breached the freedom of navigation which Panama (…) enjoyed under that provision.[253]

The tribunal concretized that the principle of exclusive flag State jurisdiction is an inherent component of the freedom of navigation under Art. 87 UNCLOS and thus,

> prohibits not only the exercise of enforcement jurisdiction on the high seas by States other than the flag State but also the extension of their prescriptive jurisdiction to lawful activities conducted by foreign ships on the high seas.[254]

In contrast to the tribunal's decisions, Judges *Cot, Pawlak, Yanai, Hoffmann, Kolodkin, Lijnzaad* and Judge ad hoc *Treves* emphasised in their joint Dissenting Opinion that first, Art. 87 was not applicable and thus not susceptible to violation, and second, even if Art. 87 (1) were applicable, it would not have been violated by Italy.[255] Especially regarding the point of prescriptive jurisdiction they found that:

---

251 Ibid para. 217, 218.
252 Ibid para. 172–177.
253 Ibid para. 226.
254 Ibid para. 225.
255 *M/V "Norstar"* (*Panama v. Italy*) (Judgment of 10 April 2019, Dis Op Cot, Pawlak, Yanai, Hoffmann, Kolodkin, Lijnzaad and Treves) ITLOS Reports 2018–2019, para. 13.

> nothing in the text of the Convention, in its *travaux préparatoires*, in other international treaties, in customary international law, or in the practice of States suggests that article 87 and its corollary article 92 altogether excludes the right of non-flag States to exercise their prescriptive criminal jurisdiction with respect to activities on the high seas.[256]

Interestingly, whereas the Tribunal relied on the *Lotus Case* to bolster its reasoning that not only enforcement jurisdiction but also prescriptive jurisdiction is prohibited, the Judges in their Dissenting Opinion referred likewise to the *Lotus Case* for supporting their counterarguments.[257] The action of concern in the *Lotus Case* was the prosecution of a French national, and hence the exercise of enforcement jurisdiction. In contrast, the legislation, on which the enforcement was based, was unobjectionable.[258] *Lotus*, therefore, provides a better precedent for the dissenting opinion than for the actual judgment. The dissenting Judges also emphasized the continuing validity of the *Lotus* principle, in particular that acts may be directed at foreign vessels "not when it is justified or allowed by international law to do so, but when it is not prohibited by international law to do so."[259] The Dissenting Opinions thus indicate that prescriptive jurisdiction on the high seas, is generally allowed, whereas enforcement jurisdiction is limited to the territorial sea. A similar approach was expressed in the Joint Separate Opinion by Judges *Wolfrum* and *Attard* stating that

> [c]onsidering the object and purpose of article 87 of the Convention, this provision first and foremost protects the free movement of vessels on the high seas against enforcement measures by States other than the flag State or States so authorized by the latter.[260]

The judgment in the *Norstar Case* and its new interpretation of the flag State's prescriptive jurisdiction for activities on the high seas has drawn a lot of criticism in scholarly literature, even labelling it as superfluous.[261] Most arguments

---

256 Ibid para. 18.

257 Ibid para. 19.

258 *Lotus Case*, para. 12–15.

259 *M/V "Norstar" (Panama v. Italy)* (Judgment of 10 April 2019, Dis. Op. Cot, Pawlak, Yanai, Hoffmann, Kolodkin, Lijnzaad and Treves) ITLOS Reports 2018–2019, para. 36.

260 *M/V "Norstar" Case (Panama v. Italy)* Preliminary Objections (Judgment of 4 November 2014, Joint Sep. Op. Wolfrum and Attard), ITLOS Reports 2014, para. 34.

261 Cameron Miles, 'The MV "Norstar" Case (Panama v. Italy' 114 AJIL 122; Richard Collins, 'Introductory Note to the M/V "Norstar" Case (Panama v. Italy)' (2019) American Society Int'l L 673–675.

highlight that the current stand of literature confines the exclusivity of the flag State's jurisdiction to enforcement jurisdiction only.[262] This radical expansion of the flag State's jurisdiction by the Tribunal leads to the result that, even where the actual movement of the vessel is not restricted, any prescriptive jurisdiction regulating acts of a vessel on the high seas is a violation of the freedom of navigation.[263] Yet, the principle of freedom of navigation cannot be understood as prohibiting States to exercise prescriptive jurisdiction over acts, which have occurred on board a vessel on the high seas.[264] *Guilfoyle* explains:

> [e]xclusivity of jurisdiction (…) creates only a prohibition on exercising enforcement jurisdiction over foreign vessels on the high seas; multiple States may still attach legal consequences to acts committed on a vessel on the high seas as a matter of prescriptive jurisdiction.[265]

The majority of the ITLOS Tribunal rested their arguments on the fact, that there is no rule in international law permitting prescriptive jurisdiction for acts occurring on the high seas and therefore, every legislative act would violate the freedom of the high seas. In contrast, some judges highlighted in their dissenting opinion the role of a prohibitive rule in international law for assessing the legality of an act.[266] This differentiation between permitting and prohibiting certain State actions in international law was also discussed by the International Court of Justice in the *Nuclear Weapons Advisory Opinion*. In the *Nuclear Weapons Advisory Opinion*, the ICJ reached the conclusion that neither conventional nor customary international law explicitly permits nor prohibits the use and threat of nuclear weapons. For this conclusion, the Court extensively examined international law and first noted, that since no principle in international law makes the legality or illegality of the use or threat of nuclear weapons dependant on authorisation, illegality can only be confirmed in case of a rule prohibiting the

262 Daniel P O'Connell, *The International Law of the Sea, Volume II* (OUP 1984) 800–801; Douglas Guilfoyle, 'Article 92 – Status of Ships' in Alexander Proelß (ed), *United Nations Convention on the Law of the Sea: A Commentary* (Nomos 2017) 700–701.

263 Cameron Miles, 'The MV "Norstar" Case (Panama v. Italy)' 114 AJIL 122–123.

264 Arron N Honniball, 'Freedom of Navigation Following the M/V "Norstar" Case', The Blog of the KG Jebsen Center for the Law of the Sea (4 June 2019).

265 Douglas Guilfoyle, 'Article 92 – Status of Ships' in Alexander Proelß (ed), *United Nations Convention on the Law of the Sea: A Commentary* (Nomos 2017) 700–701 referring to: G Gidel, Le droit international public de la mer: le temps de paix, vol. I (1932) 261; *Lotus Case*, at para 4.

266 *M/V "Norstar" (Panama v Italy)* (Judgment of 10 April 2019, Dis Op Cot, Pawlak, Yanai, Hoffmann, Kolodkin, Lijnzaad and Treves) ITLOS Reports 2018–2019, para. 36.

conduct.[267] In the end, the Court could not reach a definitive conclusion as to the legality or illegality of the use of nuclear weapons by a State in an extreme circumstance of self-defence.[268] In his dissenting opinion, Judge *Shahabudden* draws two scenarios. The first scenario describes the absence of a rule prohibiting a certain conduct, here the use of nuclear weapons. In the absence of a prohibitory rule, States have the right to use nuclear weapons. In the second, alternative scenario, the absence of a rule authorizing a conduct leads to the conclusion that States do not have the right to use nuclear weapons.[269] The reasoning of the *Norstar Case* should be seen within the context of the *Lotus Case* and the *Nuclear Weapons Advisory Opinion.*

2.4.3 Contextualization of the ITLOS Cases and Their Significance for ADIZS

The rules on the freedom of the high seas and principles of international law apply to ADIZS in international airspace subject to a balancing test.[270] These freedoms neither expressively permit nor prohibit ADIZS. For example, Art. 142 UNCLOS rules that marine scientific research in the sea bed is beyond the limits of national jurisdiction. This clearly states a prohibition of national jurisdiction in this area. A similar expression is missing in the case of aerial jurisdiction above the high seas. Any establishment of ADIZS contrary to the freedom of the high seas pursuant to Art. 87 UNCLOS would be unlawful. Concerns about the impact of ADIZS on sovereignty claims and on the freedom of overflight can be rebutted, if the role of the State is limited to that of an administrator of an ADIZ, without the State exercising coercive and punitive competences.[271]

The obligation to identify is distinct from the requirement to seek permission in order to fly through airspace in international airspace. Especially in instances where ADIZS do not impose identification procedures on aircraft not

267 *Legality of the Threat or Use of Nuclear Weapons* (Advisory Opinion) [1996] ICJ Rep 226, para. 52, referring to the reasoning in the *Lotus Case.*

268 Ibid para. 97.

269 *Legality of the Threat or Use of Nuclear Weapons* (Advisory Opinion) [1996] ICJ Rep 226, Dis. Op. Judge Shahabudden, para. 1–2.

270 Jonathan G Odom, 'A "Rule-Based Approach" to Airspace Defense: A U.S. Perspective on the International Law of the Sea and Airspace, Air Defense Measures, and the Freedom of Navigation' (2014) Revue Belge de Droit International 75; Peter Dutton, 'Caelum Liberam: Air Defense Identification Zones Outside Sovereign Airspace' (2009) 103 AJIL 3.

271 Christopher Lamont, 'Conflict in the Skies: The Law of Air Defence Identification Zones' (2014) 39 Air & Space Law 193, 194, who connects ADIZ with the exercise of sovereignty in international airspace.

intending to enter national airspace but merely crossing international airspace, there is no violation of the right of overflight.[272] In an *argumentum a maiore ad minus*, ADIZs have a less restrictive effect on the freedoms of the high seas than the creation of safety zones around artificial islands. If States are permitted to create navigation restrictions and prohibit navigation in these zones, then they should also be permitted to impose identification requirements on aircraft when traversing through an ADIZ. ADIZs have no closure-effect on international airspace for air traffic; they impose supplementary conditions for air traffic in addition to the many already existing air traffic regulations in international airspace. Even if States' prescriptive jurisdiction by the means of identification requirements targets activities on the high seas, it is not targeting the activity of overflight as such. Rather, the focus is to investigate the use of the aircraft as a potential means of attack.[273] In fact, any potential violation of the freedom of overflight would only occur in the event of a requirement to return to the airport and to land.

The primary concern in the discourse surrounding ADIZs is the exercise of enforcement jurisdiction through interception.[274] ADIZs also have to satisfy the requirements of the Chicago Convention on the interception of civil aircraft. Pursuant to Art. 3bis (b) Chicago Convention, the contracting States have to recognize that "every State, in the exercise of its sovereignty, is entitled to require the landing at some designated airport of a civil aircraft flying above its territory without authority or if there are reasonable grounds to conclude that it is being used for any purpose inconsistent with the aims" of the Chicago Convention. This provision clearly connects the authority of States to require a landing with their exercise of sovereignty and hence allows interception of aircraft only in their territory.[275] As this authority is limited to national airspace, States could not request the landing of a civil aircraft traversing through international airspace. In the event that states refrain from making such a request, no consequences arise from the non-compliance with the obligation to identify. It can therefore be argued that the freedom of overflight is only restricted when aircraft are intercepted or are forced to change their flight

272 Kay Hailbronner, 'Freedom of the Air and the Convention on the Law of the Sea' (1983) 77 AJIL 517.

273 Following the line of argumentation in the *Norstar Case*, where the Tribunal also emphasized that not he bunkering itself, as part of the freedom of navigation, was targeted, but to investigate whether the vessel is used as a means to transport and supply fuel for the purchase of which allegedly appropriate taxes were not paid in its territory, at para. 30.

274 Nicholas M Poulantzas, *The Right of Hot Pursuit in International Law* (2nd edn, Brill 2002) 345.

275 Art. 3bis(b) Chicago Convention.

path in international airspace due to the lack of identification.[276] In general, the security interests of the coastal State should accommodate the interests of other States in their free use of the airspace. It is evident that security jurisdiction must be exercised in international airspace a manner that does not result in the exercise of sovereignty, nor does it permit any undue infringement of the right of overflight. When States express their respect and application of the freedom of overflight, it could be presumed that they do not intend to extend their sovereignty claims.[277]

2.4.4 The European Court of Justice on the Extraterritorial Application of an EU Directive and the Freedom of Overflight

In *Air Transport Association of America and ors v Secretary of State for Energy and Climate Change,* the European Court of Justice (ECJ) had to decide whether an EU Directive on the EU's Emission Trading Schemes applying to aircraft operators of third States whose flights arrive at and depart from an aerodrome situated in the territory of a Member State of the European Union and which are carried out in part over the high seas and the third States' territory violates the freedom of overflight.[278] The extension of the directive to third-state aircraft prompted concern not only among the Air Transport Association of America and American, Continental and United Airlines and IATA, but also among several other countries. They expressed the disapproval and urged the EU to "exclude operations of non-European aircraft" from the scope of application.[279] Despite the political controversies, the case addressed the intensively discussed relationship between international law and EU law.[280]

---

276 Jon M Van Dyke, 'Military Ships and Planes Operating in the Exclusive Economic Zone of another Country' (2004) 28 Marine Policy 37. However, it shall be noted, that interception is a multi-layered process and sometimes also include the forced change of the flight path. This might, arguably, amount to a restriction of the freedom of overflight.

277 See for a similar argumentation *The South China Sea Arbitration* (*The Republic of Philippines v The People's Republic of China*) [2016] PCA, Case 2013–19, stating at para. 213 that because China expressed respect for both freedom of navigation and overflight, China obviously does not consider the sea areas within the 'nine-dash line' to be equivalent to its territorial sea or internal waters, as the freedoms only apply to the high seas.

278 *Air Transport Association of America and ors v Secretary of State for Energy and Climate Change,* European Court of Justice, Case C-366/10 (21 December 2011).

279 Benoit Mayer, 'Case Law' (2012) 49 Common Market Law Review 1113, 1114. Yet is has to be noted that the EU turned to a regional scheme only after the apparent failure of multilateral negotiations at the ICAO.

280 Rupert Dunbar, 'The Application of International Law in the Court of Justice of the European Union: Proportionality Rising' (2021) 22 German Law Journal 557; Geert De Baere & Cedric Ryngaert, 'The ECJ's Judgment in Air Transport Association of America and

The ECJ examined the customary international law rule on the freedom of overflight as well as the principle that aircraft are subject to the exclusive jurisdiction of the State in which they are registered in relation to the competence of the EU to apply Directive 2008/101/EC on third-State aircraft.[281] Firstly, the ECJ concluded that a violation only occurs where "institutions of the European Union made manifest errors of assessment concerning the conditions for applying those principles."[282] Secondly and most importantly, the ECJ decided that "where a flight (...) departs from an aerodrome situated in the territory of a third State (...) and arrives at an aerodrome situated in the territory of one of the Member States of the European Union" the freedom of overflight is not violated by applying the emission trade schemes to aircraft operators of third States.[283] Since the directive does not apply to international flights flying over the territory of the Member States of the European Union or of third States when such flights do not arrive at or depart from an aerodrome situated in the territory of a Member State and does also not apply to aircraft flying over third States or the high seas the freedom of overflight is not violated.[284] Therefore only where there is a connection to the territory of an EU Member State must third State aircraft report their emissions and surrender allowances.[285] That the allowances are calculated in the light of the whole of the international flight that its aircraft have performed, and hence also covers portions of the flight conducted over the high seas, does not render the directive invalid. Instead,

> The European Union legislature may in principle choose to permit a commercial activity, in this instance air transport, to be carried out in the territory of the European Union only on condition that operators comply with the criteria that have been established by the European Union.[286]

The ECJ confirmed the extraterritorial prescriptive jurisdiction of the European Union on activities of third State aircraft if there is a sufficient link to

the International Legal Context of the EU's Climate Change Policy' (2013) 18 European Foreign Affairs Review 389; See also Opinion of General Advocate Kokott para 49.

281 Opinion of General Advocate Kokott, para. 106, 107. Since the EU is not party to the Chicago Convention, the ECJ did not discuss its provisions.

282 Ibid para. 110.

283 Ibid para. 118.

284 Ibid para. 117, 122, 126.

285 Ibid para. 118.

286 Ibid para. 128.

any EU Member State's territory.[287] Consequently, the ECJ followed the General Advocate Kokott's argument that the "existence of an adequate territorial link" and the "absence of any adverse effect on the sovereignty of third countries" is central for such legislation to conform to international law on State jurisdiction.[288]

2.4.5 The International Court of Justice on the Freedom of Navigation and Overflight in the EEZ

In 2022, the ICJ rendered a judgment on the relationship between the freedoms of navigation and overflight and the jurisdiction and sovereign rights of the coastal State within its EEZ. In the case *Alleged Violations of Sovereign Rights and Maritime Spaces in the Caribbean Sea (Nicaragua v. Colombia)*,[289] the ICJ had to decide whether the exercise of enforcement jurisdiction by Colombian naval vessels in Nicaragua's exclusive economic zone is covered by the freedom of navigation and overflight. Colombian naval officers requested Nicaraguan fishing vessels to discontinue their fishing activities, alleging that those activities were environmentally harmful and were illegal or not authorized.[290] Regarding Colombia's argument that these activities are permitted as an exercise of the freedom of navigation and overflight, the ICJ observed:

> (…) in accordance with the customary rules on the exclusive economic zone, freedoms of navigation and overflight enjoyed by other States in the exclusive economic zone of the coastal State, as reflected in Article 58 of UNCLOS, do not include rights relating to the exploration, exploitation, conservation and management of the natural resources of the maritime zone, nor do they give other States jurisdiction to enforce conservation measures in the exclusive economic zone of the coastal State.[291]

The ICJ elaborated in more detail on the exact scope of sovereign rights and jurisdiction of the coastal State within its EEZ in relation to the freedoms:

287 Interestingly, the Advocate General affirmed that the EU directive "does not contain any extraterritorial provisions" as it "is concerned solely with aircraft arrivals at and departures from aerodromes in the European Union", Opinion of General Advocate Kokott, para. 145, 146. ATA, in contrast, criticizes the EU "of having exceeded the bounds of State jurisdiction in breach of principles of customary international law", at para. 143.

288 Ibid para. 150–159.

289 *Alleged Violations of Sovereign Rights and Maritime Spaces in the Caribbean Sea* (*Nicaragua v Colombia*) (Merits) [2022] ICJ Rep 155.

290 Ibid para. 92.

291 Ibid para. 94.

> According to customary international law on the exclusive economic zone, Nicaragua, as the coastal State, enjoys sovereign rights to manage fishing activities and jurisdiction to take measures to protect and preserve the maritime environment in its exclusive economic zone. (…) [Colombia's] conduct often amounted to exercising control over fishing activities in Nicaragua's exclusive economic zone, implementing conservation measures on Nicaraguan-flagged or Nicaraguan-licensed ships, and hindering the operations of Nicaragua's naval vessels. The Court considers that Colombia's legal arguments do not justify its conduct within Nicaragua's exclusive economic zone.[292]

Overall, the ICJ concluded

> In light of the foregoing considerations, the Court finds that Colombia has violated its international obligation to respect Nicaragua's sovereign rights and jurisdiction in the latter's exclusive economic zone by interfering with fishing activities and marine scientific research by Nicaraguan-flagged or Nicaraguan-licensed vessels and with the operations of Nicaragua's naval vessels, and by purporting to enforce conservation measures in that zone.[293]

For the first time, the ICJ found a State violating the obligation to respect other States' sovereign rights in the latter's EEZ. The reasoning indicates that the functional jurisdiction of the State within its EEZ is limited to the rights enshrined in Art. 56 UNCLOS respectively the customary right reflecting Art. 56 UNCLOS. It also shows that when a specific activity is not reserved for the coastal State's authority, there is no *a priori* presumption that the coastal State has the priority to regulate the activity.[294] The Court did not condemn the exercise of control and enforcement *per se* within the EEZ, but only where they created a conflict with the rights of the coastal State. However, the Court did not specify the threshold of "control" and "enforcement" and also did not offer

292 Ibid para. 100.

293 Ibid para. 101.

294 Yurika Ishii, 'Violations of Sovereign Rights at a Foreign EEZ: Alleged Violations of Sovereign Rights and Maritime Spaces in the Caribbean Sea (Nicaragua v. Colombia)' (7 July 2022), https://www.ejiltalk.org/violations-of-sovereign-rights-at-a-foreign-eez-alleged-violations-of-sovereign-rights-and-maritime-spaces-in-the-caribbean-sea-nicaragua-v-colombia/ (accessed 18 October 2022).

a definition for the terms.[295] Where there is no priority of the coastal State, namely in instances where the activity is not exclusively assigned to the coastal State's sovereign rights and jurisdiction, the competing use of the EEZ by a foreign State would not constitute a violation of the coastal State's right.[296] Even though the Applicant contested the systematic exercise of control and enforcement as being not in line with public international law, the Court refrained from clarifying whether these activities are covered by the freedom of navigation and overflight.[297] Further exploration on "control" and "enforcement" would therefore be necessary, and may also include the definition of these terms in relation to activities not covered by Art. 56 as part of competences not attributed to either the coastal State or to other States under Art. 59 UNCLOS.[298]

2.5 *Conclusion: ADIZs Do Not Necessarily Violate the Freedom of the High Seas*

This discussion on the freedom of the high seas illustrates the shift in focus from the maintenance of the freedom of the high seas for the State community to the interests of the coastal States. Similarly, *Hafner* and *Tuerk* highlight that "the pendulum has clearly swung from the principle of *mare liberum* to that of *mare clausum*".[299] One might also posit that a comparable process is underway in the realm of international airspace, evidenced by the emergence of ADIZs and a development from *caelum liberam* to that of *caelum clausum*.[300] While these broader considerations on the evolution of the freedom of the high seas are pertinent, it is important to note that ADIZs do not necessarily contravene the freedom of overflight.

---

295 Judge ad hoc McRae disagreed with the Court's reasoning and offered a narrower understanding of the terms by stating the "[d]efinitions of enforcement generally refer to the exercise of State authority to apply criminal law through arrest, detention, trial and punishment', Dissenting Opinion Judge ad hoc McRae at para. 26.

296 Ishii (2022), offering as an example of competing use the conduct of military activities using heavy weapons, https://www.ejiltalk.org/violations-of-sovereign-rights-at-a-foreign-eez-alleged-violations-of-sovereign-rights-and-maritime-spaces-in-the-caribbean-sea-nicaragua-v-colombia/.

297 *Alleged Violations of Sovereign Rights and Maritime Spaces in the Caribbean Sea (Nicaragua v. Colombia)* (Merits) [2022] ICJ Rep 155 para. 51.

298 See on the discussion whether ADIZ might be covered by Art. 59 UNCLOS below at chapter 3, 3.

299 Gerhard Hafner & Helmut Tuerk, 'The United Nations Convention on the Law of the Sea, 1982: Reflections after 40 Years' (2022) 36 Ocean Yearbook 29.

300 Peter Dutton, 'Caelum Liberam: Air Defense Identification Zones outside Sovereign Airspace' (2009) 103 AJIL 2 describing "caelum liberam" as "freedom of the skies".

In light of the substantial scope of ADIZs, the addressee of the norm as well as the subject matter of the provisions, it can be argued that they do not necessarily create a conflict with the freedom of the high seas, namely when the interception procedure is limited to national airspace.[301] This argument is also in line with the majority of ITLOS cases and the judgment of the ECJ, which differentiate between prescribing an obligation and enforcing the obligation.[302] The obligation to identify in international airspace and the freedom of overflight are not mutually exclusive when enforced in national airspace. In international airspace, aircraft are not obliged to follow national enforcement rules. *Prima facie*, ADIZs are functionally defined areas that do not give rise to a conflict if the interception procedures are strictly confined to national airspace. Any future attempts to codify the concept of ADIZs in a treaty may avoid the issue of conflicts in the first place, or at least, should include an explicit conflict clause in relation to the law of the sea.[303]

It is undeniable that specific rules may diverge from the general rule.[304] However, treaties and customary law do not exist in a legal vacuum; they are embedded within a complex system of international law. The freedom of overflight is certainly of customary nature and applies in any dispute concerning the concept of ADIZs. The challenge ahead is to find a balance between the specialized regime of ADIZs and the importance of maintaining an overall framework of legal security and coherence. In order to prevent any conflict between the law and the sea and ADIZs, it is advisable to address the issue through a process of closer cooperation and coordination between the different treaty organs, institutions, and organisations, such as ICAO and IMO.

---

301 On normative conflicts, see Dorota M Banaszewska, 'Lex specialis' in *Max Planck Encyclopaedias of Public International Law* (OUP 2015) para. 3. Normative conflicts exist where two norms are incompatible with each other, whereas the following situations can be identified: First, contradictory norms, i.e. one norm prescribes a conduct, while the other norm prohibits the same conduct; and second, opposing norms, where both norms have at least partially the same scope of application but stipulate a conduct that cannot be complied with at the same time.

302 The *Norstar Case* in this regard is an exemption to the general line of jurisprudence which in principle allows prescriptive jurisdiction in areas beyond national territory.

303 A conflict clause can, for example, be found in Art. 103 UN-Charter or Art. 8 NATO treaty, giving priority over any existing and future treaties.

304 Joost Paulweyn, 'Fragmentation of International Law' in *Max Planck Encyclopaedias of Public International Law* (Oxford University Press 2006) para. 39; Silvia Zorzetto, 'The Lex Specialis Principle and Its Use in Legal Argumentation: An Analytical Inquiry' (2012–2013) 3 Eunomía Revista en Cultura de la Legalidad 61.

3 The Dual Legal Status of Airspace above the Exclusive Economic Zone

Since the concept of an ADIZ is not explicitly regulated in any treaty text, uncertainties exist as regards the exact scope of personal and territorial application of the zone. The current debate offers three different solutions concerning the legal status of ADIZs: (1) ADIZs are limited to national airspace above the territorial sea; (2) ADIZs are part of the airspace above the high seas with exclusive security rights in favour of the coastal State; or (3) ADIZs are *sui generis* zones following the model of the EEZ.

As mentioned above, customary international law as well as conventional sources relate the status of the airspace with the legal status of the territory and the sea beneath it.[305] UNCLOS generally differentiates between sovereign waters, on the one hand, and waters not subject to sovereignty claims on the other hand, and expressively also refers to the status of the airspace above the waters.[306] For example, Art. 2 UNCLOS provides for the sovereignty of the coastal State over its territorial waters extending to the airspace above it. Similarly, sovereignty of the archipelagic State over waters enclosed by the archipelagic baseline extends to the airspace above it pursuant to Art. 49 UNCLOS. The principle of sovereignty in airspace above the territorial sea is without any doubt irrefutable and does not extend to airspace above the high seas.[307] Despite the limitation of sovereignty to national airspace in the sense of Art. 2 UNCLOS, aspects of functionality in airspace above the high seas are not *per se* excluded.[308] A comparison may be drawn with the three different types of functional marine areas provided by UNCLOS: (1) marine areas with full sovereignty and jurisdictional powers, (2) marine areas with limited jurisdiction and sovereign rights, and (3) marine areas located beyond national jurisdiction.[309] The EEZ falls within the second type of marine areas and qualifies as a *sui generis* zone with dual legal status. Sovereignty claims over the EEZ are invalid, but

305 *Nicaragua Case* (1986), para. 212.

306 Sarah Wolf, 'Territorial Sea' in *Max Planck Encyclopaedias of Public International Law* (OUP 2013) para 1.

307 For the high seas, Art. 89 UNCLOS stipulates that no State may purport to subject any part of the high seas to its sovereignty.

308 See for example Annex 2 of the Chicago Convention attributing jurisdiction to States providing air traffic services in FIR in international airspace.

309 Dorota Pyc, *The Role of the Law of the Sea in Marine Spatial Planning* (Springer 2019) 377, 378.

States can exercise jurisdiction and sovereign rights within the zone.[310] The airspace above the EEZ may likewise incur a dual legal status, namely the status of non-sovereign airspace where States enjoy functional jurisdiction and rights without risking any change of the territorial status.

3.1 *The Systemic and Evolutive Interpretation of International Air Law*

A treaty will normally be subject to interpretation and application according to its own terms, however, in certain cases, it may be necessary to refer to relevant rules outside the regime of the treaty. All international legal obligations are part of a wider legal system and the content of international law changes and develops continuously.[311] It is therefore not excluded that legal developments in the law of the sea have had an effect on the status of the airspace above the sea.[312] The concept of the EEZ and the freedom of the high seas are rules of customary international law and are likewise relevant for the interpretation of the Chicago Convention in cases where a State is not party to UNCLOS.[313] Following the two types of normative relationships, namely relationships of interpretation, and relationships of conflict,[314] the issue here at stake falls in the first category, as the law of the seas may assist in the interpretation of international air law.

The Chicago Convention as the "old treaty" has to be interpreted by taking into account deviations brought to it by the "new treaty" UNCLOS. As already described in chapter 4 of this book, the Chicago Convention does not offer a definition on the airspace above the high seas or the airspace above territorial waters. Key terms remain, therefore, unclear and open-textured. Particularly, Art. 12 of the Chicago Convention is a prime example of a norm where material sources external to the treaty, such as other treaties or customary international law, have to be taken into consideration.[315] The Chicago Convention does not

310 Alexander Proelß, 'Article 55 – Specific Legal Regime of the Exclusive Economic Zone' in Alexander Proelß (ed), *United Nations Convention on the Law of the Sea: A Commentary* (Nomos 2017) 409.

311 Campbell McLachlan, 'The Principle of Systemic Integration and Article 31(3)(c) of the Vienna Convention' (2005) 54 Int'l and Comp L Quarterly 282.

312 Peter Dutton, 'Caelum Liberam: Air Defense Identification Zones Outside Sovereign Airspace' (2009) 103 AJIL 3.

313 Mark Villiger, *Customary International Law and Treaties: A Manual on the Theory and Practice of the Interrelation of Sources* (Brill 1997) 5.

314 ILC, 'Conclusions of the Work of the Study Group on the Fragmentation of International Law: Difficulties arising from the Diversification and Expansion of International Law' (2006) para. 251 (2).

315 On the interpretation of Art. 12 and the notion of rules in force over the high seas, see chapter 2, 6.4 as well as chapter 3, 1.2.

exist independently from other relevant rules of international law.[316] Above all, customary international law has to be taken into account as it builds the foundation of the international legal order due to its pervasive and more general nature.[317]

Treaties may be interpreted by taking into consideration other primary extrinsic norms.[318] Art. 31 (3) (c) VCLT deals with the case where material sources external to the treaty are relevant in its interpretation, as "any relevant rules of international law applicable in the relations between the parties" shall be taken into account.[319] In order to achieve a consistent meaning, Art. 31 (3) (c) includes other treaties, customary rules or general principles of law.[320] The foundation of this principle is the idea that treaties are necessarily limited in scope and their application is conditioned to being part of the international law system.[321] The underlying ratio of systematic interpretation is to promote a coherent international legal system taking into account relevant developments in different fields of international law. For example, in the *Oil Platforms Case* the ICJ applied Art. 31(3) VCLT to create a bridge between a Treaty of Friendship and the customary international law of armed conflict.[322] Similarly, the ILC explained on the notion of other relevant rules:

> Such other rules are of particular relevance where parties to the treaty under interpretation are also parties to the other treaty, where the treaty rule has passed into or expresses customary international law or where they provide evidence of the common understanding of the parties as to the object and purpose of the treaty under interpretation or as to the meaning of a particular term.[323]

---

316 See on the application of Art. 31 (3) (c) VCLT; *Oil Platforms* (*Iran v United States*) (Merits) [2003] ICJ Rep 161, para. 41 (hereinafter: *Oil Platforms Case*).

317 Ibid, para. 251 (18); Campbell McLachlan, 'The Principle of Systemic Integration and Article 31(3)(c) of the Vienna Convention' (2005) 54 Int'l and Comp L Quarterly 282, 283.

318 Nele Matz-Lück, 'Norm Interpretation across International Regimes: Competences and Legitimacy' Legitimacy' in Margaret A Young (ed), *Regime Interaction in International Law: Facing Fragmentation* (Cambridge University Press 2012) 211, 212.

319 Panos Merkouris, 'Principle of Systemic Interpretation' in *Max Planck Encyclopaedias of Public International Law* (OUP 2020) para 2, stating that Art. 31 (3) VCLT is also a rules of customary international law.

320 ILC Study Group, 'Fragmentation of International Law: Difficulties arising from the Diversification and Expansion of International Law' (2006) UN Doc A/CN.4/L.702, 18.

321 Campbell McLachlan, 'The Principle of Systemic Integration and Article 31(3)(c) of the Vienna Convention' (2005) 54 Int'l and Comp L Quarterly 280.

322 *Oil Platforms Case* para. 41.

323 ILC Study Group, 'Fragmentation of International Law: Difficulties arising from the Diversification and Expansion of International Law' (2006) UN Doc A/CN.4/L.702, 21.

As already mentioned, the Chicago Convention relies on its interpretation to norms of another regime, namely the law of the sea. One can therefore argue, that the rules governing the differentiation between territorial sea, EEZ, and high seas, are relevant rules of international law for the interpretation of the Chicago Convention. In accordance with the principle of harmonization, multiple international norms are to be interpreted to give rise to coexistence.[324] When States are bound by obligations from different treaties, they ought to mutually accommodate them as far as possible.[325] *Koskenniemi* highlights the interaction between different regimes to the extent that one regime becomes part of the "daily routine and self-understanding" of another regime.[326] The point of convergence is the proximity between the rule referred to and the interpreted rule.[327] A subject matter proximity exists in this case, where the rules deal with the same issue.[328] In the *Nicaragua Case*, the ICJ pointed out the proximity between the two areas of international air law and the law of the sea:

> As to superjacent air space, the 1944 Chicago Convention on International Civil Aviation (Art. 1) reproduces the established principle of the complete and exclusive sovereignty of a State over the air space above its territory. That convention, in conjunction with the 1958 Geneva Convention on the Territorial Sea, further specifies that the sovereignty of the coastal State extends to the territorial sea and to the air space above it, as does the United Nations Convention on the Law of the Sea adopted on 10 December 1982. The Court has no doubt that these prescriptions of treaty-law merely respond to firmly established and longstanding tenets of customary international law.[329]

The reference to territorial waters and the high seas for determining the legal status of airspace shows the two regimes' tangle.[330] The principle of systemic

---

324 Ibid, 8, stating that it "is a generally accepted principle that when several norms bear on a single issue they should, to the extent possible, be interpreted so as to give rise to a single set of compatible obligations."

325 Ibid, 26, regarding the lex posterior rule.

326 Martti Koskenniemi, 'Hegemonic Regimes' in Margaret A Young (ed), *Regime Interaction in International Law: Facing Fragmentation* (Cambridge University Press 2012) 319.

327 Panos Merkouris, 'Principle of Systemic Interpretation' in *Max Planck Encyclopaedias of Public International Law* (OUP 2020) para 49.

328 *Oil Platforms Case* para. 46; Richard Gardiner, *Treaty Interpretation* (2nd edn, OUP 2015) 299.

329 *Nicaragua Case* (1986) para. 212.

330 Chicago Convention, Art. 2 and Art. 12.

integration can on occasion overlap with other principles of interpretation. Relevant to the current debate is also the principle of evolutive interpretation, which is prompted either by an evolution of fact or evolution of law.[331] It is in the latter case that a connection can be made with the principle of systemic integration.[332] The underlying idea is that the meaning of a treaty provision can be affected by subsequent developments in customary law, general principles of law as well as treaties.[333] *Merkouris* concretizes that if the parties intended the treaty and its provisions to evolve, then similarly the 'relevant rules' should be those contemporaneous to the application of the treaty.[334]

Correspondingly, the ICJ observed in the *Namibia Case* that "an international instrument has to be interpreted and applied within the framework of the entire legal system prevailing at the time of the interpretation" and that these principles are "not limited to the rules of international law applicable at the time the treaty was concluded."[335] The *corpus iuris gentium* can therefore be enriched by important legal developments.[336] This is particularly the case for a concept with a very general nature or when a concept is expressed in such general terms that it must take into account changing circumstances.[337] The impact of the EEZ on the Chicago Convention may be a good example of regime interaction in the context of the law of the sea and international air law.[338] The creation of the EEZ is without any doubt a major development influencing the status of the sea and the airspace above it. *Hafner* and *Tuerk* point out that the geographical scope of the high seas was in fact reduced by the creation of the EEZ and argue that

> By taking into account creeping national jurisdiction in the second half of the 20th century, the Convention has reduced the high seas with

---

331 Theodore Georgopoulos, 'Le Droit Intertemporel et les Dispositions Conventionnelles Évolutives – Thérapie Contre la Vieillesse des Traités?' (2004) 108 RGDIP 123ff; Eirik Bjorge, *The Evolutionary Interpretation of Treaties* (OUP 2014).

332 Panos Merkouris, 'Principle of Systemic Interpretation' in *Max Planck Encyclopaedias of Public International Law* (OUP 2020) para. 50.

333 Ibid at 50; also the traditional rule was stated in the *Island of Palmas Case* (*The Netherlands v United States of America*) [1928] UNRIAA, vol. II, at 845.

334 Ibid para. 51.

335 *Legal Consequences for States of the Continued Presence of South Africa in Namibia* (*South West Africa*) *notwithstanding Security Council Resolution 276* [*1970*] (Advisory Opinion) [1971] ICJ Rep 16 para. 53.

336 Ibid para. 53.

337 ILC Study Group, 'Fragmentation of International Law: Difficulties arising from the Diversification and Expansion of International Law' (2006) UN Doc A/CN.4/L.702 23.

338 Ibid 8.

> maritime areas 200 nautical miles from the baselines, which are within national jurisdiction, so that the high seas today cover only around 61 percent of the oceans.[339]

A similar "creeping jurisdiction" was identified by *Cuadra* in relation to the establishment of ADIZs in international airspace.[340] It can therefore be argued, that the influence of the EEZ on the interpretation of the "high seas" bears also importance for the interpretation of the notion of "high seas" as referred to in the text of the Chicago Convention.

3.2 *ADIZs as Sui Generis Zones*

In *sui generis* zones, the State proclaims and exercises specific functional rights.[341] In the law of the sea exclusive fishing zones, ecological protection zones, and the EEZ are characterized as *sui generis* zones.[342] The establishment of a sui generis zone is typically justified by special considerations, such as geographic or political factors. In the case of ADIZs, the motivation is undoubtedly political in nature, namely to guarantee national security by identifying aircraft. The absence of any treaty provision on ADIZs has the consequence of generating confusion and uncertainty regarding the extent to which national rules are applicable to them. Indeed, it is not always easy to identify the relevant ADIZ rules through official proclamations, domestic legislation, and other unilateral acts.[343]

Whether the Chicago Convention may be interpreted in accordance with the rules of UNCLOS and customary international law or may be modified by subsequent practice derived from treaty practice within a different legal field, has to be considered under the aspects of the nature of the treaty, the type of treaty obligations and provisions providing for an adaptation mechanism.[344] A balance can be achieved between the core concepts of the Chicago Convention

339 Gerhard Hafner & Helmut Tuerk, 'The United Nations Convention on the Law of the Sea, 1982: Reflections after 40 Years' (2022) 36 Ocean Yearbook 7.

340 Elisabeth Cuadra, 'Air Defense Identification Zones: Creeping Jurisdiction in the Airspace' (1977) 18 Virginia Journal of International Law 491.

341 Gemma Andreone & Giuseppe Cataldi, 'Sui Generis Zones' in David J Attard, Malgosia Fitzmaurice, & Norman A Martínez Gutiérrez (eds), *The IMLI Manual on International Maritime Law: Volume I: The Law of the Sea* (2014) 218.

342 Ibid 219.

343 This aspect is discussed in depth in chapter 3.

344 It has to be stressed that modification by the means of practice in other regimes may not undermine the object and purpose of the Chicago Convention, nor its fundamental provisions. See also, Irina Buga, *Modification of Treaties by Subsequent Practice* (2009 OUP) 107.

and norms that have emerged since its adoption in other treaty regimes as well as custom as long as it is approached with due caution.

The nature of the Chicago Convention's treaty regime is characterized as a "living, adaptable constitution" which describes the relationship between the Chicago Convention and ICAO, as well as an organizational charter for international aviation.[345] Given its nature as a "living instrument", flexibility and adaptability are the main characteristics aiming to address the demands of a rapidly changing industry.[346] The nature as a living instrument refers not to the susceptibility of the object and purpose of a treaty, as they remain unaltered, but to the regulatory framework achieving those objects and purposes.[347] The Chicago Convention's object and purpose focus on the development of civil aviation in a safe and orderly manner, but it also intends to provide a model of "neofunctionalist" institution-building for mutually beneficial rules to manage technical, apolitical issues relevant for the aviation industry.[348] The fact that the Annexes to the Chicago Convention encompass substantive provisions concerning the regulation of air traffic make the Convention susceptible to evolution.[349] Therefore, there is widespread acceptance of the method of an evolutive interpretation of the Chicago Convention.[350] The understanding of the Chicago Convention as a treaty containing evolutionary provisions implies the possibility to import rules of other fields of international law. Furthermore, the open-phrased formulation of Art. 12 Chicago Convention regarding rules for international airspace grants leeway in interpreting the Chicago Convention and facilitates regime interaction. Hence, normative uncertainties can be

345 Brian F Havel & John Q Mulligan, 'International Aviation's Living Constitution: A Commentary on the Chicago Convention's Past, Present, and Future' (2015) 15 Issues Aviation L & Pol'y 9, 11.

346 Ibid 10.

347 Malgosia Fitzmaurice, 'The Practical Working of the Law of the Treaties' in Malcom D Evans (ed), *International Law* (5th edn, OUP 2018) 158.

348 Brian F Havel & John Q Mulligan, 'International Aviation's Living Constitution: A Commentary on the Chicago Convention's Past, Present, and Future' (2015) 15 Issues Aviation L & Pol'y 12.

349 See similarly, *Whaling in the Antarctic* (*Australia v Japan: New Zealand Intervening*) (Merits) [2014] ICJ Rep 226, para. 45, in which the ICJ refers to the regulatory character of the Schedule to the International Convention of the Regulation of Whaling (ICRW) rather than to the ICRW itself to determine whether the ICRW was an evolving instrument.

350 Pablo Mendes de Leon, *Behind and Beyond the Chicago Convention: The Evolution of Aerial Sovereignty* (Kluwer 2019); Ruwantissa Abeyratne, 'Competition in Air Transport and Equality' (2018) 19 J Int'l L & Trade Pol 103; Brian F Havel & John Q Mulligan, 'International Aviation's Living Constitution: A Commentary on the Chicago Convention's Past, Present, and Future' (2015) 15 Issues Aviation L & Pol'y 10.

solved under the principle of systematic integrations and evolutive interpretation linking the Chicago Convention to its legal environment.

As mentioned in chapter 4 of this book, airspace is not defined as either national or international airspace due to the lack of these terms in the legal framework of the Chicago. The delimitation of airspace and associated rights rely on the notion of the territory, including the territorial sea and the high seas.[351] The main concern raised regarding ADIZs in international airspace pertains to the 'territorialisation' effect of ADIZs and questions related to the legal status of ADIZs.[352] Yet, this controversial aspect can be rebutted by explicitly designating an ADIZ as a functional *sui generis* zone, and in a functional sense neither part of the territorial sea nor the high seas.[353] States may only be entitled to exercise functionally limited jurisdiction in an ADIZ in line with the freedom of the high seas similar to the concept of the EEZ.[354] The persistent ambiguity concerning the legal status of ADIZs stems from the insufficient differentiation between the categories of territory and function. ADIZs are at the same time part of the high seas in a territorial sense but may also form a *sui generis* zone in a functional sense. The dichotomy as either part of national airspace or international airspace does not consider the possibility of ADIZs falling within more than one category or even in neither category.[355] As regards the territorial effect of ADIZs, the zone is clearly associated with the territorial rules of the high seas regime. This is essential to the preservation of an ADIZ as a discrete zone rather than an extension of the legal regime of the national airspace. Such differentiation leads to the perspective that ADIZs can be understood as part of international airspace in terms of territory and sovereignty, whereas in terms of function, namely identification rights, it forms a *sui generis* zone. This perspective best accommodates the risk of ADIZs as

351 Art. 2 Chicago Convention states: "For the purpose of this Convention the territory of a State shall be deemed to be the land areas and the territorial waters adjacent thereto under the sovereignty, suzerainty, protection or mandate of such State." Art. 12 Chicago Convention relates to international airspace by stating: "(…) Over the high seas, the rules in force shall be those established under this Convention."

352 Elisabeth Cuadra, 'Air Defense Identification Zones: Creeping Jurisdiction in the Airspace' (1977) 18 Virginia Journal of International Law 491.

353 The ICJ declared in the *Fisheries Jurisdiction Case*, that no sovereignty claims are attached to fishery zones and the freedom of the high seas is not infringed. Also, Donald R Rothwell, 'Fishery Zones and Limits' in *Max Planck Encyclopaedias of Public International Law* (OUP 2008) para. 4.

354 Alexander Proelß, 'Article 55- Specific legal regime of the exclusive economic zone' in Alexander Proelß (ed), *United Nations Convention on the Law of the Sea: A Commentary* (Nomos 2017) 415–419.

355 Nicolas Mateesco Matte, *Treatise on Air-Aeronautical Law* (McGill University 1981) 136.

an influential factor for territorial disputes, taking into account the security concerns of the coastal States. Overlapping ADIZs therefore would not pose a conflict of sovereignty.[356]

Any interpretation distinguishing between these two aspects is also in line with the provisions of UNCLOS. For example, Art. 86 UNCLOS differentiates between the high seas and other parts of the seas, i.e. EEZ, the territorial sea, and internal waters.[357] However, this distinction concerns only the scope of application of Part VII UNCLOS, but does not define the spatial extension of the sea.[358] In contrast to its predecessor the 1958 Convention on the High Seas and its negative definition of the high seas, Art. 86 UNCLOS omits a definition of the spatial extension of the high seas.[359] The high seas regime, such as rules on the repression of piracy or unauthorized broadcasting from the high seas, apply in the EEZ as far as it is not displaced by rights specifically allocated to the coastal State.[360] Only the high seas freedoms of Art. 87 are not curtailed in the EEZ in accordance with Art. 58 UNCLOS.[361] The establishment of the EEZ does not diminish the area of the high seas. Therefore, it cannot be assumed that the high seas begin where the EEZ ends, namely at the point of 200nm.[362] The EEZ's nature as a *sui generis* zone simply provides for the spatial scope of application of the high seas provisions contained in part VII UNCLOS. It is therefore not excluded that the EEZ is to be regarded as part of the high seas in a territorial sense.[363] Similarly, ADIZs above the EEZ are to be regarded as

356 Stefan A Kaiser, 'The Legal Status of Air Defense Identification Zones: Tensions over the East China Sea' (2016) 63 ZLW 536, stating that States do not enjoy sovereign rights in an ADIZ.

357 Art. 86 UNCLOS states: "The provisions of this Part apply to all parts of the sea that are not included in the exclusive economic zone, in the territorial sea or in the internal waters of a State (...)."

358 Alexander Proelß, 'Article 55- Specific legal regime of the exclusive economic zone' in Alexander Proelß (ed), *United Nations Convention on the Law of the Sea: A Commentary* (Nomos 2017) 417.

359 Art. 1 Convention on the High Seas (1958): "The term "high seas" means all parts of the sea that are not included in the territorial sea or in the internal waters of a State."

360 Douglas Guilfoyle, 'Article 86- Application of the Provisions of this Part' in Alexander Proelß (ed), *United Nations Convention on the Law of the Sea: A Commentary* (Nomos 2017) 676.

361 Douglas Guilfoyle, 'The High Seas' in Donald R Rothwell et al (eds), *Oxford Handbook of the Law of the Sea* (OUP 2015) 205.

362 Douglas Guilfoyle, 'Article 86 – Application of the Provisions of this Part' in Alexander Proelß (ed), *United Nations Convention on the Law of the Sea: A Commentary* (Nomos 2017), p. 676.

363 Rene-Jean Dupuy, 'The Sea under National Competence' in Rene Jean Dupuy & Daniel Vignes (eds), *A Handbook on the New Law of the Sea, Volume 1* (1991) 290.

part of the high seas in a territorial sense. This interpretation avoids exposure to the potential for ADIZs to contribute to the hardening of disputed territorial claims. A functional approach underlines that no claim of sovereignty can be derived from ADIZs, and that the high seas regime is consistent with the functions assumed by the State in relation to ADIZs. The unified character of the oceans is therefore reflected in the functional application of airspace.

3.2.1 ADIZ Do Not Exist Ipso Facto and Ab Initio

The coexistence of areas is a concept not unknown to the law of the seas, as Art. 78 (1) UNCLOS provides for the relationship between the high seas and the continental shelf beyond 200 nm.[364] Art. 78 (1) regulates the legal status of the superjacent waters and air space and the rights and freedoms of other States over the continental shelf, without clarifying whether they are part of the high seas. The main purpose of Art. 78 (1) serves to reassure States, that even though States enjoy sovereign rights and extended jurisdiction over the continental shelf, this extension does not affect the legal status of the superjacent waters and airspace over the continental shelf.[365] *Brown* proposes that this omission implies the continental shelf waters coinciding with the EEZ are not part of the high seas but are part of the *sui generis* regime of the EEZ.[366] In this line of reasoning, ADIZs may also coincide with the EEZ without contradicting the territorial status of airspace above the EEZ and issues of sovereignty. It is therefore possible to extend jurisdiction in matters of aerial security for the purpose of identifying aircraft without interfering with the rights and freedoms of the high seas and without claiming sovereignty. The airspace referred to in Art. 78 is subject to the principle that sovereign airspace is tied to its sovereign territory, and consequently, the freedom of overflight applies to the airspace above these waters.

As mentioned above, the continental shelf exists as a natural prolongation *ipso facto* and *ab initio*.[367] In contrast, the legal status of the superjacent

364 Ted L McDorman, 'The Continental Shelf' in Donald R. Rothwell et al (eds), *Oxford Handbook of the Law of the Sea* (OUP 2015) 200.

365 Amber Maggio, 'Article 78 – Legal Status of the Superjacent Waters and Air Space and the Rights and Freedoms of other States' in Alexander Proelß (ed), *United Nations Convention on the Law of the Sea: A Commentary* (Nomos 2017) 615.

366 Edward D Brown, 'The Exclusive Economic Zone: Criteria and Machinery for the Resolution of International Conflicts between Different Users of the EEZ' (1977) 4 Maritime Policy and Management 325, 339.

367 *North Sea Continental Shelf* (*Federal Republic of Germany v Denmark; Federal Republic of Germany v Netherlands*) (Merits) [1969] ICJ Rep 3, para. 19; see also, Ted L McDorman,

waters depends on the actual claim by the coastal State.[368] *Maggio* describes the relationship between the continental shelf and EEZ that "(t)he legal status of the waters above the continental shelf is not determined by reference to the shelf, but rather the limits of the EEZ of the relevant coastal State."[369] In the absence of a coastal State claiming an EEZ, no EEZ exists and the waters above the continental shelf are to be regarded as high seas.[370] Regardless of whether the superjacent waters to the continental shelf are classified as high seas or qualify as an EEZ, the freedom of overflight must be respected in both cases.[371] The EEZ can serve as a useful model for the establishment for ADIZS. Similarly, ADIZS are not regarded as autonomous legal institutions, independently and automatically attributed to the coastal State. Rather their existence depends on whether the coastal State has claimed an ADIZ.

3.2.2 Conflicts on Unattributed Rights and Jurisdiction in the EEZ

Following the "concept of dual legal status of the EEZ"[372] and its qualification as *sui generis* zone, the freedom of the high seas experiences differentiation in the EEZ. Generally, Art. 59 UNCLOS provides for a basis for the peaceful resolution of conflicts regarding unattributed rights and jurisdiction between the coastal State and other States in the EEZ.[373] Art. 59 UNCLOS reads as follows:

> In cases where this Convention does not attribute rights or jurisdiction to the coastal State or to other States within the exclusive economic zone, and a conflict arises between the interests of the coastal State and any other State or States, the conflict should be resolved on the basis of equity

'The Continental Shelf' in Donald R. Rothwell et al (eds.) *Oxford Handbook of the Law of the Sea* (OUP 2015) 183.

368 Shani Friedman, 'The Concept of Entitlement to an Exclusive Economic Zone as Reflected in International Judicial Decisions' (2020) 53 Israel L Rev 101.

369 Amber Maggio, 'Article 78- Legal Status of the Superjacent Waters and Air Space and the Rights and Freedoms of other States' in Alexander Proelß (ed), *United Nations Convention on the Law of the Sea: A Commentary* (Nomos 2017) 616.

370 Alexander Proelß, 'Article 55- Specific Legal Regime of the Exclusive Economic Zone' in Alexander Proelß (ed), *United Nations Convention on the Law of the Sea: A Commentary* (Nomos 2017) 417.

371 Amber Maggio, 'Article 78- Legal Status of the Superjacent Waters and Air Space and the Rights and Freedoms of other States' in Alexander Proelß (ed), *United Nations Convention on the Law of the Sea: A Commentary* (Nomos 2017) 617.

372 Alexander Proelß, 'Article 55- Specific Legal Regime of the Exclusive Economic Zone' in Alexander Proelß (ed), *United Nations Convention on the Law of the Sea: A Commentary* (Nomos 2017) 417.

373 Art. 59 UNCLOS.

> and in the light of all the relevant circumstances, taking into account the respective importance of the interests involved to the parties as well as to the international community as a whole.

The list of rights and freedoms enshrined in Art. 56 and 58 UNCLOS are not exhaustive, and conflicting claims can be solved on the basis of Art. 59 UNCLOS.[374] Art. 56 UNCLOS provides for jurisdiction of the coastal State but does not prescribe exhaustively the areas in which the coastal State has regulatory powers. Moreover, Art. 56 (1)(c) serves as a catch-all clause clarifying that, in addition to the rights in paragraph 1 (a) and (b), also "other rights and duties provided for in this Convention" are part of the coastal State's powers.[375] Art. 59 is applicable as backup clause in case of a conflict on rights and duties not included in Art. 56 and Art. 58.[376] It is important to mention that Art. 59 is not limited to the scope of Art. 56(1) and 58(1) UNCLOS.[377] As stated by Judge *Vukas* in his separate opinion in the *M/V Saiga Case*:

> Article 59 of the Convention itself is a confirmation of the awareness of States participating in UNCLOS III that the specific legal regime they have established has not attributed all possible rights and jurisdiction to the coastal States or to other States.[378]

The scope of the coastal State's jurisdiction has to be assessed by taking into account other rules and principles of UNCLOS, and it might be argued that the coastal State enjoys regulatory authority over aircraft. The right of overflight above the EEZ is granted in Art. 58, which provides for "the freedoms referred to in Art. 87 of navigation and overflight and the laying of submarine cables and pipelines, and other internationally lawful uses of the sea related to these freedoms."[379] In contrast, the other three freedoms of Art. 87, i.e. the freedom

374 Malcom D Evans, 'The Law of the Sea' in Malcom D Evans (ed), *International Law* (5th edn, OUP 2018) 659.

375 Alexander Proelß, 'Article 56- Rights, Jurisdiction and Duties of the Coastal State in the Exclusive Economic Zone' in Alexander Proelß (ed), *United Nations Convention on the Law of the Sea: A Commentary* (Nomos 2017) 429, 430.

376 Ibid, 460.

377 Ibid, 460.

378 *The M/V 'Saiga' (Saint Vincent and the Grenadines v Guinea)* (Judgment of 22 December 1999, Sep. Op. Vukas) ITLOS Reports 1999, 10, para. 21.

379 Art. 58 UNCLOS: "In the exclusive economic zone, all States, whether coastal or land-locked, enjoy, subject to the relevant provisions of this Convention, the freedoms referred to in article 87 of navigation and overflight and of the laying of submarine cables and pipelines (...)."

to construct artificial islands and other installations permitted under international law, the freedom of fishing, and the freedom of scientific research, are not part of the balancing test of Art. 59 UNCLOS.[380] Pursuant to Art. 58 (3) States have to comply with the laws and regulations adopted by the coastal State when exercising rights over the EEZ and hence includes rights with limiting effect on the freedom of overflight and the freedom of navigation.[381] The right of navigation and the right of overflight experience limitations within the EEZ and therefore do not have the identical spectrum of application as on the high seas.[382]

Claims of jurisdictional powers over aircraft in the airspace above the EEZ may fall within the scope of unattributed rights according to Art. 59 UNCLOS. This rule can be referred to either for competences not anticipated at the time of the adoption or where States disagree on the attribution of an established competence.[383] A prime example of rights not explicitly allocated by UNCLOS concerns military manoeuvres conducted on the high seas as well as in airspace above the EEZ.[384] Military aspects are of particular relevance for the application of the ADIZ's rules, as military aircraft are not covered by the scope of the Chicago Convention. The right to restrict or the right to conduct military manoeuvres in the EEZ is neither explicitly provided in Art. 56 nor mentioned in Art. 58 UNCLOS.[385] It can thus be argued that Art. 59 UNCLOS applies to the specific case of regulating military manoeuvres within the EEZ.[386] While one argument highlights that the freedom of overflight in general encompasses military uses of airspace, such as aerial reconnaissance or

380 Art. 78 (d)-(f) UNCLOS.

381 Jan Wouters & Bruno Demeyere, 'Overflight' in *Max Planck Encyclopaedias of Public International Law* (OUP 2008) para. 26.

382 Gemma Andreone, 'The Exclusive Economic Zone' in Donald R Rothwell et al (eds), *Oxford Handbook of the Law of the Sea* (OUP 2015) 178.

383 Rüdiger Wolfrum, 'Proportionality: Reconsidering the Application of an Established Principle in International Law' (2022) 99 Int'l Stud 684.

384 Sienho Yee, 'Sketching the Debate on Military Activities in the EEZ: An Editorial Comment' (2010) 9 Chinese Journal of International Law 3; Georg V Galdorisi & Alan G Kaufman, 'Military Activities in the Exclusive Economic Zone: Preventing Uncertainty and Defusing Conflict' (2002) 32 California Western Int'l L J 253.

385 Jon M Van Dyke, 'Military Ships and Planes Operating in the Exclusive Economic Zone of another Country' (2004) 28 Marine Policy 31.

386 Alan V Lowe, 'Some Legal Problems Arising from the Use of the Seas for Military Purposes' (1986) 10 Marine Pol J 180; Tullio Scovazzi, 'The Evolution of the International Law of the Sea: Issues, New Challenges' (2000) 286 RCADI 166–167. Contra: Zhang Haiwen, 'Is it Safeguarding the Freedom of Navigation or Maritime Hegemony of the United States? Comments on Paul Pedrozo's Article on Military Activities in the EEZ' (2010) 9 Chinese J Int'l L 31–47.

military exercises, it remains unclear whether Art. 58 includes this broad range of activities.[387] Another view proposes that the coastal State may restrict military maneuverers within its EEZ.[388] The exact scope of rights and jurisdiction stipulated by Art. 59 UNCLOS remains a controversial topic that also concerns the regulation of flights in ADIZs above the EEZ. A factual example shows the problem concerned with military activities in airspace above the EEZ and its connection with the rules of UNCLOS.

In 2001, while the United States conducted a surveillance flight along the coast of China, the US EP-3 surveillance aircraft collided with a Chinese F-8 fighter, about 70nm southeast of Hainan Island, causing the death of the Chinese pilot.[389] Following the EP-3 incident, China argued that the US flight "violated the United Nations Convention on the Law of the Sea, which stipulates that any flight in airspace above another nation's exclusive economic zone should respect the rights of the country concerned. Thus the US plane's actions posed a serious threat to the national security of China."[390] Further, China emphasized that the freedom of overflight above the EEZ has to be balanced against the security interests of the coastal State. The case-by-case assessment and the balancing test provided by Art. 59 offer the conclusion that the security situation in the airspace above the EEZ as well as the intentions of the State conducting the operation cannot be left unconsidered.[391]

While some States claim regulatory powers for foreign military vessels and aircraft, other countries do not restrict military manoeuvres within their EEZ.[392] The US position differs considerably from China's argument and emphasises that the coastal State has no right to regulate military activities within its EEZ and any limitation on military navigation would be contrary to the freedom of the high seas.[393] Part of the discussion of military activities

387 Kay Hailbronner, 'The Legal Regime of the Airspace above the Exclusive Economic Zone' (1983) 8 Air & Space Law 32.

388 Edmund J Burke & Astrid Stuth Cevallos, *In Line or out of Order? – Chinas Approach to ADIZ in Theory and Practice* (Rand 2017) 9.

389 Eric Donnelly, 'The United States–China EP-3 Incident: Legality and "Realpolitik"' (2004) 9 J Conflict & Sec L 25.

390 Spokesman Zhu Bangzao, Ministry of Foreign Affairs of the People's Republic of China (4 April 2001).

391 Alexander Proelß, 'Article 59- Basis for the Resolution of Conflicts Regarding the Attribution of Rights and Jurisdiction in the Exlusive Economic Zone' in Alexander Proelß (ed), *United Nations Convention on the Law of the Sea: A Commentary* (Nomos 2017) 462.

392 Ronald O'Rourke, 'Maritime Territorial and Exclusive Economic Zone (EEZ) Disputes Involving China: Issues for Congress' (2016) Congressional Research Service 11.

393 Raul Pedrozo, 'The Bull in the China Shop: Raising Tensions in the Asia-Pacific Region' (2014) 90 International Law Studies 83.

is the creation of "prohibited zones", "warning zones" or "temporary security zones" serving the purpose to warn ships and aircraft about military exercises on the high seas. "Warning zones" and "temporary security zones" are considered legal as they do not prohibit the entry of ships or aircraft and thus do not constitute a blockade.[394] Even though military manoeuvres in the EEZ are assessed controversially, similar considerations can be applied in the context of ADIZS, as they were initially designed to provide coastal security by identifying planes estimated to enter national airspace.

The issue of gradual expansion of the coastal States' jurisdiction and related risks of excessive restriction of the freedom of navigation has been examined in the past.[395] Previous discussions have focused on the ambiguities in the interpretation and application of maritime rights, but have not yet addressed the relevance of jurisdiction in airspace above the EEZ. Neither Art. 56 nor Art. 58 UNCLOS refer explicitly to aerial jurisdiction due to the fact that the implications of air law were not fully considered during the drafting period of UNCLOS.[396] Not only civil aircraft are affected by the identification procedures of ADIZS; these procedures likewise apply to military aircraft. Conflicts on the application of ADIZS' rules on civil as well as military aircraft may hence be solved under the mechanism of Art. 59 UNCLOS. This provision involves a weighing process on the basis of equity and taking into consideration community interests.[397] The hypothesis that an ADIZ follows the same dual legal status as the EEZ suggests that a presumption in favour of the coastal State can be assumed in terms of function.[398] In contrast, matters of territorial concerns would be solved in favour of the interest of other States due to

394 Kenneth F Schwetje, 'Protecting Space Assets: A Legal Analysis of "Keep-Out Zones"' (1987) 15 Journal of Space Law 135.

395 Albert J Hoffmann, 'Freedom of Navigation' in *Max Planck Encyclopaedias of Public International Law* (OUP 2011) para. 4.

396 John K Gamble, 'Law of the Sea: Neglected Issues' (1979) III Air Space and the Law of the Sea 119. Contra: Kay Hailbronner, 'Freedom of the Air and the Convention on the Law of the Sea' (1983) 77 AJIL 516, stating that "Article 59 must not be considered as carte blanche for claims of jurisdiction in all cases where the Convention does not attribute such rights or jurisdiction."

397 Rüdiger Wolfrum, 'Proportionality: Reconsidering the Application of an Established Principle in International Law' (2022) 99 Int'l Stud 684.

398 Alexander Proelß, 'The Law of the Exclusive Economic Zone in Perspective: Legal Status and Resolution of User Conflicts Revisited' (2012) 26 Ocean Yearbook 87–112. Contra: Douglas Guilfoyle, 'Article 86- Application of the Provisions of this Part' in Alexander Proelß (ed), *United Nations Convention on the Law of the Sea: A Commentary* (Nomos 2017) 677, stating that "there is no clear presumption in favour of either the coastal State rights or navigating States' freedoms in the EEZ in the event of any conflict."

the territorial status as airspace above the high seas. This assumption would minimize the risk of extending jurisdiction beyond the purpose of identifying aircraft or even extending sovereign claims.

Should the airspace above the EEZ no longer be considered airspace above the high seas,[399] then Art. 12 Chicago Convention could be reinterpreted. The rules in force on the high seas as established by ICAO would remain applicable in the airspace above the EEZ, however, supplemented by the ADIZ rules for its status as an independent new zone. The quasi-legislative authority of ICAO would still apply to the airspace above the high seas and need not necessarily be limited to the high seas in the understanding of UNCLOS, namely areas adjacent to the EEZ. The creation of a legal gap in the framework of the Chicago Convention can thus be avoided. The regulative authority in the airspace above the EEZ is attributed to either ICAO for rules regulating the flight and manoeuvre of aircraft in the sense of Art. 12 Chicago Convention or the coastal State for matters of national security and defence.[400] States nevertheless have to respect the freedom of overflight when establishing an ADIZ in airspace above the EEZ. Likewise, States exercising their right of freedom of navigation and overflight have the obligation to comply with the laws and regulations adopted by the coastal State in accordance with UNCLOS and other rules of international law.[401]

4 The UNCLOS Dispute Settlement Mechanism Applicable to ADIZs

In the previous subsection, the application of Art. 59 UNCLOS on ADIZs was discussed. ADIZs might be an unattributed right of the coastal State and potential conflicts with the rights of any other State have to be solved on a case-by-case analysis. Yet, if ADIZs are not encompassed by the scope of Art. 59 then it seems reasonable to evaluate whether a defence zone for identification purposes is itself part of the lawful uses of the high seas. In this case, ADIZs are subject to the balancing test of Art. 87(2) UNCLOS, and above an EEZ limited to the freedoms pursuant to Art. 58(1) UNCLOS.

399 Albert J Hoffmann, 'Freedom of Navigation' in *Max Planck Encyclopaedias of Public International Law* (OUP 2011) para. 15.

400 See on the argument that the regulatory competence of ICAO does not include matters of national security, above chapter 2, 6.6.2.

401 Albert J Hoffmann, 'Freedom of Navigation' in *Max Planck Encyclopaedias of Public International Law* (OUP 2011) para. 6.

High seas shall be open to all States with unhindered access and use of sea areas, preventing any interference from States, and prohibiting the establishment of sovereignty.[402] Under the principle of equality, all States ought to enjoy identical and equal rights on the high seas for all possible uses.[403] The freedom of the high seas is not absolute but a set of competing norms.[404] The freedom of the high seas is enjoyed by all States, and in their enjoyment restrict each other. Also, the freedoms of the high seas are subject to the specific limitations set out in UNCLOS and other relevant rules.[405] This is of relevance for the case where an ADIZ of one State overlaps with the ADIZ above the EEZ of another State, or where two or more ADIZs overlap. Art. 58 (1) UNCLOS limits the freedom of the high seas within the EEZ to navigation, overflight, and laying of submarine cables and "other internationally lawful uses of the sea related to these freedoms, such as those associated with the operation of ships, aircraft and submarine cables and pipelines". This limitation in the first place ought to concern the freedoms of other States in relation to the sovereign rights and jurisdiction of the coastal State. The wording of Art. 58 (1) UNCLOS explicitly states that "all States, whether coastal or land-locked" enjoy the freedom of navigation, overflight, and the laying of submarine cables in the EEZ. The remaining freedoms as set forth in Art. 87 UNCLOS have already been subjected to the sovereign rights and jurisdiction of the coastal State by virtue of Art. 56 UNCLOS and thus needs no further mentioning.[406] It can also be argued that a right related to these freedoms is also encompassed by the scope of the non-exhaustive list of freedoms of Art. 87 UNCLOS.

The freedom of overflight and the freedom of navigation grant States the right to commence flights or unimpeded passage but do not grant the right to actively and purposively impose obligations on other States' freedoms. The main question, therefore, is, whether the establishment of ADIZs is "related to these freedoms". Art. 58 UNCLOS does not clarify how closely related the activity and the concerned freedom have to be, and also no international court or

402 Djamchid Momatz, 'Chapter 7', in René-Jean Dupuy and Daniel Vignes (eds), *A Handbook on the Law of the Sea, Volume 1* (1991 Martinus Nijhoff) 384.

403 Ibid 385.

404 Myres McDougal & Norbert Schlei, 'The Hydrogen Bomb Test in the Perspective: Lawful Measure for Security' (1955) 64 Yale L J 356.

405 Michaela Young, 'Then and Now: Reappraising Freedom of the Seas in the Modern Law of the Sea' (2016) 47 Ocean Dev & Int'l L 165, emphasizing that it needs clear parameters for restrictions in order to avoid different interpretations among States.

406 Alexander Proelß, 'Article 58- Rights and Duties in the Exclusive Economic Zone' in Alexander Proelß (ed), *United Nations Convention on the Law of the Sea: A Commentary* (Nomos 2017) 449.

tribunal has so far dealt with this issue. The International Court of Justice was once concerned with the question of how far-reaching a State can exercise its freedoms and restrict the freedom of others at the same time as regards the testing of nuclear weapons on the high seas.[407] The issue of restricted freedoms came up when France closed off areas of the Pacific for the testing of nuclear weapons in 1973. The French Government created "Prohibited Zones" for aircraft and "Dangerous Zones" for aircraft and ships, in order to exclude aircraft and ships from the area of the tests centre; these "zones" have been put into effect during the period of testing each year in which tests have been carried out. With the creation of these zones, France temporarily occupied considerable areas of the high seas. France claimed the need to conduct nuclear tests in order to guarantee its national defence. Australia was of the opinion, that nuclear tests interfere with ships and aircraft on the high seas and thus constitute an infringement of the freedom of the high seas. In relation to the infringement of the freedom of the high seas, the activity included not only the explosion of the devices involving consequent fall-out but also the act of closure of the high seas and airspace.[408] The ICJ admitted the application of interim measures because it could not be assumed *a priori* that such claims fall completely outside the Court's jurisdiction.[409] However, the matter did not reach the merits phase of the proceeding as the Court found that the Applications of Australia and New Zealand no longer had any object because France stopped the nuclear tests.[410] The question of whether nuclear tests and the creation of zones can be subsumed under a violation of the freedom of the high seas was left unresolved.[411]

Due to the unclear terminology, it remains difficult to distinguish between a right related to the freedom of the high seas and a right within the scope of Art. 59 UNCLOS. Literature proposes to rely on the consideration of the involved actors to determine an activity as closely related. An activity is sufficiently closely related to the freedoms when the conduct is considered a regular, common, or even necessary requirement of the exercise of the freedoms.[412]

407 *Nuclear Tests* (*Australia v France*) (Merits) [1974] ICJ Rep 253.

408 Memorial on Jurisdiction and Admissibility submitted by the Government of Australia, 23 November 1973, 314.

409 *Nuclear Tests* (*Australia v France*) (Interim Protection, Order of 22 June 1973) ICJ Rep 99 para. 23.

410 *Nuclear Tests* (*Australia v France*) (Merits) [1974] ICJ Rep 253.

411 Also the International Law Commission did not make any express pronouncement on the freedom to undertake nuclear weapon development tests on the high seas, see Yearbook of the International Law Commission, vol II UN Doc A/CN/SER.A/1956 (1956).

412 Alexander Proelß, 'Article 58- Rights and Duties in the Exclusive Economic Zone' in Alexander Proelß (ed), *United Nations Convention on the Law of the Sea: A Commentary* (Nomos 2017) 452–453.

Consequently, the activity has to depend on, or is inseparably linked to one of these freedoms and an autonomous exercise would provide to be pointless.[413] As a fundamental rule, the exercise of freedoms and related rights may not contradict other freedoms. It cannot be assumed that the intention of the drafter of UNCLOS was to recognize inconsistent rights within the same regime. An implied right, which would be inconsistent with an express right, would not prevail over the express right in order to avoid that *inclusio unius* results in *exclusio alterius*.[414]

Moreover, Art. 87 (2) UNCLOS stipulates that the freedom of the high seas, including the right of navigation and overflight, needs to be exercised with due regard for the interest of other States in their exercise of the freedom of the high seas. Due regard requires the foreign State to refrain from unreasonably interfering with the exercise of the rights of the other States.[415] Likewise, other States have the duty to refrain from activities, which unreasonably interfere with the freedom of navigation and other internationally unlawful uses of the sea.[416] The principle of due regard also applies to the EEZ and the rights and duties of the coastal State.[417] "Due regard" is an obscure term and does not define criteria or legal consequences.[418] In general, State should act in a manner that does not adversely affect the freedoms of other States.[419] Extensive zones with disruptive effect on navigation have to be seen critically under the principle of due regard. In case of France's atomic test, the danger zone extended to a radius of 200sm, and intruding vessels were physically removed.[420] Physical interference as a result of the established zones seems likely to be in conflict with the principle of due regard, but it would still require a balancing test.[421] The situation remains however unclear and provides little guidance as regards ADIZS. The balancing test of the due regard principle would only be applicable if one considers ADIZS as within the scope of Art. 87(1) UNCLOS. States have a range of individual national interests in the use of the high seas,

413 Ibid 453.

414 Azadon Tiewul, 'International Law and Nuclear Test Explosions on the High Seas' (1974) 8 Cornell Int'l L J 47.

415 Albert J Hoffmann, 'Freedom of Navigation' in *Max Planck Encyclopaedias of Public International Law* (OUP 2011) para. 15.

416 Ibid para. 15.

417 Art. 58 (3) UNCLOS.

418 Zhang Guobin, 'A Discussion on Due Regard in the United Nations Convention on the Law of the Sea' (2014) 2014 China Oceans L Rev 78.

419 Ibid 80.

420 William K Ris, 'French Nuclear Testing: A Crisis for International Law' (1974) 4 Denver J Int'l Law & Pol 121.

421 Bernard H Oxman, *The Regime of Warships under the United Nations Convention on the Law of the Sea* (1983–1984) 24 VJIL 809.

such as for security and safety matters. Yet, it seems rather unlikely that an ADIZ qualifies as an activity related to the freedom of the high seas.

5 Conclusion

It was argued by ICAO and commentators that ADIZs might have a negative effect on the freedom of overflight. However, an extensive analysis of different sources of international law reveals that the freedom of overflight, and the freedom of the high seas in general, are not unlimited. While there is no consensus among international jurisprudence on the legality of extraterritorial prescriptive jurisdiction, there are several reasons that may indicate that the establishment of ADIZs does not contravene the freedom of overflight. Firstly, most cases link extraterritorial prescriptive jurisdiction with the enforcement of such rules solely within the territory of the State. In the absence of a connection between the regulated activity and the effects of such activity on the State's territory, prescriptive jurisdiction is without consequences. The discussions in the *Norstar Case* demonstrate that one might argue the lawfulness of an activity as long as it does not contravene an explicit prohibition in international law. As long as States do not intercept aircraft in international airspace, i.e. do not exercise enforcement jurisdiction, the prescription of identification procedures on aircraft bound for national airspace does not contravene the freedom of overflight.

As previously discussed at the outset of this chapter, the evolutive interpretation of international air law by taking into consideration developments in the law of the sea gives rise to the necessity to consider the airspace above the EEZ differently as the airspace above the high seas. On the example of the EEZ, there might be likewise an aerial *sui generis* zone in international airspace. In light of the dual legal status of the EEZ, namely as functional zones without implications of sovereignty, it can be argued that States may also enjoy certain jurisdictional powers in the airspace above the EEZ while not changing of the territorial status. The dual legal status of the airspace prevents territorial claims, yet simultaneously does not exclude States from exercising jurisdiction for certain functional purposes. This aligns the interests of States in establishing a functional defence zone in international airspace.

It was also briefly touched upon the question of whether ADIZs can be regarded as unattributed right pursuant to Art. 59 UNCLOS. One of the most significant advantages of addressing the ADIZ concept within the framework of UNCLOS is the application to both civil and military activities. While the issue of military manoeuvre in the EEZ remains a contested matter, security activities, including the establishment of an aerial defence zone, appear to be less problematic. In support of this argument is the right of the coastal State to create safety zones around artificial islands. The potential classification of ADIZS as a "related right" to the freedom of the high seas and the application of UNCLOS' dispute settlement mechanism would have the advantage that States may refer disputes to the ICJ and clarify the status of ADIZS. However, it seems rather unlikely that ADIZS would be characterised as a related right to the freedom of overflight.

Concluding Remarks and Outlook

The main objective was to analyse the international legal framework in relation to the legality and scope of Air Defence Identification Zones in national as well as international airspace. The effect of ADIZs on solidifying territorial claims and their influence on maritime disputed areas was discussed in every chapter separately under the respective legal source as each potential legal basis provides for specific rights with and without reference to the territory of States.

A critical examination of the methodology relates to the, regrettably, least popular field of international law among scholars, namely international air law. Hardly any material or literature discuss in detail the basic provisions of the Chicago Convention and its Annexes in detail. The aspect of necessity has not been discussed in extensively thus further research is needed to evaluate a claim under Article 25 ILC-Articles. The principal impediment to conducting a State practice analysis was the difficulty of accessing all national laws and Aeronautical Information Publications, which were in some cases not publicly available, or not available in English. This research does not purport to offer an exhaustive overview of all States claiming an ADIZ. Instead, it focused on a variety of States from different legal systems and geographical backgrounds.

The three concrete examples of problematic ADIZs, as described at the introductory part showed the legal, economic, and political aspects connected with the concept of ADIZs in international airspace. As a novel approach in the discussion on the legal basis of ADIZs in international law, the objective territorial principle could be the most suitable form for exercising prescriptive jurisdiction beyond national airspace on aircraft bound for the territory of the State. The reasoning of this argument is also reflected in the judgment of the European Court of Justice, the *Arctic Sunrise Case*, as well as several ITLOS decisions on extraterritorial prescriptive jurisdiction. From a general perspective and based on the *Lotus Case*, enforcement jurisdiction is clearly limited to national airspace if no treaty or customary international law provides for extraterritorial enforcement. As regards the application of ADIZs on traversing aircraft, which seems to be an upcoming trend in State practice, the protective principle could be applied.

A detailed analysis of national rules and Aeronautical Information Publications on ADIZs identified a uniform State practice and *opinio iuris*. This is the first time that a contribution analysed the exact scope of 25 different national rules on ADIZs in order to assess whether and to what extent a rule of customary international law exists. A number of core elements were identified

 | DOI:10.1163/9789004721005_009

namely the purpose, the geographic, temporal, and personal scope of application, the material scope of the identification obligation, the enforcement or procedure in case of non-compliance, the legal classification in international law by the States, as well as the compliance with the national regulations by other States. The most significant finding reveals a tendency to apply ADIZS rules to aircraft not bound for national airspace. This finding contradicts the majority of existing literature on this topic, which asserts that, in accordance with the US model, ADIZ rules could only be applied to aircraft bound for national airspace. A uniform State practice was identified in relation to the general claim of ADIZ in national and international airspace, the purpose of such zones, the identification requirement, and the consequence of interception in case of non-compliance. No uniform State practice yet exists on the personal scope of application, the geographical delimitation of ADIZ and the compliance of foreign military aircraft with the obligation to identify. Instead military aircraft were sent through ADIZS to protest their application. Furthermore, ADIZS vary drastically in their geographical delimitation. There seems to be an overall agreement that ADIZS do not violate the freedom of overflight if applied to aircraft bound for national airspace.

The right to self-defence under the United Nations Charter and customary international law imposes requirements which ADIZS only partly fulfil. While civil and military aircraft can generally be used for an armed attack, ADIZS are established on a permanent basis and generally anticipate future threats. The prerequisites of pre-emptive self-defence do not completely correlate with the characteristics of ADIZS, which combine two aspects: the identification of a threat by aircraft and the interception of aircraft. The occurrence of an armed attack needs to be sufficiently clear and serious to justify the use of force. The interception of aircraft as a forceful act may only be legitimate when the aircraft is bound for national airspace, cannot be passively identified and does not respond to any communication. Based on an objective ex-ante standard, the level of threat rises from latent to concrete in this context. However, the obligation to identify does not appear necessary nor proportionate under the right to self-defence. Instead, the ADIZS' identification obligation risks creating *presumptio iuris et de jure*. When an aircraft does do not comply with the obligation to identify, the State assumes a potential armed attack. Nevertheless, ADIZS are a useful mechanism to identify aircraft bound for national airspace and therefore are a beneficial for identifying the occurrence of an imminent armed attack and subsequently responding to such attack. ADIZS help to diminish the erroneous interception and shooting down of aircraft. In this context, ADIZS may provide for a meaningful response option excused under the aspect necessity pursuant to Art. 25 ILC-Articles.

The legality as well as scope and content of ADIZs under the Chicago Convention are primarily determined by the establishment of such zone in either national or international airspace. In the absence of an innocent passage regime in national airspace above the territorial sea, States may establish an ADIZ based on the principle of sovereignty pursuant to Art. 1 Chicago Convention. Art. 11 and 12 of the Chicago Conventions, along with their implementing Annexes, provide for the legal framework necessary for the contextualisation of ADIZs in international airspace. While Art. 12 Chicago Convention describes the regulatory competence of ICAO to set forth rules applicable to the airspace above the high seas, these rules only refer specifically to "rules relating to the manoeuvre and flight of aircraft". The regulation of security aspects, which are core to ADIZs, is not within ICAO's scope of regulatory authority. This interpretation correlates also with the object and purpose of Art. 11 Chicago Convention, which provides for the States' right to regulate the admission to airspace, particularly under security concerns. The protection of national security is inherently connected with the internal domain of States. Any attempt to diminish the regulatory scope of States in matters of security and to transfer certain elements of aerial security to the competence of ICAO is unlikely to be a fruitful endeavour. Moreover, Annexes 4 and 15 of the Chicago Convention, which encompass specific rules on ADIZs, are not necessarily binding on the contracting States due to the opt-out mechanism. Annexes 4 and 5 do not prohibit the establishment of ADIZs in international airspace. Even if classified as soft law, the potential exists for Annex 4 and 15 to serve an important function in the creation of a rule of customary international law on the obligation to publish all necessary information on ADIZs and to include ADIZs in Aeronautical Charts.

A comprehensive examination of international jurisprudence on violations of the freedom of the high seas as well as on relevant treaty provisions of UNCLOS leads to the conclusion that the freedom of overflight over the high seas does not preclude the establishment of ADIZs in international airspace. States, however, need to refrain from applying coercive measures on aircraft in international airspace refrain from extending territorial claims. The heavily criticised *Norstar Case* represents a departure from previous judgments and may lead to the understanding that not only enforcement jurisdiction, but also the exercise of prescriptive jurisdiction on activities on the high seas violates the freedom of the high seas. Nonetheless, in line with the objective territorial principle, the *Lotus Case* and various other judgments of ITLOS tribunals, States may assert prescriptive jurisdiction on activities beyond national territory. Another aspects relates to the interpretation of the Chicago Convention by taking into account the legal development of the law of the sea. If one denies the systematic and evolutive interpretation of the Chicago Convention, the "airspace above it lands and territorial waters" pursuant to Art. 2 Chicago Convention would still be delimitated with 3 nautical miles instead of 12 nautical miles. The concept of the EEZ and its recognition as a rule of customary international law fundamentally changed the law of the sea. The EEZ can be regarded as a third maritime zone additionally to the territorial sea and the high seas. As a novel approach, it was suggested that the concept of the EEZ influenced the legal status of the airspace above it.The airspace above the EEZ may be regarded as having a dual legal status. In concrete terms, the airspace above the EEZ could be considered to be high seas in a territorial sense, but in a functional sense be categorized differently. ADIZs could indeed be construed as a *sui generis* zone without contravening the principles of sovereignty, territoriality, and the freedoms of the high seas. The exact content of an ADIZ *sui generis* should then take into account elements of the relevant State practice. Furthermore, ADIZs may fall within the scope of "unattributed rights" in the sense of Art. 59 UNCLOS and thereby becoming subject to the dispute settlement mechanism of UNCLOS.

The general effect of exercising control in airspace above the disputed Senkaku/Diaoyu islands was discussed, with reference to the broader and multi-faceted dispute surrounding the islands. While some influence might be derived from aerial claims, these claims are nevertheless part of a larger dispute that must be assessed in its entirety. In general, the creation of ADIZs in international airspace cannot be based on the principle of sovereignty and have to exclude, prima facie, territorial aspects. Likewise, State practice indicated that States do not view these zones as an effective means to strengthen territorial claims. The discussion under the law of the sea reveals, that if the airspace above the EEZ has a dual legal status, then no territorial effect can be assumed. ADIZs can be clearly associated with the territorial rules of the high seas regime, while in terms of function may form a *sui generis* zone. Instead of strictly following the dichotomy as either part of the airspace above the territorial sea or the high seas, ADIZs may fall in more than one category. In terms of territory and sovereignty, ADIZs are regarded as airspace above the high seas, while still forming a functional *sui generis* zone. This argument accommodates the risk that ADIZs may influence territorial disputes, while taking into account the security concerns of States.

Overall, ADIZs can be very well integrated into the international legal system without creating a conflict with other essential principles of international law. ADIZs represent a complex State practice attempting to adequately encompass meaningful responses to aerial threats. Since the 1950s, the development of ADIZs has been observed, since 2013 and the establishment of the Chinese

ECS ADIZ, a newly increased engagement of States can be seen. These observations indicate that ADIZs have become gradually accepted by the State community. It can be argued that ADIZs are on the brink of forming a *sui generis* zone in international airspace. While China was heavily criticised for applying the ADIZ's rules on traversing aircraft not intending to enter national airspace, reality shows that it would be very difficult to pre-emptively obtain evidence on the intention of the aircraft to enter national airspace. As evidenced by the case of Japan, a State that purports to apply ADIZ rules solely to aircraft destined for national airspace, interception of aircraft is nevertheless occurring in international airspace when it is unclear if the aircraft is actually intending to enter Japanese airspace. In conclusion, the overarching purpose of ADIZs is to ascertain whether an aircraft has the intention to reach national airspace. This also serves the States' interest in identifying any potential armed attack conducted with an aircraft and may therefore be seen to fill the gap left by the right to self-defence in situations where the attack is not yet imminent. While self-defence cannot be applied for the establishment of an ADIZ, they still fulfil the essential aim of obtaining evidence on the occurrence of an imminent armed attack. A continuous analysis of State practice can lead to more legal clarity on the exact scope of a *sui generis* ADIZ and its functioning in relation to self-defence.

It is imperative that the international community clarify the discrepancies in the interpretation of the scope of application of ADIZs to prevent a conflict of international norms governing activities beyond national boundaries. The establishment of a new ADIZ by a State should be meticulously coordinated with ICAO to ensure clear and unambiguous instructions for civil and military aircraft to adhere to the established rules. In particular, where States lack the capacity to respond effectively to aerial threats, discussion of a more precise and uniform ADIZ concept has the potential to reshape acceptable interactions between States in international airspace. At the centre of discussions should be the rule of law and the non-arbitrary use of powers. In a further step, it could be considered to offer the civil aviation industry, as the primary subject of ADIZ's rules, direct access to an administrative and juridical procedure dedicated to legal protection and the examination of ADIZ's rules and interception orders.

Annex 1: Overview of State Practice

	Legal basis	Nat. airspace	Int. airspace	Flight plan	ADC	Interception
1. Argentina	FUA	x FIR		x before departure		x
2. Australia	Safety of aviation		x	x + position report; 60' before entry		x instructed to land + destroy
3. Bangladesh	Chicago Convention		x		x 10' prior to entry in ADIZ	x no details
4. Brazil		x FIR		x		
5. Canada	Entry regulation		x	x +position report; "as soon as possible after take off"		x instructed to land
6. China	Custom, UN Charter		x	x		x „defensive measures"
7. Cuba		x FIR		"Overflight Permit"		
8. Finland	ICAO SARPS, Annex 2 and 11	x FIR		x		
9. Greece		x FIR		x		
10. Iceland			x			
11. India	FUA; in line with ICAO SARPS		x	x	x 10' prior to entry Indian Airspace	x
12. Indonesia	Custom, self-defence	x	x Plan: EEZ	x		x forced to land
13. Iran			x FIR	"Obtain permission", position report; 10' prior to entry FIR Iran		x

 | DOI:10.1163/9789004721005_010

TABLE 1 Overview of state practice (*cont.*)

	Legal basis	Nat. airspace	Int. airspace	Flight plan	ADC	Interception
14. Japan			x FIR			x
15. Myanmar	Annex 2		x FIR	x	x 30' prior to departure + 10' prior to entry ADIZ	x
16. Pakistan		x (application to aircraft in int airspace)		x	x 15' prior to entry ADIZ/ national airspace	x
17. Panama		x		x +position report		
18. Peru	Sovereignty	x		x		x
19. Poland	FUA	x		x		
20. South Korea			x EEZ	x + position report		x
21. Sri Lanka		x (application to aircraft in int airspace)		x	x 15' prior to entering ADIZ	x
22. Taiwan			x	x 60' before departure		x
23. Thailand	Annex 2, 11		x	x 10' prior to entry ADIZ		x
24. US	Entry regulation for defence; ICAO Standards		x	x + position report; 1h before entering		x escorted + forced to land
25. Uruguay	Sovereignty, FUA	x		x before or during the flight		x

Annex 2: Personal Scope of Application in International Airspace

Australia (*1988*): traversing aircraft	*Bangladesh* (*2018*): traversing aircraft	*Canada* (*1950*): traversing aircraft	*China* (*2013*): traversing aircraft
***India* (*1950ies*):** aircraft bound for nat. airspace	*Iran* (*2018*): traversing aircraft	*Japan* (*1950, 1969*): aircraft bound for nat. airspace	*Myanmar* (*2017*): traversing aircraft
South Korea (*1950, 2013*): aircraft bound for nat. airspace	*Taiwan* (*1950*): aircraft bound for nat. airspace	*Thailand* (*2010*): traversing aircraft	*United States* (*1950*): aircraft bound for nat. airspace

 | DOI:10.1163/9789004721005_011

List of Authorities

Treaties

Agreement between India and Pakistan on Prevention of Air Space Violations and for Permitting Over Flights and Landings by Military Aircraft (1994) 60 UNTS
Charter of the United Nations (1945) 1155 UNTS 331
Convention against Torture and Other Cruel, Inhuman or Degrading Treatment or Punishment (1984) 1465 UNTS 85
Convention on the Prevention and Punishment of Crimes against Internationally Protected Persons, including Diplomatic Agents (1973) 15410 UNTS 168
Convention on Civil Aviation ("Chicago Convention") (1944) 15 UNTS 295
Convention on the Territorial Sea and the Contiguous Zone (1958) 516 UNTS 205
Convention on the High Seas (1958) 459 UNTS 11
Convention on Fishing and Conservation of the Living Resources of the High Seas (1958) 559 UNTS 285
Convention on the Continental Shelf (1958) 499 UNTS 311
Convention on the Prevention of Marine Pollution by Dumping of Wastes and Other Matter (London Convention) (1972) 1046 UNTS 120
Convention on Jurisdictional Immunities of States and Their Property, A/RES/59/38 (2 December 2004)
Hague Convention for the Suppression of Unlawful Seizure of Aircraft (1973) 1973 UNTS 106
International Air Services Transit Agreement (1944) 84 UNTS 389
International Air Transport Agreement (1944) 502 UNTS 171
Protocol to the Convention on the Prevention of Marine Pollution by Dumping of Wastes and Other Matter (1996)
Rome Convention on Damages Caused by Foreign Aircraft to Third Parties on the Surface (9 September 1958) 310 UNTS 181
Statute of the International Court of Justice (1945) 1155 UNTS 331
Tokyo Convention on Offences and Certain Other Acts Committed on Board Aircraft (Tokyo Convention) (1969) 1969 UNTS 220
United Nations Convention on the Law of the Sea (UNCLOS) (1994) 1833 UNTS 397
Vienna Convention on the Law of the Treaties (VCLT) (1980) 1155 UNTS 331

International Court of Justice Cases & Advisory Opinions

Aerial Incident of 10 March 1953 (*United States of America v Czechoslovakia*) (Order) [1953] ICJ

Aerial Incident of 7 October 1952 (*United States of America v Union of Soviet Socialist Republics*) (Order) [1952] ICJ

Aerial Incident of 4 September 1954 (*United States of America v Union of Soviet Socialist Republics*) (Order) [1954] ICJ

Aerial Incident of 7 November 1954 (*United States of America v Union of Soviet Socialist Republics*) (Order) [1954] ICJ

Aerial Incident of 27 July 1955 (*Israel v Bulgaria*) (Order) [1955] ICJ

Aerial Incident of 27 July 1955 (*United Kingdom v Bulgaria*) (Order) [1955] ICJ

Aerial Incident of 27 July 1955 (*United States of America v Bulgaria*) (Order) [1955] ICJ

Aerial Incident of 3 July 1988 (*Islamic Republic of Iran v United States of America*) (Order) [1988] ICJ

Aerial Incident of 10 August 1999 (*Pakistan v India*) (Questions of Jurisdiction and Admissibility) [2000] ICJ Rep 12

Alleged Violations of Sovereign Rights and Maritime Spaces in the Caribbean Sea (*Nicaragua v Colombia*) (Merits) [2022] ICJ Rep 155

Appeal Relating to the Jurisdiction of the ICAO Council (*India v Pakistan*) (Merits) [1972] ICJ Rep 46

Appeal Relating to the Jurisdiction of the ICAO Council under Article II, Section 2, of the 1944 International Air Services Transit Agreement (*Bahrain, Egypt and United Arab Emirates v Qatar*) (Merits) [2020] ICJ Rep 172

Appeal Relating to the Jurisdiction of the ICAO Council under Article 84 of the Convention on International Civil Aviation (*Bahrain, Egypt, Saudi Arabia and United Arab Emirates v Qatar*) (Merits) [2020) ICJ Rep 81

Application of the Convention on the Prevention and Punishment of the Crime of Genocide, Bosnia and Herzegovina v Yugoslavia (Order, Provisional Measures) [1993] ICJ Rep 3

Armed Activities on the Territory of the Congo (*Congo v Ruanda*) [2005] ICJ Rep 168

Barcelona Traction, Light and Power Company, Ltd (*Belgium v Spain*) [1970] ICJ Rep 3

Certain Expenses of the United Nations (Advisory Opinion) [1962] ICJ Rec 151

Continental Shelf (*Tunisia v Lybian Arab Jamahiriya*) (Merits) [1982] ICJ Rep 18

Continental Shelf (*Libyan Arab Jamahiriya v Malta*) (Merits) [1984] ICJ Rep 3

Delimitation of Maritime Boundary in the Gulf of Maine Area (*Canada v United States of America*) (Merits) [1984] ICJ Rep 246

Fisheries (*United Kingdom v Norway*) (*Merits*) [1951] ICJ Rep 116

Fisheries Jurisdiction (*United Kingdom v Iceland*) (Merits) [1974] ICJ Rep 3

Frontier Dispute (*Benin/Niger*) (Merits) [2005] ICJ Rep 90

Gabcikovo-Nagymaros Project (*Hungary v Slovakia*) (Merits) [1997] ICJ Rep 7

Gabčikovo-Nagymaros Project (*Hungary v Slovakia*), Sep Opinion Vice-President Weeramantry [1997] ICJ Rep 8

LaGrand (*Germany v United States*) (Merits) [2011] ICJ Rep 466

Land, Island and Maritime Frontier Dispute (*El Salvador v Honduras*) (Merits) [1992] ICJ Rep 351

Legal Consequences for States of the Continued Presence of South Africa in Namibia (*South West Africa*) *notwithstanding Security Council Resolution 276* [*1970*] (Advisory Opinion) [1971] ICJ Rep 16

Legality of the Threat or Use of Nuclear Weapons (Advisory Opinion) [1996] ICJ Rep 226

Lotus Case, Judgment No. 9 (1927) PCIJ Series A, No. 10

Maritime Delimitation and Territorial Questions between Qatar and Bahrain (*Qatar v Barain*) (Merits) [1994] ICJ Rep 112

Military and Paramilitary Activities in and against Nicaragua (*Nlcaragua v United States of America*) (Merits) [1986] ICJ Rep 14

Military and Paramilitary Activities in and against Nicaragua (*Nicaragua v United States of America*) (Jurisdiction and Admissibility) [1984] ICJ Rep 392

Nationality Decrees Issued in Tunis and Morocco (*France v Great Britain*) (Advisory Opinion) [1923] PCIJ

North Sea Continental Shelf (*Federal Republic of Germany v Denmark; Federal Republic of Germany v Netherlands*) (Merits) [1969] ICJ Rep 3

Nuclear Tests (*Australia v France*) (Merits) [1974] ICJ Rep 253

Oil Platforms (*Iran v United States*) (Merits) [2003] ICJ Rep 161

Pulp Mills on the River Uruguay (*Argentina v Uruguay*) (Merits) [2006] ICJ Rep 156

Question of Interpretation and Application of the 1971 Montreal Convention Arising from the Aerial Incident at Lockerbie (*Libyan Arab Jamahiriya v United Kingdom and the United States*) (Provisional Measures) [1992] ICJ Rep 3

Right of Passage over Indian Territory (*Portugal v India*) (Merits) [1960] ICJ Rep 6

Sovereignty over Certain Frontier Land (*Belgium v Netherlands*) (Merits) [1958] ICJ Rep 28

South West Africa Cases (*Ethiopia v. South Africa; Liberia v. South Africa*) (Merits) [1966] ICJ Rep 6

Treatment in Hungary of Aircraft and Crew of the United States of America (*United States of America v Hungarian People's Republic*) (Order) [1954] ICJ

Voting Procedure on Questions relating to Reports and Petitions concerning the Territory of South West Africa (Advisory Opinion) [1955] ICJ Rep 67

Whaling in the Antarctic (*Australia v Japan: New Zealand Intervening*) (Merits) [2014] article 86ICJ Rep 226

Western Sahara (Advisory Opinion) [1975] ICJ Rep 12

International Tribunal for the Law of the Sea Cases

ARA Libertad (*Argentina v Ghana*) (Provisional Measures, Order of 15 December 2012) ITLOS Reports 2012

'Arctic Sunrise' (Netherlands v. Russia) (Provisional Measures Order, 22 November 2013) ITLOS Reports 2013

'Arctic Sunrise' (Netherlands v. Russia) (Provisional Measures, Order of 22 November 2013, Joint Sep. Op. Wolfrum and Kelly) ITLOS Reports 2013

'Arctic Sunrise' (Netherlands v. Russia) (Provisional Measures, Order of 22 November 2013, Dis. Op. Golitsyn) ITLOS Reports 2013

Dispute concerning Delimitation of the Maritime Boundary between Bangladesh and Myanmar in the Bay of Bengal (Bangladesh/Myanmar) ITLOS Reports 2002

The M/V 'Saiga' (Saint Vincent and the Grenadines v Guinea) (Judgment of 22 December 1999) ITLOS Reports 1999

The *M/V "SAIGA" (No. 2)* (*Saint Vincent and the Grenadines v. Guinea*) (Merits) [1999] ITLOS Reports 1999

M/V "Louisa" (Saint Vincent and the Grenadines v *Kingdom of Spain*) (*Judgment of 28 May 2013*), *ITLOS Reports 2013*

M/V "Norstar" (Panama v Italy) (Judgment of 10 April 2019) ITLOS Reports 2018–2019

M/V "Virginia G" (Panama v Guinea-Bissau) (*Judgment of 14 April 2014*) *ITLOS Reports 2014*

Permanent Court of Arbitrations Cases

The Island of Palmas Case (Netherlands v USA) [1928] Permanent Court of Arbitration, Case No. 1925–01

Arctic Sunrise' (Netherlands v Russia) (Award on Jurisdiction) [2013] Permanent Court of Arbitration, Case No. 2014–02

Arctic Sunrise' (Netherlands v Russia) (Merits) [2015] Permanent Court of Arbitration, Case No. 2014–02

The South China Sea Arbitration (The Republic of Philippines v The People's Republic of China) [2016] Permanent Court of Arbitration, Case No. 2013–19

European Court of Justice Cases

Swiss Confederation v European Commission, European Court of Justice, Case C-547/10 P (7 March 2003)

Air Transport Association of America and ors v Secretary of State for Energy and Climate Change, European Court of Justice, Case C-366/10 (21 December 2011)

National Decision

Naim Molvan v. Attorney General for Palestine (The "Asya"), [1948] 81 Ll L Rep 277, United Kingdom: Privy Council (Judicial Committee)

International Law Commission Documents and Reports

Report of the ILC, Yearbook of the International Law Commission, Vol. II (1955), A/CN.4/SER.A/1955/ADD.L

Report of the ILC, Yearbook of the International Law Commission, Vol. II (1956), A/CN.4/SER.A/1956/ADD.L

ILC, 'Commentary to the ILC Articles concerning the Law of the Sea' (1956), Yearbook of the International Law Commission, Vol II, UNGOAR UN Doc A/3159

ILC, 'Report of the International Law Commission on the Work of its Thirty-Second Session' Yearbook of the International Law Commission, Vol II (5 May–25 July 1980) UN Doc. A/35/10

ILC Articles on Responsibility of States for Internationally Wrongful Acts, A/56/10 (2001)

ILC, 'Responsibility of States for Internationally Wrongful Acts, with commentaries' UN Doc A/56/10 (2001)

ILC, 'Report of the Study Group on Fragmentation of International Law' Yearbook of the International Law Commission, Vol II (2006) UN Doc A/CN.4/L.682

ILC, 'Conclusions of the Work of the Study Group on the Fragmentation of International Law: Difficulties arising from the Diversification and Expansion of International Law' Yearbook of the International Law Commission, Vol II (2006) UN Doc A/61/10

ILC 'Fragmentation of International Law: Difficulties Arising from the Diversification and Expansion of International Law' Yearbook of the International Law Commission, Vol II (2006) UN Doc A/CN.4/L.702

ILC, 'Fifth Report on International Liability for Injurious Consequences arising out of Acts not prohibited by International Law, by Mr. Robert Quentin Baxter, Special Rapporteur', Yearbook of the International Law Commission, Vol II (12 and 19 June 1984) UN Doc A/CN.4/383

ILC, 'Second Report on State Responsibility by Mr. James Crawford, Special Rapporteur' UN Yearbook of the International Law Commission, Vol II (30 April 1999), UN Doc. A/CN.4/498/ADD.2

ICAO Documents

ICAO Assembly Resolution A15–6, Appendix E (1965)

ICAO Doc 8724 A16-P/3 'Annual Report of the Council to the Assembly for 1967' (1968)

ICAO Doc 8869 A18-P/2 'Annual Report of the Council to the Assembly for 1969' (1970)

ICAO, Doc 9061 A19-Res., Min. (Nineteenth Session – Extraordinary; 27 February – 2 March 1973)

ICAO Doc Ref. LE 4/19.4 – 93/68 (1993)
ICAO Council Res, Doc 9790 (4 June 1973)
ICAO Doc 7600/3 'Standing Rules of Procedure of the Assembly of the International Civil Aviation Organization' (1977)
ICAO Doc. AN 13/4.3–897 (1989)
ICAO Doc 9470 AT-Conf/3-WP/71, Third Air Transport Conference (22.10.-7.11.1985)
ICAO Doc. LC/29-WP/2–1, Secretariat Study on 'Civil/State Aircraft' (1994)
ICAO Council Res, Doc/1996/509 (1 July 1996)
ICAO, Doc 9790 'Assembly Resolutions in Force' (5 October 2001)
ICAO Doc 9800, High-level, Ministerial Conference on Aviation Security (Montreal, 19–20.2.2002)
ICAO Council C-MIN 166/5, 166th Session (June 2002)
ICAO Doc ATConf/6-WP/80 'Airspace Sovereignty' Sixth Meeting of the Worldwide Air Transport Conference (18.3–21.3.2013)
ICAO Doc AN-Conf/11-WP/142, A-1. 'SARPS "Notification of Differences" Procedures and PANS Status', Eleventh Air Navigation Conference (8.9.2013)
ICAO Doc, SAM ASTRO/6-NI/03 (24 October 2014)
ICAO Doc LC/36-WP/2–6, 'State/Civil Aircraft Definition and its Impact on Aviation', Legal Committee – 36th Session (29.9.2015)
ICAO Doc 4444 PANS-ATM 'Air Traffic Management' (16th edn 2016)
ICAO Doc SAIOACG/8 and SEACG/25 WP 22, 'Imposition Of Military Requirements And Restrictions On International Civil Aviation', Combined Eighth Meeting of the South Asia/Indian Ocean ATM Coordination Group (SAIOACG/8) and Twenty – Fifth Meeting of the South East Asia ATS Coordination Group (SEACG/25) (30.03.2018)
ICAO Doc ATMSG/6 WP 26, 'Civil/Military Cooperation Update', Sixth Meeting of the APANPIRG ATM Sub-Group (ATM/SG/6) (03.08.2018)
ICAO Doc SAIOACG/9 – WP29, 'Civil/Military Update' Ninth Meeting of the South Asia/Indian Ocean ATM Coordination Group (26.03.2019–29.03.2019)
ICAO Doc APANPIRG 29, 'Final Report', Twenty Ninth Meeting Of The Asia/Pacific Air Navigation Planning And Implementation Regional Group (30.09.2019)
ICAO Assembly Resolution A35–9, Appendix E, 'The ICAO Universal Security Audit Programme'
ICAO Doc 8973 'Aviation Security Manual'
ICAO Res A33–1, 'Declaration on Misuse of Civil Aircraft as Weapons of Destruction and other Terrorist Acts Involving Civil Aviation'
ICAO Doc. S/i5g66/Rev. i
ICAO Doc 4444, Procedure for Air Navigation Services – Air Traffic Management (15th edn, 2007)

UN General Assembly Resolutions & Security Council Resolutions

UNGA Res 380 (V) 'Peace through Deeds Resolution' (17 November 1950)
UNSC Res 83, UN Doc S/RES/83 (27 June 1950)
UNSC Res 85, UN Doc S/RES/85 (7 July 1950)
UNGA Res/927 'Question of the safety of commercial aircraft flying in the vicinity of, or inadvertently crossing, international frontiers' (14 December 1955)
UNGA Res 2625 (XXV) 'Declaration on Principles of International Law concerning Friendly Relations and Co-operation among States in accordance with the Charter of the United Nations' (24 October 1970)
UNGA Res 3314 (XXIX) 'Definition of Aggression' (14 December 1974)
UNGA, Res/55/959 S/2001/531, 'Letter dated 2001/05/29 from the Permanent Representative of Lebanon to the United Nations addressed to the Secretary-General' (29 May 2001)
UNGA Res A/ES-10/PV.21, 'Emergency Special Session' (20 October 2003)
UNGA Res A/59/565, 'A More Secure World: Our Shared Responsibility Report of the Secretary-General's High-level Panel on Threats, Challenges and Change' (2 December 2004)
UNSC, UN Doc S/PV/.2470 (2470th Meeting, 2 September 1983)
UNSC, UN Doc 1986/3, UN Chron 16–19
UN Security Council, 'Provisional Verbatim Record of the 2655th Meeting', S/ PV.2655 (6 February 1986)
UNSC, UN Doc S/PV.2818 (3 July 1988)
UNSC Res 616 (20 July 1988)
UNSC Res 1967 (26 July 1996)
UNSC Res 1368 (12 September 2001)
UNSC Res 1373 (28 September 2001)
UNSC, Press Release SC/7242 'Security Council Fails To Adopt Resolution On Middle East Situation, To Condemn Use Of Force, Encourage Monitoring Mechanism' (14 December 2001)

International Documents

United Nations Conference on the Law of the Sea, UN Doc A/CONF.13/4, 'The Law of the Air and the Draft Articles Concerning the Law of the Sea Adopted by the International Law Commission at its Eight Session' by A. Pepin (4 October 1957)
United Nations Conference on the Law of the Sea, UN Doc A/CONF.31, 'Comments by the International Civil Aviation Organization on the Draft Articles Concerning the Law of the Sea Adopted by the International Law Commission at Its Eighth Session'

United Nations Conference on the Law of the Sea, A/CONF.13/40, 'Volume IV: Second Committee (High Seas: General Regime) (Geneva 24 February – 27 April 1958)

'Comments by Governments on the Provisional Articles Concerning the Regime of the High Seas and the Draft Articles on the Regime of the Territorial Sea adopted by the International Law Commission at its Seventh Session', UN Doc. A/CN.4/99 and Add.1–9

International Maritime Organisation, 'General Provisions on Ships Routeing', Res A.572/14, 14th (20 January 1985)

'International Civil Aviation Organization: Resolution And Report Concerning The Destruction Of Iran Air Airbus On July 3, 1988' (1989) 28 International Legal Materials 896

'Documents Concerning the Korean Air Lines Incident' (1983) 22 International Legal Materials 1109

Kenya: Draft Articles on the Concept of an Exclusive Economic Zone Beyond the Territorial Sea' (1973) 12 International Legal Materials 33

Books & Chapters in Books

Abeyratne, Ruwantissa, *Convention on International Civil Aviation – A Commentary* (Springer 2014)

Akande, Dapo, 'International Organizations' in Malcom D Evans(ed), *International Law* (5th edn, Oxford University Press 2018)

Ammann, Odile, *Domestic Courts and the Interpretation of International Law* (Brill 2020)

Andreone, Gemma & Cataldi, Guiseppe, 'Sui Generis Zones' in *Max Planck Encyclopaedias of Public International Law* (Oxford University Press 2014)

Andreone, Gemma & Cataldi, Giuseppe, 'Sui Generis Zones' in David J Attard, Malgosia Fitzmaurice, & Norman A Martínez Gutiérrez (eds), *The IMLI Manual on International Maritime Law: Volume I: The Law of the Sea* (Oxford University Press 2014)

Anghie, Antony, 'Asia in the History and Theory of International Law' in Simon Chesterman et al (eds), *The Oxford Handbook of International Law in Asia and the Pacific* (Oxford University Press 2019)

Aust, Anthony, *Handbook of International Law* (Cambridge University Press 2005)

Banaszewska, Dorota M, 'Lex specialis' in *Max Planck Encyclopedias of Public International Law* (Oxford University Press 2015)

Bartsch, Ronald, *International Aviation Law: A Practical Guide* (2nd edn, Ashgate 2012)

Beaulac, Stephane, 'The Lotus Case in Context – Sovereignty, Westphalia, Vattel and Positivism' in Stephen Allen, Daniel Costelloe, Malgosia Fitzmaurice, Paul Gragl & Edward Guntrip (eds), *Oxford Handbook of Jurisdiction in International Law* (Oxford University Press 2019)

Beckman, Robert & Phan, Hao D, 'Air Defence Identification Zones: Implications For Freedom Of Overflight And Maritime Disputes' in Truong Tran, John Welfield &Thuy Le (eds), *Building a Normative Order in the South China Sea* (Edward Elgar Publishing 2019)

Bjorge, Eirik, 'The Vienna Rules, Evolutionary Interpretation and the Intentions of the Parties, Interpretation in International Law', in Bianchi, Andrea et al (eds), *Interpretation in International Law* (Oxford University Press 2015)

Bjorge, Eirik, *The Evolutionary Interpretation of Treaties* (Oxford University Press 2014).

Blumenkron, Jimena, 'International Safety Requierments', in Paul S Dempsey & Ram S Jakhu (eds), *Routledge Handbook of Public Aviation Law* (Routledge 2017)

Boyle, Alan, 'Soft Law in International Law-Making' in Malcom D Evans (ed), *International Law* (5th edn, Oxford University Press 2018)

Boyle, Alan, 'The Choice of a Treaty: Interaction between Hard Law and Soft Law in the United Nations Law-Making' in Simon Chesterman, David Malone and Santiago Villalpando (eds), *Oxford Handbook of UN Treaties* (Oxford University Press 2018)

Breuer, Marten, 'Effektivitätsprinzip' in Burkhard Schöbener et al (eds), *Völkerrecht: Lexikon zentraler Begriffe und Themen* (Müller 2014)

Broude, Tomer & Shany, Yuval (eds), *Multi-Sourced Equivalent Norms in International Law* (Oxford University Press 2011)

Brown, Edward D, *The International Law of the Sea, Volume 1* (Dartmouth Publishing 1994)

Brownlie, Ian, *International Law And The Use Of Force By States* (Oxford University Press 2012)

Buergenthal, Thomas, *Law Making in the International Civil Aviation Organization* (Syracuse Univ Press 1969)

Buga, Irina, 'Between Stability and Change in the Law of the Sea Convention: Subsequent Practice, Treaty Modification, and Regime Interaction' in Donald R Rothwell et al (eds), *Oxford Handbook of the Law of the Sea* (Oxford University Press 2015)

Burke, Edmund J & Stuth Cevallos, Astrid, *In Line or out of Order? – Chinas Approach to ADIZ in Theory and Practice* (Rand 2017)

Cameron, Iain, 'International Criminal Jurisdiction, Protective Principle', *Max Planck Encylopedia of Public International Law* (Oxford University Press 2012)

Cassese, Antonio, *International Law* (2nd edn Oxford University Press 2005)

Cassese, Antonio, *Terrorism, Politics and The Law: The Achille Lauro Affair* (S J K Greenleaves 1989)

Cheng, Bin, *The Law of International Air Transport* (Stevens 1965)

Cheng, Chia-Jui (ed), *Studies in International Air Law* (Brill 2018)

Chung, Chien, 'Military Culture and Air Force Restructuring' in Martin Edmonds & Michael Tsai (eds) *Taiwan's Security and Air Power* (Routledge 2003)

Churchill, Robin R & Lowe, Vaughan, *The Law of the Sea* (Manchester University Press 1999)

Churchill, Robin R, 'The 1982 United Nations Convention on the Law of the Sea' in Donald R Rothwell et al (eds) *Oxford Handbook of the Law of the Sea* (Oxford University Press 2015)

Constantinou, Avra, *The Right to Self-Defence under Customary International Law and Article 51 of the UN Charter* (Sakkoulas Athenes 2000)

Cooper, John, 'The Chicago Convention – After Twenty Years' in Ivan A Vlasic (ed), *Explorations in Aerospace Law* (1968)

Cooper, John, *Roman Law and the Maxim „Cujus est Solum" in International Air Law* (McGill University 1952)

Corten, Oliver, *The Law against War* (Oxford University Press 2010)

Crawford, James & Olleson, Simon, 'The Character and Forms of International Responsibility' in Malcom D Evans (ed), *International Law* (5th edn, Oxford University Press 2018)

Crawford, James, *Brownlie's Principles of Public International Law* (8th edn, Oxford University Press 2012)

Crawford, James, *The International Law Commission's Articles on State Responsibility* (Cambridge University Press 2001)

Crawford, James; *The Creation of States in International Law* (2nd edn, Oxford University Press 2007)

Damrosch, Lori et al, *International Law – Cases And Materials* (5th edn, West Academic Publishing 2009)

Davies, Kirk, Johnson, Eric, Desio, Laura, Kidd, Sam & Paul, Thomasa, *Air Force Operations and the Law* (3rd ed., Maxwell Air Force Base, Ala.: Judge Advocate General's School 2014)

Deeks, Ashley S, 'Taming the Doctrine of Pre-Emption' in Marc Weller (ed), *The Oxford Handbook of the Use of Force in International Law* (OSAIL 2015)

Dempsey, Paul S, *Public International Air Law* (2nd edn, McGill University 2017)

De Lucia, Vito, Elferink, Alex Oude, & Nguyen, Lan Ngoc (eds), *International Law and Marine Areas beyond National* Jurisdiction (Brill 2022)

Diederiks-Verschoor, Philipina I H and Mendes De Leon, Pablo, *Introduction to Air Law* (9th edn Kluwer 2012)

Dinstein, Yoram, *War, Aggression and Self-Defence* (3rd edn, Cambridge University Press 2001)

Dörr, Oliver & Randelzhofer, Albrecht, 'Purpose and Principles, Art 2(4)' in Bruno Simma et al (eds), *The Charter of the United Nations: A Commentary, Volume 1* (3rd edn, Oxford University Press 2012)

Dupuy, Rene-Jean, 'The Sea under National Competence' in Rene Jean Dupuy & Daniel Vignes (eds), *A Handbook on the New Law of the Sea, Volume 1* (Martinus Nijhoff 1991)

Evans, Malcom D, 'The Law of the Sea' in Malcom D Evans (ed), *International Law* (5th edn, Oxford University Press 2018)

Fellmeth, Aaron & Horwitz, Maurice *A Guide to Latin in International Law* (Oxford University Press 2011, online version)

Fietta, Stephen & Cleverly, Robin, *A Practitioner's Guide to Maritime Boundary Delimitation* (Oxford University Press 2016)

Fischer, Paula, *Das Irrtumsrisiko bei den Ausnahmen des völkerrechtlichen Gewaltverbotes* (Nomos 2020)

Fitzmaurice, Malgosia, 'The Practical Working of the Law of the Treaties' in Malcom D Evans (ed), *International Law* (5th edn, Oxford University Press 2018)

Freeland, Steven, 'The Role of 'Soft Law' in Irmgard Marboe (ed), *Soft Law in Outer Space* (Böhlau 2012)

Frowein, Jochen, 'Recognition' in *Max Planck Encyclopedias of Public International Law* (Oxford University Press 2010)

Gaeta, Paola, Viñuales, Jorge E & Zappalá, Salvatore, *Cassese's International Law* (3rd edn, Oxford University Press 2020)

Gamble, John K., *Law of the Sea: Neglected Issues* (The Law of the Sea Institute University of Hawaii 1979)

Gardam, Judith, *Necessity, Proportionality and the Use of Force by States* (Cambridge Studies in Int'l and Comp L 2004)

Gardiner, Richard, *Treaty Interpretation* (2nd edn, Oxford University Press 2015)

Gavouneli, Maria, *Functional Jurisdiction in the Law of the Sea* (Brill 2007)

Giemullar, Elmar M & Weber, Ludwig, *International and EU Aviation Law* (Wolters Kluwer Law & Business 2011)

Gray, Christine, 'The Use of Force and the International Legal Order' in Malcom D Evans (ed), *International Law* (5th edn, Oxford University Press 2018)

Gray, Christine, *International Law and Use of Force* (4th edn, Oxford University Press 2018)

Greenwood, Christopher, 'Self-defence' in *Max Planck Encyclopaedias of Public International Law* (Oxford University Press 2011)

Groenewege, Adrianus D, *Compendium of International Civil Aviation Organisation* (Intl Air Transport Assn 1999)

Grotius, Hugo, *The Freedom of the High Seas: Or, the Rights which Belong to the Dutch to Take Part in the East Indian Trade* (translated by R van Deman Magoffin, Oxford University Press 1916)

Grytsenko, Anatoliy, 'Political Irresponsibility and Lack of Transparency in Ukrainian Defence Reform' in Hans Boern et al (eds), *Civil-Military Relations in Europe* (Routledge 2006)

Guilfoyle, Douglas, 'Article 111- Right of Hot Pursuit', in Alexander Proelß (ed), *United Nations Convention on the Law of the Sea: A Commentary* (Nomos 2017)

Guilfoyle, Douglas, 'Article 86 – Application of the Provisions of this Part' in Alexander Proelß (ed), *United Nations Convention on the Law of the Sea: A Commentary* (Nomos 2017)

Guilfoyle, Douglas, 'Article 87 – Freedom of the High Seas' in Alexander Proelß (ed), *United Nations Convention on the Law of the Sea: A Commentary* (Nomos 2017)

Guilfoyle, Douglas, 'Article 92 – Status of Ships' in Alexander Proelß (ed), *United Nations Convention on the Law of the Sea: A Commentary* (Nomos 2017)

Guilfoyle, Douglas, 'The High Seas' in Donald R Rothwell et al (eds), *Oxford Handbook of the Law of the Sea* (Oxford University Press 2015)

Hailbronner, Kay, *Der Schutz der Luftgrenzen im Frieden* (Heymann 1972)

Hanks, Patrick (ed), *Collins Dictionary of the English Language* (Collins 1960)

Harris David, *Cases and Materials on International Law* (7th edn, Sweeth & Maxwell 2010)

Hartzenberg, Belinda, *The Rights and Obligations of a State under Article 3bis of the Chicago Convention pursuant to an Intrusion of its sovereign Air Space by Civilian Aircraft* (LL.M. Thesis 2019)

Havel, Brian F & Sanchez, Gabriel S, *The Principles and Practice of International Air Law* (Cambridge University Press 2014)

Henkin, Louis, *International Law: Politics and Values* (Springer 1995)

Heraclis Alexis, *The Greek-Turkish Conflict in the Aegean* (Springer 2010)

Herdegen, Matthias, 'Interpretation in International Law', in *Max Planck Encyclopedias of Public International Law* (Oxford University Press 2020)

Higgins, Rosalyn, *Problem & Process, International Law and How We Use It* (Oxford University Press 1999)

Hilpold, Peter (ed), *Responsibility to Protect: A new Paradigm of International Law?* (Brill Nihjoff 2015)

Hobe, Stephan, 'Airspace' in *Max Planck Encyclopedias of Public International Law* (Oxford University Press 2019)

Hoffmann, Albert J, 'Freedom of Navigation' in *Max Planck Encyclopedias of Public International Law* (Oxford University Press 2011)

Hoffmann, Julia & Nollkaemper, Aandre, *Responsibility to Protect: From Principle to Practice* (Pallas Publication 2012)

Huang, Jiefang, 'Security Regulations' in Paul S Dempsey & Ram Jahku (eds), *Routledge Handbook of Public Aviation Law* (Taylor Francis 2016)

Hutchkinson, Charles D, 'The Air Bridge Denial Program and the Shootdown of Civil Aircraft under International Law' (LL.M. Thesis 2004)

Janik, Ralph, *International Law and the Use of Force- Cases and Materials* (Routledge 2019)

Jennings, Robert & Watts, Arthur (eds), *Oppenheim's International Law, Volume 1* (9th edn, Longman 1996)

John Noyes, 'The Territorial Sea and Contiguous Zone' in Donald Rothwell et al (eds), *The Oxford Handbook of the Law of the Sea* (OUP 2015)

Jürgens, Friedrich, *International Environmental "Soft Law": The Functions and Limits of Nonbinding Instruments in International Environmental Governance and Law* (Springer 2013)

Kamminga, Menno T, 'Extraterritoriality' in *Max Planck Encyclopedias of Public International Law* (Oxford University Press 2012)

Keenan, Peter, Lester, Anthony & Martin, Peter, *Shawcross and Beaumont on Air Law* (3rd edn, Butterworths 1966)

Kentaro Serita, *The Territory of Japan* (Springer 2023) Shaw, Malcom N, *International Law* (9th edn, Cambridge University Press 2021)

Klabbers, Jan, *International Law* (3rd edn, Cambridge University Press 2021)

Kolesnik, Dimitri, 'The Development of the Right to Self-Defence' in William Butler (ed), *The Non-Use of Force in International Law* (Brill 1989)

Koplow, David, 'Legal Aspects of the Use of Nuclear Explosive Devices in Planetary Defence' in Irmgard Marboe & Cordula Panosch (eds) *Legal Aspects pf Planetary Defence* (Brill Nijhoff 2021)

Koskenniemi, Martti, 'Hegemonic Regimes' in Margaret A. Young (ed), *Regime Interaction in International Law: Facing Fragmentation* (Cambridge University Press 2012)

Kraska, James & Pedrozo, Raul, *International Maritime Security Law* (Brill Nijhoff 2013)

Krisch, Nico, 'Ch.VII Action with Respect to Threats to th Peace, Breaches of the Peace, and Acts of Aggression, Article 39' in Bruno Simma et al (eds), *The Charter of the United Nations: A Commentary, Volume 2* (Oxford University Press 2012)

Kunig, Philip, 'Prohibition of Intervention' in *Max Planck Encyclopedias of Public International Law* (Oxford University Press 2008)

Laeiae, Johann Ruben & Paulus, Andreas, 'Ch.XVI Miscellaneous Provisions, Article 103' in Bruno Simma et al (eds), *The Charter of the United Nations: A Commentary, Volume 2* (Oxford University Press 2012)

Larsen, Paul, Sweeney, Joseph & Gillick, John, *Aviation Law: Cases, Law and Related Sources* (2nd edn, Martinus Nijhoff 2012)

Lubell, Noam, 'The Problem of Imminence in an Uncertain World' in Marc Weller (ed), *The Oxford Handbook of the Use of Force in International Law* (OSAIL 2015)

Maggio, Amber, 'Article 78 – Legal Status of the Superjacent Waters and Air Space and the Rights and Freedoms of other States' in Alexander Proelß (ed), *United Nations Convention on the Law of the Sea: A Commentary* (Nomos 2017)

Mann, Frederick A, *The Doctrine of Jurisdiction in International Law* (AW Sijthoff 1964)

Marboe, Irmgard (ed), *Soft Law in Outer Space – The Importance of Non-Binding Rules in International Space Law* (Böhlau Verlag 2012)

Marlin, Ruth, *Understanding Air Traffic Control Financing* (National Air Traffic Controllers Association 2005)

Matte, Nicolas M, *Treatise on Air-Aeronautical Law* (McGill University 1981)

Matz-Lück, Nele, 'Norm Interpretation across International Regimes: Competences and Legitimacy' Legitimacy' in Margaret A Young (ed), *Regime Interaction in International Law: Facing Fragmentation* (Cambridge University Press 2012)

McDorman, Ted L, 'The Continental Shelf' in Donald R Rothwell et al (eds), *Oxford Handbook of the Law of the Sea* (Oxford University Press 2015)

Meessen, Karl (ed), *Extraterritorial Jurisdiction in Theory and Practice* (Springer 1996)

Mendelson, Michael, 'Right of Passage over Indian Territory' in *Max Planck Encylopedias of Public International Law* (Oxford University Press 2007)

Mendes de Leon, Pablo, *Behind and Beyond the Chicago Convention: The Evolution of Aerial Sovereignty* (Kluwer Law International 2019)

Mendes de Leon, Pablo, *Introduction to Air Law* (10th edn Kluwer 2017)

Merkouris, Panos, 'Principle of Systemic Interpretation' in *Max Planck Encyclopaedias of Public International Law* (Oxford University Press 2020)

Milde, Michael, *International Air Law and ICAO* (4th edn Eleven International Publishing 2023)

Milde, Michael, *Rendition Flights and International Law* (Redress 2008)

Mölksoo, Lauri, *Illegal Annexation and State Continuity* (Brill Nijhoff 2003)

Momatz, Djamchid, 'Chapter 7', in René-Jean Dupuy & Daniel Vignes (eds), *A Handbook on the Law of the Sea, Volume 1* (Martinus Nijhoff 1991)

Nelson, Dolliver, 'Maritime Jurisdiction' in *Max Planck Encyclopedias of Public International Law* (Oxford University Press 2010)

Nolte, Georg & Randelzhofer, Albrecht, 'Ch.VII Action with Respect to Threats to the Peace, Breaches of the Peace, and Acts of Aggression' in Bruno Simma et al (eds), *The Charter of the United Nations: A Commentary, Volume 2* (Oxford University Press 2012)

Nordquist, Myron H, Nandan, Satya N, and Shabtai, Rosenne (eds), *United Nations Convention on the Law of the Sea 1982: A Commentary, Volume III* (Brill 1995)

Noyes, John E, 'Interpreting the 1982 Law of the Sea Convention and Defining it Terms' in Georg E Walker (ed), *Definitions for the Law of the Sea* (Martinus Nijhoff 2012)

Nuñez, Jorge E, *Territorial Disputes and State Sovereignty: International Law and Politics* (Taylor and Francis 2020)

O'Conell, Mary E, Tams, Christian J & Tladi, Dire (eds), *Self-Defence against Non-State Actors* (Cambridge University Press 2019)

O'Connell, Daniel P, *The International Law of the Sea, Volume II* (Oxford University Press 1984)

Oduntan, Gbenga, *Sovereignty and Jurisdiction in the Airspace and Outer Space* (Routledge 2012)

Ohnuki-Tierney, Emiko, *Kamikaze Diaries: Reflections of Japanese Student Soldiers* (Chicago University Press 2006)

Ohnuki-Tierney, Emiko, *Kamikaze, Cherry Blossoms, and Nationalisms* (Chicago University Press 2002)

Olufemi Elias, 'Persistent Objector' in *Max Planck Encyclopedias of Public International Law* (Oxford University Press 2006)

Oxman, Bernhard M, 'Jurisdiction' in *Max Planck Encyclopedias of Public International Law* (Oxford University Press 2007)

Paulwelyn, Joost, *Conflict of Norms in Public International Law* (Cambridge University Press 2003)

Paulweyn, Joost, 'Fragmentation of International Law' in *Max Planck Encyclopaedias of Public International Law* (Oxford University Press 2006)

Poulantzas, Nicholas M, *The Right to Hot Pursuit in International Law* (2nd edn, Brill 2002)

Price, Jeffrey & Forrest, Jeffrey, *Practical Airport Operations, Safety and Emergence Management* (Butterworth-Heinemann 2016)

Proelß, Alexander, 'Article 55 – Specific Legal Regime of the Exclusive Economic Zone' in Alexander Proelß (ed), *United Nations Convention on the Law of the Sea: A Commentary* (Nomos 2017)

Proelß, Alexander, 'Article 56 – Rights, Jurisdiction and Duties of the Coastal State in the Exclusive Economic Zone' in Alexander Proelß (ed), *United Nations Convention on the Law of the Sea: A Commentary* (Nomos 2017)

Proelß, Alexander, 'Article 58 – Rights and Duties in the Exclusive Economic Zone' in Alexander Proelß (ed), *United Nations Convention on the Law of the Sea: A Commentary* (Nomos 2017)

Proelß, Alexander, 'Article 59 – Basis for the Resolution of Conflicts Regarding the Attribution of Rights and Jurisdiction in the Exclusive Economic Zone' in Alexander Proelß (ed), *United Nations Convention on the Law of the Sea: A Commentary* (Nomos 2017)

Proelß, Alexander, 'Article 60 – Artificial Islands, Installations and Structures in the Exclusive Economic Zone' in Alexander Proelß (ed), *United Nations Convention on the Law of the Sea: A Commentary* (Nomos 2017)

Pyc, Dorota, *The Role of the Law of the Sea in Marine Spatial Planning* (Springer 2019)

Rajput, Aniruddha, 'Standard of Proof' in *Max Planck Encyclopedias of Public International Law* (Oxford University Press 2021)

Ramcharan, Bertrand G, 'The Foundations' in Carla Ferstman et al (eds), *Contemporary Human Rights Challenges: The Universal Declaration of Human Rights and its Continuing* Relevance (Routledge 2019)

Reinicke, Wolfgang & Witte, Jan Martin,' Interdependence, Globalization, and Sovereignty: The Role of Non-binding International Legal Accords' in Dinah Sheldon (ed), *Commitment And Compliance: The Role Of Non-Binding Norms In The International Legal System* (Oxford University Press 2000)

Ridell, Ana & Brendan Plant, *Evidence before the International Court of Justice* (British Institute of International and Comparative Law 2009)

Ritchie, Jean H, *Prohibited Areas in International Air Law* (LLM Thesis 1969)

Roach, Ashley, 'Air Identification Zones' in *Max Planck Encyclopedias of Public International Law* (Oxford University Press 2017)

Rothwell, Donald R, 'Fishery Zones and Limits' in *Max Planck Encyclopedias of Public International Law* (Oxford University Press 2008)

Rothwell, Donald R, & Stephens, Tim, *The International Law of the Sea* (Hart Publishing 2023)

Ruys, Tom, 'The Cuban Missile Crisis – 1962' in Tom Ruys, Oliver Corten, & Alexandra Hofer (eds), *The Use of Force in International Law: A Case-Based Approach* (Oxford University Press 2018)

Ruys, Tom, *Armed Attack and Article 51 of the UN Charter* (Cambridge University Press 2010

Ryngaert, Cedric, *Jurisdiction in International Law* (2nd edn, Oxford University Press 2015)

Schenkman, Jacob, *International Civil Aviation Organization* (Droz 1955)

Scott, Benjamyn I & Trimarchi, Andrea, *Fundamental of International Aviation and Policy* (Routledge 2009)

Scovazzi, Tullio (ed), *Marine Specially Protected Areas. The General Aspects and the Mediterranean Regional System* (Kluwer Law International 1999)

Shubber, Sami, *Jurisdiction over Crimes on Board Aircraft* (Martinus Nijhoff 1973)

Sochor, Eugene, *The Politics of International Aviation* (Springer 1991)

Spiermann, Ole, 'Lotus and the Double Structure of International Legal Argument' in Philippe Sands & Laurence Boisson de Chazournes (eds), *International Law, the International Court of Justice and Nuclear Weapons* (Cambridge University Press 1999)

Stadlmeier, Sigmar, 'Luftverkehr' in August Reinisch (ed), Österreischisches Handbuch des Völkerrechts (5th edn, Manz 2013)

Stadlmeier, Sigmar, 'The Shooting Down of the Malaysian Airlines Flight MH17' in *The Case of Crimea's Annexation under International Law* (2017 Wladislaw Czaplinski et al)

Staker, Christopher, 'Jurisdiction' in Malcom D Evans (ed), *International Law* (5th edn, Oxford University Press 2018)

Tams, Christian J, 'Self-Defence against Non-State Actors: Making Sense of the 'Armed Attack' Requirement' in Mary E O'Conell, Christian J Tams & Dire Tladi (eds), *Self-Defence against Non-State Actors* (Cambridge University Press 2019)

Tanaka, Yoshifumi, *The International Law of the Sea* (3rd edn, Cambridge University Press 2019)

Tanzi, Attila, 'State of Necessity' in *Max Planck Encyclopedias of Public International Law* (Oxford University Press 2021)

Thürer, Daniel, 'Soft Law' in *Max Planck Encyclopedias of Public International Law* (Oxford University Press 2009)

Tomas, Lisa, 'Air Law' in *Max Planck Encyclopedias of Public International Law* (Oxford University Press 2008)

Tomka, Peter, 'Fisheries Jurisdiction Cases (United Kingdom v Iceland; Federal Republic of Germany v Iceland)' in *Max Planck Encyclopedias of Public International Law* (Oxford University Press 2007)

Trent, Mercedes, 'Appendix A: List of Publicized PLA ADIZ Intrusions from 2016–2020' in Federation of American Scientists (eds), *Over the Line: Implications of China's ADIZ Intrusions in Northeast Asia* (2020)

Trent, Mercedes, 'Overview of ADIZ in East Asia' in Federation of American Scientists (eds), *Over the Line – The Implications of China's ADIZ Intrusions in North East* (2020)

Treves, Tullio, 'Chapter 17' in Rene Jean Dupuy & Daniel Vignes (eds), *A Handbook on the New Law of the Sea, Volume 2* (Martinus Nijhoff 1991)

Treves, Tullio, 'Historical Development of the Law of the Sea' in Donald R Rothwell et al (eds), *Oxford Handbook of the Law of the Sea* (Oxford University Press 2015)

Treves, Tullio, 'Law of the Sea' in *Max Planck Encyclopedias of Public International Law* (Oxford University Press 2011)

Tzou, Byron N, *China and International Law – The Boundary Disputes* (Prager 1990)

Verdross, Alfred & Bruno Simma, *Universelles Völkerrecht: Theorie und Praxis* (3rd edn, Duncker & Humblot) 1984

Villiger, Mark E, *Commentary on the 1969 Vienna Convention on the Law of Treaties* (Brill 2009)

Villiger, Mark E, *Customary International Law and Treaties: A Manual on the Theory and Practice of the Interrelation of Sources* (Brill 1997)

Waldock, Humphrey, *The Regulation of the Use of Force by Individual States in International Law* (Collected Course 1952)

Walker, George K, *Definitions for the Law of the Sea – The Terms not Defined by the 1982 Convention* (Martinus Nijhoff 2012)

Watts, Arthur, & Jorritsma, Remy, 'Israeli Wall Advisory Opinion (Legal Consequences of the Construction of a Wall in the Occupied Palestinian Territory)' in *Max Planck Encylopedias of Public International Law* (Oxford University Press 2019)

Weber, Ludwig, 'The Chicago Convention' in Paul S Dempsey & Ram S Jakhu (eds), *Routledge Handbook of Public Aviation Law* (Routledge 2017)

Williamson, Myra, *Terrorism, War and International Law: The Legality Of The Use Of Force Against Afghanistan In 2001* (Ashgate 2009)

Wolf, Sarah, 'Territorial Sea' in *Max Planck Encyclopaedias of Public International Law* (Oxford University Press 2013)

Wolfrum, Rüdiger, 'Ch.I Purposes and Principles, Article 1' in Bruno Simma (ed), *The Charter of the United Nations – A Commentary* (Oxford University Press 2012)

Wood, Michael, 'The Caroline Incident -1873' in Tom Ruys, Oliver Corten & Alexandra Hofer (eds), *The Use of Force in International Law: A Case-Based Approach* (Oxford University Press 2018)

Wouters, Jan, & Demeyere, Bruno, 'Overflight' in *Max Planck Encyclopedias of Public International Law* (Oxford University Press 2008)

Young, Margaret A (ed), *Regime Interaction in International Law: Facing Fragmentation* (Cambridge University Press 2012)

Zemanek, Karl, 'Armed Attack' in *Max Planck Encyclopedia of Public International Law* (Oxford University Press 2013)

Articles in Journals

Abeyratne, Ruwantissa, 'Competition in Air Transport and Equality' (2018) 19 Journal of International Law and Trade Policy 85

Abeyratne, Ruwantissa, 'The Legal Status of the Chicago Convention and its Annexes' (1994) XIX Air& Space Journal 113

Abeyratne, Ruwantissa, 'In Search of Theoretical Justification for Air Defence Identification Zones' (2011) 5 Journal of Transportation Security 87

Abramovitch, Yehuda, 'The Maxim "Cujus Est Solum Ejus Usque Ad Coelum" as Applied in Aviation' (1962) 8 McGill Law Journal 247

Akande, Dapo & Liefländer, Thomas, 'Clarifying Necessity, Imminence, and Proportionality in the Law of Self-Defense' (2013) 107 American Journal of International Law 563

Allen, Craig H, 'The Peacetime Right of Approach and Visit and Effective Security Council Sanctions Enforcement at Sea' (2019) 95 International Law Studies 401

Allen, Craig H, 'The Doctrine of Hot Pursuit: A Functional Interpretation Adaptable to Emerging Maritime Law Enforcement' (1989) 20 Ocean Development & International Law 309

Akehurst, Micheal, 'Jurisdiction in International Law' (1972) 46 British Yearbook of International Law 145

Almond, Roncevert, 'Clearing the Air above the East China Sea: The Primary Elements of Aircraft Defense Identification Zones' (2017) 7 Harvard National Security Journal 126

Barber, Nicholas W, 'Self-Defence for Institutions' (2013) 72 Cambridge Law Journal 558

Bellamy, Alex 'Libya and the Responsibility to Protect: The Exception and the Norm' (2011) 25 Ethics & International Affairs 263

Bethlehem, Daniel, 'Principles Relevant to the Scope of a State's Right of Self-Defense against an Imminent or Actual Armed Attack by Nonstate Actors' (2012) 106 American Journal of International Law 6

Bhatti, DS, Drion, H & Heller, P 'Prohibited Areas in International Civil Aviation' (1953) U.S. and Canadian Aviation Reports 109

Binder, Martin & Heupel, Monika, 'The Legitimacy of the UN Security Council: Evidence from Recent General Assembly Debates' (2015) 59 International Studies Quarterly 247

Borgen, Christopher J, 'Resolving Treaty Conflicts' (2005) 37 George Washington International Law Review 573

Bothe, Michael, 'Terrorism and the Legality of Pre-emptive Force' (2003) 14 European Journal of International Law 229

Bourbonniere, Michel & Haeck, Louis, 'Military Aircraft And International Law: Chicago Opus' (2000) 66 Journal of Air Law & Commerce 885

Brown, Edward D, 'The Exclusive Economic Zone: Criteria and Machinery for the Resolution of International Conflicts between Different Users of the EEZ' (1977) 4 Maritime Policy and Management 325

Brown, Phillip M, 'The Legal Effects of Recognition' (1950) 44 American Journal of International Law 617

Brownlie, Ian, 'The Use of Force in Self-Defence' (1961) 37 British Yearbook of International Law 279

Burra Srinivas, 'Use of Force as Self Defence against Non-State Actors and TWAIL Considerations: A Critical Analysis of India's State Practice' (2018) 24 Asian Yearbook of International Law 106

Calvo, Alex, 'China's Air Defense Identification Zone: Concept, Issues at Stake and Regional Impact' (2013) Naval War College Press 1

Carroz, Jean, 'International Legislation on Air Navigation over the High Seas'(1959) 26 Journal of Air Law & Commerce 158

Cassese, Antonio, 'Is the Bell Tolling for Universality? A Plea for a Sensible Notion of Universal Jurisdiction' (2003) 1 Journal of International Criminal Justice 589

Charbonneau, Joëlle, Heelis, Katie & Piereder, Jinelle, 'Putting Air Defense Identification Zones on The Radar' (2015) CIGI Graduate Fellows Series 1

Chinkin, Christine M, 'The Challenge of Soft Law: Development and Change in International Law' (1989) 38 The International and Comparative Law Quarterly 850

Collins, Richard, 'Introductory Note to the M/V "Norstar" Case (Panama v. Italy)' (2019) 58 International Law Materials 673

Cooper, John, 'Legal Problems of Upper Space' (1965) 23 Journal of Air Law and Commerce 308

Coppel, Jason, 'A Hard Look at the Effects Doctrine of Jurisdiction in Public International Law' (2009) 6 Leiden Journal of International Law 73

Crawford, James, 'The Creation of the State of Palestine' (1990) 1 European Journal of International Law 309

Cuadra, Elisabeth, 'Air Defense Identification Zones: Creeping Jurisdiction in the Airspace' (1977) 18 Virginia Journal of International Law 485

De Baere, Geert & Ryngaert, Cedric, 'The ECJ's Judgment in Air Transport Association of America and the International Legal Context of the EU's Climate Change Policy' (2013) 18 European Foreign Affairs Review 389

De Luca, Maj Ann, 'Using the Air Force against Civil Aircraft – From Air Terrorism to Self-Defense' (2012) ASPJ Africa & Francophonie 45

De Oliveira, Ricardo, 'Does the Current Legal Framework Provide Sufficient Clarity of Law with Regard to Civil and State Aircraft in Relation to Aviation Practicalities?' (2016) 41 Air & Space Law 329

Dempsey, Paul S, 'Compliance & Enforcement in International Law: Achieving Global Uniformity in Aviation Safety' (2004) 30 North Carolina Journal of International Law and Commercial Regulation 1

Dempsey, Paul S, 'The Role of the International Civil Aviation Organization on Deregulation, Discrimination, and Dispute Resolution' (1987) 52 Journal of Air Law and Commerce 529

Dinstein, Yoram, 'Computer Network Attacks and Self-defence' (2001) 76 International Law Studies, Naval War College 99

Donnelly, Eric, 'The United States–China EP-3 Incident: Legality and "Realpolitik"' (2004) 9 Journal of Conflict & Security Law 25

Dunbar, Rupert, 'The Application of International Law in the Court of Justice of the European Union: Proportionality Rising' (2021) 22 German Law Journal 557

Dutton, Peter, 'Caelum Liberam: Air Defense Identification Zones Outside Sovereign Airspace' (2009) 103 Americna Journal of International Law 1

Ferry, James E, 'Towards Completing the Charm: The Woodpulp Judgment' (1989) EIPLR 21

FitzGerald, Gerald, 'The Use of Force against Civil Aircraft: The Aftermath of the KAL Flight 007 Incident' (1984) 38 Canadian Yearbook of International Law 291

Flint, Colin & Xiaotong, Zhang, 'Historical – Geopolitical Contexts and the Transformation of Chinese Foreign Policy' (2019) 12 Chinese Journal of International Politics 300

Foont, Brian, 'Shooting down Civilian Aircraft: Is there an International Law?' (2007) 72 Journal of Air Law and Commerce 695

Friedman, Shani, 'The Concept of Entitlement to an Exclusive Economic Zone as Reflected in International Judicial Decisions' (2020) 53 Israel Law Review 101

Galdorisi, George V, & Kaufman, Alan G, 'Military Activities in the Exclusive Economic Zone: Preventing Uncertainty and Defusing Conflict' (2002) 32 California Western International Law Journal 253

Gariepy, Richard N, & Botsford, David L, 'The Effectiveness of the International Civil Aviation Organization's Adjudicatory Machinery' (1976) 42 Journal of Air Law and Commerce 351

Geiß, Robin, 'Civil Aircraft as Weapons of Large-Scale Destruction: Countermeasures, Article 3bis of the Chicago Convention, and the Newly Adopted German "Luftsicherheitsgesetz"' (2005) 27 Michigan Journal of International Law 227

George, Ann Mary, 'Constructing the China threat: the Indian strategic community's discursive interpretation of the East China Sea ADIZ' (2021) 59 Commonwealth & Comparative Politics 297

Georgopoulos, Theodore, 'Le Droit Intertemporel et les Dispositions Conventionnelles Évolutives – Thérapie Contre la Vieillesse des Traités? (2004) 108 Revue Générale de Droit International Public 123

Gerber, David, 'Beyond Balancing: International Law Restraints on the Reach of National Laws' (1984) 10 Yale International Law 185

Gibney, Mark, 'The Downing of MH17: Russian Responsibility?' (2015) 15 Human Rights Law Review 169

Gill, Terry, 'The Law of Armed Attack in the Context of the Nicaragua Case' (1988) 1 Yearbook of International Law 30

Gill, Terry, 'The Temporal Dimension of Self-Defence: Anticipation, Pre-emption, Prevention and Immediacy' (2006) 11 Journal of Conflict & Security Law 361

Gooding, Gregory V, 'Fighting Terrorism in the 1980's: The Interception of the Achille Lauro Hijackers ' (1987) 12 Yale Journal of International Law 158

Gordon, Edward, 'Grotius and the Freedom of the Seas in the Seventeenth Century' (2008) 16 Willamette Journal of International Law & Dispute Resolution 252

Green, James & Francis Grimal, 'The Threat of Force as an Action in Self-Defence under International Law' (2011) 44 Vanderbilt Journal of Transnational Law 276

Green, James A, 'The Oil Platforms Case: An Error in Judgment?' (2004) 9 Journal of Conflict & Security Law 380

Grieger, Gisela, 'Sino-Japanese controversy over the Senkaku/Diaoyu/Diaoyutai Islands' (2021) European Parlament Research Service 1

Grimal, Francis, 'Missile Defence Shields: Automated and Anticipatory Self-Defence' (2014) 19 Journal of Conflict & Security Law 317

Guobin, Zhang, 'A Discussion on Due Regard in the United Nations Convention on the Law of the Sea' (2014) 2014 China Oceans Law Review 70

Hafner, Gerhard & Tuerk, Helmut, 'The United Nations Convention on the Law of the Sea, 1982: Reflections after 40 Years' (2022) 36 Ocean Yearbook 1

Hafner, Gerhard, 'Pros and Cons Ensuing from Fragmentation of International Law' (2004) 25 Michigan Journal of International Law 849

Hailbronner, Kai, 'Freedom of the Air and the Convention on the Law of the Sea' (1983) 77 American Journal of International Law 490

Hailbronner, Kai, 'The Legal Regime of the Airspace above the Exclusive Economic Zone' (1983) 8 Air & Space Law 30

Handeyside, Hugh, 'The Lotus Principle in ICJ Jurisprudence: Was the Ship ever Afloat?' (2007) 29 Michigan Journal of International Law 71

Hassan, Farooq, 'A Legal Analysis of the Shooting of Korean Airlines Flight 007 by the USSR' (1984) 49 Journal of Air Law and Commerce 555

Havel, Brian F, & Mulligan, John Q, 'International Aviation's Living Constitution: A Commentary on the Chicago Convention's Past, Present, and Future' (2015) 15 Issues Aviation Law & Policy 7

Hayton, Robert D, 'Jurisdiction of the Littoral State' (1964) III Philippine International Law Journal 369

Head, Ivan, 'ADIZ, International Law, and Contiguous Airspace' (1964) 3 Alberta Law Review 182

Heere, Wybo, 'Problems of Jurisdiction in Air and Outer Space' (1999) XXIV Air & Space Law 70

Henderson, Christian, 'The Bush Doctrine: from Theory to Practice' (2004) 9 Journal of Conflict and Security Law 3

Hobe, Stephan & Fremuth, Michael L, 'No Fly Zones: Connectivity between International Law and Air Law in the Case of Lybia' (2001) 60 Zeitschrift für Luft- und Weltraumrecht 389

Honniball, Arron N, 'The Exclusive Jurisdiction of Flag States: A Limitation on Pro-active Port States' (2016) 31 International Journal of Marine & Coastal Law 499

Hsieh Pasha L, 'An Unrecognized State in Foreign and International Courts: The Case of China and the Republic of Taiwan' (2007) 28 Michigan Journal of International Law 765

Hughes, William J, 'Aerial Intrusions by Civil Airliners and the Use of Force' (1980) 45 Journal of Air Law and Commerce 595

Ikeshima, Taisaku, 'China's Air Defense Identification Zone (ADIZ) and its Impact on the Territorial and Maritime Disputes in the East and South China Seas' (2016) 3 Tanscommunication 151

Jaisuk, Ewa et al, 'The Responsibility of a State in the Shooting down of Malaysian Airlines Flight MH17' (2019) 43 Transport Research Procedia 113

Jamenjad, Maziar & Wood, Michael, 'The Principle of Non-Intervention' (2009) 22 Leiden Journal of International Law 345

Juqian, Li, 'Air Defense Identification Zone: The Restriction on the Free Sky Due to the Residual Right Principle' (2014) 2 China Legal Science 12

Kaiser, Stefan A, 'The Legal Status of Air Defense Identification Zones: Tensions over the East China Sea' (2016) 63 Zeitschrift für Luft- und Weltraumrecht 527

Kaiser, Stefan A., 'No-Fly Zones Established by the United Nations Security Council' (2011) 60 Zeitschrift für Luft- und Weltraumrecht 402

Kazemi, Hamid & Asiabipourimani, Naser, 'Reparation of Aerial Accidents under International Law with Emphasize On 752 Ukrainian Flight' (2021) 24 Legal Research Quarterly 369

Knauth, Andreas, 'Bulgarian Destruction of El Al Airliner' (1955) 22 Journal of Air Law and Commerce 356

Kontorovich, Eugene, 'Arctic Sunrise (Netherlands v. Russia); In re Arctic Sunrise (Netherlands v. Russia)' (2016) 110 American Journal of International Law 96

Kraska, James, 'The "ARA Libertad" (Argentina v. Ghana)' (2013) 107 American Journal of International Law 404

Krizek, Monika B, 'The Protective Principle of Extraterritorial Jurisdiction: A Brief History and Application of the Principle to Espionage as an Illustration of Current United States Practice' (1988) 6 BU International Law Journal 337

Kuperman, Alan J, 'Rethinking the Responsibility to Protect' (2008) 19 The Whitehead Journal of Diplomacy and International Relations 19

Lagoni, Rainer, 'Die Errichtung von Schutzgebieten in der ausschließlichen Wirtschaftszone aus völkerrechtlicher Sicht, Natur und Recht' (2002) 24 Natur und Recht 124

Laina, Eustathia, 'The Arctic Sunrise Case – Provisional Measures Ordered' (2015) 45–46 Environmental Policy & Law 266

Lamont, Christopher, 'Conflict in the Skies: The Law of Air Defence Identification Zones' (2014) 39 Air & Space Law 187

Laposi, Alexandra L, 'Anticipatory Self-Defence' (2014) Caiete de Drept Penal 107

Lee, Jaw Woon, 'Tension on the Air: The Air Defence Identification Zones on the East China Sea' (2014) 7 Journal of East Asia & International Law 274

Lee, Jaw Woon, 'Revisiting Freedom of Overflight in International Air Law: Minimum Multilateralism in International Air Transport' (2013) 38 Air and Space Law 351

Lissitzyn, Oliver, 'The Treatment of Aerial Intruders in Recent Practice and International Law' (1953) 47 American Journal of International Law 559

Lowe, Alan V, 'Some Legal Problems Arising from the Use of the Seas for Military Purposes' (1986) 10 Marine Policy Journal 195

Lowe, Vaughan, 'International Law and the Effects Doctrine in the European Court of Justice' (1989) 48 Cambridge Law Journal 9

Lowenfeld, Andreas, 'Conflict, Balancing of Interests and the Exercise of Jurisdiction to Prescribe: Reflections on the Insurance Antitrust Case' (1995) 89 American Journal of International Law 42

A Majid, 'Legal Capacity of Eurocontrol to Ensure Smooth Aviation in Europe' (1991) 16 Air Law 267

Majiel, Amir, 'Impact of Current U.S. Policy On International Civil Aviation' (1983) 32 Zeitschrift für Luft- und Weltraumrecht 295

Maogoto, Jackson, 'New Frontiers, Old Problems: The War on Terror and the Notion of Anticipating the Enemy' (2004) 51 Netherlands International Law Review 1

Marsono, Deni, 'Determination of Air Defense Identification Zone (ADIZ) in order to Support Sovereignty of National Air Region' (2018) 8 Journal of Defense & State Defense 17

Mayer, Benoit, 'Case Law' (2012) 49 Common Market Law Review 1113

McDougal, Myres & Schlei, Norbert, 'The Hydrogen Bomb Test in the Perspective: Lawful Measure for Security' (1955) 64 Yale Law Journal 648

McLachlan, Campbell, 'The Principle of Systemic Integration and Article 31(3)(c) of the Vienna Convention' (2005) 54 International and Comparative Law Quarterly 279

McGinley, Gerald P, 'The Achille Lauro Affair-Implications for International Law' (1985) 52 Tennessee Law Review 691

Meessen, Karl, 'Antitrust Jurisdiction under Customary International Law' (1984) 78 American Journal of International Law 783

Metzger, Stanley D, 'The "Effects" Doctrine of Jurisdiction' (1967) 61 American Journal of International Law 1015

Milde, Michael 'The Chicago Convention – After Forty Years' (1984) 9 Annals of Air & Space Law 119

Milde, Michael, 'The Chicago Convention – Are Major Amendments Necessary or Desirable 50 Years Later?' (1994) 19 Annals of Air & Space Law 401

Miles, Cameron, 'The MV "Norstar" Case (Panama v. Italy)' (2020) 114 American Journal of International Law 116

Mills, Alex, 'Rethinking Jurisdiction in International Law' (2014) 84 British Yearbook of International Law 187

Morris, Justin & Wheeler, Nicholas J, 'The Security Council's Crisis of Legitimacy and the Use of Force' (2007) 44 International Politics 219

Murphy, Sean D, 'The Doctrine of Preemptive Self-Defence' (2005) 50 Villanova Law Review 720

Murphy, Sean D, 'Self-Defense and the Israeli Wall Advisory Opinion: An Ipse Dixit from the ICJ?' (2005) 99 American Journal of International Law 62

Myres, S McDougal, 'The Soviet-Cuban Quarantine and Self-Defense' (1963) 57 American Journal of International Law 597

Nagan, Winston P & Haddad, Aitza M, 'Recognition of Palestinian Statehood: A Clarification of the Interests of the Concerned Parties' (2012) 40 Georgia Journal of International & Comparative Law 341

Najeeb, Samie, 'The Doctrine of "Effects" and the Extraterritorial Application of Antitrust Laws' (1982) 14 U Miami Intern-American Law Review 23

O'Rourke, Ronald, 'Maritime Territorial and Exclusive Economic Zone (EEZ) Disputes Involving China: Issues for Congress' (2016) Congressional Research Service 1

Odom, Jonathan G, 'A "Rule-Based Approach" to Airspace Defense: A U.S. Perspective on the International Law of the Sea and Airspace, Air Defense Measures, and the Freedom of Navigation' (2014) Revue Belge de Droit International 65

Oxman, Bernard, 'The Regime of Warships under the United Nations Convention on the Law of the Sea' (1983–1984) 24 Virginia Journal of International Law 809

Oxman, Bernard & Bantz, Vincent, 'The M/V "Saiga" (No. 2) (Saint Vincent and the Grenadines v. Guinea), Judgment (ITLOS Case No. 2)' (2000) 94 American Journal of International Law 140

Paddeu, Federica, 'Self-Defence as a Circumstance Precluding Wrongfulness: Understanding Article 21 of the Articles on State Responsibility' (2015) 85 British Yearbook of International Law 1

Paddeu, Federica & Waibel, Michael, 'Necessity 20 Years On: The Limits of Article 25' (2022) 37 ICSID Review – Foreign Investment Law Journal 160

Papp, Zoltan, 'ADIZ in the Light of Public International Law' (2015) Pécs Journal of International and European Law 28

Paulsen, Gordon W, 'An Historical Overview of the Development of Uniformity on International Maritime Law' (1983) 57 Tulane Law Review 1065

Pedrozo, Raul, 'Preserving Navigational Rights and Freedoms: The Right to Conduct Military Activities in China's Exclusive Economic Zone' (2010) 9 Chinese Journal of International Law

Pedrozo, Raul, 'The Bull in the China Shop: Raising Tensions in the Asia-Pacific Region' (2014) 90 International Law Studies 66

Pepin, Eugen, 'ICAO and Other Agencies Dealing with Air Regulation' (1952) 19 Journal of Air Law and Commerce 152

Petras, Christopher, 'The Law of Air Mobility-the International Legal Principles behind the U.S. Mobility Air Forces' Mission' (2010) 44 in Air Force Law Review 1

Proelß, Alexander, 'The Law of the Exclusive Economic Zone in Perspective: Legal Status and Resolution of User Conflicts Revisited' (2012) 26 Ocean Yearbook 87

Purwanto, Harry & Yustitianingtyas, Levina, 'The Establishment of an Air Defence Identification Zone as an Opportunity in Enforcing the Sovereignty of the State and Law in Indonesia' (2019) 85 Journal of Law, Policy & Globalization 76

Reisman, Michael, & Armstrong, Andrea, 'The Past and Future of the Claim of Preemptive Self-Defense' (2006) 100 American Journal of International Law 525

Ris, William K, 'French Nuclear Testing: A Crisis for International Law' (1974) 4 Denver Journal of International Law and Policy 111

Roach, Ashely, 'Today´s Customary International Law of the Sea'(2014) 45 Ocean Development & International Law 239

Ronzitti, Natalino, 'The Expanding Law of Self-Defence' (2006) 11 Journal of Conflict & Security Law 343

Roscini, Marco, 'Threats of Armed Force and Contemporary International Law' (2007) 54 Netherland International Law Review 273

Rose, Cecily, 'Appeal Relating to the Jurisdiction of the ICAO Council' (2021) 115 American Journal of International Law 301

Rossi, Christopher R, 'Ex Injuria Jus Non Oritur, Ex Factis Jus Oritur, and the Elusive Search for Equilibrium after Ukraine' (2015) 24 Tul Journal of International Law & Comparative Law 155

Ryngaert, Cedric, 'Territorial Jurisdiction over Cross Frontier Offences: Revisiting a Classic Problem of International Criminal Law' (2009) 9 International Criminal Law Review 187

Sand, Peter, Lyon, James & Pratt, Geoffrey, 'An Historical Survey of International Air Law since 1944' (1960) 7 McGill Law Journal 125

Sato, Koichi, 'The Senkaku Island Dispute: Four Reasons of the Chinese Offensive' (2019) 8 Journal Contemporary East Asia Studies 50

Schmitt, Michael N, 'Aegean Angst – The Greek-Turkish Dispute' (1996) 49 Naval War College Review 61

Schmitt, Michael N, 'Wings over Lybia- The No Fly Zone in Legal Perspective' (2011) 36 The Yale Journal Of International Law Online 45

Schwetje, Kenneth F, 'Protecting Space Assets: A Legal Analysis of "Keep-Out Zones"' (1987) 15 Journal of Space Law 131

Scovazzi, Tullio, 'The Evolution of the International Law of the Sea: Issues, New Challenges' (2000) 286 RCADI 39

Sofaer, Abraham D, 'On the Necessity of Pre-emption' (2003) 14 European Journal of International Law 209

Sopilko, Iryna & Shevchuk, Yevhenii, 'Jurisdiction Over Crimes Committed On Board Aircraft In Flight Under The Tokyo Convention 1963' (2016) 69 National Aviation University 121

Stubbs, Matthew & Stephens, Dale, 'Dredge Your Way to China? The Legal Significance of Chinese Reclamation and Construction in the South China Sea' (2017) 2 Asia-Pacific Journal Of Ocean Law And Policy 25

Su, Jinyuan, 'Is the Establishment of Air Defence Identification Zones Outside National Airspace in Accordance with International Law?' (2020) 32 European Journal of International Law 1309

Su, Jinyuan, 'The East China Sea Air Defense Identification Zone and International Law' (2015) 14 Chinese Journal of International Law 271

Su, Jinyuan, 'The Delineation Between Airspace and Outer Space and the Emergence of Aerospace Objects' (2013) 78 Journal of Air Law & Commerce 369

Su, Jinyuan, 'The Practice of States on Air Defence Identification Zones: Geographical Scope, Object of Identification, and Identification Measures' (2019) 18 Chinese Journal International Law 811

Taft IV, William H, 'Self-Defense and the Oil Platforms Decision' (2004) 29 Yale Journal of International Law 295

Tams, Christian J, 'Light Treatment of a Complex Problem: The Law of Self-Defence in the Wall Case' (2006) 16 European Journal of International Law 963

Tiewul, Azadon, 'International Law and Nuclear Test Explosions on the High Seas' (1974) 8 Cornell International Law Journal 45

Theutenberg, Bo J, 'Mare Clausum et Mare Liberum' (1984) 37 Arctic 481

Tuerk, Helmut, 'Some Developments and Issues after the Adoption of UNCLOS' (2021) 9 Korean Journal of International Law 1

Van Dyke, Jon M, 'An Analysis of the Aegean Disputes' (2005) 36 Ocean Development & International Law 63

Van Dyke, Jon M, 'Military Ships and Planes Operating in the Exclusive Economic Zone of another Country' (2004) 28 Marine Policy 29

Vanhullebusch, Matthias & Shen, Wei, 'China's Air Defence Identification Zone: Building Security through Lawfare'(2016) 16 China Review 133

Vaugeois, Mathieu, 'Settlement of Disputes at ICAO and Sustainable Development' (2016) IV Occasional Paper Series 1

Watson, Geoffrey R, 'The Passive Personality Principle' (1993) 28 Texas International Law Journal 1

Wedgewood, Ruth, 'Unilateral Action in the UN System' (2000) 11 European Journal of International Law 355

Wedgwood, Ruth, 'The Fall of Saddam Hussein: Security Council Mandates and Preemptive Self-Defense' (2003) 97 American Journal of International Law 584

Williams, Andrew, 'The Interception of Civil Aircraft over the High Seas in the Global War on Terror' (2007) 59 Air Force Law Review 1

Wright, Quincy, 'The Cuban Quarantine' (1963) 57 Law and Conflict: Changing Patterns and Contemporary Challenges 9

Wolfrum, Rüdiger, 'Proportionality: Reconsidering the Application of an Established Principle in International Law' (2022) 99 International Studies 684

Yee, Sienho, 'Sketching the Debate on Military Activities in the EEZ: An Editorial Comment' (2010) 9 Chinese Journal of International Law 1

Young, Michaela, 'Then and Now: Reappraising Freedom of the Seas in the Modern Law of the Sea' (2016) 47 Ocean Development & International Law 165

Zhang, Haiwen, 'Is it Safeguarding the Freedom of Navigation or Maritime Hegemony of the United States?' Comments on Paul Pedrozo's Article on Military Activities in the EEZ' (2010) 9 Chinese Journal of International Law 31

Zorzetto, Silvia, 'The Lex Specialis Principle and Its Use in Legal Argumentation: An Analytical Inquiry' (2012–2013) 3 Eunomía Revista en Cultura de la Legalidad 61

Online Sources

Archive of the Website of the White House, https://georgewbush-whitehouse.archives.gov/nsc/nss/2002/

Bronk, Justin, 'China's Air Defence Identification Zone and its Role in Chinese Geo-Strategic Policy' (2013) RUSI Analysis, Royal United Services Institute, https://stage.rusi.institute/explore-our-research/publications/commentary/chinas-air-defence-identification-zone-and-its-role-chinese-geo-strategic-policy

Campbell, Brian F, 'Record-Setting Incursions into Taiwan's Air Defense Identification Zone: The People's Republic of China's Psychological Operations Designed to Erode US Support for Taiwan' (2022) J Indo Pacific Affairs https://www.airuniversity.af.edu/JIPA/Display/Article/3111071/record-setting-incursions-into-taiwans-air-defense-identification-zone-the-peop/

Ching, Chang, 'An Embarrassing Fact. The Legal Basis of the PCR East China Sea ADIZ' (23 November 2015) http://cimsec.org/an-embarrassing-fact-the-legal-basis-of-the-prc-east-china-sea-adiz/19804

Comando Conjunto Aeroespacial, 'Respaldo y compromiso' https://www.fuerzas-armadas.mil.ar/cocaes/pesta%C3%B1as/queressabermas.html

Council of the EU, 'Belarus: fourth package of EU sanctions over enduring repression and the forced landing of a Ryanair flight' (21 June 2021) available at https://www.consilium.europa.eu/en/press/press-releases/2021/06/21/belarus-fourth-package-of-eu-sanctions-over-enduring-repression-and-the-forced-landing-of-a-ryanair-flight/

Deutsche Digitale Bibliothek, Air Defence Identification Zone https://www.deutsche-digitale-bibliothek.de/item/JVQVW66LLGEUJ4YARJVUAFAFSFUYDMHV

Kiessling, Elizabeth, 'Gray Zone Tactics and the Principle of Non-Intervention: Can "One of the Vaguest Branches of International Law" Solve the Gray Zone Problem?' (1 February 2021) Harvard NSJ online

Laksmana, Evan, 'Is an Indonesian Air Defence Identification Zone Forthcoming?' (10 April 2018) https://amti.csis.org/indonesian-adiz-forthcoming/

Milanovic, Marko, 'What is an Imminent Armed Attack? A Hopefully Helpful Hypo' (12 January 2017) www.ejiltalk.org/what-is-an-imminent-armed-attack-a-hopefully-helpful-hypo/

Min, Gyo, 'China's Proclamation of its Air Defense Identification Zone and South Korea: The International Legal Perspective' (17 December 2013) http://www.eai.or.kr/main/english/search_view.asp?intSeq=8929&board=eng_multimedia

Nagaiwa, Toshimichi, 'A Technical Aspect of ADIZ' (2014)109 The Japanese Institute of International Affairs, www.jiia.or.jp/en/ajiss_commentary/column-209.html

Tladi, Dire, 'The Use of Force in Self-Defence against Non-State Actors' UN Lecture Series https://legal.un.org/avl/ls/Tladi_PS.html

Waxman, Matthew, 'The 'Caroline' Affair in the Evolving International Law of Self-Defense' (28 August 2018) https://www.lawfareblog.com/caroline-affair

Yun-hyung, Gil, The History of Air Defense Identification Zones in Northeast Asia' (27 November 2013), https://english.hani.co.kr/arti/english_edition/e_international/612953.html

Yurika, Ishii, 'Violations of Sovereign Rights at a Foreign EEZ: Alleged Violations of Sovereign Rights and Maritime Spaces in the Caribbean Sea (Nicaragua v. Colombia)' (7 July 2022), https://www.ejiltalk.org/violations-of-sovereign-rights-at-a-foreign-eez-alleged-violations-of-sovereign-rights-and-maritime-spaces-in-the-caribbean-sea-nicaragua-v-colombia/

Newspaper Articles and Press Releases

Ang U-jin, Adrian, 'Are ADIZ Incursions China's New Response to US Arms Sales to Taiwan?', The Diplomat (23 July 2022) https://thediplomat.com/2022/07/are-adiz-incursions-chinas-new-response-to-us-arms-sales-to-taiwan/

Ang U-jin, Adrian & Pekka Suorsa, Olli, 'Understanding China's Aerial Incursions Into Taiwan`s ADIZ', The Diplomat (2 June 2021) https://thediplomat.com/2021/06/understanding-chinas-aerial-incursions-into-taiwans-adiz/

BBC, 'China establishes 'air-defence zone' over East China Sea', BBC NEWS (23 November 2013) http://www.bbc.co.uk/news/world-asia-25062525

Brown, David, 'China and Taiwan – A Really Simple Guide', BBC News (8 August 2022) https://www.bbc.com/news/world-asia-china-59900139

Carpenter, Ted G, 'US Response to China's ADIZ Biased' (23 December 2013) https://www.cato.org/commentary/us-response-chinas-adiz-biased

Chang, Eric, '21 Chinese Military Aircraft enter Taiwan's ADIZ', Taiwan News (3 August 2022) https://www.taiwannews.com.tw/en/news/4614891

Cenciotti, David, 'Why the Russian Tu-95 bombers that intruded US air space weren't intercepted' (4 May 2015) https://www.businessinsider.com/why-the-russian-tu-95-bombers-that-intruded-us-air-space-werent-intercepted-2015-5

Chrysopoulos, Philip, 'Turkish Fighter Jets Violate Greek Airspace, Again' (17 July 2015) https://greekreporter.com/2015/07/17/turkish-fighter-jets-violate-greek-airspace-again/

CNN, 'Israel shoots down Lebanese civil plane' (24 May 2001) http://edition.cnn.com/2001/WORLD/meast/05/24/israel.plane.02/index.html

Cockburn, Alexander & Silverstein, Ken, 'The System that Brought Down Flight 655' (1988) HARPERS 64 https://harpers.org/archive/1988/09/the-system-that-brought-down-flight-655/

Demetri Sevastopulo, 'Q&A: What is an air defence identification zone?', Financial Times, 29 November 2013

Dutch Aviation Society, 'New intercepts in Taiwan ADIZ' (7 December 2020) https://www.scramble.nl/military-news/new-intercepts-in-taiwan-adiz

Huang, Kristin, 'US bombers enter Chinese air defence zone as Beijing's navy mounts massive exercises' (17 November 2020) https://www.scmp.com/news/china/military/article/3110262/us-bombers-enter-chinas-adiz-pla-navy-mounts-massive-exercises

ICAO Council 'Statement on Ukraine International Airlines Flight PS752' (8 January 2021) https://www.icao.int/Newsroom/Pages/Statement-on-Ukraine-International-Airlines-Flight-PS752.aspx

ICAO Council, 'ICAO Council to pursue fact finding investigation into Ryanair FR4978' (27 May 2021) https://www.icao.int/Newsroom/Pages/ICAO-Council-agrees-to-pursue-fact-finding-investigation-into-Belarus-incident.aspx

ICAO Council, 'ICAO Council urges Iran to complete PS752 accident investigation Final Report' (6 November 2020) https://www.icao.int/Newsroom/Pages/ICAO-Council-urges-Iran-to-complete-PS752-accident-investigation-Final-Report.aspx

ICAO Council, 'Update on fact-finding investigation on Ryanair flight FR478' (16 June 2021) https://www.icao.int/Newsroom/Pages/Update-on-factfinding-investigation-into-Ryanair-flight-FR4978.aspx

Japantimes, 'South Korea scrambles Jets as Chinese and Russian Warplanes enter Air Defense Zone' (19 November 2021) https://www.japantimes.co.jp/news/2021/11/19/asia-pacific/south-korea-china-russia-aircraft-air-defense-zone/

Kachi, Hiroyuki & Takahashi, Yoshio, 'Japan asks Airline to Ignore China Flight-Plan Rule' (26 November 2013, Wall Street journal) https://www.wsj.com/articles/SB10001424052702304281004579221681641322204

Kamimura, Kenta, 'Tensions Rising Around Maritime Border Claimed by China; Globally Recognized 'Freedom of Overflight' Under Threat', The Japan News (29 January 2024) https://japannews.yomiuri.co.jp/politics/defense-security/20240129-165259/.

Lee, Yimou, 'Taiwan Vows Counter-Attack If Chinese Forces Enter Its Territory' (31 August 2022) https://www.reuters.com/world/asia-pacific/chinese-military-continues-high-intensity-patrols-near-taiwan-taiwanese-defence-2022-08-31/

Martinez Luis, 'Russian bombers intercepted 8 miles from US airspace' (10 June 2020) https://abcnews.go.com/Politics/russian-bombers-intercepted-miles-us-airspace/story?id=71171943

NORAD Press Release, 'NORAD intercepts Russian bombers and fighters entering Alaskan Air Defense Identification Zone' (22 May 2019)

Perez, Jane, 'China Accuses Japan of Stealing After Purchase of Group of Disputed Islands' New York Times (11 September 2012)

Qin, Lee 'U.S Plane Grossly Violated International Law' (3 April 2001) https://www.fmprc.gov.cn/ce/cegv/eng/premade/11437/article040401.html

R.O.C. Air Force, 'PLA activities in the waters and airspace around Taiwan Apr. 10, 2024' (10.04,2024) https://air.mnd.gov.tw/EN/News/News_Detail.aspx?CID=214&ID=56950

Reuters, 'China says its coast guard patrols around Taiwan islands 'beyond reproach' (28 February 2024) https://www.reuters.com/world/asia-pacific/china-says-its-coast-guard-patrols-around-taiwan-islands-beyond-reproach-2024-02-28/

Reuters, 'China says U.S. should respect China's air defense zone' (23 March 2017) https://www.reuters.com/article/us-china-usa-defence-idUSKBN16U0SB

Reuters, 'China trying to 'normalise' military drills near Taiwan: island's top security official' (11 March 2024) https://www.reuters.com/world/asia-pacific/china-trying-normalise-military-drills-near-taiwan-islands-top-security-official-2024-03-11/

Reuters, 'Six U.N. Security Council members condemn Belarus plane interception' (26 May 2021) available at https://www.reuters.com/world/europe/six-un-security-council-members-condemn-belarus-plane-interception-2021-05-26/

Reuters, 'U.N. Security Council to discuss Belarus plane interception–diplomats' (25 May 2021) https://www.reuters.com/article/belarus-politics-un/u-n-security-council-to-discuss-belarus-plane-interception-diplomats-idUSL2N2NC1TU

'Time to Regulate Air Defence Zones to Prevent Conflict', South China Morning Post (29 November 2013) http://www.scmp.com/comment/insight-opinion/article/1368612/time-regulate-airdefence-zones-prevent-conflict

The Times of Israel, 'Disastrous mistake': Iran admits it mistakenly downed Ukraine plane, killed 176' (11 January 2020) https://www.timesofisrael.com/iran-admits-it-unintentionally-shot-down-ukrainian-jetliner/

Ye, Zang, 'Air Defense ID Zone to Deter Those with Designs on China's Territory' (26 November 2013, People's Daily Online) http://en.people.cn/90883/8466523.html

Official Statements

Announcement of the Aircraft Identification Rules for the East China Sea Air Defence Identification Zone of the P.C.R. (23 November 2013) http://us.china-embassy.gov.cn/eng/zt_120777/cadiz/201312/t20131205_4911505.html

EU Press Statement, 'Declaration by the High Representative Catherine Ashton on behalf of the European Union on the establishment by China of an "East China Sea Air Defence Identification Zone"' (28 November 2013) 17082/1/13/REV 1

Japanese Ministry of Foreign Affairs, 'Situation of the Senkaku Islands' https://www.mofa.go.jp/a_o/c_m1/senkaku/page1we_000010.html

Ministry of Foreign Affairs of the People's Republic of China, 'Statement of the Ministry of Foreign Affairs of the People's Republic of China' (10 September 2012), https://www.fmprc.gov.cn/mfa_eng/topics_665678/diaodao_665718/201209/t20120911_701817.html

Ministry of Foreign Affairs of the People's Republic of China, "Foreign Ministry Spokesperson Qin Gang's Remarks on Japan's Representations About China's Establishment of an Air Defense Identification Zone in the East China Sea," (25 November 2013) https://www.fmprc.gov.cn/mfa_eng/xwfw_665399/s2510_665401/2535_665405/201311/t20131125_696274.html

Ministry of Foreign Affairs Taiwan, 'MOFA condemns Taiwan ADIZ intrusions by PLA, urges vigilance against threats' (11 September 2020)

Ministry of Foreign Affairs Japan, Press Conference by Foreign Press Secretary Yoshida, 'Situation in Taiwan (Intrusion by Chinese Military Aircraft into Taiwan's Air Defence Identification Zone' (6 October 2021)

Newsletter No.0107, Embassy of the PCR in the United States of America (15 April 2011) https://www.mfa.gov.cn/ce/ceus//eng/sgxx/sggg/sstx/2001/t35019.html

Statement by the Ministry of Foreign Affairs of the People's Republic of China (2 August 2022) https://www.fmprc.gov.cn/eng/zxxx_662805/202208/t20220802_10732293.html

Türkiye Ministry of Foreign Affairs, 'Airspace Related Problems' https://www.mfa.gov.tr/air-space-related-related-problems.en.mfa

U.S. Dep't of Defense Press Release, 'Hagel Issues Statement on East China Sea Air Defense Identification Zone' (23 November 2013) www.defense.gov/news/newsarticle.aspx?id_121223

Miscellaneous

Council of Europe, 'Recommendation No. R (97) 11 of the Committee of Ministers to Member States on the Amended Model Plan for the Classification of Documents Concerning State Practice in the Field of Public International Law' (12 June 1997)

Declaration Of The Latin American States On The Law Of The Sea [1970]

Eighth Report on State Responsibility by Mr. Roberto Ago, Special Rapporteur – The Internationally Wrongful Act of the State, Source of International Responsibility (Part 1), Yearbook of the International Law Commission 1980, Vol. II(1)

EUROCONTROL, *The EUROCONTROL Concept of the Flexible Use of Airspace* (2002)

EUROCONTROL, 'Advanced Flexible Use of Airspace', https://www.eurocontrol.int/publication/advanced-flexible-use-airspace-afua-concept

EUROCONTROL, *European Action Plan for Airspace Infringement Risk Reduction* (2022)

Guidelines for Navigation and Overflight in the Exclusive Economic Zone (2005) https://nippon.zaidan.info/seikabutsu/2005/00816/pdf/0001.pdf

Ho, Duc L, 'A South China Sea ADIZ – Vietnam's Next Challenge' (Master Thesis, 2016, Naval Postgraduate School)

Honniball, Arron N, 'Freedom of Navigation Following the M/V "Norstar" Case', The Blog of the K.G. Jebsen Center for the Law of the Sea (4 June 2019)

Int'l Institute Of Humanitarian Law, *San Remo Manual On International Law Applicable To Armed Conflicts At Sea* (1994)

Japanese Ministry of Defense, *Defense White Paper* (2022)

Marchisio, Sergio, 'National Jurisdiction for Regulating Space Activities of Governmental and Non-Governmental Entities' (United Nations/Thailand Workshop on Space Law, Bangkok, 16–19 November 2010)

Memorandum of Understanding on the Rules of Behavior for the Safety of Air and Maritime Encounters (Supplement) (15 September 2015)

Montevideo Declaration on the Law of the Sea [1970]

NAM 2006/Doc.1, '14th Summit of Heads of State or Government of the Non-Aligned Movement' (16. September 2006, Havana, Cuba)

Territorial Sovereignty and Scope of the Dispute (Eritrea v Yemen) XXII RIAA (1998)

U.S. Navy, U.S. Coast Guard & U.S. Marine Corps, NTTP3–07.11M/CGTTP3–93.3/MCIP3–33.04, 'Visit, Board, Search, And Seizure Operations' (2013) 1–2

United States Army Air Defense Artillery School, 'Small Arms Defense Against Air Attack' (2006)

National Legislation & Aeronautical Information Publications

Argentina AIP (5 November 2020)
Argentina Decreto 1054/18 del Poder Ejecutivo Nacional
Australian Civil Aviation Act 1988, Act No 63
Australian Civil Aviation Safety Amendment (Part 91) Regulations 2018 https://vfrg.casa.gov.au/operations/air-defence-identification-zone/general-2
Australian Government – Civil Aviation Safety Authority, *Understanding the Legislative Framework* (May 2021)
Australia AIP (16 June 2022)
Bangladesh AIP SUPP 01/18 (1 February 2018)
Brazil Aeronautical Information Circular, AIC-N 16/17 (4 August 2017). https://publicacoes.decea.mil.br/publicacao/aic-n-1617
AIP Brazil (09 Mar 2019)
Canadian Aviation Regulation (SOR/96–433) 600.01 (last amended 2017)
Canadian Aviation Regulation 602.145 2
Canadian Designated Airspace Handbook, Issue No 289 (12 June 2021)
Canadian Aeronautical Information Manual (AIM) (2022)
Cuba AIP (25 April 2019)
Finland AIP (26 April 2018)
Finnish Aviation Act (864/2014)
Indian Manual on Flexible Use of Airspace, ATFM/SG/5-WP13 Attachment A (2015)
Indonesian Regulation No. 4 of 2018 on Airspace Security (Peraturan Pemerintah) (19 February 2018)
Iran AIP (August 2018)
Japan AIP (1 March 2018)
Myanamar General Rules and Procedures https://www.ais.gov.mm/eAIP/2017-08-03-AIRAC/html/eAIP/ENR-1.1-en-GB.html
Myanamar AIP https://www.ais.gov.mm/eAIP/2017-08-03-AIRAC/html/eAIP/ENR-1.1-en-GB.html
Pakistan AIP (20 April 2020) https://caapakistan.com.pk/eAIP/01-22/eAIP/index.html.
Pakistan Air Navigation Order (4.12.2009)
Panama AIP https://www.aeronautica.gob.pa/PAGINA%20NUEVA3/aac/racp/zip/RACP_LIB_XXXI.pdf
Peru, La Junta Directiva de la Autoridad Aeronautica Civil, Articulo 2 (16 August 2017)
Peru, Decreto Supremo que regula la Zona de Identificación de Defensa Aérea (ADIZ PERÚ), N° 005–2016-DE (3 April 2016)
Peru, Directorial Resolution No. 0041–94-MTC /15.12 of 4 August 1994
Poland AIP (24 February 2022)
South African Civil Aviation Authority, AIRAC AIP Sup S060/12

South Korea, BMS KTO AIP (2015)

South Korea AIP (27 September 2018)

Sri Lanka AIP (30 January 2015)

Taiwan Rules of the Air https://law.moj.gov.tw/ENG/LawClass/LawAll.aspx?pcode=K0090014.b

AIP Taipei FIR (14 May 2015)

Thailand AIP https://aip.caat.or.th/2020-02-27-AIRAC/html/eAIP/VT-GEN-3.3-en-GB.html

Thailand Act on Conduct of Violating Aircraft, B.E.2553 (2010)

Uruguay, Reglamento Aeronáutico Latinoamericano, LAR 211 (01 August 2020) Gestión Del Tránsito Aéreo

Uruguay Circular de Asesoramiento, CA.UY.ANS/ATM/011 (7 May 2021)

Uruguay Reglamento Aeronáutico Latinoamericano, LAR 211 (01 August 2020)

Uruguay Article 112 to 117, Espacio Aéreo Nacional, Law No. 19.889 (9 July 2020)

US Federal Aviation Regulation, Part 99 (September 1993), P-10

US Code of Federal Regulations, Title 14, §99.43 (1 January 1966)

US 69 Federal Register No. 40 (2004) 16754 on the amendment of Civil Aviation Act

US Doc. No. FAA-2001–10693, 66 FR 49822, 28 September 2001

US Federal Aviation Act 14 CFR §99.3.

US 14 CFR §49.43

US Aeronautical Information Manual 5–6-2, https://www.faa.gov/air_traffic/publications/atpubs/aim_html/chap5_section_6.html

US Department of the Navy, *The Commander's Handbook on the Law of Naval Operations* (2008)

Index

Essential Air and Space Law

Dr. Marietta Benkö

Volumes 1–29 published by Eleven International, The Hague.
Continued by De Gruyter Brill, Leiden and Berlin

Volumes

1. *Natalino Ronzitti & Gabriella Venturini (eds.)*, The Law of Air Warfare – Contemporary Issues. (2006)
2. *Marietta Benkö & Kai-Uwe Schrogl (eds.)*, Space Law: Current Problems and Perspectives for Future Regulations (2005)
3. *Tare Brisibe*, Aeronautical Public Correspondence by Satellite (2006)
4. *Michael Milde*, International Air Law and ICAO (2008)
5. *Markus Geisler & Marius Boewe*, The German Civil Aviation Act (2009)
6. *Ulrich Steppler & Angela Klingmüller*, EU Emissions Trading Scheme and Aviation (2010)
7. *Heiko van Schyndel (ed.)*, Aviation Code of the Russian Federation (2010)
8. *Zang Hongliang & Meng Qingfen*, Civil Aviation Law in the People's Republic of China (2010)
9. *Ronald M. Schnitker & Dick van het Kaar*, Aviation Accident and Incident Investigation. Concurrence of Technical and Judicial Inquiries in the Netherlands (2010)
10. *Michael Milde*, International Air Law and ICAO, second edition. (2012)
11. *Ronald Schnitker & Dick van het Kaar*, Safety Assessment of Foreign Aircraft Programme. A European Approach to Enhance Global Aviation Safety (2013)
12. *Marietta Benkö & Engelbert Plescher*, Space Law: Reconsidering the Definition/Delimitation Question and the Passage of Spacecraft through Foreign Airspace (2013)
13. *Heiko van Schyndel (ed.)*, Aviation Code of the Russian Federation, second edition (2015)
14. *Alejandro Piera Valdés*, Greenhouse Gas Emissions from International Aviation: Legal and Policy Challenges (2015)
15. *Peter Paul Fitzgerald*, A Level Playing Field for "Open Skies": The Need for Consistent Aviation Regulation (2016)
16. *Jae Woon Lee*, Regional Liberalization in International Air Transport: Towards Northeast Asian Open Skies (2016)

17. *Tanveer Ahmad,* Climate Change Governance in International Civil Aviation: Toward Regulating Emissions Relevant to Climate Change and Global Warming (2016)
18. *Michael Milde,* International Air Law and ICAO, third edition, 2016. (Available also in Russian and Korean.)
19. *Nataliia Malysheva,* Space Law and Policy in the Post-Soviet States (2018)
20. *Philippe Clerc,* Space Law in the European Context (2018)
21. *Benjamyn Scott,* Aviation Cybersecurity: Regulatory Approach in the European Union (2019)
22. *Dick van het Kaar,* International Civil Aviation: Treaties, Institutions and Programmes (2019)
23. *Lasantha Hettiarachchi,* International Air Transport Association (IATA): Structure and Legitimacy of its Quasi-International Regulatory Power (2020)
24. *Masataka Ogasawara & Joel Greer,* Japan in Space (2021)
25. *Ronald Schnitker & Dick van het Kaar,* Drone Law and Policy (2021)
26. *Marietta Benkö & Kai-Uwe Schrogl* (eds.), Outer Space, Future for Humankind – Issues of Law and Policy (2021)
27. *Wu, Xiaodan,* China's ambition in Space, Programs, Policy and Law (2022)
28. Milde's International Air Law and ICAO, 4th edition. Revised by *Attila Sipos* (2023)
29. *Dick van het Kaar,* The Aircraft Commander in International Air Transportation. Legal Powers, Duties and Decision Making (2024)
30. *Stipsits, Stephanie,* Air Defense Identification Zones, Legality and Maritime Frontier Disputes (2024)

Awards

Volume 1 received the Basic Science Book Award by the International Academy of Astronautics (IAA).
Volume 20 won the IAA Social Sciences Book Award.

Translations

Volume 2
Chinese (Law Press China, Bejing), Russian (Aerohelp, St. Petersburg) and Korean (Bobmunsa Publishing House, Paju Book City). A translation into Arabic is in progress.

Volume 18
is in the process of being translated into Chinese (China International Book Trading Corp., Bejing)

Volume 24
Japanese (Zelo, Foreign Joint Enterprise, Tokyo)

www.ingramcontent.com/pod-product-compliance
Lightning Source LLC
LaVergne TN
LVHW010659300926
849161LV00005B/1165